International Arctic Petroleum Cooperation: Barents Sea scenarios

The Arctic region contains large amounts of natural resources considered necessary to sustain global economic growth, so it is unsurprising that it is increasingly susceptible to political, economic, environmental and even military conflicts. This book looks in detail at the preconditions and outlook for international cooperation on the development of Arctic petroleum resources, focusing on Norwegian–Russian cooperation in the Barents Sea towards 2025.

The authors provide a cross-disciplinary approach including geopolitical, institutional, technological, corporate and environmental perspectives to analyze the underlying factors that shape the future development of the region. Three future scenarios are developed, exploring various levels of cooperation and development influenced by and resulting from potential political, commercial and environmental circumstances. Through these scenarios, the book improves understanding of the challenges and opportunities for Arctic petroleum resource development and promotes further consideration of the possible outcomes of future cooperation.

The book should be of interest to students, scholars and policy-makers working in the areas of Arctic studies, oil and gas studies, energy security, global environmental governance, environmental politics and environmental technology.

Anatoli Bourmistrov is professor and Head of Section at Bodø Graduate School of Business, University of Nordland, Norway, and project manager at the High North Center for Business.

Frode Mellemvik is Director of the High North Center and professor at Bodø Graduate School of Business, University of Nordland, Norway.

Alexei Bambulyak is Country Manager, Russia, at the research company Akvaplan-niva, Norway.

Ove Gudmestad is professor of marine technology at the University of Stavanger, Norway.

Indra Overland is head of the Russia, Eurasia and Arctic Research Group at the Norwegian Institute of International Affairs and Professor II at Bodø Graduate School of Business, University of Nordland, Norway.

Anatoly Zolotukhin is Counsellor on International Affairs, Research Director of the Institute of Arctic Petroleum Technologies and Professor of Petroleum Reservoir Engineering at Gubkin University, Moscow, Russia.

Routledge Studies in Environmental Policy

International Arctic Petroleum Cooperation

Barents Sea scenarios

Edited by Anatoli Bourmistrov, Frode Mellemvik, Alexei Bambulyak, Ove Gudmestad, Indra Overland and Anatoly Zolotukhin

Routledge
Taylor & Francis Group
LONDON AND NEW YORK

First published 2015

by Routledge
2 Park Square, Milton Park, Abingdon, Oxon OX14 4RN

and by Routledge
711 Third Avenue, New York, NY 10017

First issued in paperback 2016

Routledge is an imprint of the Taylor & Francis Group, an informa business

© 2015 Anatoli Bourmistrov, Frode Mellemvik, Alexei Bambulyak, Ove Gudmestad, Indra Overland and Anatoly Zolotukhin, selection and editorial material; individual chapters, the contributors

The right of the editors to be identified as the authors of the editorial material, and of the authors for their individual chapters, has been asserted in accordance with sections 77 and 78 of the Copyright, Designs and Patents Act 1988.

With the exception of Chapters 1, 2 and 6 no part of this book may be reprinted or reproduced or utilised in any form or by any electronic, mechanical, or other means, now known or hereafter invented, including photocopying and recording, or in any information storage or retrieval system, without permission in writing from the publishers.

Chapters 1, 2 and 6 of this book is available for free in PDF format as Open Access at www.tandfebooks.com. It has been made available under a Creative Commons Attribution-Non Commercial-No Derivatives 4.0 license.

Trademark notice: Product or corporate names may be trademarks or registered trademarks, and are used only for identification and explanation without intent to infringe.

British Library Cataloguing-in-Publication Data
A catalogue record for this book is available from the British Library

Library of Congress Cataloging-in-Publication Data
International Arctic petroleum cooperation : Barents Sea scenarios / edited by Anatoli Bourmistrov, Frode Mellemvik, Alexei Bambulyak, Ove Gudmestad, Indra Overland and Anatoly Zolotukhin.
    pages cm. — (Routledge studies in environmental policy)
    Includes bibliographical references and index.
  1. Petroleum industry and trade—Barents Sea Region. 2. Petroleum industry and trade—Norway. 3. Petroleum industry and trade—Russia (Federation)   4. Petroleum—Barents Sea Region. 5. Petroleum—Norway. 6. Petroleum—Russia (Federation)   I. Bourmistrov, Anatoli.
    HD9576.B392I58 2015
    333.8'2309163'24—dc23
    2014048376

ISBN 13: 978–1–138–62927–1 (pbk)
ISBN 13: 978–1–138–78326–3 (hbk)

Typeset in Bembo
by Apex CoVantage, LLC

Contents

PART I
Introduction and scenarios   1

PART II
Politics, economics and experience of cooperation   33

List of Figures

List of Tables

Abbreviations

1P, 2P, 3P, 1C, 2C, 3C	resource classification by the Petroleum Resources Management System
AC	alternating current
ACAP	Arctic Contaminants Action Program
AMAP	Arctic Monitoring and Assessment Programme
AMIGE	Arctic Marine Engineering–Geology Expedition
AMNGR	"Arktikmorneftegazrazvedka," is a Russian exploration company located in Murmansk
B2B	business-to-business
BAP	best available practice
BAT	best available technology
Bboe	billions of barrels of oil equivalent
bcm	billion cubic meters
b/d	barrels per day
BEAC	Barents Euro–Arctic Council
BEAR	Barents Euro–Arctic Region
BNKMT	Barents–North Kara megatrough
boe	barrel of oil equivalent
BTEX	benzene, toluene, ethylbenzene, and xylenes
btoe	billion tons of oil equivalent
Btu	British thermal unit
BUNKER	International Convention on Civil Liability for Bunker Oil Pollution Damage
CAFF	Conservation of Arctic Flora and Fauna
CAPEX	capital expenditures
CBA	Central Barents anticline
CDP	Common Depth Point Method
CDU	central distribution unit
CEMP	Coordinated Environmental Monitoring Program 2002–2011
CLC	International Convention on Civil Liability for Oil Pollution Damage
CNPC	China National Petroleum Corporation

CUREN	Central Department of Fishery Review and Norms on Protection and Restoration of Water Biological Resources and Acclimatization
DS	Diploma Supplement
DSHA	defined situations of hazard and accident
EBM	Ecosystem Based Management
ECTS	European Credit Transfer and Accumulation System
EEZ	exclusive economic zones
EFTA	European Free Trade Association
EIA	environmental impact assessment
ELS	unitary command system
EOR	enhanced oil recovery
EPC	engineering, procurement and construction
EPPR	Emergency Prevention, Preparedness and Response Working Group
ESPO	East Siberia–Pacific Ocean
EUR	expected ultimate recovery
FEED	Front-End Engineering Design
FJL	Franz Joseph Land
FPAL	First Point Assessment
FUND	International Convention on the Establishment of an International Fund for Compensation for Oil Pollution Damage
GBS	gravity-based structures
GM	metacentric height
GVF	gas volume fraction
HC	hydrocarbon
HHB	Bodø Graduate School of Business at the University of Nordland
HQ	headquarter
HSE	health, safety, and the environment
HSEQ	health, safety, environmental, and quality
Hz	hertz
ICT	information and communication technology
IEA	International Energy Agency
IMO	International Maritime Organization
IMRF	International Maritime Rescue Federation
IR spectrum	infrared spectroscopy
JIP	Oil in Ice Joint Industry Program
JIP OGP	joint industry project of the International Association of Oil and Gas Producers
kW	kilowatt
LCC	life cycle cost
LNG	liquefied natural gas
M2	major tidal component

Ma	million years
MAGE JSC	Marine Arctic Geological Expedition Joint Stock Company
MARPOL	International Convention on the Prevention of Pollution from Ships
MBA	Master of Business Administration
mb/d	millions of barrels per day
mD	millidarcy, unit of permeability
MIEP	International Institute of Energy Politics and Diplomacy at MGIMO University
Minprirody	Ministry of Natural Resources and Environment of the Russian Federation
MoU	memorandum of understanding
MPC	maximum permissible concentration
Mtoe	million tons of oil equivalent
mt/y	million tons per year
MW	megawatt
NAREC	Norwegian and Russian Education and Research Consortium for International Business Development in the Energy Sector
NCS	Norwegian continental shelf
NEBA	net environmental benefit analysis
NGO	nongovernmental organization
NIC ARM	National Information Center for Academic Recognition and Mobility
NOEC	no observable effect concentration
NOFO	Norwegian Clean Seas Association for Operating Companies
NOKUT	Norwegian Agency for Quality Assurance in Education
NPD	Norwegian Petroleum Directorate
NUPI	Norwegian Institute of International Affairs
O&G	oil and gas
OECD	Organization for Economic Co-operation and Development
OEM	original equipment manufacturer
OGP	International Association of Oil and Gas Producers
OPEC	Organization of the Petroleum Exporting Countries
OPRC	International Convention on Oil Pollution Preparedness, Response and Cooperation
ORF	oil recovery factor
OSCAR	Oil Spill Contingency and Response

OSPAR	Convention for the Protection of the Marine Environment of the North-East Atlantic
OSR	oil-spill response
P90, P50, Pmean	proved, probable and mean resources. Measure of uncertainty, or maturity of resources
PAH	photo-oxidation of certain polyaromatic hydrocarbons
PAME	Protection of the Arctic Marine Environment
PCA	Pollution Control Act
PCM	phase change materials
ppm	parts per million
PPR	possibly petroleum region
PR	petroleum region
PRMS	Petroleum Resources Management System
PSA	production sharing agreement
Roshydromet	Federal Service on Hydrometeorology and Environmental Monitoring of Russia
Rosmorrechflot	Federal Agency of Marine and River Transport
Rosnedra	Federal Subsoil Resource Management Agency
Rosprirodnadzor	Federal Service for Supervision of Natural Resources Use
S&P	Standard & Poor's
SAR	search and rescue
SDWG	Sustainable Development Working Group
SEVMORGEO	Northern State Enterprise on Marine Geological Works
SIU	Norwegian Centre for International Cooperation in Higher Education
SMNG	SevMorNefteGeophysica (Northern Marina Oil Geophysics)
SPE	Society of Petroleum Engineers
SPS	subsea production system
SPV	special project vehicle
STOOIP	stock tank oil originally in place
tcm	trillion cubic meters
toe	tons of oil equivalent
UCube	Upstream Cube, Internet-based software, developed by Rystad Energy, a Norwegian company
UHR	Norwegian Association of Higher Education Institutions
UiN	University of Nordland
UiS	University of Stavanger
UNCLOS	United Nations Convention on the Law of the Sea

VNIGNI	All-Russian Research Geological Oil Institute
VNIIOkeangeologia	All-Russian Scientific Research Institute for Geology & Mineral Resources of the Ocean
VSEGEI	Russian Geological Research Institute
WAF	water accommodated fraction
WCI	wind chill index
W/m²	watts per square meter
XMT	Christmas tree template

Contributors

Andrea Bagi (PhD) is currently employed at the University of Stavanger as a postdoctor and laboratory engineer. She studied hydrocarbon biodegradation under psychrophilic conditions during her PhD at the University of Stavanger, from which she graduated in June 2013. Bagi is originally from Hungary, where she obtained her master of science level diploma in 2007 as an environmental engineer at the Budapest University of Technology and Economics (abbreviated as BME), the most significant university of technology in the country.

Alexei Bambulyak is Country Manager, Russia, at the research company Akvaplan-niva, and a PhD candidate at the Norwegian University of Science and Technology (NTNU). Bambulyak has the MSc degree of an engineer-physicist from Petrozavodsk State University, and he is a certified environmental auditor in Russia. He has 20-years' experience in running international capacity building and research projects in the Barents region. Bambulyak is an author of joint reports on environmental and resource management in Norway and Russia, and on marine shipping and oil pollution issues in the Arctic. His research topics are within the areas of environmental risk assessments, resource management and international cooperation.

Javad Barabady is professor of safety and technology at the Department of Safety and Engineering, UiT – The Arctic University of Norway. He obtained his BSc degree in mining engineering from Azad University of Shahrood and his MSc degree in mining engineering from the University of Tehran, Iran. After working for more than five years as a lecturer at Azad University of Shahrood, he gained a PhD degree in operation and maintenance engineering from the Luleå University of Technology. His research interests include reliability and risk analysis, operation and maintenance engineering and planning, production assurance analysis and management.

Anatoli Bourmistrov is professor and head of section at Bodø Graduate School of Business, University of Nordland (Norway), project manager at the High North Center for Business and program coordinator for the joint degree master of science programs in energy management (in cooperation with MGIMO University, Moscow). He has a doctoral degree from the Norwegian School of Economics (NHH). He was awarded the David Solomons Prize for the best paper in the annual volume of *Management Accounting Research*. His research interests are in the areas of energy management, management control, public sector management, international business and education.

Maria Bulakh is a PhD candidate in Arctic & Cold Climate Subsea Development at the Gubkin University of Oil and Gas and is employed as a full-time Subsea Engineer in Aker Solutions, Norway. Her research interests focus on the feasibility of the subsea-to-shore oil and gas field developments with subsea processing units located under ice conditions. The author has participated in a number of international conferences with the emphasis on offshore and subsea field developments. She has been chosen by Aker Solutions' Arctic Hub Center as subject matter expert related to challenges with oil and gas field development in Arctic conditions.

June Borge Doornich holds a PhD in business economics from Bodø Graduate School of Business, University of Nordland. Her academic field of expertise is strategic management and management control within international business. Doornich is engaged at the High North Center and is involved in NAREC as a research coordinator. She has close ties with the business environment through participation at seminars, conferences and board representations. She is also actively engaged in various fora for Norwegian–Russian cooperation in higher education, among others, through a positon as a project board member at the Norwegian Centre for International Cooperation in Higher Education (SIU).

Svetlana Golubeva is Director General of the System Development Agency. She holds MSc degrees in Economic Cybernetics and in Environmental Protection and Rational Nature Resources' Management from the Lomonosov Moscow State University. She is a leading Russian expert in environmental impact assessment and state environmental review. She cochaired working and expert groups on industrial pollution and environmental impact assessment under the Joint Norwegian–Russian Environmental Commission. Golubeva is an author of guidelines and methodological recommendations on a wide range of environmental issues, including impact assessment, strategic environmental assessment, environmental review, environmental standards, public participation and economics of nature resources' management.

Ove Gudmestad has been professor of marine technology at the University of Stavanger since 2008. He worked at Statoil from 1975 to 2008 and began Statoil's research activities related to technology for the Arctic oil and gas developments. Gudmestad has a PhD in hydrodynamics from the University of Bergen and spent two years at Massachusetts Institute of Technology undertaking research work. He has published papers on Arctic-related technologies, often in cooperation with staff and students from Gubkin

University of Oil and Gas in Moscow, where he was granted an honorary doctor's degree in 2002.

Tor Hemmingsen is a professor in chemistry and corrosion at the University of Stavanger, and has been prorector for the last four years. He holds an MSc in organic chemistry from the University of Tromsø and a PhD in electrochemistry from the University of Bergen. He has been employed at IRIS – International Research Institute of Stavanger – for eight years as a research manager in petroleum technology and as a research manager in oil field chemistry at Schlumberger for two years.

Gennady Ivanov is an assistant director general for research at JSC "MAGE" (Marine Arctic Geophysical Expedition) and a doctor of geological-mineralogical sciences. After graduating from the Leningrad Mining Institute in 1980, Ivanov worked for 27 years in VNIIOkeangeologia in the area of surveying, prospecting and exploration of the ocean floor. In 1990 he defended his PhD thesis and in 2004, his doctor of science dissertation. Ivanov has published more than 450 scientific works, including six monographs. He has participated in more than 20 Arctic marine expeditions. In recent years Ivanov has been working in the area of forecasting petroleum resources in shallow waters of the Arctic shelf on the basis of integrated geochemical studies. Together with coauthors, he developed and tested trans-regional transects and applied this approach to the shallow waters of the Kara Sea.

Roald Kommedal is currently associate professor in environmental science and technology at the University of Stavanger. He holds a PhD in environmental biotechnology and an MSc in marine resource development and protection. Research areas include biodegradation of natural and synthetic organics, bioprocess modelling and aquatic micriobial ecology.

Andrey Krivorotov (born 1964 in Moscow) graduated from MGIMO in 1987. His career record includes diplomatic missions in Norway, the Russian parliament and the Council of Europe in Strasbourg. Since 1997, he has worked in the petroleum industry, including Tyumen Oil Company, Gazprom, Shtokman Development AG and two professional journals. He also lectures in MGIMO and in 2004 defended his PhD there on Norwegian economic policies in the High North. Krivorotov is an author of nearly 70 publications and a member of the NAREC Advisory Board. His inputs in this book represent his personal expert opinions, summing up his varied experience.

Lars-Henrik Larsen is head of the Marine Environment department at Akvaplan-niva, and a PhD candidate at UiT – the Arctic University of Norway. He holds an MSc degree in resource biology from the University of Tromsø. Larsen has worked on a variety of aspects on documenting and risk-evaluating human activities influencing the Arctic marine environment and its biological resources with special attention on the Barents Sea and the Norwegian–Russian cooperation. Most of his work has been related to petroleum activity, fisheries and shipping. Larsen has participated in, and developed methods for, environmental risk and impact assessments and associated research.

Tore Markeset is professor of mechanical engineering (operations and maintenance) at the University of Stavanger (UiS) and adjunct professor at the University of Tromsø, both in Norway. Currently he is head of the Department of Industrial Economics, Risk Management and Planning, UiS. He received a BSc in petroleum engineering from the University of Stavanger in 1985, and a BSc and MSc in mechanical engineering from the University of Minnesota, USA, in 1989 and 1991 respectively. He received his Dr.-Ing. in Offshore Technology – Operations and Maintenance from UiS in 2003. His research interests include operations, maintenance and support management, Arctic engineering, industrial services and product support.

Frode Mellemvik is Director of the High North Center and Professor at Bodø Graduate School of Business, University of Nordland. Mellemvik holds a PhD and has written books and articles on management and High North related topics. He has worked at academic institutions in Europe and the US, and is Honorary Doctor and Honorary Professor at several universities. Mellemvik has been rector of Bodø University College (University of Nordland) for 10 years. He has participated in several boards and councils, for instance in the Norwegian Government's Expert Committee for the High North, and been chairperson of the Norwegian Government's High North Council.

Ove Njå is professor of risk and emergency management at the University of Stavanger. Njå is a principal researcher at the International Research Institute of Stavanger and a visiting professor at Stord/Haugesund University College. Njå's doctoral thesis is related to safety management and emergency preparedness planning. His professional career includes five years in the civil engineering industry, 10 years in the petroleum industry and more than 15 years in research and education. Njå has participated in and led a large number of risk and safety related projects. The research covers risk analysis, risk analysis methods, risk acceptance, risk management, emergency preparedness, emergency response performance and crisis management. Njå's research also includes learning from accident and incident investigations, studying various fields such as the crisis management, transport and petroleum sectors.

Indra Overland is head of the Russia, Eurasia and Arctic Research Group at the Norwegian Institute of International Affairs and Professor II at Bodø Graduate School of Business, University of Nordland. He did his PhD at the Scott Polar Research Institute at the University of Cambridge and has since published extensively on post-Soviet energy issues. He was awarded the Toby Jackman Prize for best PhD dissertation, the Marcel Cadieux Prize for an article on Russia's Arctic energy policy in the *International Journal*, the Stuland Prize, and coauthored the most-cited article published by the *Journal of Eurasian Studies* (analyzing the constraints on Russia's foreign energy policy).

Valery Salygin is Director of the International Institute of Energy Policy and Diplomacy (MIEP) at MGIMO University of the Ministry of Foreign Affairs of the Russian Federation. His scientific interests are in the fields of energy diplomacy and geopolitics, system analysis, corporate governance, fuel and energy complex regulation. The author of more than 450 publications, under his guidance and mentorship more than 40 students have received their PhDs. A graduate of the Mining Institute, in 1974 he received his doctor of science degree. For several years he served as Deputy Minister of Education of the Russian Federation and board member. He has been a corresponding member of the Russian Academy of Sciences since 1990. He was also elected vice president of the International Fuel and Energy Development Academy.

Nodari Simonia is the former Director of the Institute of World Economics and International Relations of the Russian Academy of Sciences, professor of MGIMO University and member of the Russian Academy of Sciences. Born in 1932, he graduated from MGIMO University in 1955. From 2001–2006 he served as a Special Presidential Envoy on African Issues at the G8. Simonia is a recognized expert in international relations. His current area of expertise is global energy issues. He is the author of 17 books and monographs, and of hundreds of articles in Russian and international periodicals.

Vlada Streletskaya is the Executive Assistant to the Rector of Gubkin Russian State University of Oil and Gas. She holds a BSc in engineering from the Faculty of Oil and Gas Field Development at Kazakh National Technical University (named K.I. Satpaev) and an MSc degree in engineering and technology from Gubkin University. Assistant professor in the Offshore Field Development Technology department, she is also the director of Students' Programs at SPE's Moscow section. Streletskaya is a third-year PhD student at Gubkin University, specializing in environmental protection study.

Per-Arne Sundsbø is professor of cold climate technology at Narvik University College (NUC). He gained his PhD in 1997 at the Norwegian University of Science and Technology, with the title "Numerical modeling and simulation of snow drift – application to snow engineering." He has also held positions as postdoc and Dean of the Faculty of Technology at the NUC. He has been involved in the research and development of winterization measures for the Snøhvit process plant at Melkøya, land development on Sakhalin, offshore development on Goliat and Shtokman and a variety of residential-, road-, railroad- and airport projects in Norway. In addition to research and development of new winterized solutions, Sundsbø's background includes the provision of advisory services concerning winterization strategies for onshore and offshore developments.

Anton Sungurov is Head of Representation at Rystad Energy, responsible for business development in Russia & Commonwealth of Independent States. He holds a master's degree in petroleum geology from Moscow State University, received in 2006. A petroleum geologist by background, Sungurov started his career at the Moscow office of Roxar (now Emerson), a Norwegian developer of subsurface modeling software. He worked at Roxar for six years in the positions of geologist, senior geologist, leading geologist (expertise: modeling and simulation, user training, project management, presale) and finally in the position of business development manager with responsibility for sales in several regions in Russia and CIS. Before joining Rystad Energy, Sungurov worked in IHS as Regional Director, sales (subsurface software part of the company).

Are Kristoffer Sydnes, PhD, is a professor in societal safety at UiT – the Arctic University of Norway. His research has a particular focus on Arctic issues. Sydnes has led international research and education development projects in the Barents region. He has published widely on topics related to the Law of the Sea, maritime transport, oil-spill response, safety management and the marine environment.

Maria Sydnes, PhD, is an associate professor in societal safety and environment at UiT – the Arctic University of Norway. Her research topics lie within the political sciences with a focus on international cooperation issues in the Arctic. She has published a number of articles on Norwegian and Russian oil-spill preparedness policies and oil-spill response organization in the Barents Sea region.

Anette Sæland (former Larsen) obtained an MSc degree in marine operations/marine construction from the Norwegian University of Science and Technology in 1999. Sæland has worked in the industry as a topside piping inspection planner, design and construction engineer, flow line and umbilical project engineer, and has also worked as a faculty member and research fellow in arctic maintenance engineering at the Tromsø University College (now part of UiT – the Arctic University of Norway).

Sergey Vasiliev is a deputy director at the International Institute of Energy Policy and Diplomacy (MIEP) of the MGIMO University and Head of Center for Specialized Linguistic Training. He is a candidate of science (PhD) philology and Honored Worker of the High Education of the Russian Federation. He graduated from the Military Institute of Foreign Languages, Moscow, Russia, in 1974. Vasiliev is also the director of the Russian–Norwegian executive MBA Program for the Rosneft, Russian–Italian, Russian–German, Russian–British and Russian–Norwegian joint/double degree master's programs. His areas of expertise are sustainable development, energy management, indigenous peoples and disarmament.

Mark Verba is a graduate of the Leningrad Mining Institute (1958). He holds a PhD in geology and exploration of oil and gas deposits as well as a doctorate in geological sciences (1993). Chief Geologist of the PMGRE (Polar Marine Geological Exploration Expedition) from 1969–1972 and of MAGE (Marine Arctic Geological Expedition) from 1973–1983, he was Head of Division at VNIIOkeangeologiya from 1983–1994 and Chief Geologist from 1994–2001. Verba is currently Chief Scientific Officer of Sevmorgeo. He has carried out geological and geophysical surveys in 29 field expeditions and participated in the opening of the Barents gas province and the discovery of the Leningradskoye and Skuratovskoye gas fields in the Kara Sea and the North Kildinskoye field in the Barents Sea. He developed the concept of the riftogenesis origin of the Barents–Northkara megabasin and its petroleum model and is the author of over 300 scientific works, including 18 monographs.

Elana Wilson Rowe is a senior research fellow at the Norwegian Institute of International Affairs (NUPI), where she leads the Emerging Powers and Global Development Research Group. She is also an adjunct professor at Bodø Graduate School of Business, University of Nordland in Bodø, Norway. She holds a PhD from the University of Cambridge, where she was affiliated with the Scott Polar Research Institute. Her research interests include circumpolar relations, international climate politics and Russia's foreign, northern and climate policymaking. A common theme in her research is attention to science diplomacy and the politics of expertise.

Anatoly Zolotukhin holds the position of counsellor on International Affairs, research director of the Institute of Arctic Petroleum Technologies and professor of Petroleum Reservoir Engineering at Gubkin University. Being a member of the Russian Academy of Natural Sciences, he is the chief researcher at the Oil and Gas Institute of the Russian Academy of Sciences. Zolotukhin is an adjunct professor at Stavanger University, a chaired professor at the Northern Arctic Federal University (Arkhangelsk) and holds the title Doctor *Honoris Causa* from Murmansk and Arkhangelsk. Holding a PhD in the mechanics of liquids, gases and plasma, he is a doctor of technical sciences in petroleum reservoir engineering. Publications include 16 textbooks and monographs and around 130 technical papers.

Foreword

We need to de-mystify the Arctic.

True, the Arctic, and what we in Norway call the High North, is to many a new region, inspiring dreams and anxieties. But this is no terra *nullius*; international rules and regulations apply, such as the UN Convention on the Law of the Sea. In recent years, closer cooperation between the Arctic coastal states has helped fill the gaps; the Arctic is gradually becoming subject to advanced international and regional cooperation.

One illustration of this normal state of affairs came with the conclusion of almost 40 years of negotiations on the delimitation of the sea boundaries between Norway and Russia in 2010. Following the guide and spirit of the UN Convention, we devised a modern, balanced and just treaty on the delimitation, proving that overlapping claims can be settled through constructive negotiations. Gradually we are seeing the emergence of a regulatory framework that can guide and regulate human activity in these vast and vulnerable waters.

Management of natural resources will continue to be a key feature of developments in the High North. We will have to deal with this in a responsible manner, especially as we are bound to experience ups and downs in economic as well as political expectations. Sustainable management of the renewable fish resources will continue to be of the utmost importance. Exploration of oil and gas will be subject to complex considerations as the energy markets undergo structural change. At the end of 2014 a geopolitical freeze emanating from the conflict in Ukraine can be felt all the way to the Arctic.

Politically, everything is linked; nothing is frozen, not even in the Arctic.

Norway and Russia are neighbors. In 1,000 years, the two countries have never been at war with each other. It is the responsibility of both Norway and Russia to manage relations and activities in the same constructive manner as we have seen in recent decades. The future lies open, and we need to reflect on scenarios for how things may develop, not least in the light of predicted climate change; we can expect to see much greater implications of rising temperatures in the north compared to further south. How we manage to mitigate and adapt to climate change will be a decisive factor for the development of the Barents Sea.

For Norway and Russia, how the Barents Sea develops as a petroleum province will influence the prosperity and environmental conditions in the northernmost parts of our countries. It is a welcome sign that Norwegian and Russian researchers from many different disciplines have come together to reflect about the future of this region. By taking into account the full range of possible futures, we can prepare to shape the future as we would like it to be.

Ten years ago, in 2004, the book *Big Oil Playground, Russian Bear Preserve or European Periphery?* was published. It presented three scenarios looking 10 years ahead to the Russian Barents Region in 2015. I had the honor to be part of the fine team that initiated that project, which stimulated much debate about the High North at that time. The findings served as an important inspiration to me as I named the High North as the priority for Norway's foreign policy in 2005. The project was skillfully led by one of Norway's leading scenario experts, Bjørn Brunstad.

Now a decade has passed and the world is a different place. But the High North remains a key interest for Arctic nations such as Norway and Russia, and the Barents Sea remains important to the development of both countries. The publication now of a new scenario project looking at the next decade into the future is therefore timely and welcome. We became wiser and better informed back in 2004, and I am pleased to see that excellent researchers have again put their brains together to ponder what the next 10 years may look like. In these times of complex political relations between East and West, I truly welcome researchers from both countries continuing to reach out and work together.

No doubt, this is another piece of work that helps de-mystify the Arctic.

Jonas Gahr Støre
Oslo, December 2014

Part I

Introduction and scenarios

1 Introduction

Anatoli Bourmistrov and Frode Mellemvik

Will Arctic states cooperate in the development of Arctic petroleum resources? This is what they declare, but the barriers to the cooperative development of Arctic petroleum resources are intensifying and the future is unclear. This book looks in detail at the preconditions and outlook for the cooperative development of Arctic petroleum resources.

Arctic oil and gas figure prominently in the regional economic hopes and strategies of many of the Arctic states. However, if and how these resources are developed depends on the political and economic choices made by relevant national actors, the technology developed and global trends outside the circumpolar region.

The Barents Sea is a microcosm and indicator of what can happen elsewhere in the Arctic: the Gulf Stream makes it largely ice-free; it is closer to oil and gas markets than most other parts of the Arctic and many different countries are present in the broader Barents region, while it is divided between Russia and western Europe.

Applying a cross-disciplinary approach, including geopolitical, institutional, technological, corporate and environmental perspectives, a team of Norwegian and Russian researchers offer the reader three scenarios as possible ways of thinking about the future of Norwegian–Russian petroleum cooperation in the Barents Sea towards 2025, taking the Murmansk Treaty signed in 2010 by Norway and Russia as the point of departure. This treaty delineated the maritime boundary between the two countries in the Barents Sea, creating new opportunities for petroleum development in a large, previously disputed, area, while creating a framework for Norwegian–Russian cooperative exploitation of trans-boundary oil and gas fields.

It is essential to remember that while oil and gas resources are valuable, they are also expensive to extract, especially in a harsh-climate frontier environment like the Arctic. The Shtokman project in the Russian part of the Barents Sea – which Western companies once competed excitedly to access, but later put on ice – has already shown that even the greatest projects may be commercially vulnerable. Regional economies of scale can be decisive for project costs: a project realized on its own will often be far more expensive than if it is carried out in coordination with other projects in the same area, sharing infrastructural facilities (pipelines, LNG facilities, electricity supply, etc.); mobile infrastructure (rigs, ships, etc.); a skilled labor pool; rescue services and so on. Without Norwegian–Russian cooperation across the Barents Sea border, many such opportunities for economies of scale may be lost, and the development of the resources below the seabed will be less likely. The lower the price of oil and gas, the more acute this point becomes. Accordingly, cooperation may be both a possible outcome and a chosen strategy.

We have written this book at a time when the barriers to the cooperative development of Arctic petroleum resources are intensifying and the future is unclear. The core question addressed by this book is thus all the more pressing: What factors would need to fall into place for the cooperative development of Arctic petroleum resources?

In order to speak to this question, this book is centered on scenarios – a range of possible futures of Norwegian–Russian petroleum cooperation in the Barents Sea towards 2025 – developed by a team of Norwegian and Russian researchers. The aim of scenarios is not to attempt to forecast or make projections, but rather to identify alternative possible developments with an emphasis on the unpredictable interaction between multiple factors.

These scenarios are based on the thematic chapters that make up the majority of this book. Part I (Chapters 1–2) introduces and presents the scenarios. In the belief that the underlying analysis of trends and possible developments is an equally important aspect of scenarios as the scenarios themselves, we have given the thematic chapters much space in the book and kept the scenarios correspondingly brief. Parts II and III are dedicated to unveiling in detail the building blocks for the scenarios presented in Chapter 2 and provide extensive background knowledge on the Barents Sea developments. In particular, Part II (Chapters 3–7) examines economic and political factors that may influence the development of the Barents Sea as well as experience from past cooperation. Part III (Chapters 8–14) focuses on technology and the natural environment.

This book is a result of the joint effort of the core group of Norwegian and Russian researchers who are involved in NAREC – the Norwegian and Russian Education and Research Consortium for International Business Development in the Energy Sector – and who have cooperated on different research and education programs for several years. NAREC was formally established in October 2009 with the purpose of strengthening education and research cooperation between Norwegian and Russian institutions with support from the Norwegian and Russian Ministries of Foreign Affairs. This cooperation gives the book strength in that it brings into close conversation different views on similar issues from researchers in both countries.

Summaries of the chapters

Part I of the book contains this introduction and Chapter 2. In Chapter 2, a six-person scenario-building team – Indra Overland, Alexei Bambulyak, Anatoli Bourmistrov, Ove Gudmestad, Frode Mellemvik and Anatoly

Zolotukhin – discusses the assumptions, uncertainties and three scenarios for the development of the petroleum sector in the Barents Sea. Drawing on a time-honored methodology for scenario building used by Royal Dutch Shell and the points made in the thematic chapters (3–14), the team identifies 10 assumptions and 12 major uncertainty factors that the authors see as shaping the future of cooperation and petroleum development in the Barents Sea. Putting these different uncertainties together, three scenarios are developed providing different understandings of the future.

The scenario "After You, Sir" describes a situation in which unconventional oil and gas reduce the prices of oil and gas in global energy markets, and Norway and Russia are therefore hesitant to make a first move in order to make petroleum-related investments in the region. Thus, two countries are like two British gentlemen in front of a door, each politely ushering the other to enter first but neither of them actually going through the door.

In contrast, in the scenario "Parallel Play", oil and gas prices are relatively high, but there is a freeze in political relations leading to the noncooperative development of the Barents Sea.

Finally, the scenario "Let's Dance" envisages a possible future where a breakthrough has been made in noncarbon energy sources. In spite of relatively good cooperation between Norway and Russia, only a few big gas projects are developed in the Barents Sea.

Part II of the book comprises five thematically specific chapters dedicated to issues of politics, economics and experiences from past cooperation between Norway and Russia. In Chapter 3, Indra Overland, Nodari Simonia, Sergei Vasiliev and Elana Wilson Rowe examine the international context for Barents oil and gas. According to their analysis, the global context will be more important than Arctic politics for the development of the Barents Sea. In identifying relevant factors, the authors conclude that Asia in spite of its remoteness is particularly important as it may have a double effect on developments in the Barents Region. On the one hand, Asian economic growth is important because it can drive rising demand for oil and gas, and thus make challenging projects in the Barents Sea financially attractive. On the other, Asian economic growth may change Russia's internal priorities, causing it to develop the eastern parts of the country rather than the Barents Sea. Furthermore, any financial downturn in China and other Asian countries will have complex and unforeseeable effects. The future of the Barents Sea will therefore depend on how the Asian economies develop and how the impact plays out in international oil and gas markets and Russian priorities. Two other factors examined by the authors are the development of unconventional oil and gas and the possibility of a new global climate policy regime.

In Chapter 4, Alexei Bambulyak, Svetlana Golubeva, Maria Sydnes, Are Kristoffer Sydnes, Lars-Henrik Larsen and Vlada Streletskaya identify similarities and differences in petroleum resource management in Norway and Russia. They demonstrate that the petroleum industry in both countries is moving northwards and in order to secure environmentally safe oil and gas exploration and production in the Barents Sea region, both countries are developing new regulations. The authors examine the current management regimes in both countries in terms of licensing, environmental control and oil-spill response with especial focus on the Barents Sea. They conclude that, despite the fact that the resource management systems in the two countries are different, they also have many similarities in terms of basic principles of licensing, impact and risk assessment and pollution control. Implications for potential regulatory harmonization between Norway and Russia are also discussed.

In Chapter 5, Anatoli Bourmistrov, June Borge Doornich and Andrey Krivorotov discuss the driving forces for Norwegian–Russian business-to-business cooperation in the petroleum sector. The chapter shows that the rich oil and gas resources in the Barents Sea – including the expected trans-boundary resources in the previously disputed area – are a driving force for business-to-business cooperation. Opportunities for knowledge and technology transfer, as well as sharing expertise, represent benefits for cooperation that can provide the advantages of economy of scale and economy of scope in developing demanding areas of the Barents Sea. By describing historical aspects of business-to-business cooperation between the petroleum industries in the High North, key driving forces and factors that can promote and limit future cooperation in the Barents Sea are illuminated. It is argued that in the short term cooperation will most probably occur in the southwestern part of the Barents Sea in Norway because of this area's accessibility in terms of climate, logistics and finances. In the long run, cooperation may be focused on the exploration and development of the southeastern part of the Barents Sea on the Russian side. It is further argued that oil and gas resources in the delimitation-line areas, and particularly trans-boundary resources, will be explored and developed last because of lack of experience in cooperation and differences between the regulative frameworks of the two countries.

In Chapter 6, Indra Overland and Andrey Krivorotov take as their point of departure the 2010 Murmansk Treaty and discuss the history, present and possible future of Norwegian–Russian political relations and their implications for the development of Barents Sea oil and gas resources. The authors argue that a good political relationship between the two countries can facilitate oil and gas projects in the Barents Sea, while noncooperative relations will slow them down. The authors also discuss how the Barents Sea may interact with other factors and priorities inside Norway and Russia, and how Norwegian–Russian relations are influenced by the broader Russian–Western relationship.

In Chapter 7, Anatoli Bourmistrov, Ove Gudmestad, Valery Salygin and Anatoly Zolotukhin describe the experience of Norwegian–Russian cooperation on education in the areas of energy management and petroleum technology. The chapter shows how favorable political attention in both Norway and Russia directed towards the development of Arctic petroleum resources, joint political initiatives in both countries and the possibility of the international harmonization of education brought by the Bologna process have created space for cooperation in the field of oil and gas education between Norwegian and

Russian universities. Despite considerable differences in education standards and cultures, two universities in Norway and two in Russia strategically developed joint degree/dual degree education programs in energy management and petroleum technology for the benefit of the authorities and industries in both countries. Reviewing this experience, the authors conclude that, in the case of education and research, it has been possible to establish long-term and beneficial cooperation based on the continuous search for synergies, respect for differences, experimentation and the involvement of dedicated individuals.

Part III of the book comprises seven chapters dedicated to technology and the natural environment. In Chapter 8, Mark Verba, Gennady Ivanov and Anatoly Zolotukhin describe the structure of the geological and geophysical profiles and the main features of oil and gas content in the Barents Sea. In Chapter 9, Anatoly Zolotukhin, Anton Sungurov and Vlada Streletskaya describe and compare the Barents Sea hydrocarbon resource base and production potential on both the Norwegian and Russian sides of the boundary. Both chapters indicate a great discovered and undiscovered potential of hydrocarbon resources in the Barents Sea that can contribute to the global energy supply. The development of these resources can be an important driving force to stimulate the development of domestic and international petroleum industries and active collaboration between those. However, the authors conclude that it also requires a much clearer understanding of the market potential for Arctic gas and oil in the global energy supply picture including issues related to e.g. demanded volumes, project development time frames and transportation routes.

In Chapter 10, Maria Bulakh, Ove Gudmestad and Anatoly Zolotukhin describe how hydrocarbon fields in the newly delineated border area in the Barents Sea of Norway and Russia can be developed based on subsea technology. Founded on data from previous geological surveys, the authors describe the physical environmental conditions in the most promising area of the Barents Sea – the Fedynsky High, analyze the main challenges for exploration and production and suggest possible scenarios for oil and gas fields' technical development and arrangements. The authors conclude that subsea development is the most promising approach for gas fields; the corresponding technology for oil is still premature.

In Chapter 11, Tore Markeset, Anette Sæland, Ove Gudmestad and Javad Barabady discuss the design and use of petroleum production facilities in conditions of Arctic operational environments. The authors demonstrate how remote Arctic locations affect an industrial production facility's design, construction and installation, as well as its operation, maintenance, support and decommissioning phases. Criteria for the efficient design of facilities for the Arctic that help avoid injuries and prevent loss of human life, prevent environmental disasters, mitigate high costs and improve performance efficiency are presented and discussed.

In Chapter 12, Ove Njå and Ove Gudmestad address problems of crisis management in cold climate areas. Because the Arctic is associated with a harsh climate, environmental vulnerability and limited experience in emergency response, the authors discuss the design of appropriate technical safety systems in the petroleum industry and related shipping sectors. They emphasize the known and potential uncertainty dimensions and recommend how these can be addressed by the design approach based on all available knowledge to identify, recognize and prevent hazards. The chapter also explores structures that are already employed to work close to or in transit through the Barents Sea. Furthermore, the chapter describes the efficiency of different emergency response equipment, the consequences of the long distances to shore bases and the limited infrastructure of Northern Norway and northwestern Russia.

In Chapter 13, Roald Kommedal, Andrea Bagi and Tor Hemmingsen address potential environmental effects of oil and gas exploration and production in the Barents Sea related mainly to offshore operations. The chapter starts by addressing both general and Arctic-specific environmental issues, and then highlights the challenges of creating safe working conditions on offshore Arctic installations followed by a discussion of oil behavior in open water and the effects of oil on marine organisms. A description of specific Arctic environmental issues focusing on the Barents Sea and its natural ecosystem follows, together with an overview of management strategies to tackle operational and accidental emissions of pollutants under Arctic conditions. The authors conclude that potential oil spills represent the largest threat to the Barents Sea and, therefore, it is essential to plan in detail for possible scenarios and to develop appropriate contingency strategies in order to achieve the necessary level of preparedness.

Finally, in Chapter 14, Per-Arne Sundsbø discusses issues of the winterization of onshore facilities and outdoor work areas. Because wind and drifting snow are among the most essential characteristics of the Arctic climate, increasing petroleum activity means that proper winterization of equipment is an indispensable condition for successful operations in Arctic conditions. The author describes and reviews different winterization measures. The chapter also provides design guidelines for wind and snow control, while illustrating that selected control measures should be carefully designed and implemented according to a systematic and overall wind and snow control strategy for petroleum facilities.

Use of this book

We hope that this book will be useful for many readers, including researchers, NGO representatives, students, policymakers and business actors concerned with the development of the Arctic petroleum resources. The development of Arctic resources requires multidisciplinary knowledge. Engineers must understand the geopolitical, environmental and managerial complexities involved in petroleum projects, and managers and politicians need to be equipped to understand the engineering and operational challenges of the Arctic. We also hope that this book will interest scholars in the fields of political science, international and cross-cultural management, geography, petroleum, cold climate technology, geopolitics, Arctic studies, energy policy and Russian studies. This book can also be useful as a syllabus for both petroleum technology and petroleum management oriented introductory Arctic resource management courses for students at graduate and postgraduate levels.

Finally, the book's application may be related directly to the scenarios it contains. Chapter 2 highlights three qualitatively different descriptions of the future. These are three pictures of what may happen, not what will happen. Still, these pictures of the possible future may be relevant for readers, who can help to think through possible consequences for their organization, institution or company in case each scenario materializes.

However, the book highlights only three out of many conceivable scenarios for the development of the petroleum resources in the Barents Sea. In this sense, the aim of this book is also to demonstrate the many uncertainties involved in the development of the Barents Sea and examples of how scenario methodology may be applied. The range of assumptions and uncertainties identified in the thematic chapters provide ample ground for scenario development beyond those three presented here. In this regard, we hope that the book will inspire readers who would like to construct their own scenarios for the Barents Sea and/or to apply scenario methodology to the discussion of petroleum development in other parts of the Arctic.

Although the book relates to interaction on the border between Norway and Russia, we think its relevance extends beyond those geographical limits. Similar analysis can be used to pave the way to a better understanding of the opportunities and challenges for cooperative development of Arctic petroleum resources in other Arctic regions as well as in the Arctic as a whole. Ultimately, the book should prove valuable also to policymakers and entrepreneurs outside the Arctic countries dealing or wishing to deal with Russia and Norway in the energy sector.

Acknowledgements

We would like to thank all the authors of the chapters included in this book for their dedication to the project. All papers submitted went through several rounds of review by the editors, internal and external reviewers. The external reviewers had two especially important functions: to ensure that the thematic chapters reached a high standard and to secure the relevance of those chapters for the scenario building.

Next, special thanks go to our colleagues, Alexei Bambulyak, Ove Gudmestad, Indra Overland and Anatoly Zolotukhin, who are coeditors of the book and who functioned as members of the core scenario-building group. For many of us, this project started in January 2012 when the very first idea was launched at a NAREC workshop in Tromsø and followed up during the September 2012 NAREC seminar in St. Petersburg. Since then, members of the core group attended countless meetings to discuss and clarify the book content, assign responsibilities to contributors, invite authors for the thematic chapters, organize reviews and provide feedback. We are thankful to all of you for making this project a priority, especially during its final and most critical phase.

In particular, this concerns our joint work on the scenarios during and between the internal scenario-building workshops held in Oslo (May 20, 2014), Bodø (September 4 and 5, 2014) and Gardermoen (September 26, 2014). We appreciate our fruitful and sometimes challenging discussions based on different and sometimes contrasting views regarding e.g. the issues of the climate change, the role of authorities and the relative importance of different factors. This book is evidence that we managed to reach a consensus.

We are thankful to the people who dedicated their time to review and comment on individual chapters and scenarios. In this respect, we would like to express our gratitude to experts on different issues related to Arctic petroleum in international, Norwegian and Russian perspectives, especially those who have provided written comments and/or actively participated in discussions during the book seminars in Moscow (October 22, 2014) and Oslo (October 31, 2014): *Morten Anker* (Counselor for Energy and Environment, Norwegian Embassy in Moscow), *Odd Jarle Borch* (Professor, Bodø Graduate School of Business, University of Nordland), *Daniel Fjærtoft* (Partner and Managing Director, Sigra Group), *Jarle Forbord* (Managing Director, the Norwegian Russian Chamber of Commerce), *Jakub Godzimirski* (Research Professor, Norwegian Institute of International Affairs), *Marsel Gubaidullin* (Professor, Northern Arctic Federal University, Arkhangelsk), *Andrey Kulikov* (Second Secretary, Embassy of the Russian Federation in Norway), *Petter Nore* (Chief Energy Analyst, Ministry of Foreign Affairs of Norway), *Iryna Roddvik* (Vice President External Affairs, Region Europe, Telenor), *Sverre Rustad* (Counselor for Education, Research and Technology, Royal Norwegian Embassy in Moscow), *Antonina Stoupakova* (Professor, Lomonosov Moscow State University, Geological Adviser to Statoil) and *Erik Øverland* (Senior Advisor, Ministry of Education and Research of Norway). Thank you all – you have given us valuable comments and feedback that strengthen the book.

We would like to thank the Norwegian Ministry of Foreign Affairs for supporting the initial stage of the NAREC network project through the Barents 2020 program; and we are grateful to the Norwegian Centre for International Cooperation in Education (SIU) for financial support for book workshops and meetings.

Special thanks go to Helen Bell from Routledge for her support and appreciation of the book idea but also for her effort to ensure the completion of the project. For language editing and consultation, we are very thankful to Linda March from the Good English Company. We extend our appreciation to Kris Kommedahl from the University of Nordland and Valeria Sungurova from the All-Russian Research Geological Oil Institute (VNIGNI) for excellent work on the design of figures and tables.

Finally, this book would be impossible without a very special person – Petter Gullmark at the Bodø Graduate School of Business, University of Nordland. His dedication and ability to stay attentive to detail and deadlines have been a guarantee for delivering the project on time.

2 Barents Sea oil and gas 2025

Three scenarios

Indra Overland, Alexei Bambulyak, Anatoli Bourmistrov,
Ove Gudmestad, Frode Mellemvik, and
Anatoly Zolotukhin

Introduction to the scenarios

What are some of the possible futures for Barents Sea oil and gas? This chapter draws upon the key trends and issues covered by the book's thematic chapters and presents three scenarios on the prospects for Norwegian–Russian cooperation in the Barents Sea. Ultimately human interaction will play a large part in how the Barents Sea is developed, and we have therefore given the scenarios metaphorical titles related to interaction between people.

In the first scenario – called "After You, Sir" – petroleum development in the Barents Sea region is a respectful and cooperative enterprise between Norway and Russia. However, both countries are also hesitant to make first moves on investments, because growing production of unconventional resources has suppressed oil and gas prices. Thus we think of Norway and Russia as two British gentlemen in front of a door, each politely ushering the other to enter first, but neither of them actually going through the door:

"After you, Sir."
"No, no, after you, Sir."

In contrast, the second scenario – "Parallel Play, Not Only for Children" – is centered on the combination of high oil and gas prices and noncooperative relations between Norway and Russia in times of growing energy demand and oil/gas prices. The result is "parallel play", a term borrowed from the pedagogical literature to describe the stage at which toddlers take an interest in playing with other children, but are incapable of interacting directly with them because of their limited social and language skills.

The third scenario – "Let's Dance, but Where Is the Music?" – envisages a future where Russia and Norway cooperate on the development of a few big petroleum projects, but broader development is hindered by a strict and effective global climate regime that reduces profits from the sale of oil and gas and makes smaller Arctic fields commercially unviable.

Figure 2.1 plots the three scenarios on the 12 main uncertainties we have identified. The shape of each scenario on the radar diagram can be thought of as its unique fingerprint.

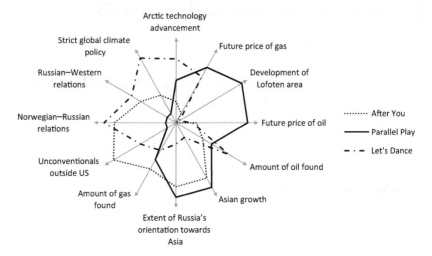

Figure 2.1 Scenario star with all three scenarios

Approach

In developing the scenarios we have applied the time-honored approach made famous by Royal Dutch Shell (Cornelius, Van de Putte, & Romani, 2005; Jefferson, 2012; Varum & Melo, 2010). Rather than probability – which cannot be quantitatively estimated with any degree of accuracy for complex future developments – the criteria for the scenarios are instead plausibility and internal coherence. That means that the scenarios are not attempts at forecasting or projection but rather at identifying alternative possible developments, emphasizing the unpredictable interaction between multiple factors. The aim is not to predict the future but to prepare mentally for a full range of possible futures. Neither is it decisive whether the reader agrees with the scenarios or not, as long as he or she is stimulated to make his or her own reflections on the future.

The scenarios were developed through four stages. First, the book's thematic chapters (3–14) were written to provide input on different topics of relevance for the future development of the oil and gas resources in the Barents Sea. In addition to the chapters as they are published here, the authors of each chapter were requested to provide specific written input for the scenarios. Second, we held a series of internal intensive scenario-building discussions among the six authors of the scenarios. The authors include both Norwegians and Russians, and social scientists, natural scientists, and experts on technology, making for rich and dynamic discussions. Third, the scenarios were presented at two dedicated seminars, one in Norway and one in Russia. The participants in these seminars were well-informed non-academic actors who are involved in petroleum cooperation between Norway and Russia. These sessions were also interactive, with ample room for feedback and discussion. Fourth and finally, the written scenarios were submitted to three knowledgeable people for review.

In developing the scenarios we first identified developments that we believe are likely. These we refer to as "assumptions", not because it is certain that they will take place but because we think they are significantly more probable than many other developments. An example is rising energy demand. Having laid out our assumptions, we attempted to identify key uncertainties – developments that we think are fundamentally uncertain and could easily tip one way or the other. An example is the future price of gas. Subsequently, we pieced together the three scenarios, each consisting of contrasting combinations of the assumptions and uncertainties.

Finally, we added a series of wild cards. These are events that have low probability but would have a great impact. They are difficult to fit into the scenarios and are more like miniature scenarios in their own right. We believe that wild cards are one of the most important components in scenario building, because they help expose the full range of possible future developments. Unexpected things often do happen and play an important role in how the world develops. To prepare for the future one therefore needs to prepare for the unexpected, and wild cards are a good way of remaining attuned to the future's unforeseeable nature.

Assumptions

In this section, we briefly outline the main assumptions identified in the book's thematic chapters and taken into the scenarios. By "assumptions" we mean things that we are reasonably confident about and therefore choose to treat as givens. This does not mean that they are guaranteed, just that we see them as significantly more probable than other factors we have considered.

Global markets vs. international political bodies

According to Chapter 3 (Overland, Simonia, Vasiliev, and Wilson Rowe), the Arctic, and especially the Barents Sea, is unlikely to be the setting for a major geopolitical conflict, and circumpolar political bodies are unlikely to propose binding agreements that would restrict oil and gas development. The Arctic Council is an important institution of political discussions but has no power over the Arctic nation-states and lacks power of enforcement. Also UN organizations cannot stop Norwegian and Russian Arctic offshore petroleum activities. For the development of the Barents Sea, we therefore assume that the global market and global geopolitical context will be more important than circumpolar or other international political bodies.

Demand for energy

According to major world energy market forecasts, including those of the IEA and OPEC reviewed in Chapter 3 (Overland, Simonia, Vasiliev, and Wilson

Rowe), global energy demand is going to continue growing, driven by a combination of population growth and economic growth. Forecasts also assume that oil and gas will remain an important part of the world energy supply, even if their consumption is reduced. The composition of the energy resources portfolio to cover this increasing demand is, however, uncertain. For example, coal may or may not be phased out, and the balance between oil and gas is uncertain.

Asian market growth

We also assume that the importance of Asian markets will continue to grow and that Russia will continue diversifying its exports by expanding infrastructure to sell oil and gas to the Asia–Pacific region. Although we are relatively confident about this development and have therefore included it among our assumptions, we are far from sure how far it will go and its extent is therefore included in the uncertainties listed below.

Global climate policy

Although we do not know whether an effective new climate agreement will be reached to follow up and improve on the Kyoto Protocol, we do assume that climate change will remain on the political agenda. The pressure for transformation towards a low carbon economy comes from many directions. The UN report *Better Growth, Better Climate* (Global Commission on the Economy and Climate [GCEC], 2014) focuses on how major economies through innovation and changing regulations can combine continued economic growth with reduced carbon emissions. The question is how quickly such policies will be developed and what impact they will have on the development and use of oil and gas resources.

Barents petroleum exploration

Exploration drilling will be extended to cover all parts of the southern Norwegian Barents Sea. On the Russian side, the Dolginskoye, Varandey-More, Medin-More, and Pomorskoye fields will be explored (see Figure 9.4 in Chapter 9 – Zolotukhin, Sungurov, and Streletskaya). However, outside the potentially interesting structures that have already been identified for test drilling, very large fields are not very likely to be found, especially on the Norwegian side.

Arctic petroleum production

Oil and gas resources in the Arctic will continue to be explored and developed. Even though many environmentalists and fishermen are critical regarding Arctic petroleum developments, exploration and production have already started and further development of new licenses is probable. Probably, the Dolginskoye oilfield will come into the production phase between 2015 and 2025. It is therefore likely that there will be significant oil and gas production from the Arctic, although how much will be produced remains uncertain.

The cost of operations, maintenance, and logistics will be higher than in other parts of the world due to the harsh climate and longer distances that infrastructure and human resources need to travel. Subsea processing factories can be hooked up to production centers located relatively far away (say 200 km), making integrated area development possible (see Chapter 10 – Bulakh, Gudmestad, and Zolotukhin).

Arctic marine bio-resources

Although biodiversity and catches may be influenced downwards or upwards by climate change, the Barents Sea will remain an important marine habitat for Arctic marine species, both in terms of the planet's ecology and in terms of commercial fisheries (see Chapter 13 – Kommedal, Bagi, and Hemmingsen).

Arctic weather conditions

Regardless of how the climate changes, Arctic weather conditions will challenge personnel and hardware (see Chapter 11 – Markeset, Sæland, Gudmestad, and Barabady). Greater physical and mental pressure on personnel will necessitate higher wages and more time off. For hardware, there will be higher failure rates as well as higher maintenance costs also when there are no failures (see example Chapter 14 – Sundsbø). The cost of petroleum exploration and production under these conditions will remain high, even if significant technological progress is made and the climate heats up.

Northern Sea Route

The Northern Sea Route will remain secondary as a transport route for oil and gas from the Barents Sea to Asia. It will only be used in summer. Less ice may actually be more difficult to handle than a firm ice cover that it is possible to plow a channel through. There will be a limited number of icebreakers, and they will have the capacity to take a limited number of ships in each convoy because the broken ice slips back into the channel they have created. This is disadvantageous for the development of the Barents Sea because it limits the volume of hydrocarbon resources that can be exported via the Northern Sea Route to Asia and therefore reduces possible synergies that the petroleum industry in the region can have by building and using a common infrastructure with the Northern Sea Route.

Business-to-business cooperation

Norwegian and other Western oil companies will continue to want access to the Russian part of the Barents Sea; and Russian oil companies will want access to the Norwegian part of the Barents Sea (see Chapter 5 – Bourmistrov, Borge Doornich, and Krivorotov). However, there will be limited room for small supply companies to play a role in the Barents Sea petroleum province, especially local small players and especially on the Russian side – except if there are very many large developments and the authorities make a special effort to facilitate their participation.

Uncertainties

Having presented the points that we are relatively sure about in the previous section, here we summarize the points that we see as most uncertain. When forecasting the future, the aim is to reduce uncertainty as much as possible. This is of course not the aim in a scenario project such as this one. Uncertainties are rather at the core of the project and actively cultivated in order to define the range of possible scenarios. The uncertainties discussed here are also presented visually in Figure 2.1.

Price of gas and oil

As discussed in Chapter 3 – Overland, Simonia, Vasiliev, and Wilson Rowe – some of the uncertainties that will affect the development the Barents Sea are related to energy demand: will the prices of oil and gas rise, stabilize, or fall, and will they be high enough to justify the development of Barents Sea fields? Historically, the prices of oil and gas were tightly correlated, in large part due to the linking of gas contracts to oil prices. However, from 2005 to 2015, the prices of oil and gas increasingly diverged, as increasing amounts of gas were traded in spot markets and shale gas in the US pressed gas prices downwards. Thus, in our work on the uncertainties, we treated the future price of oil and future price of gas as two separate factors. This does not mean that they will not interact with each other, just that they will not necessarily move in tandem.

Asian growth

Although oil, and increasingly gas, is traded in global markets, location still makes some difference. As the Barents Sea is located as far away as it is possible to get from the Asia–Pacific region, it makes some difference whether demand for oil and gas imports will be concentrated in the Atlantic basin area or Asia. The effect of Asian growth on the development of the Barents Sea is nonetheless uncertain. Currently, import growth is concentrated in Asia, but if there is a slowdown in China's growth, Asia's importance may diminish (which might be positive for the Barents Sea) at the same time as oil prices would fall (which would be negative for the Barents Sea). On the other hand, if growth continues unabated in China, it could have a converse double effect on the Barents Sea: on the one hand it would help support higher oil and gas prices, which would promote the development of the Barents Sea; on the other hand it would continue to drive Russian prioritization of its eastern provinces. Thus, the total impact of this double effect on the development of the Barents Sea is an important uncertainty.

Unconventionals outside the US

Another key question is whether the rapid development of unconventional oil and gas will spread beyond the United States, and how expensive unconventionals will be. If they are cheap enough, they will be prioritized over Arctic resources, as they are less risky and available to more countries. Even if unconventionals stall, will there be room for large volumes of Barents Sea gas in the EU market, given the growing EU imports of LNG from Qatar and other countries, possible LNG deliveries from the US, coupled with deliberate EU efforts to cut dependence on Russian energy? This is not only a market question, but also a political one: will the EU show any serious interest in supporting developments in the Barents Sea, and would the support only apply to the Norwegian part of the sea (in an effort to reduce import dependency on Russia) or also extend to the Russian side (in an effort to maximize overall supply)?

Global climate policy

A focus on green growth policies during the decade 2015–2020 could result in a new set of incentives and mechanisms that simultaneously promote growth and reduce carbon emissions. However, there is uncertainty as to whether and how quickly governments can produce a common international agreement on those issues. Will there be a global, binding, and strict agreement to follow up the Kyoto Protocol, and what would its impact be on demand for oil and, especially, gas? Coal is an obvious priority target for such an agreement, oil could be, but its status is less clear, and natural gas even more so. A stricter climate regime might even end up promoting natural gas.

Moreover, how will global climate change affect climatic conditions for petroleum activities in the Barents Sea, especially north of Bjørnøya? Will there be less ice but more dispersed icebergs and storms? In spite of a long-term trend towards global warming, could there be shorter-term (e.g. 20-year) oscillations that make the region colder?

Amount of oil and gas found

As we can see from Chapter 8 – Verba, Ivanov, and Zolotukhin – and Chapter 9 – Zolotukhin, Sungurov, and Streletskaya – the Barents Sea has important hydrocarbon resource potential both in terms of oil and gas. The Fedynsky High prospect is being drilled by Norwegian and Russian companies, but the outcome is not known. If there is a major find, this may spearhead developments in the Barents Sea due to proximity to land and infrastructure in

Kirkenes. It may be important whether it is oil or gas that is found, depending on which is better priced in the market. Gas is also more difficult and expensive to transport long distances.

Development of Lofoten area and infrastructure

As explained in Chapter 6 – Overland and Krivorotov – the Lofoten Islands area in Norway can be an important factor in the development of petroleum fields in the Barents Sea by serving as the gas transportation infrastructure bridge between well-developed southern gas fields in the Norwegian Sea and prospective gas fields in the Barents Sea. If the Lofoten area is opened, the effect on the Barents Sea is still not certain. At first it might distract attention from the Barents Sea, but if major gas resources are found and the Norwegian pipeline grid is extended northwards to the Lofoten Islands, it could provide an important bridge to the Barents Sea that could make many more natural gas projects there feasible in the long term.

As discussed in Chapter 3 – Overland, Simonia, Vasiliev, and Wilson Rowe – during the entire post-Soviet period, Gazprom has had a monopoly on exports, but there has been some discussion of unbundling the company and moving the control over exports to an independent government body. Novatek has already been permitted to export LNG from the Yamal Peninsula, but this is considered an exception from the rule that was only possible for LNG. If Gazprom loses the monopoly, it could open up the way for more dynamism in the Barents Sea, as other companies could handle the opportunities there more creatively. On the other hand, if Gazprom keeps the export monopoly, it may result in other companies being forced to produce more LNG if it is seen as easier to get exemptions from the monopoly for LNG than pipeline exports. Therefore, an important question is: will there be a gas pipeline to the European market in place providing access for Barents Sea gas to this market and facilitating further developments in the area? Related questions are: will this pipeline go through Norwegian waters or through the Republic of Karelia, and will the Norwegian and/or Russian governments reduce taxes in order to kick-start field developments and infrastructure?

Arctic petroleum technology development

As follows from Chapter 10 – Bulakh, Gudmestad, and Zolotukhin – another important uncertainty is how fast remote operation and subsea technologies will develop in the future. These technologies can lower the cost of field operation and be decisive for whether fields are sufficiently profitable to be brought online. For instance, will the Johan Castberg oilfield and nearby fields be developed together, creating enough infrastructure to spearhead other developments?

The technology to be developed should reflect growing environmental, preparedness, and safety concerns related to expanding petroleum operations in the Arctic (see Chapter 10 – Bulakh, Gudmestad, and Zolotukhin – Chapter 11 – Markeset, Sæland, Gudmestad, and Barabady – and Chapter 12 – Njå and Gudmestad). For instance, the effect of hydrocarbon pollution on Arctic species and ecosystems and especially the effect of long-term exposure have not been researched thoroughly. Future research may show that it is worse or better than thought. It is also not clear whether environmental legislation will be developed adequately for the Arctic environment, and whether effective legislation will be adopted and upheld by Arctic states and operators. If environmental and safety demands are strict, they will push up the cost of petroleum projects. If they are not coordinated by Norway and Russia, they can create obstacles to cooperation and joint development (see Chapter 4 – Bambulyak, Golubeva, Sydnes, Sydnes, Larsen, and Streletskaya).

When there is another major oil spill somewhere in the world it could contribute to holding back the development of the Barents Sea, especially if it is an Arctic offshore oil spill that looks bad on television. Spills that have occurred in the past, such as the Exxon Valdez and Deepwater Horizon accidents, have received broad media coverage but have, nonetheless, only briefly slowed down petroleum sector developments. The main route of influence for such an incident on the development of the Barents Sea would most likely be through a tightening of environmental regulations that drive up the need for new technology and thus the cost of field development.

Russian–Western relations

It will be difficult to build good Russian–Western relations during the first half of the decade from 2015–2025. Over time, the EU will attempt to steadily reduce energy imports from Russia. Although news fades fast and, for example, the conflict in South Ossetia was forgotten quite easily, the conflict in Ukraine has brought some serious negative components into Russian–Western relations and could turn the relationship into a self-reinforcing negative spiral.

Thus, due to the conflict over Ukraine, Western–Russian relations could potentially be bad for a long period of time, especially if Russia succeeds in reorienting its economic focus towards Asia and the EU reduces its economic dependence on Russia. At the same, there is also a possibility that the conflict over Ukraine will subside and relations improve. So the question is first, will Russian–Western relations improve or worsen, and, second, how will that affect Norwegian–Russian relations?

Understanding Russian–Western relations is particularly important because it will affect Russian attitudes towards the role of Western companies in the development of Russian Arctic offshore fields (see Chapter 5 – Bourmistrov, Borge Doornich, and Krivorotov). To what extent will Russia allow for direct foreign investment in developing its Arctic offshore fields, and how actively will Norwegian companies pursue these opportunities? What changes might there be in elite attitudes in either country towards the other, due to a change of government or other political developments?

Norwegian–Russian relations

The relationship between Norway and Russia will never be entirely divorced from the broader Russian–Western relationship, but neither is it entirely dependent on it either (see Chapter 6 – Overland and Krivorotov). Countries other than Norway are more likely to be at the forefront of Western quarrels with Russia. In spite of asymmetries, it will be in the shared interest of both Russia and Norway, as the two countries sharing the Barents Sea, to cooperate in meeting common challenges, e.g. exploration and development, environmental protection, resource management, and promoting regional growth and employment. However, the degree of cooperation depends on the approaches of both sides, as well as all the other contextual factors discussed here.

Although we do not expect Russia's relationship with Norway to be one of its worst European relationships, there is a considerable range within which it can move. One of the great successes of Norwegian–Russian cooperation was the partial decentralization of the bilateral relationship to the local and regional level through the Barents Euro-Arctic Region. As Russian–Western relations have soured, there has been a de facto recentralization of Norwegian foreign policy towards Russia. A question for the future is therefore whether the provinces near the Barents Sea will have the possibility to cooperate locally across the border and especially in the traditional areas of cooperation such as education, research, and people-to-people (see Chapter 7 – Bourmistrov, Gudmestad, Salygin, and Zolotukhin). A related question is whether Norway will continue to have ambition to be a leading Arctic state focusing on Arctic oil and gas and relations with Russia in the North, or might an emphasis on climate change under a future Norwegian government alter Norway's strategic priorities?

Extent of Russia's orientation towards Asia

Giving the potential for Chinese–Russian petroleum cooperation described in Chapter 3 – Overland, Simonia, Vasiliev, and Wilson Rowe – if Russian–Western and Norwegian–Russian relations stay negative or worsen, Russia could diversify and give Chinese companies an important role in the Barents Sea. This could affect the prospects for Norwegian–Russian cooperation. The relevant uncertainty in this respect is: will political relations between Russia and the West and the instability and risks that they bring deter Norwegian and Russian companies from investing in each other's countries in the long term?

As noted in Chapter 9 – Zolotukhin, Sungurov, and Streletskaya – Russia is the world's largest country by surface area and has many locations to choose between for hydrocarbon production. Thus Russia may prioritize the Barents Sea or other areas such as the Russian Far East, the Yamal Peninsula, or enhanced oil recovery from its old West Siberian fields.

One strength of Norwegian–Russian cooperation is that previous cooperative initiatives between the two countries are already close to institutionalization,
particularly attempts to harmonize education (see Chapter 7 – Bourmistrov,
Gudmestad, Salygin, and Zolotukhin) and some business practices (see Chapter 5 – Bourmistrov, Borge Doornich, and Krivorotov). However, the extent to
which Russia can shift towards Asia will also depend on how active and efficient
the Norwegian and Russian authorities will be in promoting petroleum-related
joint industrial investments in the coastal Barents Sea region: cross-border
Russian–Norwegian business-to-business and people-to-people contacts (creating cooperative institutions, lifting administrative and cultural barriers, etc.).

Interaction between different uncertainties

The uncertainties identified in the previous section can be thought of as the
building blocks for a time machine: how each of them works out and how they
interact with each other will determine what the future looks like. Figure 2.2
is a simplified illustration of how we have thought about this interaction. The
darker an arrow, the more strongly we assume a factor influences another. Dotted lines indicate that a factor reinforces the effect of another factor.

Scenarios

In line with Shell's methodology, we have striven to avoid scenarios that are
simply optimistic or pessimistic. Instead, each of them is meant to be balanced

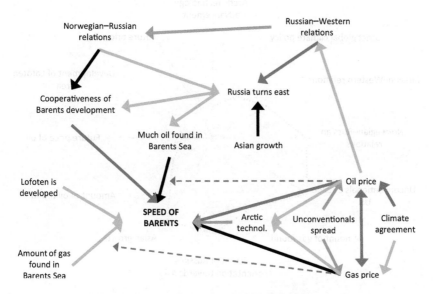

Figure 2.2 Time machine – how the future may be shaped by the interaction of factors

and multifaceted. We tried to avoid getting caught up in discussions of current events or simply extending current trends. That is always difficult. An informed observer can often make good predictions for the coming six or 12 months, and while we have worked on our scenarios we have experienced that some of our visions have already become true. Although that gives one the feeling that one is on the right track, it is not necessarily a good thing, as the scenarios should strive to relate to a future beyond what we know now. It is also worth noting that the diversity of the people involved in making the scenarios, while enriching and providing a sound basis for them, has also had a limiting effect as it was necessary to compromise between sometimes highly divergent worldviews. Tables 2.1 and 2.2 provide an overview of how the different assumptions and uncertainties are related to each other in the three scenarios.

Scenario 1: "After You, Sir"
– Good relations, but surging unconventionals reduce oil and gas prices

In the scenario "After You, Sir", Russian–Western relations had not fully recovered from the Ukrainian crisis, but the crisis did not have a similar degree of influence on the cooperation between the two states in the Arctic. Because of this, the relationship between Norway and Russia was respectful, and their interaction in the Barents Sea was cooperative. But the price of oil and, especially, natural gas, was low and combined with the high costs of infrastructure

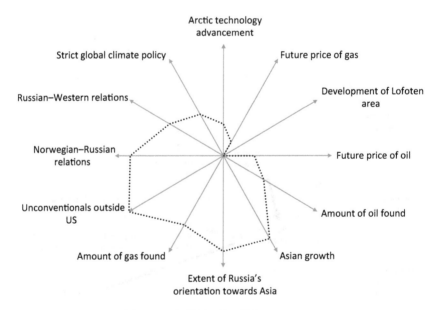

Figure 2.3 Fingerprint of the scenario "After You, Sir"

that meant that many fields were not commercially viable. Thus, in spite of the cooperative atmosphere, the two countries were like two British gentlemen in front of a door, each politely ushering the other to enter first, but neither of them actually going through the door.

A new climate regime was agreed upon in Paris in 2015, but it lacked teeth and failed to limit greenhouse gas emissions seriously. Unconventionals, especially shale gas, spread across the world as the Chinese, Argentineans, and others successfully copied the US approach, flooding the market with gas. The interest of companies in developing Arctic petroleum technology was consequently low. Even in Russia, unconventional natural gas became more interesting than the expensive Arctic offshore developments – especially as the Chinese came to fully master shale gas technology and not only used it to expand their own production but in parallel flooded the world market with cheap drilling rigs, often leased along with cheap, disciplined Chinese engineers.

In the Russian part of the Barents Sea, the Russian authorities and companies were slow to act, while Rosneft and Gazprom continued monopolizing all opportunities. On the Norwegian side, the authorities and Statoil disagreed on infrastructure choices and environmental principles, and the Lofoten Islands area remained closed for exploration. Both the Norwegian and Russian authorities were reluctant to give tax breaks. The 1.8 trillion-bcm trans-boundary gas field identified in the Fedynsky High in 2016 was developed jointly by Gazprom and Statoil and is due to come on stream in 2029. The gas would be piped through Russia to the EU and partly replace volumes from West Siberia that were being diverted to Russia's Altai pipeline to western China.

A number of smaller oilfields were identified on the Norwegian side, whereas exploration stalled on the Russian side. But beyond Johan Castberg and Fedynskoye fields, there were few actual field developments.

As there were not so many projects, the development of the local supply industry in North Norway and Russia was slow. Fields were mostly developed from the Norwegian side, where Kirkenes was used as a main supply hub. The volume of contracts had not been high enough to justify a high level of local content and therefore most of the contracts were awarded to internationally well-positioned Norwegian firms that used only a few local Russian subcontractors, mostly those who had cooperated with Gazprom/Shtokman Development AG previously.

Scenario 2: "Parallel Play, Not Only for Children"
– Intensified but noncooperative development of the Barents Sea under conditions of rising energy demand and political polarization

In this scenario – "Parallel Play" – the market context for the development of the Barents Sea was good, especially because of continuous economic growth in Asia and correspondingly growing demand for energy. But the relationship between Norway and Russia was not so good, and the two countries both tried to go it on their own. The result was parallel play, a term borrowed from the

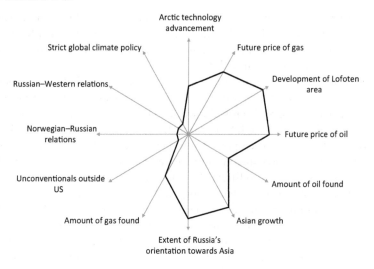

Figure 2.4 Fingerprint of the scenario "Parallel Play"

pedagogical literature, where it refers to the stage at which small children want to play but are unable to interact directly with each other.

In this scenario, no climate agreement had been reached. Unconventionals failed to spread significantly outside the US because other countries failed to adopt the legislation necessary to secure the property rights that were indispensable for the success of unconventionals in the US. Especially the oil price, but also the gas price, was high, providing strong market support for field developments in the Barents Sea. But the Norwegian–Russian relationship had been drawn into the maelstrom of persistently worsening Russian–Western relations, and, beyond the regulation of cod stocks, there was little cooperation in the Barents Sea.

In 2022 there was a military confrontation off the coast of the Svalbard archipelago over a fisheries incident. Although the violence was minor, it was not good for cooperation in the Barents Sea. As a result both sides were working actively but not in coordination, and Russian activity in the Barents Sea had been weakened by the intensive efforts to develop Far East and East Siberia as the country reoriented itself towards Asia.

It also turned out that the procedure for unitization of trans-boundary oil and gas fields under the 2010 Murmansk Treaty was not quite clear after all, and in the prevailing atmosphere the sides were unable to iron out the wrinkles. Combined with the generally negative political atmosphere, this made it difficult to develop any trans-boundary fields. The major oil finds happened to straddle the boundary delimitation line, meaning that little happened on the oil front. Some smaller fields deeper into the Norwegian part of the sea were however developed.

The Chinese company, CNPC, had taken a central role on the Russian side after it offered to take full responsibility for the Shtokman field in return for a 49% stake and little security apart from assurances from Russia's top politicians.

Norway's conservative coalition government was reelected in 2017, with, among other things, a strong vote in North Norway based on a promise to finally open the Lofoten area for exploration. Although the pro-oil part of the North Norwegian population was dissatisfied with the government's recent performance, the green turn of the competing coalition led by the Labor Party gave pro-oil voters little choice.

An unprecedented number of blocks were opened for exploration on the Norwegian side in 2018 and the industry grasped the opportunity and went on a hectic exploration campaign. On both sides, companies heavily invested in the development of Arctic petroleum technologies, but the lack of cooperation across the border limited progress on both sides as well as the potential market for new technologies. There were sufficient discoveries to extend the Norwegian pipeline grid northwards to the Lofoten archipelago, but there were insufficient gas finds in the Norwegian part of the Barents Sea to extend it any further, and the Chinese and Russian companies working in the Russian part of the Barents Sea opted for LNG instead, deploying a floating LNG plant to export the gas from the Shtokman field.

Supply industries on both the Norwegian and Russian sides had developed, aimed at delivering products and services to the fields in each country. On both the Norwegian and Russian sides, the volume of contracts awarded to the local supply industries had increased considerably because of the high volume of contracts awarded. However, local content policies motivated Chinese companies to work mainly with Russian partners, while the Norwegians worked with Western oil companies – there was little cooperation between Norwegian and Russian companies.

Scenario 3: "Let's Dance, but Where Is the Music?"
– Good cooperation in the Barents Sea, but demand is hampered by climate policy

In the scenario "Let's Dance", Norway and Russia were keen to cooperate in the development of the Barents Sea, but the international market conditions were not conducive for investment.

Russian–Western relations were reasonably good and Norwegian–Russian relations were even better. Asian growth had stagnated, resulting in lower demand for energy. Consequently Russia had reduced its interests in Asia beyond keeping up deliveries of gas to China in accordance with the agreement on the Power of Siberia Pipeline reached in 2014. The Altai pipeline was only partially filled. The world had also become increasingly worried about climate change – and willing to do something about it. Both the Norwegian and Russian governments had

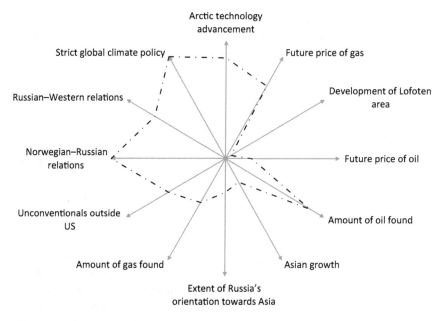

Figure 2.5 Fingerprint of the scenario "Let's Dance"

answered the call of the UN for green growth policies and implemented those. The Lofoten area was permanently closed for petroleum development, mainly due to local environmental concerns and fisheries interests.

At the global level, a serious follow-up agreement to the Kyoto Protocol was finally agreed upon just before the extension of the Kyoto Protocol ran out in 2020. Strict measures were swiftly ratcheted up, putting downward pressure on the price of oil. The price of natural gas was higher, as gas was used to replace coal, which had become prohibitively expensive under the new climate regime. This also put pressure on the development of unconventionals, especially shale oil.

The new climate regime was accompanied by much stricter environmental regulations and requirements for Arctic offshore petroleum operations in Norway and Russia. This put pressure on companies to advance their Arctic petroleum technologies. Due to the cooperative climate, the Russian and Norwegian petroleum majors managed to develop new advanced technologies at a reasonable cost, due only to close research cooperation. However, the lack of development in the Lofoten area meant that there was no infrastructure to connect the Barents Sea with the rest of the Norwegian continental shelf. Instead, a pipeline was finally completed in 2025 to take Shtokman gas from Murmansk through Karelia to Vyborg, and Shtokman was to come on stream in 2026 – with the same consortium of companies as in the initial agreement: Gazprom, Statoil, and Total. However, apart from the Shtokman and Johan Castberg projects, there were few developments, especially oilfields, in the Barents Sea as demand was subdued by the new climate agreement. Faced with limited capacity and uncertainty about the future of the petroleum industry in the High North, the local supply industry in both Norway and Russia had to make U-turns in their strategic priorities to answer the call for green growth policies. Most of the firms had chosen to diversify market portfolios and to develop and supply products and services for projects other than petroleum industrial ones, related to, for example, green cities, building wind turbines, etc. There were several interesting examples of how technological innovation had stimulated Norwegian and Russian companies to cooperate.

Wild cards

Wild cards are events that have low probability, but high impact if they do occur – similar to the concept of "black swans". They are, thus, clustered in the top left corner of the graph in Figure 2.6. The fact that such unexpected events do happen all the time is one of the reasons for using Shell's imaginative scenario-building methodology rather than forecasting and projecting trends.

Frequently – but not always – they are exogenous to the system and trends that underpin the main scenarios. Alternatively, they may arise when a trend reaches a threshold or tipping point (cf. Anker, Baev, Brunstad, Overland, & Torjesen, 2010, p. 131; Brunstad, Magnus, Swanson, Hønneland, & Overland, 2004, p. 163). Wild cards are thus often stand-alone events that would throw other variables into the air and impact on many different trends. In that regard they are mini-scenarios in their own right, therefore standing alone rather than being integrated into the main scenarios.

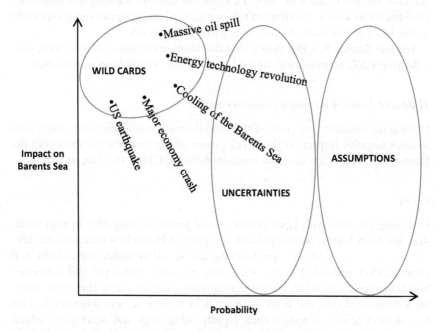

Figure 2.6 Wild cards in the development of petroleum resources in the Barents Sea

In working on the wild cards for this book, it was noticeably difficult to think of unpredictable events that would lead to rapid petroleum development in the Barents Sea. Most events that we have managed to think of would reduce the likelihood of rapid petroleum development.

Wild card 1: a massive oil spill

We have considered an oil spill per se as only an uncertainty rather than a wild card, but a massive oil spill is a wild card, especially if it occurs somewhere in the Arctic. It is not certain how it would affect the oil and gas industry, as there have previously been big spills that did not lead to major changes in the industry in spite of broad media coverage and changes in regulations. However, changes in regulations could make fields more expensive to develop, and the Lofoten area is already closed (at least for the time being) due to environmental concerns, showing that such concerns can in fact have an impact.

For the development of the Barents Sea, the massive oil spill was the death knell. Oil had been the most attractive resource due to higher oil than gas prices, but, due to the costly new regulations, only very large oilfields could be developed.

Wild card 2: a big earthquake in the US blamed on fracking

A 2017 earthquake in Oklahoma City killed 12 people and brought down many buildings, as well as several railway and highway bridges. The event received television coverage around the world. It led to a temporary ban against fracking near residential areas in the US and all-out bans on fracking in many other countries. The knock-on effect of this was that oil and gas prices rose, especially in the US, but gradually also in other parts of the world.

For the Barents Sea, this meant that the Shtokman project was revived, with a floating LNG terminal and aimed largely at the North American market.

Wild card 3: one of the major economies crashes

During the coming years, one of the world's major economies may crash, with a major negative impact on the development of the petroleum resources in the Barents Sea. The economies we consider here are China, the EU, and the US.

China

Escalating tensions with Japan finally caused Japanese companies to start withdrawing from China. Municipal and company debt reached unsustainable levels, and, in a series of attempts to bring the situation under control, the real estate market unraveled at the same time as many municipal and corporate bonds matured. China had been on an upward spiral for a long time, now it was on a downward one and from 2018 to 2021 it went steeply downwards. This forced the Chinese to reduce their rapidly rising wage and other costs, which in turn led to (even) lower imports and to social unrest in China, which in turn further undermined Chinese growth. The Chinese threw out their environmental ambitions, stopped replacing coal with natural gas, and reduced oil imports. At the same time, the West was reducing its consumption of fossil fuels, both for economic and climate reasons. This brought oil and gas prices down, which in turn brought developments in the Barents Sea almost to a halt.

The United States

The US economy had been the first to overcome the financial crisis that started in 2008. However, the US recovery was driven by printing money, which led to a new stock market bubble rather than sustainable growth. Although US exports improved with the lower value of the dollar and lower energy costs from shale gas, the trade balance continued to be seriously off balance, and the US could not pay its debt. When attempts were made to reduce the printing of money, economic growth quickly slowed, so the printing was resumed again. This led to an economic crash in the US in November 2018. As the markets were no longer convinced by promises of quantitative easing, the crash was even worse than that in 2008 and the American dollar lost more than half its value. The Chinese lost one of their main export markets and the whole world economy fell two years in a row. Along with the world economy, oil and gas prices fell, undermining the development of the Barents Sea.

The EU

There was stagnation, continued high unemployment, debt, and increasing political instability in some countries. Increasingly unruly member countries saw less and less benefit in the union and started challenging it – in particular Denmark, Hungary, and the UK. These developments led to a downward spiral, including another economic crisis, the rise of Euroskeptic parties (mostly right-wing, but, in a few places, left-wing), the weakening of environmental policy, and increased use of coal. For the Barents Sea this meant chaos and low demand in its main gas market, making it even more difficult to develop new gas fields.

Wild card 4: an energy technology revolution

There was a breakthrough in Canada in 2015 in the storage of CO_2 from a coal-fired electricity plant, leading to a revival for coal. Electricity companies joined forces to develop a pipeline network for capturing and transporting CO_2 to suitable locations for storage, and managed to cut costs for the production of the necessary materials for the pipelines. This led to reduced investment in the oil and gas sector. Furthermore, in 2020 another energy technology breakthrough was achieved when Lockheed Martin finalized the technology for mass production of mobile fusion reactors. The prospect of cheap and abundant electricity led to a substantial reduction in the development of new gas fields. For the Barents Sea, the effect was that all new field developments were put on hold and further exploration drilling in the prospective Fedynsky High area was abandoned.

Wild card 5: cooling of the Barents Sea

After a volcano eruption in Indonesia in 2018, a large cloud of volcano ash covered most of the earth's atmosphere. The result was a global cooling that lasted for six years. During the cooling period the ice cover in the Arctic increased considerably, causing a setback in development work. The cooling also caused reduced temperatures worldwide, increasing the need for fuel for heating. For the Barents Sea projects, the situation resulted in an increased interest in Arctic technology, with a delay, however, in exploration drilling and development studies due to the increased ice coverage.

Table 2.1 Overview of common assumptions for the three scenarios

Assumptions	Scenario 1 "After You, Sir"	Scenario 2 "Parallel Play"	Scenario 3 "Let's Dance"
World markets vs. international political bodies	World markets and the geopolitical context will be more important than circumpolar or other international political bodies		
Demand for energy	Global energy demand is going to continue growing, driven by a combination of population growth and economic growth		
Asian market growth	Asian markets will continue to grow. Russia will continue diversifying its exports by expanding exports to the Asia–Pacific region		
Global climate policy	Climate change will remain on the political agenda		
Barents petroleum exploration	Large fields are not very likely to be found outside the potentially interesting structures that have already been identified for exploration, especially on the Norwegian side		
Arctic petroleum production	There will be significant interest in oil and gas production from the Arctic, but development will be dependent on the costs of operations, maintenance, and logistics. The cost of petroleum exploration and production will remain high in the Arctic, even if significant technological progress is made.		
Arctic marine bio-resources	The Barents Sea will remain a globally important marine habitat important for Arctic marine species and commercial fisheries		
Arctic weather conditions	Arctic weather conditions will continue to challenge personnel and hardware		
The Northern Sea Route	The Northern Sea Route will remain secondary as a transport route for oil and gas from the Barents Sea to Asia		
Business-to-business cooperation	Oil companies will continue to want access to each other's parts of the Barents Sea, but there will be limited room for small players, especially on the Russian side		

Table 2.2 Overview of uncertainties for the three scenarios

Uncertainty factors	Scenario 1 "After You, Sir"	Scenario 2 "Parallel Play"	Scenario 3 "Let's Dance"
Future price of gas	Low	High	High
Future price of oil	Low	High	Low
Asian growth	High	High	Low
Unconventionals outside US	High	Low	Medium
Strict global climate policy	Medium	Lax	Strict
Amount of oil found	Medium	Medium	High
Amount of gas found	High	Medium	Medium
Development of Lofoten area	No	Yes	No
Arctic technology advancement	Low	Medium	High
Norwegian–Russian relations	Good	Bad	Good
Russian–Western relations	Medium	Bad	Good
Extent of Russia's orientation towards Asia	Yes	Yes	No

References

Anker, M., Baev, P., Brunstad, B., Overland, I., & Torjesen, S. (2010). *The Caspian Sea region towards 2025: Caspia Inc., national giants or trade and transit?* Delft, Netherlands: Eburon.

Brunstad, B., Magnus, E., Swanson, P., Hønneland, G., & Overland, I. (2004). *Big oil playground, Russian bear preserve or European periphery? The Russian Barents Sea region towards 2015.* Delft, Netherlands: Eburon.

Cornelius, P., Van de Putte, A., & Romani, M. (2005). Three decades of scenario planning in Shell. *California Management Review, 48*(1), 92–110.

Global Commission on the Economy and Climate. (2014). *Better growth, better climate: The new climate economy report.* Washington, DC: World Resources Institute.

Jefferson, M. (2012). Shell scenarios: What really happened in the 1970s and what may be learned for current world prospects. *Technological Forecasting & Social Change, 79*(1), 186–197. doi:10.1016/j.techfore.2011.08.007

Varum, C.A., & Melo, C. (2010). Directions in scenario planning literature – A review of the past decades. *Futures, 42*(4), 355–369. doi:10.1016/j.futures.2009.11.021

Part II

Politics, economics and experience of cooperation

3 The international context for Barents oil and gas – Asia's double impact

Indra Overland, Nodari Simonia, Sergey Vasiliev, and Elana Wilson Rowe

Introduction

This chapter lays out the global and regional context for oil and gas developments in the Barents Sea. The international context – and how this context is interpreted and understood by decision-makers – will play a decisive role in determining how the Barents Sea evolves as a petroleum province. Whatever oil and gas is found in the Barents Sea, it will only be exploited if there is sufficient demand for it. With the technological challenges and high cost of extracting oil and gas under remote Arctic conditions, that is an important "if". The Shtokman project has already been shelved for the time being, partly because American demand for liquefied natural gas (LNG) did not live up to expectations.

We suggest that influences from Asia may be decisive for the development of the Barents Sea. This may seem paradoxical, considering that this sea is about as far away as one can get by ship from the rapidly growing economies of East and South Asia. Consequently, a good deal of this chapter is devoted to introducing the reader to this line of reasoning, which can be summarized as follows: Barents Sea oil and gas development will be technically difficult and expensive compared to competing sources. Consequently, the overall demand for oil and gas will need to be high in order for such developments to be financially viable, and the rapidly growing Asian economies are essential drivers of global demand. At the same time, much of what happens in the Barents Sea will depend on Russia. Russia is the world's largest country and faces choices between Eastern and Western orientation that no other countries face in the same way. This manifests itself in several ways. As a geographic giant, Russia has a range of undeveloped oil and gas reserves to choose between, some of which are closer to Asia than to the Barents Sea. Politically, Russia is out of step with its European gas customers and may seek to export to countries that are more politically compatible. Thus if Asian demand is high, Russia may choose to invest in its eastern fields oriented towards Asian markets rather than in the Barents Sea.

In addition to our focus on Asia as a key factor in global developments of relevance to the Barents Sea, we look at both Norwegian and Russian perspectives on the Arctic region. Russia – with the longest Arctic coastline of all littoral states and the undisputed majority of Arctic oil and gas reserves – garners an added level of attention.

The chapter starts at the global level, with an overview of the oil and gas market projections of the International Energy Agency (IEA) for the coming years. Unconventional oil and gas and climate policy receive particular attention. It then moves to the regional level, where it casts a brief glance at the European and Asian gas markets and Arctic politics.

The chapter has important interfaces with Chapter 6 on the bilateral relationship between Norway and Russia, where the impact of the Russian–Western conflict over Ukraine on Norwegian–Russian relations is discussed, and with Chapter 5 on Norwegian–Russian business-to-business cooperation. It could benefit from being read in conjunction with those chapters.

Global demand and supply projections: IEA and OPEC

As a starting point for understanding the evolving international context for the development of the Barents Sea, we take the IEA's *World Energy Outlook 2013* projections for the world in 2035. We also make some comparisons with projections of the Organization of the Petroleum Exporting Countries (OPEC) and find that they point in the same direction, although there are some interesting differences. We then discuss unconventional hydrocarbons and attempt to give the reader an appreciation of how the uncertainties at play in this field can influence oil and gas developments in the Barents Sea.

According to the primary projection of the IEA, regardless of new policies and programs that will be put in place to encourage energy savings and reduce greenhouse gas emissions, global energy consumption will keep growing and will increase by around one-third in 2035 compared to 2011. This is based on the assumption that the world population will grow by 1.7 billion and the world economy nearly double by 2035 (International Energy Agency [IEA], 2013, p. 33). This is in spite of a projected drop in the relative share of fossil fuels in the world's energy mix from 82% to 76% (IEA, 2013, p. 57). The absolute consumption of natural gas will grow continuously, and gas demand is projected to rise almost 50% by 2035. Although this is clearly a picture of continued growth, there is a geography to this increased demand – it is not evenly spread around the globe, and international supply/demand patterns are likely to continue to change. The share of global energy demand in non–OECD countries in 2035 will be 64%, with fossil fuels continuing to meet most of the demand (IEA, 2013, p. 481).

The emerging economies with their rapidly growing populations, industrial production, and increasing urbanization will account for more than 90% of net energy demand growth (IEA, 2013, p. 55). China is projected to account for the largest share of this growth, followed by India, where demand will more than double, and finally by the Middle East. To be more specific, Middle Eastern countries will be the second-largest group of gas consumers by 2020 and the third-largest group of oil consumers by 2030 (IEA, 2013, p. 55). China has already become the largest oil-importing country in 2013. Its share of world energy consumption is projected to amount to 33%, as Chinese energy demand rises by 60% between 2010 and 2035. By contrast, OECD energy demand in 2035 is expected to be only 3% higher than in 2010. Furthermore, unconventional domestic resources in some OECD countries will further change the import/export picture. The United States, for example, is projected to meet almost all of its energy needs from domestic resources by 2035. China will therefore play a decisive role in global energy markets over the projected period.

Global oil demand

The IEA expects that the growth in global demand for oil will be slowed by energy efficiency measures and higher prices: the crude oil price is expected to rise to 125 USD per barrel in 2035. Overall, the share of oil in the primary energy mix is likely to drop from 32% in 2012 to 27% in 2035 (IEA, 2013, p. 61). Nonetheless, absolute global oil demand will reach almost 100 mb/d in 2035, up from 87 mb/d in 2011 (IEA, 2013, p. 55).

The reduction in US oil imports on the one hand, and the rising oil consumption in emerging economies on the other hand, will have consequences for trade flows along some key strategic maritime and pipeline transportation routes: Asia–Pacific markets are already exerting a powerful pull on oil, drawing it away from North Atlantic consumers. Over the projection period towards 2035, Middle Eastern supplies for Asia will be supplemented by growing volumes produced in Russia and Kazakhstan, and possibly Brazil and Canada.

Global natural gas demand

The IEA expects that new sources of gas, both conventional and unconventional, will bring greater diversity to global supply. In the LNG market,

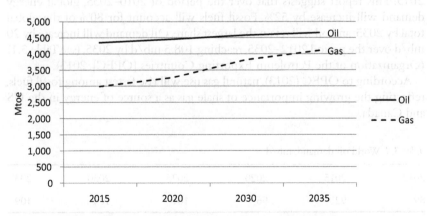

Figure 3.1 Global oil and gas demand growth over projection period (in Mtoe)
Source: Based on data from IEA (2013).

which is particularly relevant for the Barents Sea as long as there is no pipeline connecting the sea to markets, the IEA believes that growing supplies of LNG will create new linkages between regional gas markets, gradually making the market for natural gas more global and leveling prices. But there will still be differences between the prices in different parts of the world, and above all there will remain a large discrepancy between the transportation cost for LNG and piped gas. Thus, gas extracted in the Barents Sea and gas extracted in the Russian Far East may not have the same value – especially if the former must be transported as LNG and the latter can be transported via pipeline.

Natural gas demand is projected to grow from 3.3 trillion cubic meters (tcm) in 2010 to over 5 tcm in 2035, an increase of almost 50% (IEA, 2013, p. 99). The IEA expects its share in the energy mix to rise from 22% in 2010 to 24% in 2035 (IEA, 2013, p. 100). The natural gas supply–demand balance will significantly depend on the extent to which the North American experience in producing shale gas, a development discussed in detail below, is replicated elsewhere. For countries currently reliant on imported gas, there is certainly a temptation to develop indigenous resources, whenever possible. Consequently, the IEA projects that the global supply of shale gas will expand significantly, accounting for almost half the increase in global gas production (IEA, 2013, p. 108). Such a development would certainly put pressure on exporters of conventional natural gas and challenge the traditional oil-linkage pricing mechanism for gas (IEA, 2013, pp. 108, 128–129).

Demand for natural gas is expected to exceed that for oil during the projection period, since natural gas is cleaner both in terms of greenhouse gas emissions and local air pollution and is therefore seen in many countries as a replacement for coal. Natural gas is also seen as an alternative to nuclear energy, which is being phased out (at least for the time being) in some countries following the 2011 Fukushima Daiichi nuclear power plant accident.

For purposes of comparison, we turn now to OPEC's *World Oil Outlook 2013*. This report suggests that over the period of 2010–2035, global energy demand will increase by 52%. Fossil fuels will account for 80% of the global total by 2035, and oil will retain the largest share. Oil demand will increase by 20 mb/d over the period 2012–2035, reaching 108.5 mb/d by 2035, (see Table 3.1) (Organization of the Petroleum Exporting Countries [OPEC], 2013).

According to OPEC (2013), natural gas use will rise fastest among fossil fuels, reflecting the growing importance of shale gas as a source of energy in the US and Canada.

Table 3.1 World oil demand, mb/d

2012	2015	2020	2025	2030	2035
89	92	96	101	105	109

Source: Based on data from OPEC (2013).

Table 3.2 IEA and OPEC forecasts compared

INDICATOR	IEA	OPEC
WORLD ENERGY DEMAND INCREASE BY 2035	33%	52%
GLOBAL OIL DEMAND IN 2035	100 mb/d	109 mb/d

Source: Based on data from IEA (2013) and OPEC (2013).

OPEC represents the majority of the world's major oil exporters, and thus its projections may have a bias towards their perspective, i.e. expecting high oil demand. The IEA represents most of the world's major oil importers, and thus its projections may have a bias towards their perspective, i.e. expecting low oil demand. When their predictions are largely in line with each other, as in this case, it is an important signal about expectations for the future, and this signal is observed by oil and gas companies taking decisions about whether and how to invest in the Barents Sea (see Table 3.2).

Unconventional hydrocarbons

Regardless of which set of projections policymakers and company executives rely upon, it is clear that they must operate in an environment of increased dynamism and uncertainty. Oil and gas companies need to accurately assess how the energy market situation unfolds and adapt rapidly to changes in forecasts and realities, the rapid-growth markets evolution being one of them. How oil and gas companies interpret current global developments will be decisive for whether they choose to invest in the Barents Sea or not. A key uncertainty that we explore in this section is the varied opinions on the medium- and long-term significance of unconventional hydrocarbons in order to give the reader an appreciation of the challenges involved in projecting trends in energy markets.

Estimates of ultimately recoverable resources of oil continue to increase as technologies unlock new types of resources, such as light tight oil, that were not considered recoverable only a few years ago. Declining output from existing fields is a major driver of upstream investment in unconventional sources. The latest IEA estimates for remaining recoverable resources show 2,670 billion barrels of conventional oil (including natural gas liquids), 345 billion barrels of light tight oil, 1,880 billion barrels of extra-heavy oil and bitumen, and 1,070 billion barrels of kerogen oil (IEA, 2013, p. 421). The share of conventional crude oil in total oil production is expected to fall from 80% in 2012 to two-thirds in 2035 (IEA, 2013, p. 457).

Unconventional sources of petroleum also change the geography of the market. For example, according to the IEA's *World Energy Outlook 2012*, the United States is projected to become the largest global oil producer, overtaking Saudi Arabia in the mid-2020s and a net oil exporter around 2030, all thanks to the advanced upstream technologies that allow large-scale production of light tight oil and shale gas.

Brazil's deepwater oil likewise makes the country a heavyweight in the global energy picture. While the US attracts quite a few newspaper inches on the topic of unconventional sources, if one is to use the term "revolution" about developments in the natural gas sector based on the criterion of fast growth, it is also applicable to Qatar. In 2002, this small country produced only 29 billion cubic meters (bcm) and exported 19 bcm as LNG. By 2012, Qatar's LNG exports amounted to 105 bcm (of which 67 bcm went to the Asia–Pacific region), bypassing Saudi Arabia, Algeria, Indonesia, and Nigeria and seeking to become the number one exporter in the world. In addition, Qatar supplied another 19 bcm of gas to its Middle Eastern neighbors by pipeline. So, currently not only shale gas but also Qatar constitutes a challenge to Russian and Norwegian future gas exports from the Barents Sea. Similar developments may also happen elsewhere: Australian exports of LNG are expected to reach 88 million tons per year (equivalent to 121 bcm natural gas) by 2017, with even more coming online by 2021 (Tsafos, 2013), and major new finds off the coast of East Africa will likely also be turned into LNG one day. Thus, the most important upstream factor in the global gas market may not be shale gas in itself but rather new sources of LNG (some of which may also be sourced from shale gas). For US shale gas to play a role beyond North America, it will in any case have to be turned into LNG, and any LNG made from unconventional gas is likely to be more expensive than LNG from large conventional gas fields.

The potential significance of unconventional resources also needs to be balanced against the possibility that they may not prove as revolutionary outside the United States as inside. For example, there was much ado about shale gas in Poland. ConocoPhillips and 40 other companies arrived to prospect for it. They promised energy independence to the Polish government and said Polish gas would oust Russian gas from the EU market. In 2011, the US Department of Energy estimated that Poland could have 5.3 trillion cubic meters of shale gas, which would be sufficient for 300 years of Polish consumption. However, Exxon Mobil withdrew from Poland in 2012, and in May 2013 another three companies withdrew from shale gas in Poland – Marathon Oil, Talisman Energy, and Polish state-run Lotos. ConocoPhillips is still deciding whether to stay or go. In 2014 there was still no shale gas in the country's commercial energy mix and it was not clear when, if ever, any major projects would be realized. One of the few things that might change that is the conflict in Ukraine, but Polish shale gas would still have to compete against LNG, which the country plans to import through a new LNG terminal on the Baltic.

Around 2012 the attention shifted from unconventional gas to unconventional oil. Oil is more valuable than natural gas, and it is easier and cheaper to transport. The shale oil revolution is even more likely than shale gas to have consequences beyond the United States in places like the Barents Sea.

There are different views on the promise of shale oil. The IEA (2014) has predicted that it will spread beyond North America by 2020. Others are more skeptical. Arthur Berman argues that many numbers and forecasts are exaggerated and that oil companies do this because their conventional oil reserves are falling and they do not have anything other than shale oil to point to. He states, "There have been some truly outrageous claims made by some executives about the Permian basin in recent months that I suspect have their general counsels looking for a defibrillator" (Berman cited in Stafford, 2014). In another analysis, Spencer, Sartor, and Mathieu (2014) argue that the changes in the US industrial sector attributed to shale gas and shale oil are in fact due to other causes and that the growth of unconventionals therefore will not go as far as some expect. Yet others argue that shale oil and gas will encounter growing environmental resistance and fear related to earthquakes (Kolb, 2014, p. 121; Maugeri, 2013, p. 61).

How shale oil and gas develop in the future depends on how the geology of new exploratory areas works out, what progress is made in equipment and engineering, how environmental concerns evolve, and to what extent governments of different countries facilitate such developments through legal and economic frameworks. We are therefore not in a position to pass final judgment on the potential of shale oil and gas but can only note that there are starkly opposing views on the phenomenon, and scenarios for the future of the Barents Sea must therefore take into account a range of possibilities.

Russia investing in eastward exports

Despite major uncertainties about the role of unconventionals in the global energy supply picture, the projections reviewed above are clear about global demand trends and place great weight on the growing Asian economies. Developments in Asia are decisive for the global petroleum sector, and thus for both Norway and Russia as major oil and gas exporters to international markets. But more than 75% of Russia's own territory lies in Asia, and in this respect Russia is itself a major power in Asia. As a consequence, the pull of Asia plays a role for Russia not only in terms of international markets, but also as a factor in its domestic priorities. In this section we take a closer look at some of the options and factors that shape how Russia approaches the growing export opportunities along its eastern borders – and the consequences they could have for the Barents Sea.

Traditionally the Russian oil export balance has been in favor of the West. The same applies to the other two major oil-exporting former Soviet republics, Kazakhstan and Azerbaijan. In 2012, out of total oil exports from post-Soviet countries amounting to 424 million tons, Europe and North America received 313 million tons, while the Asia–Pacific countries took 93 million tons (BP, 2013). Driven by the developments outlined in the previous section, this pattern has started to change, and this section briefly addresses Russian export relations/plans with China, Japan, and the Korean peninsula.

Since the first part of the main East Siberia–Pacific Ocean (ESPO) pipeline and its China spur were put in operation, under a USD 25-billion (Figure 3.2 and

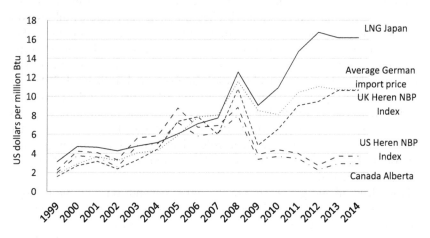

Figure 3.2 Natural gas prices highlighting strength of demand in the Asia–Pacific countries (US dollars per million Btu)

Source: Based on data from BP (2010, p. 30); BP (2011, p. 28); BP (2012, p. 28); BP (2013, p. 28); BP (2014, p. 28).

Figure 3.3) Chinese credit line for Rosneft and Transneft, 15 million tons of oil have been delivered through this pipeline to China annually. The second part of ESPO was completed in late 2012, and the pipe's capacity has already reached 80 million tons per year. Simultaneously Rosneft became the main driver in Russia's East Siberia–Far East petroleum sector and concluded an agreement on an additional broad Chinese credit line with the China National Petroleum Corporation (CNPC) in October 2013 (USD 270 billion including prepaid nearly USD 70 billion). According to this agreement, Rosneft would deliver 365 million tons of oil to China during a 25-year period (Starinskaya, 2014).

Besides, oil from Skovorodino is delivered to the terminal at Kozmino Bay by rail. This has had a considerable impact on Japan's oil imports. In 2006, when Japan began purchasing oil from Sakhalin, the share of these shipments in its oil imports was just 0.7%. A year later it increased fivefold, reaching 3.5%. In 2010, with the start of ESPO shipments from Kozmino, Japanese imports of oil from Russia amounted to 14.5 million tons, or 6.4% of its total oil imports. Simultaneously, for the first time ever, the Middle Eastern share fell below 80% (Bustelo, 2008; BP, 2011). Statistics on LNG produced by Sakhalin Energy, the operator of the Sakhalin-2 project, tell a similar story.

Although the first major long-term Chinese–Russian energy deals concerned oil, major natural gas projects are also being added. After more than a decade of intransigent negotiations, in 2014 the two countries agreed to build a pipeline to carry 38 bcm of gas per year from Russia to China over a 30-year period. Although the parties did not disclose the price, the deal has been estimated to be worth USD 400 billion, of which 55 billion will be invested by Gazprom in giant Siberian fields (Mazneva & Kravchenko, 2014). Part of the

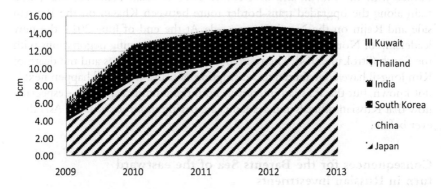

Figure 3.3 LNG exports from Russia (bcm)
Source: Based on data from BP (2010), (2011), (2012), (2013), and (2014).

Chinese payment for the gas is to be made in advance, meaning that Russia is essentially borrowing money to invest in Siberian fields for export to China. The question is how much it will be able to invest in a place like the Barents Sea in addition.

China and Russia are also negotiating over the possible building of a pipeline to take gas from West Siberia to Western China via Altai. This is more difficult because the density of population and industry are far less in the western part of China that this pipeline would first reach. If realized, this pipeline would further orient Russian investments towards China, but at the same time it would add an Asian outlet to the West Siberian fields that currently serve the European market, thus possibly freeing up space for Barents gas in the European market.

The Japanese–Russian energy trade is also likely to increase in the coming years. In connection with the Fukushima accident and the shutting down of other Japanese nuclear power reactors, the discussion of the old proposal to build an underwater gas pipeline to Hokkaido has been revived in Russia. Along the same lines, the Trans-Korean Gas Pipeline is also worth mentioning as an illustration of Russia's efforts to increase its energy exports to Asia. This pipeline is planned to become 1,100 kilometers long and to serve as an extension of the Sakhalin 1–Khabarovsk–Vladivostok pipeline. This project is usually discussed as part of a package with the Trans-Korean Railroad (planned as an extension of the Trans-Siberian one). Implementation of the Trans-Korean projects might contribute to a new atmosphere of cooperation on the peninsula and eventually contribute to reducing one of the major geopolitical impediments to economic integration in East Asia.

Both projects had been offered more than once to both the North and the South, and more than once both the North and the South expressed their approval (Gabuev, 2011). South Korea demonstrated its seriousness towards the projects by building its own section of the railway that now ends near the border with the North, and in October 2011 Russian Railroads ran a trial train along the upgraded trans-border route between Khasan on the Russian side and Rajin on the North Korean side. At the end of June 2014, the new leadership of North Korea unexpectedly proposed resuming negotiations with the South (Strokan, 2014). The resistance of the United States and the death of Kim Jong-il have contributed to a disruption of plans. What will happen next is not known, but the Russian interest in both these projects is high – especially now that Russian officials and academia are paying more attention to Asia than ever before.

Consequences for the Barents Sea of the eastward turn in Russian investments

However, Russia is not the only country paying attention to these growing Asian economies. Australia is also projected to greatly increase its supply of LNG to the region, and further down the line new large discoveries off the coast of East Africa may also come into play. Demand from China and other Asian countries may easily grow to absorb these new volumes, or they may fail to do so, depending on the policies of those countries. The development of shale gas in China could also impact strongly on the supply–demand balance if the Chinese manage to copy the American shale success. China is estimated to have the world's largest recoverable shale gas reserves, almost twice as large as those of the United States (Energy Information Administration [EIA], 2013). The price that Russia will get for future LNG exports in Asia will therefore depend on the balance between the growth in LNG from other sources and the energy policies and other developments in the purchasing countries. What the outcome will be is impossible to predict. Should Asian LNG exports turn out to be less lucrative than hoped, and less lucrative than Atlantic LNG exports, it could invigorate Russian interest in the Barents Sea as a gas province. Should Asia turn out to provide a good revenue stream, it could reduce Russian interest in Barents Sea gas.

The Asian countries are also the main drivers of the growing global oil exports and have helped, and may or may not continue to help, keep oil prices high. High prices can facilitate the implementation of costly Barents projects. At the same time, for Russia as a country with much territory and many resources right next door to the growing markets in Asia, the growth is a driver of a shift away from investment in the Barents Sea and towards investment in fields and infrastructure in the eastern part of the country. In spite of the low levels of Russian government debt, Russian companies are heavily indebted and do not have unlimited amounts of capital to invest or skilled personnel to deploy. The squeeze on capital is further exacerbated by Western sanctions against Russia and the knock-on effect of capital flight from the country. The Russians will have to prioritize.

But what then if there is a change in China's economic fortune? China has experienced 30 years of steep economic growth, as well as dramatic demographic and social changes. Although it is beyond the scope of this article to assess the likelihood of a downturn in the Chinese economy, in a scenario-building exercise such a possibility must be taken into account. Should it happen, the impact on the Barents Sea might again be dual: a lowering of world oil prices that makes it more difficult to carry through Barents projects, at the same time as it might increase Russian interest in the Barents Sea relative to East Siberia and the Russian Far East. The market for oil is global and location is normally not decisive, but in practice location can still play a role at the level of psychology and infrastructure priorities. For gas the market is still more regionalized, and a China crash might promote Russian interest in Barents gas over that in the Far East. A broke China is unlikely to enjoy paying the European prices that Russia wants for its eastern gas exports.

Russia's newfound interest in the East is mirrored in Statoil's new deal with Rosneft. In May 2012, Rosneft and Statoil signed a comprehensive cooperation agreement that included exploration for oil and gas, not only in the Barents Sea but even more in the Sea of Okhotsk, off Russia's Pacific coast. In the same month, it was reported that Statoil would withdraw from its joint project with Gazprom and Total to develop the Shtokman gas and condensate field in the Russian part of the Barents Sea (Lorentzen, 2012).

These moves surprised many. The Shtokman field had been the most talked about project in Statoil's global portfolio and one to which the company had worked hard to gain access. The 2007 merger between Statoil and Hydro was the largest ever in Norwegian history; one of the main reasons for it had been the desire to join forces in order to improve the chance of getting access to Shtokman (Awaiting imminent Hydro/Statoil-merger, 2006; Buanes et al., 2006; Noreng, 2008). Whereas the Shtokman field is located just over 200 kilometers from the Norwegian–Russian maritime boundary and thus near many other Statoil projects, the Sea of Okhotsk lies 10 time zones east of Norway on the other side of the planet (Overland, in press).

It could seem that Statoil was making a shift away from the previously so powerful Gazprom to the ascendant Rosneft and at the same time a geographical shift from the Barents Sea to the Sea of Okhotsk. The former may have been true, the latter not. Although Statoil was clearly giving up on Shtokman for the time being, the deal with Rosneft included other components such as the shale oil near Samara and the North Komsomolskoe field in West Siberia, which is a complex gas and condensate field with a thin band of oil. It appears that for Statoil these were the real draws. The deal also included the Perseevskiy area in the northernmost part of the previously disputed area in the Barents Sea, but the companies would have to make a very big find indeed, and it would have to be oil rather than gas, to be able to develop anything in that area if Shtokman was not viable. Thus Perseevskiy may have been included more as a matter of principle (Statoil also likely wanted more southern parts of the formerly disputed area, which were given to the Italian company ENI instead). Thus, rather than reflecting Statoil's priorities, the inclusion of Okhotsk in the new deal reflected the priorities of Rosneft and the Russian state.

While Statoil has been enticed by Rosneft into looking towards the Russian Far East, much of the company's investment is in other parts of the world, especially the United States, Angola, and Brazil. Thus, while Russia's national oil company is increasingly looking east, Norway's is looking west and south, and, in addition, to the Norwegian continental shelf. Should these two trends continue and strengthen, the Barents Sea might fall between two chairs.

Another aspect of Asia's development that could impact on the Barents Sea is likely to be the growing importance of Chinese and possibly other Asian oil companies in the Arctic. Especially if Russia continues to be subject to Western sanctions and to orient itself towards the East, Chinese companies are likely to play an increasingly prominent role in the Barents Sea and other parts of the Russian Arctic. We think this is, however, mainly about business rather than geopolitics and our space is limited so we do not deal with it in depth here.

Norwegian and Russian supplies to the European gas market

In spite of Asia's pull, both Norway and Russia have longstanding and to some extent interplaying commitments to the European gas market. However, the centrality of Russian gas in the EU is easily overplayed. In the decades following the signing of the historical "gas for pipes" agreements between the USSR and Germany in 1970, 1972, and 1974, in spite of increased physical volumes of gas deliveries from the Soviet Union, the Soviet Union's share in total volume of European gas imports more than halved. This happened due to diversification of import sources (from Norway and Algeria as well as other North African countries, plus Qatar, Trinidad and Tobago, among others). Russian gas now represents about one-third of EU imports, yet this corresponds to only 5–6% of total EU energy consumption (Eurostat, 2014).

Norway, by contrast, exports smaller volumes but its share in the EU gas market has been increasing steadily. In 2002, Norway supplied the EU with 61 bcm gas, nearly half as much as Russia, which was then supplying over 128 bcm (Eurostat, 2014). But Norway, whose oil production is declining and gas production rising, gradually increased its gas exports to Europe and precisely during the worst years of the financial crisis, 2008–2011. Norwegian exports jumped to approximately 93 bcm and finally to 107 bcm in 2012 (Qatar also experienced an increase in exports to the EU). At the start of the financial crisis, Gazprom's exports to the EU also increased to 154 bcm in 2008. But Russian exports did not steadily increase as did Norwegian exports to the EU – by 2011 there was a decline to 141 bcm (Eurostat, 2014). That was probably partly driven by negativity towards Russia after the 2008 War in South Ossetia and the 2009 gas quarrel between Russia and Ukraine.

Irrespective of this competition between the two countries in the EU gas market, there is a lot of potential for Russia and Norway to cooperate, not only in the Barents Sea but also in a broader Arctic framework. Economies of scale can be gained through cooperation, enabling Barents Sea projects that would otherwise not be commercially viable. This is especially true when it comes to the highly expensive transport infrastructure for natural gas. For more on this, see Chapter 6.

In the years after the financial crisis, EU gas demand oscillated and stagnated (EIA, 2014), but in the longer term it is set to rise, something that is of interest to both Norway and Russia. However, it remains to be seen whether Russian gas producers will benefit from this increasing demand. The Russian–Western relationship after Russia's takeover of Crimea and the war in eastern Ukraine is significantly worse, and a greater effort to reduce dependence on Russian gas can be expected from the EU.

As a consequence of the Ukraine crisis, the European gas sector will likely be reorganized to minimize its dependence on Russian gas. Efforts may be made to speed up the commencement of indigenous shale gas production as well as the reorientation of gas imports, though so far European shale has been no success and LNG will remain more expensive than piped Russian gas. Though it is hard to forecast how and how fast the evolution of the European gas market will occur, it is obvious that the crisis in Ukraine will accelerate change. Although the EU is generally slow to reformulate policy and it may therefore take a while, the changes may potentially be dramatic.

The Arctic context

Having reviewed some of the global political landscape to gain a sense of the broader picture, we will now focus on the politics of the Arctic region. Are there political or security aspects of regional Arctic affairs that could slow (or accelerate) the interest in Barents Sea oil and gas?

"Race for the Arctic" and the "New Cold War" are common newspaper headlines when it comes to coverage of Arctic affairs. In popular media, the Arctic is often portrayed as a zone of potential conflict – with unresolved boundary issues, rapidly changing sea ice cover, and tempting natural resources forming a potentially explosive political cocktail (Wegge, 2011; Wilson Rowe, 2012; Young, 2009). However, the region possesses a strong track record of peace and cooperation. Following the end of the Cold War, the governments and peoples of the Arctic increasingly engaged in a range of cooperative activities designed to address issues of shared concern and to raise the profile of the Arctic as a political and geographical region, such as the Arctic Council and the Barents Euro–Arctic Region (BEAR). The Arctic Council has high-level representatives from all eight Arctic states (Canada, Finland, Denmark/Greenland, Iceland, Norway, Russia, Sweden, and the US); indigenous peoples of the Arctic region participate as "permanent participants"; and a number of non-Arctic states and NGOs have observer status. The BEAR is a regional initiative in the European North, involving national and local governments, civil society, and indigenous peoples.

The subsequent proliferation of activities aimed at promoting stable and ongoing cooperation in the circumpolar North was associated with the Arctic being a relatively secure source of nonrenewable resources (oil, gas, and minerals), awareness of the heightened impact of global environmental problems (such as global warming and trans-boundary pollutants) on the Arctic environment, and the increased politicization of Arctic indigenous peoples (Keskitalo, 2004; Kraska, 2011; Stokke & Hønneland, 2007; Tennberg, 2000; Young, 1992, 2009).

Political leaders and civil servants representing Arctic states have, in recent years, become a seemingly coordinated chorus extolling the peacefulness of the region. The key policy documents of the five Arctic coastal states (Canada, Denmark/Greenland, Norway, Russia, US) are striking in the extent to which they overlap in highlighting problems and opportunities of importance for the Arctic region (Wilson Rowe, 2012). For example, most country statements point to climate change, increased human traffic and presence (e.g. shipping), and the promise of natural resources extracted in a fragile environment as drivers of political attention to the Arctic. All of the documents point to the peacefulness of the Arctic region and the cooperative nature with which potential conflicts of interests are resolved (Wilson Rowe, 2012). It is thus unlikely that the Arctic will become an arena for military confrontation. All Arctic littoral states have economic interests in the Arctic, and armed confrontation in the region would worsen the prospect for profit from the region.

All Arctic states also have a professed interest in sustainable and responsible stewardship of the Arctic environment in their key policy documents. A binding agreement has been signed "On Cooperation on Marine Oil Pollution Preparedness and Response in the Arctic" that addresses accident preparedness and response (2013), as well as a set of best-practice guidelines for the petroleum development produced in 2007 (Arctic Monitoring and Assessment Programme [AMAP], 2007). However, it is unlikely that they will adopt policies in circumpolar regional bodies, like the Arctic Council, that could eventually act as a brake on Arctic petroleum development. In fact, one of the main points of divergence in their Arctic policy documents is exactly about whether the Arctic Council should be a "decision-making" or "decision-shaping" body, with the majority landing on today's milder version of decision-making (Solli, Wilson Rowe, & Yennie Lindgren, 2013). While Arctic regional bodies will remain an important site for the formation and discussion of best practices, it is likely that national environmental debates (and possibly even more local debates) will be the most influential in shaping Barents Sea outcomes.

The framings of the political Arctic as a smoothly coordinated zone indicate that the Arctic coastal states see their own northern interests as best served through today's arrangements, which award primacy to existing international law and the littoral states themselves. Emphasizing the peacefulness and cooperative nature of the region is one way of casting the outside actors' suggestions of expanded participation or additional layers of governance (including environmental governance) as superfluous. It also makes it easier to draw attention to the economic possibilities of the region, rather than emphasizing security concerns.

Conclusions

In this chapter, we have noted the particular importance of Asia for developments in the Barents Region, and that it may represent two contradictory effects. First, most of the growth in global demand for oil and gas during the coming decades will be found in the Asian countries (along with the countries of the Middle East, but that region has its own supplies). How demand develops in Asia will therefore be decisive for whether prices are high enough to support oil and gas extraction under the harsh (and expensive) climatic conditions of the Barents Sea. Second, the growth of Asia is changing Russia's internal priorities. Russia has many oil and gas fields from which to choose and vast areas that have not been explored properly. As Russian actors increasingly look to Asia, they are prioritizing the development of resources closer to Asian markets, and this may lead to slower development and fewer opportunities for Norwegian–Russian cooperation in the Barents Sea. On the other hand, if the Altai Pipeline is built, it will feed off the same West Siberian gas fields that also supply Europe, possibly making space for gas from the Barents Sea. The question is: which of these Asian effects will be strongest?

The projections of the IEA and OPEC foresee steady growth in the demand for oil and gas. On the one hand it is possible that unconventionals could oversupply the market, on the other hand climate policy might undermine demand. It is difficult to judge the likelihood of either of these developments, but, interestingly, many Russian experts remain skeptical of both. In the short term it is the perceptions of Norwegian and Russian actors that are most important for the development of the Barents Sea. Russian experts' divergent opinions on the significance of these trends may open up more possibilities for investments in the oil and gas sector in the Barents Sea than a more pro-climate and pro-unconventionals perspective would have done, as they are associated with expectations of higher oil and gas prices in the future.

The discussion above clearly indicates that the future of Arctic hydrocarbons cannot be analyzed or projected just on the basis of simple arithmetic equations and calculations using demand–supply projections, no matter how accurate and reliable initial source data might be. Technological, geological, and, to an even greater extent, political factors create a whole array of uncertainties and easily make any assumption or projection obsolete and irrelevant.

The Arctic and especially the Barents Sea is unlikely to be the setting for a major geopolitical conflict, and Arctic political bodies are unlikely to propose binding agreements that would restrict oil and gas development. For the development of the Barents Sea, the global context will therefore be more important than Arctic politics.

Climate change mitigation will remain on the agenda. But as coal produces greater emissions than oil and gas, if there is an effective follow-up agreement to the Kyoto Protocol it is most likely to affect coal, and it could possibly even give natural gas a boost.

In the aftermath of the Ukraine crisis, the EU will attempt to reduce energy imports from Russia, and the collapse of the Ukrainian economy combined with efforts to increase energy efficiency will also reduce the market for Russian gas. Meanwhile, Russia will continue to invest in the expansion of its exports to Asia.

References

Arctic Monitoring and Assessment Programme. (2007). *Arctic oil and gas 2007.* Retrieved from www.amap.no/documents/doc/arctic-oil-and-gas-2007/71

[Awaiting imminent Hydro/Statoil-merger] Venter snarlig Hydro/Statoil-fusjon. (2006, October 16). *Dagens Næringsliv.* Retrieved from www.dn.no/

BP. (2010). *BP statistical review of world energy June 2010.* Retrieved from Thayer School of Engineering at Dartmouth website http://engineering.dartmouth.edu/~d30345d/courses/engs41/BP-StatisticalReview-2010.pdf.

BP. (2011). *BP statistical review of world energy June 2011.* Retrieved from www.bp.com/content/dam/bp-country/de_de/PDFs/brochures/statistical_review_of_world_energy_full_report_2011.pdf

BP. (2012). *BP statistical review of world energy June 2012.* Retrieved from www.bp.com/content/dam/bp/pdf/Statistical-Review-2012/statistical_review_of_world_energy_2012.pdf

BP. (2013). *BP statistical review of world energy June 2013.* Retrieved from www.bp.com/content/dam/bp/pdf/statistical-review/statistical_review_of_world_energy_2013.pdf

BP. (2014). *BP statistical review of world energy June 2014.* Retrieved from www.bp.com/content/dam/bp/pdf/Energy-economics/statistical-review-2014/BP-statistical-review-of-world-energy-2014-full-report.pdf

Buanes, F., Hjertenes, Ø., Øyehaug, O., Strand, T., Mørseth, T.O., Østerbø, K., . . . Berg-Olsen, M. (2006, December 19). Samtaler siden sommeren [Talks since the summer]. *Bergens Tidene.* Retrieved from www.bt.no/

Bustelo, P. (2008). *Energy security with a high external dependence: The strategies of Japan and South Korea* (MPRA Paper No. 8323). Retrieved from Munich University Library website http://mpra.ub.uni-muenchen.de/8323/1/MPRA_paper_8323.pdf

Energy Information Administration. (2013). *Technically recoverable shale oil and shale gas resources: An assessment of 137 shale formations in 41 countries outside the United States.* Retrieved from www.eia.gov/analysis/studies/worldshalegas/

Energy Information Administration. (2014). *Dry natural gas consumption.* Retrieved from www.eia.gov/cfapps/ipdbproject/iedindex3.cfm?tid=3&pid=26&aid=2&cid=r3,&syid=1990&eyid=2013&unit=BCF

Eurostat. (2014). *EU energy imports.* Retrieved from http://appsso.eurostat.ec.europa.eu/nui/submitViewTableAction.do

Gabuev, A. (2011, November 30). Гарантией станет заинтересованность Пхеньяна и Сеула в успехе проекта [The interest of Beijing and Seoul guarantee the success of the project]. *Kommersant.* Retrieved from http://kommersant.ru/

International Energy Agency. (2013). *World energy outlook 2013.* Paris, France: Author.

International Energy Agency. (2014). *Medium-term oil market report 2014.* Paris, France: Author.

Keskitalo, E.C.H. (2004). *Negotiating the Arctic: The construction of an international region.* New York, NY: Routledge.

Kolb, R.W. (2014). *The natural gas revolution: At the pivot of the world's energy future.* Upper Saddle River, NJ: Pearson.

Kraska, J. (Ed.). (2011). *Arctic security in an age of climate change*. Cambridge, England: Cambridge University Press.

Lorentzen, M. (2012, May 25). Statoil kan forlate Shtokman [Statoil can leave Shtokman]. *E24*. Retrieved from http://e24.no/

Maugeri, L. (2013). *The shale oil boom: A US phenomenon*. Retrieved from http://belfercenter.ksg.harvard.edu/files/draft-2.pdf

Mazneva, E., & Kravchenko, S. (2014, May 21). Russia, China sign $400 billion gas deal after decade of talks. *Bloomberg*. Retrieved from www.bloomberg.com/

Noreng, Ø. (2008, December 11). Oljegigantens utfordringer [Oil giant's challenges]. *BI Norwegian Business School*. Retrieved from www.bi.no/

Organization of the Petroleum Exporting Countries. (2013). *World oil outlook 2013*. Retrieved from www.opec.org/opec_web/static_files_project/media/downloads/publications/WOO_2013.pdf

Overland, I. (in press). Joining Rosneft in the Sea of Okhotsk – Statoil's pivot to Asia? In J. Huang & A. Korolev (Eds.), *International cooperation and development of Russia's Siberia and Far East*. Basingstoke, England: Palgrave Macmillan.

Solli, P.E., Wilson Rowe, E., & Yennie Lindgren, W. (2013). Coming into the cold: Asia's Arctic interests. *Polar Geography, 36*(4), 253–270. doi: 10.1080/1088937X.2013.825345

Spencer, T., Sartor, O., & Mathieu, M. (2014). *Unconventional wisdom: An economic analysis of US shale gas and implications for the EU* (Policy Brief No. 05/14). Retrieved from www.iddri.org/Publications/Collections/Syntheses/PB0514.pdf

Stafford, J. (2014, March 21). Interview with Arthur Berman: "Shale is not a revolution, it's a retirement party". *Energy Post*. Retrieved from www.energypost.eu/

Starinskaya, G. (2014, May 5). Роснефть обслуживает долг благодаря предоплате от CNPC – аналитики [Rosneft serves its debt thanks to advance payment from CNPC – analysts]. *Vedomosti*. Retrieved from www.vedomosti.ru/

Stokke, O., & Hønneland, G. (Eds.). (2007). *International cooperation and Arctic governance: Regime effectiveness and northern region building*. Abingdon, England: Routledge.

Strokan, S. (2014, July 1). Корейский полуостров сбросил напряжение [The Korean Peninsula shed its tensions]. *Kommersant*. Retrieved from http://kommersant.ru/

Tennberg, M. (2000). *Arctic environmental cooperation: A study in governmentality*. Aldershot, England: Ashgate.

Tsafos, N. (2013). The new geography of Asian LNG. In M. Bradshaw, M. Herberg, M. Myers Jaffe, D. Ma, & N. Tsafos (Eds.), *Asia's uncertain LNG future* (pp. 7–22). Seattle, WA: NBAR.

Wegge, N. (2011). The political order in the Arctic: Power structures, regimes and influence. *Polar Record, 47*(241), 165–176. doi:10.1017/S0032247410000331

Wilson Rowe, E. (2012). A dangerous space? Unpacking state and media discourse on the Arctic. *Polar Geography, 36*(3), 232–244. doi: 10.1080/1088937X.2012.724461

Young, O.R. (1992). *Arctic politics: Conflict and cooperation in the circumpolar north*. Hanover, Germany: University Press of New England.

Young, O.R. (2009). Whither the Arctic 2009? Further developments. *Polar Record, 45*(2), 179–181. doi:10.1017/S0032247408008061

4 Resource management regimes in the Barents Sea

Alexei Bambulyak, Svetlana Golubeva, Maria Sydnes, Are Kristoffer Sydnes, Lars-Henrik Larsen, and Vlada Streletskaya

Introduction

The Barents Sea petroleum industry, on both the Norwegian and Russian sides, is in its early phase. The 2010 agreement on the delimitation line opened new possibilities for the implementation of joint projects throughout the previously disputed area. How these projects can be realized in practice in the case of trans-boundary fields remains unclear, as the resource management systems in the two countries are different. However, they also have many similarities and, to a large extent, build on the same declared basic principles: licensing, impact and risk assessment, no pollution without permission, "zero discharge", etc.

The hydrocarbon resources of the Barents Sea have long been noted as promising and prospective. While the petroleum industry is moving north and approaching those resources, Norway and Russia are developing regulations aimed at safe and sustainable oil and gas exploration and production in the region; they are also discussing the possibilities for establishing common or harmonized rules. Significant changes in environmental management and licensing procedures have been implemented in Russia during the last 15 years and more are still to come; at the same time, Norwegian rules have been adjusted for the Barents Sea compared to traditional petroleum regions in the North and Norwegian Seas.

We start this chapter with general information on the hydrocarbon resources in Norway and Russia and on the resource classification systems of the two countries; elements of the resource management regimes established in Norway and Russia in terms of licensing, environmental control of the petroleum industry and oil-spill response, focusing on the Barents Sea as a target area, are then described. We also present a structure and mention some Norwegian–Russian environmental cooperation projects. In the conclusion, we reflect on the resource management systems established in the two countries: their fundamentals, similarities and differences.

Hydrocarbon resources estimation and classification

Hydrocarbon resources in Russia

Official Russian data on the country's oil reserves was classified as a state secret from Soviet times until 2013. Oil and gas resources were excluded from the list of state secrets by a governmental resolution in July 2013 (Government of the Russian Federation, 2013a), and in the same year the Ministry of Natural Resources and Environment of the Russian Federation (henceforth: Minprirody) published data on the country's oil and gas reserves and resources (Ministry of Nature Resources and Environment of the Russian Federation, 2013a). Official Russian estimations of the country's hydrocarbon reserves, however, were two to three times higher than those of international assessments, like those published by BP (BP, 2013) (see Table 4.1). To a large extent, this can be explained by the different calculation systems used.

Hydrocarbon reserves classification systems in Russia and Norway

In 2013, the Minister of Natural Resources, Sergey Donskoy, stated that the existing Russian classification of oil and gas reserves and resources calculation (see Table 4.2) was outdated and should be brought closer to the Petroleum Resources Management System (PRMS) definitions of the Society of Petroleum Engineers (SPE) or a Norwegian system (Kezik, 2013). Minprirody has developed and approved a new classification system for hydrocarbon reserves and resources (see Table 4.2) to be applied from 1 January 2016 (Ministry of Natural Resources and Environment of the Russian Federation, 2013b). It takes into consideration not only the geological characteristics of a deposit but also the economic parameters for its development. License owners should recalculate hydrocarbon reserves and resources for their fields during 2014–2015 (Ministry of Natural Resources and Environment of the Russian Federation, 2014).

In the Norwegian petroleum resource classification system introduced in 2001, resources are divided into classes and project status categories, and comprise recoverable resources. The classes are: historical production (S), reserves (R), contingent resources, (C) and undiscovered resources (P). The project

Table 4.1 Russian oil and gas reserves at the end of 2012

Russian reserves estimation	Oil and gas condensate (billion tons)	Natural gas (trillion cubic meters)
Minprirody (ABC1 + C2)	20.1 + 12.3	49.1 + 19.9
BP	11.9	32.9

Source: Based on Ministry of Natural Resources and Environment of the Russian Federation (2013a); BP (2013).

Table 4.2 Current and future classifications of oil and gas reserves and resources in Russia

Category and definition until 2016		Category and definition from 2016	
A	reserves calculated on a deposit (its part) drilled within an approved project for development	A	producing, drilled reserves
B	reserves calculated on a deposit (its part) drilled within an approved technological scheme or research-and-industrial development project	B1	producing, undrilled, explored reserves
		B2	producing, undrilled, estimated reserves
C1	reserves of a deposit (its part) determined on the basis of commercial flows of oil or gas obtained in wells and results of geological and geophysical research of non-probe wells	C1	explored reserves
C2	reserves of a deposit (its part) preliminarily estimated on the basis of geological and geophysical research of unexplored parts of a deposit or non-probe deposits of a field	C2	estimated reserves
C3	prospective resources of oil and gas prepared for drilling of contoured traps and undrilled petroleum-bearing beds	D0	prepared resources
D1L	forecasted localized resources of traps determined by geological and geophysical exploration methods	DL	localized resources
D1	forecasted resources estimated on results of regional geological, geophysical and geochemical research	D1	prospective resources
D2	forecasted resources estimated on the basis of general geological evaluations	D2	forecasted resources

Source: Based on Ministry of Natural Resources of the Russian Federation (2001); Ministry of Natural Resources and Environment of the Russian Federation (2013b).

status categories are numbered from 0 to 9, and some also have attributes F for "first" and A for "additional" (see Table 4.3) (Norwegian Petroleum Directorate [NPD], 2001).

Legal framework

Licensing in Russia

According to amendments to the Russian legislation enacted in 2008, the licenses on the Russian continental shelf are granted for exploration and production of oil and gas on a nontender basis (President of the Russian Federation, 2008). The license holders and users are chosen among Russian companies with more than 50% of their shares controlled by the Russian Federation, and companies with at least five years' experience of project development on the Russian continental shelf. However, foreign companies may still act as operators.

Table 4.3 Norwegian classification of petroleum resources

Resources class	Project status		Description
	Category		
S	0		Sold and delivered petroleum
	1		Reserves in production
R	2	F A	Reserves with approved plan for development and operation
	3	F A	Reserves: recovery is decided by the licensees
	4	F A	Resources: recovery is in the planning phase
C	5	F A	Resources: recovery is likely, but not clarified
	6		Resources: recovery is not very likely
	7	F	Resources: new discoveries that have not been evaluated
		A	Resources: possible future measures to improve recovery
P	8		Resources in prospects
	9		Resources in leads and unmapped resources

Source: Based on Norwegian Ministry of Petroleum and Energy & Norwegian Petroleum Directorate (2014); Norwegian Petroleum Directorate (2001).

Those changes in the legislation granted exclusive rights for oil and gas exploration and production on the Russian continental shelf to the largest Russian companies, state-owned Gazprom and Rosneft. In 2012, the state-owned company, Zarubezhneft, merged with the AMNGR company, which had over five years' experience of petroleum exploration and production on the Russian continental shelf and, therefore, joined Gazprom and Rosneft in this exclusive list of possible license owners. Zarubezhneft applied to the Federal Subsoil Resource Management Agency (Rosnedra) for exploration licenses on the continental shelf of the Barents Sea, where it intended to work with Statoil and Total (Starinskaya, 2011).

By the end of 2010, 45 licenses had been granted on the Russian continental shelf, among them, 12 to the Gazprom Group, 16 to Rosneft, 6 to LUKOIL, 5 for the production sharing agreement (PSA) in Sakhalin and 14 to other petroleum companies (Bambulyak & Frantzen, 2011).

At the end of 2013, Gazprom owned 36 licenses on the Russian continental shelf, while Rosneft had 46, including licenses in the Russian part of the former disputed area with Norway in the Barents Sea (Birg, 2014). The entire Russian part of the former disputed area was divided into three large blocks – Fedynsky in the south (38.1 thousand square kilometers), Central-Barents (15.8 thousand square kilometers) in the middle and Perseevsky (23 thousand square kilometers) in the north. The licenses on these three blocks were granted to

Rosneft in 2012, the same year the company signed cooperation deals with Eni for two southern blocks and with Statoil for the northernmost one (Shelf projects, n.d.).

Rosneft signed the largest deal on the Russian continental shelf, the so-called Arctic Deal, with ExxonMobil in 2011 (after the similar deal with BP was revoked). Now, the deal includes 10 license blocks in the Kara, Laptev and Chukchi Seas with a total area of over 760 thousand square kilometers (Shelf projects, n.d.).

All the above-mentioned deals made by Rosneft for joint work on the Russian continental shelf have the same terms – 66.7% of the shares are owned by Rosneft and 33.3% by cooperating partners (Shelf projects, n.d.).

Liberalization or monopolization

In April 2012, four large Russian private oil companies – LUKOIL, Surgutneftegaz, Bashneft and TNK-BP – addressed a letter to then Prime Minister Vladimir Putin, arguing that the limitations put on private petroleum companies to access the Russian continental shelf might have a decisive negative impact on the implementation of the state program for offshore exploration. The same month, Rosneft subsequently invited those companies to join the state oil major in 12 licensed areas on the Russian shelf, including those in the Barents Sea, on the same terms that were offered to foreign companies (Staalesen, 2012). In July 2012, the Federal Antimonopoly Service of Russia published proposals for changing federal legislation so that it would allow any Russian company with relevant experience to work on the continental shelf. In August 2012, Minister Sergey Donskoy presented the draft program for exploration and development of the Russian continental shelf up to 2030 and stated the importance of allowing access to exploration and production licenses to private petroleum companies (Ernst & Young, 2012). In September 2012, the heads of Rosneft and Gazprom, Igor Sechin and Alexey Miller, sent a letter to President Vladimir Putin, in which they expressed their concern over governmental plans to liberalize access for private companies to explore the continental shelf; they also asked for an acceleration of the process of granting their companies the licenses for which they applied in 2010–2012 ("Gazprom and Rosneft express concern", 2012). In January 2013, Igor Sechin and Alexey Miller sent a letter to Prime Minister Dmitry Medvedev, in which they again asked the government to maintain the monopoly of state-owned companies over the continental shelf licenses and not to allow private companies to even carry out seismic surveys ("Heads of Rosneft and Gazprom", 2013). In September 2014, Gazprom and Rosneft were granted new exploration and production licenses in the Okhotsk and Barents Seas (Government of the Russian Federation, 2014). As of now, the position regarding state companies' monopoly over the continental shelf projects remains unchanged.

Licensing in Norway

In Norway, the Petroleum Act (LOV, 1996) provides the legal basis for the licensing system. Exploration and production licenses are awarded through licensing rounds. Prior to that, the area must be opened for petroleum activities by the parliament's decision. The licensing round for a number of blocks is announced by the Norwegian Petroleum Directorate. Only companies that meet certain criteria can apply and be granted a license. As stated by the Norwegian Ministry of Petroleum and Energy, these qualification criteria are relevant, objective, nondiscriminatory and announced (Norwegian Ministry of Petroleum and Energy, & Norwegian Petroleum Directorate [MPE & NPD], 2014). The Ministry grants a license to a company or a group of companies based on applications received and designates a responsible operator. The production license regulates the rights and obligations of the companies and grants them exclusive rights for exploration and production of hydrocarbon resources within the licensed area. Oil and gas produced within the license is owned by licensees, proportionate to their shares in the joint venture.

Oil and gas activities on the Norwegian continental shelf started in the North Sea and then moved north to the Norwegian and Barents Seas. The major part of the Barents Sea is regarded by the petroleum authorities as a frontier area (MPE & NPD, 2014) with limited geological information, significant technological challenges and lack of infrastructure. In 2004, with the eighteenth license round, the principles of relinquishment in frontier areas were amended. In spring 2013, the twenty-second license round was completed, and 24 licenses in the Barents and Norwegian Seas were granted to 29 out of the 37 participating companies. Two Russian companies have shares in three licenses in the Barents Sea. LUKOIL has a 30% share in the joint venture with Centrica (50%) and North (20%) in license PL709, and 20% with Lundin (40%), Edison (20%) and North (20%) for license PL708, close to the border with Russia. Rosneft has a 20% share in license PL713 operated by Statoil (40%), where Edison and North have 20% each (NPD, 2013).

The twenty-third licensing round, with invitations to nominate areas on the shelf, began in August 2013. By the nomination deadline in January 2014, the Ministry of Petroleum and Energy had received proposals from 40 companies, including LUKOIL's and Rosneft's Norwegian subsidiaries, for 160 blocks as candidates for the licensing round (NPD, 2014).

Environmental regulations

In both Norway and Russia (see Table 4.4), pollution without permission is not allowed (LOV, 1981; President of the Russian Federation, 2002); each offshore oil and gas project should undergo a state environmental review procedure with the necessary environmental impact and risk assessments (Dahle, Shagarova, Sander, & Larsen, 2000; Golubeva & Svensen, 2001). In Norway, the

Table 4.4 State environmental pollution control in Norway and Russia with polluter pays principle realized

Norway	Russia
No pollution without permission	No pollution without permission
Baseline EIA study	Regular state monitoring
Risk-based and BAT principles for permission	Pollution norms and limits principle/BAT to be introduced in 2015
No payment for permitted discharges and emissions (special taxes on CO_2 and NO_x)	Fees for environmental pollution – discharges and emissions based on threshold values – maximum permissible concentration (MPC)
Monitoring of external environment	Monitoring of pollution sources
Compensation for acute pollution – paying all costs for clean-up and direct losses	Fines for acute pollution – compensation for documented and calculated environmental damage

environmental impact assessment (EIA) procedure is applied at all project implementation stages. In Russia, since January 2007, the EIA and state environmental review are applied at the project design stage only (Golubeva, 2013). Public participation is guaranteed but realized differently in Norway and Russia (Moe, 2010).

Environmental control of petroleum industry in Norway

Norway has an integrated national system for environmental control, and the Norwegian continental shelf is divided into 11 regions for environmental monitoring of the petroleum industry (Bambulyak & Dahle, 2014; MPE & NPD, 2014). Environmental pollution and the use of chemicals by the oil and gas industry offshore are regulated by national laws: the Pollution Control Act (PCA), the Climate Quota Act, the Product Control Act, the Petroleum Act and other regulations and guidelines of the responsible national authorities.

Prior to opening an area of the Norwegian shelf to exploration for petroleum hydrocarbons, the government initiates a strategic impact assessment for the region in question. The Ministry of Petroleum and Energy is responsible for the collection and presentation to the parliament of all necessary information. The parliament then makes a decision whether to open that particular region for hydrocarbon exploration or not. Norway has introduced an ecosystem approach for the integrated management of the continental shelf, taking into account all kinds of man's impact on marine areas (Dahle & Shagarova, 1999; Lukin, Pavlenko, Bambulyak, & Larsen, 2012).

The petroleum industry in general is not permitted to discharge any environmentally harmful substances to the sea on the Norwegian continental shelf (Bambulyak & Dahle, 2014; MPE & NPD, 2014). All compounds being discharged must have a certificate showing that the compound does not harm the environment (acute toxicity and bioaccumulation) at the given concentrations; the documentation is based upon standard environmental toxicology tests. The industry must have permits for all the compounds being used and discharged during their operations and deliver detailed annual reports on the amounts and types of chemicals discharged. The industry does not pay for these permitted discharges. However, financial compensation to Norwegian fishermen is regulated by the Petroleum Act. In the case of accidental pollution, the industry should pay all necessarily costs for the clean-up and recovery of the polluted area ("polluter pays" principle). Best available technology (BAT) and best available practice (BAP) principles must be used to improve the production circle and reduce the environmental impact of the activities (Lukin et al., 2012).

When a petroleum company has been awarded a license for exploration and production of hydrocarbons covering a specific area, the company must carry out a baseline survey prior to any exploitative drilling. In the Barents Sea, an exploratory well has to be preceded by a visual inspection of the seabed, to discover sensitive habitats like coral reefs and sponges, and frequently also by a sediment survey. The industry also has to provide an environmental risk assessment as part of the application for a discharge permit and a consent permit, presenting information on the possible environmental impacts of their activities. The Norwegian Environment Agency is the responsible authority for maintaining the guidelines and overseeing the environmental monitoring of petroleum activities on the Norwegian continental shelf. The monitoring regions, principles and procedures for environmental control and monitoring are described in the national guidelines (Iversen et al., 2011) elaborated from the basis of international standards under the Convention for the Protection of the Marine Environment of the North-East Atlantic (OSPAR) (OSPAR Commission, 2012). The petroleum industry organizes a regional survey for each monitoring region every third year and pays the costs, while the environmental monitoring itself is carried out by independent accredited scientific consultants on a contract base. The reports are delivered to the Environment Agency and made available to the public at the agency's website (Bambulyak & Dahle, 2014).

Environmental monitoring of offshore petroleum activities in Norway is organized as an ecosystem-based and dynamic tool, and it is one of key elements of the state and industrial environmental control system in the country (Bambulyak & Dahle, 2014).

The sediment monitoring includes taking samples of the seabed, analyzing sediments for given heavy metals and oil compounds, as well as analyzing the biodiversity of the macro benthic community. Norwegian ISO-based standards are used for carrying out the program. The combined results from the sediment analyses, the operators' reported discharges since the previous survey and the state of the benthic communities are used for calculating the degree and size of the sea floor being impacted by the oil and gas activities. Data from the offshore environmental monitoring is also used in connection with Norwegian reporting to OSPAR (Bambulyak & Dahle, 2014; Iversen et al., 2011).

Environmental monitoring offshore includes both monitoring of the sediments and monitoring of the water column. Measurements of concentration levels of given compounds in selected organisms and in the water are key elements for environmental monitoring in the water column in the vicinity of petroleum facilities offshore (Bambulyak & Dahle, 2014; Iversen et al., 2011).

Environmental monitoring and control system in Russia

The state environmental management and control system in Russia has been built around the "polluter pays" principle and the introduction of environmental payments as financial compensation for industrial pollution. The environmental payments are divided into payments for regular (permitted) industrial pollution (emission, discharge and waste disposal) and payments (fines) for violation of environmental regulations (accidental acute pollution) (President of the Russian Federation, 2002).

The system for environmental payments in Russia consists of methods for defining and calculating costs for environmental protection measures, economic assessment of environmental impacts and calculation of losses due to violation of environmental regulations. Environmental payments are calculated as a sum of economic losses through environmental damage assessment, and/or payments to cover certain environmental protection and restoration measures, like environmental payments for indisputable losses, such as losses of fishery resources, occurring due to offshore petroleum activities, are paid to the federal budget or a special fund for fish stock restoration (Lukin et al., 2012).

With the basic Federal Law on Environmental Protection, Russian environmental legislation set principles for defining limits for industrial environmental pollution as an impact to be allowed through ecologically based maximum permissible concentration (MPC) for each pollutant to be emitted or discharged. The state also establishes rules and guidelines for calculating environmental payments for pollution below and above permissible levels, as well as for violation of environmental regulations. Basic norms of payments (fees) for pollutants' emission to air, discharge into waters and waste management (treatment and disposal) are set by the Russian government (President of the Russian Federation, 2002). The state and industrial environmental management systems are built to control and monitor the industrial pollution for each regulated (with defined MPC) contaminant.

State environmental supervision of the industrial activities in Russia is carried out by the Federal Service for Supervision of Natural Resources Use (henceforth: Rosprirodnadzor) agency under Minprirody (Government of the Russian Federation, 2004a; Bambulyak, Golubeva, & Savinov, 2013). This agency controls implementation of the environmental regulations (permissions to pollute within certain limits) set for the industry and supervises industrial environmental control and monitoring systems, including inspection of pollution reports and verification of industrial laboratories. Since 2010, Rosprirodnadzor is also the responsible state authority for carrying out environmental reviews of petroleum projects on the Russian continental shelf (Kirillov, 2013).

Industrial environmental control is obligatory for oil and gas activities and is part of the industrial environmental management system. The company operator is responsible for identifying sources of pollution (emission to air, discharge to water, waste disposal) for each regulated pollutant, measuring the pollution load (mass of emitted/discharged pollutant per year) and calculating environmental payments – fees to be paid to the state (Aleksandrov, 2005; Buhgalter & Ilyakova, 2013).

Waste management is based on provisions of the Federal Law on Industrial and Household Waste (President of the Russian Federation, 1998). In Russia, waste is divided into five hazard classes. Projects on waste management, recycling or disposal go through EIA and state environmental review procedures.

State environmental monitoring of the Russian continental shelf, including the Russian part of the Barents Sea, is established according to the Federal Laws: on Environmental Protection, on the Continental shelf, on the Exclusive Economic Zone (Aleksandrov, 2005; Buhgalter & Ilyakova, 2013). The agency of the Minprirody – the Federal Service on Hydrometeorology and Environmental Monitoring of Russia (henceforth: Roshydromet) – is the responsible authority for managing the Unified State Environmental Monitoring System (Government of the Russian Federation, 2004b). The environmental monitoring system of Roshydromet is region- (regional network of offices and monitoring points) and pollution-based. Research institutes under Minprirody also run state projects for monitoring offshore environmental pollution on requests from the ministry. The state monitoring of marine biological resources in Russia is the responsibility of the Federal Agency of Fisheries and carried out by its subordinated research institutes (Lukin et al., 2012). For example, any new technology or equipment to be applied offshore that may impact marine biological resources should be reviewed by the Central Department on Fishery Review and Norms on Protection and Restoration of Water Biological Resources and Acclimatisation (CUREN), and the environmental monitoring program should be approved (Aleksandrov, 2005; Golubeva, 2013).

Industry is obliged to establish and carry out environmental monitoring of environmental impact sources within its industrial environmental pollution control system. Industry monitors the sources of pollutants permitted for emission or discharge, and waste disposal places in areas of impact. An environmental monitoring program (with a list of pollutants to be monitored, terms, measurements or calculation methods) is developed for each pollution source (Buhgalter & Ilyakova, 2013).

In 2013, changes to the federal regulations came into force, obliging all operators of offshore petroleum projects to elaborate their oil-spill contingency plans and present them for state environmental review, to implement an oil-spill response system according to the adopted plan and to provide a financial guarantee for paying all costs in the case of accidental oil pollution, including

Table 4.5 Environmental requirement for offshore petroleum industry in Norway and Russia

Impact	Norway	Russia
Emission to air		
CO_2	reduction, reinjection, tax	fee: MPC 27000 mg/m^3
NO_x	reduction, tax	fee: MPC 0.1–5 mg/m^3
nmVOC	reduction	fee: MPC 300–900 mg/m^3
CH_4	reduction	fee: MPC 7000 mg/m^3
SO_2	reduction	fee: MPC 0.5 mg/m^3
Discharge to water		
Produced water – oil	reinjection, treatment to < 30 mg/l	reinjection, fee: MPC 0.05 mg/l
Chemicals	Reduction, substitution	fee: MPC 0.001–0.05 mg/l
Drill cuttings	Discharge or onshore disposal, reinjection	removal onshore, reinjection
Waste management		
Liquid	treatment and discharge	removal onshore
Solid	removal onshore	removal onshore

Source: Based on Federal Agency of Fisheries (2010); LOV (1981); Ministry of Health Protection of the Russian Federation (2003); OSPAR Commission (2012).

compensation for environmental damage (President of the Russian Federation, 2012). Environmental damage assessment is challenging, as it may combine costs for oil-spill recovery and fines for nature resource and environmental quality losses (Bambulyak, von Bock und Polach, Ehlers, & Sydnes, 2014).

According to the Federal Law on the Continental shelf of the Russian Federation (President of the Russian Federation, 1995), waste disposal and discharge of pollutants is not permitted on the Russian continental shelf. This means that all drill cuttings, chemicals and produced water cannot be disposed of on the sea floor or discharged to the sea waters within the continental shelf area and must be transported and treated onshore (see Table 4.5).

Norwegian–Russian environmental cooperation

The agreement between the Governments of the Kingdom of Norway and the Russian Federation on Environmental Matters was signed in 1992 as a renewal of the first bilateral governmental agreement on environmental cooperation signed between Norway and the Soviet Union in 1988. At the political level, the cooperation operates through the Norwegian–Russian Environmental Commission, co-led by state environmental authorities, the Norwegian Ministry of Climate and Environment and the Ministry of Natural Resources and Environment of the Russian Federation. Bilateral activities are carried out as projects within the joint work program agreed every second year (Norwegian–Russian environmental cooperation, n.d.). The management of resources in the Barents Sea in a sustainable way, based on scientific knowledge and an ecosystem approach, has been one of the main focuses in the bilateral discussions. The Environmental Commission initiated and supported a number of projects aimed at analyses, improvement and harmonization of environmental requirements and standards for the oil and gas industry prior to their operations in the Barents Sea, e.g. the exchange of competence on EIA processes in Russia and Norway, started in 1999 (Dahle et al., 2000; Golubeva & Svensen, 2001; Lukin et al., 2012), Coordinated Environmental Monitoring Program 2002–2011 (CEMP) (Savinov et al., 2011) and Joint Guidelines for Post Oil-Spill Damage Assessment 2006–2010 (Dahle, Larsen, Bambulyak, & Studenov, 2011; Studenov et al., 2009). In 2009, the Joint Norwegian–Russian Environmental Status Report on the Barents Sea Ecosystem was presented (Stiansen et al., 2009); this addressed all aspects of the sea's ecosystem and highlighted increases in petroleum and shipping activities as significant challenges (Norwegian–Russian environmental cooperation, n.d.).

In June 2006, the Norwegian parliament ratified the integrated management plan for the Barents Sea and Lofoten; this was updated in 2011 (Government of Norway, 2011; von Quillfeldt, 2012). One of the issues stated in the management plan is the establishment of special marine protection areas, where oil exploration will not be permitted (Moe, 2010). The Norwegian management plan for the Barents Sea has been presented and promoted on the Russian side within the Joint Environmental Commission meetings, and development of the common principles for resource and environmental management for the whole Barents Sea has been discussed (Moe, 2010; von Quillfeldt, 2012). On the other side, the State Oceanographic Institute under Minprirody elaborated the Methodology for Marine Spatial Planning and Comprehensive (Integrated) Nature Resources Management Plan in the Barents Sea, taking into account international experience and the best practices of trans-border resources use (Zemlyanov et al., 2013), which is under discussion now. The methodology and the plan were elaborated within the Russian Federal Target Program "World Ocean" and are based on the Large Marine Ecosystem (Protection of the Arctic Marine Environment [PAME], 2013) concept and ecosystem approach in management (Zemlyanov et al., 2013).

Norwegian and Russian environmental authorities, research institutes and nongovernmental organizations (NGOs) collaborate and also implement joint projects to study and protect the Barents Sea ecosystem within other bilateral and international platforms, including the Joint Norwegian–Russian Fisheries Commission, established by the decision made in 1974 (The Fisheries Commission, n.d.); the Arctic Council with its working groups (AMAP, PAME, ACAP, CAFF, EPPR, SDWG); EU–Russia cooperation programs, such as Kolarctic; the Barents Euro–Arctic Region with environmental working groups and subgroups operating at national and regional levels; NATO–Russia Science for Peace and Security ("frozen" at the moment); Norwegian Research Council and the Russian Foundation for Basic Research cooperation programs; petroleum industry associations and projects, like INTSOK RU-NO Barents project; Barents-2020 Harmonization of Health, Safety and Environmental Protection Standards for the Barents Sea; joint industry project of the International Association of Oil and Gas Producers (JIP OGP) on Arctic oil-spill response technologies; and others.

Oil-spill response in the Barents Sea

Oil-spill response system for the Russian Barents Sea

In the Russian Federation, all issues related to emergency prevention, response and security, including oil-spill response (OSR), are organized within the Unified State System of Emergency Prevention and Response (Government of the Russian Federation, 2003; President of the Russian Federation, 1994). OSR in Russia is a tiered system (International Petroleum Industry Environmental Conservation Association [IPIECA], 2007; Semanov & Ivanchin, 2004), in which the first level responds to local and/or municipal spills, the second to regional ones and the third to federal spills. It has been characterized as a complex, multiorganizational structure and regulated by an extensive legislative framework (Ivanova, 2011; Rambøll Barents, 2010; Sydnes, Bambulyak, & Sydnes, 2013).

Russian legislation ranks emergencies caused by oil spills in terms of their potential severity, based on the volume of oil spilled (Government of the Russian Federation, 2000), with five categories of oil spills on land and three at sea (Ivanova, 2011). Contingency plans are based on the maximum possible volume of oil spilled and are enacted depending on the category of a spill (Government of the Russian Federation, 2000).

All activities related to OSR are carried out according to contingency plans established at the federal, regional and local/object levels. Initially OSR in Russia is the responsibility of the industrial operators, who are obliged to have and implement oil-spill contingency plans for their projects (Government of the Russian Federation, 2002; President of the Russian Federation, 2012). If an oil spill at the offshore facility shifts from the local to the regional level of emergency, the regional plan comes into action. A similar procedure is applied if an oil spill extends up to the federal level. Contingency plans at regional and federal levels at sea are elaborated and managed by the State Marine Coordination and Emergency Rescue Service of the Russian Federation (henceforth: Gosmorspassluzhba). These are to be approved by federal authorities, including the Ministry of Transport, the Ministry of Emergencies and Minprirody (Government of the Russian Federation, 2002).

Industrial operators are also to establish oil-spill response teams (Government of the Russian Federation, 2002; President of the Russian Federation, 2012). As few operators have their own response teams, the majority outsource these services to private or state OSR providers. In addition, operators are to establish an environmental monitoring system, including an oil-spill detection system, and ensure that they have a system for early warning and communications. Finally, operators are obliged to have financial provisions to cover OSR costs including compensation for environmental damage (President of the Russian Federation, 2012).

The OSR system in the Barents Sea is established by the Ministry of Transport of Russia and its subordinate authorities, including the Federal Agency of Marine and River Transport (henceforth: Rosmorrechflot), the Rosmorport and Gosmorspassluzhba (Government of the Russian Federation, 2013b;

Ministry of Transport of the Russian Federation, 2009, 2013). These agencies operate at the federal level. Gosmorspassluzhba's head office is in Moscow, while nine branches operate in all sea basins in Russia (About SMPCSA, n.d.). The Northern branch of Gosmorspassluzhba, with headquarters in Murmansk, is responsible for OSR operations from the Norwegian–Russian border in the west to 125°E in the east, i.e. covering the whole Russian part of the Barents Sea (Bambulyak et al., 2014; Korenev & Vassiliev, 2013). It is the main provider of search and rescue and OSR services at sea in the Russian Arctic (Government of the Russian Federation, 2013b; Ministry of Transport of the Russian Federation, 2013). OSR activities in the Barents Sea are coordinated through the state Marine Rescue Coordination Centers and communicated with relevant authorities in the case of incidents (Ivanova, 2011).

Oil-spill response in Norway

The Pollution Control Act (PCA) is the legal basis that establishes the general requirements for the OSR system and the basic principles, demands and obligations to the organizations involved in activities that may cause acute pollution in Norway (LOV, 1981). The PCA establishes the "polluter pays" principle in Norwegian OSR. Another cornerstone of the Norwegian policy against acute pollution is the use of preventive and risk-reducing measures (Bjerkemo, 2010).

The Norwegian OSR system is a tiered system based on private, municipality and state systems (IPIECA, 2007). All levels of contingency act in accordance with their contingency plans that provide guidance for acting in emergency situations. The contingency plans of private industry and municipalities are based on requirements set by the Norwegian Environment Agency, which also approves the plans. The Department of Emergency Response of the Coastal Administration under the Ministry of Transport is responsible for maintaining the national contingency, including all three levels (Sydnes & Sydnes, 2011). The Coastal Administration, in cooperation with the Climate and Pollution Agency (now, the Norwegian Environment Agency) and the Norwegian Directorate for Civil Protection, have developed a "unitary command system" (ELS) for fire, rescue and acute pollution that is to be applied during operations (Norwegian Directorate for Civil Protection, 2011).

As stated in the PCA, oil-spill response is primarily the responsibility of the polluter, who is in charge of emergency operations in the event of acute pollution resulting from its activity, regardless of the size of an oil spill. Petroleum operators are obliged to establish contingency plans and OSR systems to ensure safe operations. Contingency plans are to ensure that response organizations and procedures are established (Sydnes & Sydnes, 2011). In Norway, private offshore operators are members of the Norwegian Clean Seas Association for Operating Companies (henceforth: NOFO) (Bjerkemo, 2010). The NOFO's main task is to maintain oil-spill emergency preparedness on the Norwegian Continental Shelf and coordinate the activities of private companies (Norwegian Clean Seas Association for Operating Companies [NOFO], 2013). The

NOFO is a part of the national OSR system and can mobilize significant resources in the event of acute pollution (Bjerkemo, 2010; INTSOK, 2014; NOFO, 2013).The NOFO's OSR capacity is organized as "Clean Seas Association" systems, including equipment and personnel, located along the coastline in five different regions (NOFO, 2013; Sydnes & Sydnes, 2011).

Municipalities and intermunicipal response regions are primarily responsible for minor incidents of acute pollution within the municipality, but they are also to provide assistance if the polluter is unable to handle the incident on its own. In addition, municipalities are obliged to provide each other with assistance in the case of oil spills from shipping, offshore installations and other sources (LOV, 1981). Intermunicipality OSR coordination is organized through 32 intermunicipal regions, established by the government and covering the entire country. These act when municipalities need assistance and are also obliged to assist each other in cases of emergency. The Norwegian Environment Agency sets the requirements for the level of contingency both at the municipal level and that of intermunicipal regions (Sydnes & Sydnes, 2011).

State contingency is the core of the Norwegian OSR system.The Norwegian Coastal Administration, under the Ministry of Transport, is responsible for the enforcement of the PCA in the case of acute oil pollution. It is also the national administrative authority on maritime safety and the maintenance of national preparedness against acute pollution. Under its auspices, the state contingency plan includes national, international and private agreements with actors to provide resources. State contingency is based on a regularly revised and updated environmental risk assessment (DNV GL, 2011; Norwegian Environment Agency, 2001) and is primarily focused on maritime traffic and responding to accidents along the coast (DNV GL, 2011).The PCA, further, gives the Coastal Administration the right to mobilize and coordinate all national resources into one national OSR organization in the event of large oil spills, irrespective of their origin.This is ensured by a compensation scheme that guarantees that all costs derived from providing such assistance will be reimbursed. As such, the three levels of contingency are to operate as a single integrated response operation when required.There are no formally established criteria for when the Coastal Administration may take control over OSR operations (Sydnes & Sydnes, 2011).

Oil-spill response cooperation in the Barents Sea

Norway and Russia have organized cooperation to combat accidental oil spills in the Barents Sea on an intergovernmental level.This cooperation is built on the basis of the bilateral Agreement on Maritime Safety and Environmental Protection against Oil Pollution signed in 1994, with a Joint Norwegian–Russian Contingency Plan for the Combatment of Oil Pollution in the Barents Sea as its integral part.This agreement was based on the 1990 International Convention on Oil Pollution Preparedness, Response and Cooperation (OPRC) that encourages its parties to "co-operate and provide advisory services, technical support and equipment for the purpose of responding to an oil pollution incident" (International Convention on Oil Pollution Preparedness, Response and Cooperation, 1990; Sydnes & Sydnes, 2013). The agreement gives a platform to responsible authorities from both countries to run practical joint activities, including joint exercises that are arranged annually, one year in Norway and another in Russia (Bambulyak & Frantzen, 2011). State departments responsible for oil-spill preparedness and response at sea lead the cooperation, the Norwegian Coastal Administration, from one side, and Gosmorspassluzhba from the other. Other state departments, like units of the Norwegian Coast Guard, Russian Ministry of Emergencies and regional environmental authorities, as well as professional private companies and environmental NGOs take part in workshops and exercises. The cooperation is managed by the Joint Norwegian–Russian Steering Group, established in 2006 with a Memorandum on Maritime Safety, and the Planning and Policy Group (INTSOK, 2014; Sydnes & Sydnes, 2013).

The joint oil-spill contingency plan establishes the four steps to be taken during the stages of an oil-spill response operation: discovery and alarm; evaluation and plan invocation; containment, counter measures, clean-up and disposal; and documentation and cost recovery. So far, the joint contingency plan has not been implemented in a real case, as there has not been an oil spill to activate it, and joint exercises, called Exercise Barents, provided the only opportunity to assess the regime's effectiveness and reveal possible gaps in preparedness. These exercises are also important for professional training, experience exchange and capacity improvement. Since 2006, Exercise Barents can also be combined with Barents Rescue and Norwegian–Russian search-and-rescue exercises. The authorities also arrange education and training courses and provide technical support to oil-spill response units (Sydnes & Sydnes, 2013).

In addition to the bilateral cooperation, both Norway and Russia are participants of the multilateral cooperation established under the Arctic Council. Its Emergency Prevention, Preparedness and Response Working Group (EPPR) facilitates the exchange of information and practical experience among the Arctic states on issues related to the prevention of, preparedness for and response to all kinds of environmental emergencies in the Arctic, including oil spills (INTSOK, 2014). Both Norway and Russia are parties to the 2013 Agreement on Cooperation on Marine Oil Pollution Preparedness and Response in the Arctic (Agreement on Cooperation on Marine Oil Pollution Preparedness and Response in the Arctic, 2013).

Norway and Russia have ratified the United Nations Convention on the Law of the Sea (UNCLOS), as well as the international conventions adopted by the International Maritime Organization (IMO) to prevent and compensate environmental damage by oil pollution from seagoing vessels: on the Prevention of Pollution from Ships (MARPOL); on Civil Liability for Oil Pollution Damage (CLC); on the Establishment of an International Fund for Compensation for Oil Pollution Damage (FUND); and on Civil Liability for Bunker Oil Pollution Damage (BUNKER) (Bambulyak et al., 2014). The IMO is currently developing an international code of safety for ships operating in polar waters (Polar Code), which should cover the full range of design, construction, equipment, operational, training, search and rescue and environmental protection matters relevant to ships operating in Arctic and Antarctic waters (INTSOK, 2014).

Conclusions

In this final section, we outline the main principles on which Norwegian and Russian resource management systems are based. We further discuss not only whether these principles conform or differ but also how they are acted upon. This is important as it provides a basis on which future harmonization and cooperation can be built.

The Barents Sea and its resources have been historically shared and utilized by Norway and Russia, and both countries are motivated to harmonize their rules for sustainable and responsible resource management of the sea. Norway and Russia are developing laws and regulations following national priorities and international principles, formulated in key conventions and agreements for the protection of the sea, such as UNCLOS or CLC. We can see that the oil and gas industry is moving north in both countries, moving step-by-step and taking those steps differently. Norway has longer experience of the exploration and exploitation of offshore petroleum resources, while Russia has gained some experience operating in all-year-round ice conditions. Moreover, the economically important fisheries of the Barents Sea are shared between the countries. That lays the basis for a dialogue on common rules and standards.

However, there is not yet a harmonized approach to industrial control and environmental protection. Whether we take the licensing regime, environmental control or oil pollution prevention systems, we will see that Norway and Russia build those systems on the same principles of sustainable development and pollution prevention. Nevertheless, those principles are realized differently. In Norway, the state grants licenses for exploration and production through open competitions, although companies must qualify for entry, and production sharing agreements (PSA) are commonly used in consortiums. In Russia, the continental shelf is shared by two state majors – Gazprom and Rosneft – which may compete from time to time but act as one team when they need to secure their duopoly. On one hand, the Norwegian system is a more open and transparent process, whereas the Russian one is centralized and closed; on the other hand, both systems are built on trust and knowledge to realize state interests. And in both cases they give a clear message about what to do to operate in the Barents Sea: either follow qualification procedures and licensing in Norway or join Gazprom or Rosneft in Russia. It is, however, unclear how cooperation between Norwegian PSAs and Russian Rosneft-based consortiums can be realized in case of trans-boundary field development.

We can say that there are similar system differences in environmental management and control of offshore oil and gas projects in Norway and Russia. The "polluter pays" principle is realized in both countries, but the "pay lists" for polluters are different. In both countries, industry needs to obtain permission from the state to pollute. And while special taxes have been introduced for air emission of CO_2 and NO_X by the petroleum industry in Norway, in Russia each polluter has to pay for the release of each contaminant within approved limits. In Norway, permissions are given through the implementation of a risk-based approach and BAT principles; in Russia, threshold values (maximum permissible levels of contamination) provide the basis for assessments and decisions, and the BAT principle that should be applied to projects starting from 2018 (President of the Russian Federation, 2014) is introduced, not instead of, but on the basis of, the existing MPC system.

Norway has announced a "zero discharge" rule for the Barents Sea, but Russian legislation has set an absolute zero discharge rule for the whole country's continental shelf, including produced water and drill cuttings. Note that produced water accounts for 90% of all discharges from Norwegian petroleum activities; over 150 million m3 of produced water was discharged to the sea in 2013, while 85 million cubic meters of oil was produced (Bambulyak & Dahle, 2014; MPE & NPD, 2014).

Prior to full-scale oil and gas production in the Barents Sea, an economically reasonable and environmentally safe "zero discharge" principle should be documented and agreed upon in both Norway and Russia. Environmental requirements and standards for the industry should be based on a common understanding of environmental quality, industrial impacts and risks. Therefore environmental quality, impact and risk assessments criteria should be harmonized (otherwise, one will be motivated to discharge produced water on one side of the border and emit climatic gases on the other).

We see more similarities when examining the organization of oil pollution prevention and response systems in Norway and Russia. There are certain differences in risk assessment, contingency planning, capacity distribution, coordination and technology application; but basic goals regarding oil-spill management are the same – prevention, recovery, clean-up. These goals stimulate practical cooperation between authorities, response units and respective institutions. That cooperation has been seen as successful, although it has not been tested in a real-case oil spill (Bambulyak & Frantzen, 2011; Sydnes & Sydnes, 2013). Nevertheless, lack of harmonization in technologies and methods that can be used for oil-spill clean-up offshore and onshore, i.e. technologies approved on both sides, may result in the limitation of oil-spill clean-up capabilities by a short list of traditional means that can be applied.

Though there is much common ground between Norway and Russia, in terms of the international laws and general principles applied as a basis for national management systems, there are also differences in how these are applied in practice through national regulations. Research institutes from Russia and Norway have been working together in the Barents Sea for decades; they have a dialogue, speaking the same language. Harmonization of standards for oil and gas operations in the Barents Sea should also be brought about in a dialogue, establishing harmonized understandings of what "zero", "harmful", "safe" and "clean" imply. This is required as a basis for further, productive cooperation and development.

References

About SMPCSA. (n.d.). Retrieved from: http://gmssr.ru/en/smpcsa/about/

Agreement on Cooperation on Marine Oil Pollution Preparedness and Response in the Arctic. (May 15, 2013). Retrieved from www.arctic-council.org/eppr/agreement-on-cooperation-on-marine-oil-pollution-preparedness-and-response-in-the-arctic/

Aleksandrov, A.K. (2005). *Законодательная и нормативная база, регламентирующая природоохранные требования при разведке, обустройстве и эксплуатации нефтегазовых месторождений на шельфе России* [Legal and normative base regulating nature protection requirements during exploration, construction and exploitation of oil-and-gas fields on the shelf of the seas of Russia]. Retrieved from Priroda.ru website: www.priroda.ru/lib/detail.php?ID=5244

Bambulyak, A., & Dahle, S. (April 2014). *Environmental monitoring as a management tool for oil-and-gas projects in the Arctic: Norwegian practices and joint Norwegian–Russian activities.* Paper presented at the Fourth Russian Arctic Oil & Gas Conference, Moscow, Russia.

Bambulyak, A., & Frantzen, B. (2011). *Oil transport from the Russian part of the Barents region. Status per January 2011.* Retrieved from: www.barents.no/Filnedlasting.aspx?MId1=2504&FilId=1717

Bambulyak,A., Golubeva, S., & Savinov,V. (2013). *Assessment of the Barents hot spot report describing the state of 42 original Barents environmental "hot spots". Analysis.* Retrieved from Barentsinfo website: www.barentsinfo.fi/beac/docs/Environment_Ministers_Meeting_4_5_Nov_2013_Inari_HotSpots_Assessment_Report_ENG.pdf

Bambulyak, A., von Bock und Polach, R.U.F., Ehlers, S., & Sydnes, A. (June 2014). *Challenges with oil spill risk assessment in Arctic regions: Shipping along the Northern Sea Route.* Paper presented at the ASME 2014 33rd International Conference on Ocean, Offshore and Arctic Engineering, San Francisco, CA. Abstract retrieved from http://proceedings.asmedigitalcollection.asme.org/proceeding.aspx?articleid=1911683

Birg, G. (August 8, 2014). *Газпром и Роснефть – на шельф вне очереди* [Gazprom and Rosneft – to the shelf out of turn]. *RBC daily.* Retrieved from http://rbcdaily.ru/

Bjerkemo, O.K. (March 2010). *Norwegian oil spill response organization, training and exercise – Are we prepared?* Paper presented at the Petroleum Association of Japan (PAJ) Oil Spill Symposium 2010, Reality and Formality in Oil Spill Response and Training/Exercise, Tokyo, Japan. Abstract retrieved from: www.pcs.gr.jp/p-kokusai/epaj2010.html

BP. (2013). *BP statistical review of world energy. June 2013.* Retrieved from: www.bp.com/content/dam/bp/pdf/statistical-review/statistical_review_of_world_energy_2013.pdf

Buhgalter, E.B., & Ilyakova, E.E. (2013). *Нормативные аспекты экологического мониторинга при нефтегазодобыче в Арктике* [Normative aspects of ecological monitoring with oil-and-gas production in the Arctic]. *Gas Science Tribune Scientific-and-Technical Journal, 2,* 82–87. UDK: 504.06:622.276.04(98)

Dahle, S., Larsen, L.H., Bambulyak, A., & Studenov, I. (2011). Norwegian–Russian cooperation on reducing environmental risk of accidental oil spills on Arctic coasts. In A. Bourmistrov, F. Mellemvik, & S. Vasiljev (Eds.), *Perspectives on Norwegian–Russian energy cooperation* (pp. 147–159). Oslo: Cappelen Akademisk Forlag.

Dahle, S., & Shagarova, L. (Eds.). (1999). *Exchange of competence on environmental impact assessment of offshore oil and gas exploration and extraction in Russia and Norway* (Akvaplan-niva report No. 1447). Tromsø, Norway: Akvaplan-niva.

Dahle, S., Shagarova, L., Sander, G., & Larsen, L.H. (June 2000). *Bilateral Russian–Norwegian cooperation on environmental impact assessment.* Paper presented at the SPE International Conference on Health, Safety and the Environment in Oil and Gas Exploration and Production,

Stavanger, Norway. Abstract retrieved from: www.onepetro.org/conference-paper/SPE-61129-MS

DNV GL. (2011). *Miljørisiko ved akutt oljeforuresning fra skiptrafikken langs kysten af Fastlands-Norge for 2008 og prognoser for 2025* [Environmental risk of acute oil spills from ships along the coast of mainland Norway] (Report No. 2011–0850). Retrieved from Kystverket website: www.kystverket.no/Nyheter/2011/Oktober/Miljorisikoanalyse/

Ernst & Young. (2012). *Arctic oil and gas*. Retrieved from: www.ey.com/Publication/vwLU Assets/Arctic_oil_and_gas/$FILE/Arctic_oil_and_gas.pdf

Federal Agency of Fisheries. (2010). *Об утверждении нормативов качества воды водных объектов рыбохозяйственного значения, в том числе нормативов предельно-допустимых концентраций вредных веществ в водах водных объектов рыбохозяйственного значения* [On adoption of norms of water quality of water objects of fishery importance, including norms of maximum permissible concentrations of harmful substances in waters of water objects of fishery importance]. Order dated January 18, 2010 N 20. Moscow: Author.

Gazprom and Rosneft express concern over plans to let private companies explore Russian shelf. (October 18, 2012). *Gazeta.ru English*. Retrieved from: http://en.gazeta.ru/

Golubeva, S. (2013). *Анализ нормативных требований по проведению экологической оценки при разработке проектной документации* [Analyses of legal requirements for environmental impact assessment of project documentation]. Moscow, Russia: System Development Agency.

Golubeva, S., & Svensen, I. (2001). *EIA in Norway and Russia*. Oslo, Norway: Norwegian Pollution Control Authority.

Government of Norway. (2011). Updated version of the integrated management plan for the Barents Sea–Lofoten area [Press release]. Retrieved from: www.regjeringen.no/en/archive/Stoltenbergs-2nd-Government/Office-of-the-Prime-Minister/Nyheter-og-pressemeldinger/pressemeldinger/2011/updated-version-of-the-integrated-manage.html?id=635620

Government of the Russian Federation. (2000). *О неотложных мерах по предупреждению и ликвидации аварийных разливов нефти и нефтепродуктов* [On urgent measures for oil spill prevention and emergency response]. Decree dated August 21, 2000 N 613. Moscow: Author.

Government of the Russian Federation. (2002). *О порядке организации мероприятий по предупреждению и ликвидации разливов нефти и нефтепродуктов на территории Российской Федерации* [On organizing measures for oil spill prevention and response on the territory of the Russian Federation]. Decree dated April 15, 2002 N 240. Moscow: Author.

Government of the Russian Federation. (2003). *О единой государственной системе предупреждения и ликвидации чрезвычайных ситуаций* [On a unified state system of emergency prevention and response]. Decree dated December 30, 2003 N 794. Moscow: Author.

Government of the Russian Federation. (2004a). *Об утверждении положения О Федеральной службе по надзору в сфере природопользования и внесении изменений в Постановление Правительства Российской Федерации от 22 июля 2004 г. N 370* [On approval of the regulation on Federal Service on Supervision in the Sphere of Nature Use and introducing changes in the Decree of the Government of the Russian Federation dated 22 July 2004 N 370]. Decree dated July 30, 2004 N 400. Moscow: Author.

Government of the Russian Federation. (2004b). *О Федеральной службе по гидрометеорологии и мониторингу окружающей среды* [On Federal Service on

Hydrometeorology and Environmental Monitoring]. Decree dated July 23, 2004 N 372. Moscow: Author.

Government of the Russian Federation. (2013a). *О внесении изменений в постановление Правительства Российской Федерации от 2 апреля 2002 года N 210* [On introducing changes in the Decree of the Government of the Russian Federation dated April 2, 2002 N 210]. Decree dated July 5, 2013 N 569. Moscow: Author.

Government of the Russian Federation. (2013b). *О реорганизации федерального государственного унитарного предприятия "Балтийское бассейновое аварийно-спасательное управление"* [On reorganization of the state unitary enterprise Baltic basin emergency rescue and salvage department]. Resolution dated January 17, 2013 N 12-r. Moscow: Author.

Government of the Russian Federation. (2014). *О предоставлении ОАО "Газпром" и ОАО "НК Роснефть" права пользования участками недр в Баренцевом и Охотском морях* [On granting JSC Gazprom and JSK OC Rosneft the right to use licensed blocks in Barents and Okhotsk Seas]. Resolution dated September 4, 2014 N 1722-r. Moscow: Author.

Heads of Rosneft and Gazprom renewed their appeal to Medvedev about the shelf. (January 30, 2013). *Arctic-Info Internet News Agency*. Retrieved from: www.arctic-info.com/

International Convention on Oil Pollution Preparedness, Response and Cooperation. (November 30, 1990). Retrieved from: https://treaties.un.org/doc/Publication/UNTS/Volume%201891/volume-1891-I-32194-English.pdf

International Petroleum Industry Environmental Conservation Association. (2007). *Guide to tiered preparedness and response* (Vol. 14). London, England: Author.

INTSOK. (2014). *Russian–Norwegian oil and gas industry cooperation in the High North. Environmental protection, monitoring systems and oil spill contingency*. Oslo, Norway: Author.

Ivanova, M. (2011). Oil spill emergency preparedness in the Russian Arctic: A study of the Murmansk region. *Polar Research, 30*, 1–13. doi: 10.3402/polar.v30i0.7285.

Iversen, P.E., Vik Green, A.M., Lind, M.J., Hedegaard Petersen, M.R., Bakke, T., Lichtenthaler, R., Ersvik, M. (2011). *Guidelines for offshore environmental monitoring on the Norwegian continental shelf* (Report No. TA-2849). Retrieved from: www.miljodirektoratet.no/old/klif/publikasjoner/2849/ta2849.pdf

Kezik, I. (July 15, 2013). Минприроды раскрыло запасы газа и нефти в России [Minprirody opened reserves of oil and gas in Russia]. *Vedomosti.ru*. Retrieved from: www.vedomosti.ru/

Kirillov, V.V. (May 2013). *Предложения по организации и ведению экологического надзора объектов на шельфе* [Proposals for organization and implementation of environmental supervision on the shelf]. Poster session presented at the Scientific-practical Conference Monitoring of Natural and Man-made Processes – the Basis for Emergency Prevention in the Murmansk Region, Murmansk, Russia.

Korenev, V., & Vassiliev, A. (December 2013). *Northern branch of the Murmansk Salvage Service*. Poster session presented at the Norwegian–Russian Search-and-Rescue in the Barents Sea workshop, Murmansk, Russia.

LOV. (1981). *Lov om vern mot forurensninger og om avfall (Forurensningsloven)* [Act on protection against pollution and on waste (Pollution Control Act)]. Act dated March 13, 1981 N 6. Oslo, Norway.

LOV. (1996). Lov om petroleumsvirksomhet (Petroleumsloven) [Act on petroleum activities (Petroleum Act)]. Act dated November 29, 1996 N 72. Oslo, Norway.

Lukin, A., Pavlenko, V., Bambulyak, A., & Larsen, L.H. (2012). Перспективные направления развития российско-норвежских исследований в области охраны природной среды

Арктики [Prospects for Russian–Norwegian research development in Arctic environmental protection]. *The Arctic: Ecology and Economy, 2*(6), 44–57.

Ministry of Health Protection of the Russian Federation. (2003). *О введении в действие ГН 2.1.6.1338–03 "Предельно допустимые концентрации (ПДК) загрязняющих веществ в атмосферном воздухе населенных мест"* [On enactment of GN 2.1.6.1338-03 maximum permissible concentrations (MPC) of pollutants in atmospheric air of populated places]. Resolution dated May 30, 2003 N 114. Moscow, Russia: Author.

Ministry of Natural Resources of the Russian Federation. (2001). *Об утверждении временных положения и классификаций* [On approval of temporary regulation and classifications]. Order dated February 7, 2001 N 126. Moscow, Russia: Author.

Ministry of Natural Resources and Environment of the Russian Federation. (2013a). *О состоянии и использовании минерально-сырьевых ресурсов Российской Федереции в 2012 году* [On status and use of mineral resources in the Russian Federation in 2012]. Moscow, Russia: Author.

Ministry of Natural Resources and Environment of the Russian Federation. (2013b). *Об утверждении Классификации запасов и ресурсов нефти и горючих газов* [On approval of the classification of reserves and resources of oil and fossil gases]. Order dated November 1, 2013 N 477. Moscow, Russia: Author.

Ministry of Natural Resources and Environment of the Russian Federation. (2014). Новая Классификация запасов и прогнозных ресурсов нефти и горючих газов будет введена с 1 января 2016 г [New classification of reserves and prospective resources of oil and fossil gases will be introduced from January 1, 2016] [Press release]. Retrieved from: www.mnr.gov.ru/news/detail.php?ID=132240

Ministry of Transport of the Russian Federation. (2009). *Об утверждении Положения о функциональной подсистеме организации работ по предупреждению и ликвидации разливов нефти и нефтепродуктов в море с судов и объектов независимо от их ведомственной и национальной принадлежности* [On approval of the provision on the functional subsystem of the organization of work on oil spill prevention and response at sea from vessels and facilities regardless of their departmental and national affiliation]. Order dated April 6, 2009 N 53. Moscow, Russia: Author.

Ministry of Transport of the Russian Federation. (2013). *О реорганизации федерального бюджетного учреждения "Государственная морская аварийная и спасательно-координационная служба Российской Федерации в форме присоединения к нему федерального бюджетного учреждения "Морская спасательная служба"* [On reorganization of the Federal Budgetary Institution "State Marine Emergency Rescue and Salvage Coordination Service of the Russian Federation in the form of a merge with the Federal Budgetary Institution Marine Salvage Service"]. Order dated December 31, 2013 N 492. Moscow, Russia: Author.

Moe, A. (2010). Russian and Norwegian petroleum strategies in the Barents Sea. *Arctic Review on Law and Politics, 1*(2), 225–248.

Norwegian Clean Seas Association for Operating Companies. (2013). *NOFO: Effective and robust oil spill response tailored to the operator's preparedness plans*. Retrieved from: www.nofo.no/Documents/V%C3%A5r%20virksomhet/NOFO_brosjyre_eng_smallest2.pdf

Norwegian Directorate for Civil Protection. (2011). *Veileder om enhetlig ledelsessystem (ELS)* [Guidelines on united unitary command system]. Oslo, Norway: Author.

Norwegian Environment Agency. (2001). *Risikobasert dimensjonering av statlig beredskap mot akutt forurensning* [Risk-based dimensioning of state preparedness against acute pollution] (SFT report 1755/2000). Oslo: Norwegian Pollution Control Authority. Retrieved from: www.miljodirektoratet.no/old/klif/publikasjoner/vann/1755/ta1755.pdf

Norwegian Ministry of Petroleum and Energy & Norwegian Petroleum Directorate. (2014). *Facts 2014. The Norwegian petroleum sector* (Report No. Y-0103/15 E). Retrieved from: www.npd.no/Global/Engelsk/3-Publications/Facts/Facts2014/Facts_2014_nett_.pdf

Norwegian Petroleum Directorate. (2001). *Guidelines to classification of the petroleum resources on the Norwegian continental shelf.* Retrieved from: www.npd.no/Global/Engelsk/5-Rules-and-regulations/Guidelines/Ressursklassifisering_e.pdf

Norwegian Petroleum Directorate. (2013). Offers for ownership interests in the 22nd licensing round [Press release]. Retrieved from: www.npd.no/en/Topics/Production-licences/Theme-articles/Licensing-rounds/22-nd-Licencing-round/Offers-for-owner ship-interests-in-the-22nd-licensing-round/

Norwegian Petroleum Directorate. (2014). Nominations for the 23rd licensing round [Press release]. Retrieved from: www.npd.no/en/Topics/Production-licences/Theme-articles/Licensing-rounds/23rd-Licencing-round/Nominations-for-the-23rd-licensing-round/

(n.d.). Retrieved from: www.regjeringen.no/en/dep/kld/Selected-topics/svalbard_og_polaromradene/Norwegian-Russian-environmental-cooperation.html?id=451246

OSPAR Commission. (2012). *OSPAR guidelines in support of recommendation 2012/5 for a risk-based approach to the management of produced water discharges from offshore installations* (Annex 19). Retrieved from: www.ospar.org/v_measures/get_page.asp?v0=11–08e_amending %20Rec%202001–1.doc&v1=4

President of the Russian Federation. (1994). *О защите населения и территорий от чрезвычайных ситуаций природного и техногенного характера* [On protection of population and territories from natural and man-made emergencies]. Federal Law dated December 21, 1994 N 68-FZ. Moscow, Russia: Author.

President of the Russian Federation. (1995). *О континентальном шельфе Российской Федерации* [On continental shelf of the Russian Federation]. Federal Law dated November 30, 1995 N 187-FZ. Moscow, Russia: Author.

President of the Russian Federation. (1998). *Об отходах производства и потребления* [On industrial and household waste]. Federal Law dated June 24, 1998 N 89-FZ. Moscow, Russia: Author.

President of the Russian Federation. (2002). *Об охране окружающей среды* [On environmental protection]. Federal Law dated January 10, 2002 N 7-FZ. Moscow, Russia: Author.

President of the Russian Federation. (2008). *О внесении изменений в отдельные законодательные акты Российской Федерации и признании утратившими силу отдельных положений законодательных актов Российской Федерации в связи с принятием Федерального закона "О порядке осуществления иностранных инвестиций в хозяйственные общества, имеющие стратегическое значение для обеспечения обороны страны и безопасности государства"* [On amendments to certain legislative acts of the Russian Federation and annulment of certain provisions of legislative acts of the Russian Federation in connection with adoption of the Federal Law "On foreign investments in business entities of strategic importance for country's defence and state security"]. Federal Law dated April 29, 2008 N 58-FZ. Moscow, Russia: Author.

President of the Russian Federation. (2012). *О внесении изменений в Федеральный закон О континентальном шельфе Российской Федерации и Федеральный закон О внутренних морских водах, территориальном море и прилежащей зоне Российской Федерации* [On amendments to the Federal Law on the continental shelf of the Russian Federation and the Federal Law on internal sea waters, territorial sea and adjacent zone of the Russian Federation]. Federal Law dated December 30, 2012 N 287-FZ. Moscow, Russia: Author.

President of the Russian Federation. (2014). *О внесении изменения в Федеральный закон Об охране окружающей среды и отдельные законодательные акты Российской*

Федерации [On amendments to the Federal Law on environmental protection and selected legal acts of the Russian Federation]. Federal Law dated July 21, 2014 N 219-FZ. Moscow, Russia: Author.

Protection of the Arctic Marine Environment. (2013). *Large Marine Ecosystems (LMEs) of the Arctic area. Revision of the Arctic LME map. May 15, 2013. Second Edition.* Retrieved from: www.pame.is/images/03_Projects/EA/EA/PAME_revised_LME_map_with_explanatory_text_15_Aug_2013_-_Vefur.pdf

RamBøll Barents. (2010). *Improvement of the emergency oil spill response system under the Arctic conditions for protection of sensitive coastal areas (Case study: The Barents and the White Seas). Pilot project* (Vol. I). Murmansk, Russia: Author.

Savinov, V., Larsen, L.H., Green, N., Korneev, O., Rybalko, A., & Kochetkov, A. (2011). *Monitoring hazardous substances in the White Sea and Pechora Sea: Harmonization of OSPAR's Coordinated Environmental Monitoring Programme (CEMP)* (Akvaplan-niva report 414.5124, KLIF report TA 2757/2011). Tromsø, Norway: Akvaplan-niva.

Semanov, G.N., & Ivanchin, A.A. (June 2004). *Russian legislation and oil spill response.* Paper presented at the Interspill Conference, Trondheim, Norway. Abstract retrieved from: www.interspill.com/previous-events/2004/session5.php

[Shelf projects] Шельфовые проекты. (n.d.). Retrieved from: http://rosneft.ru/Upstream/offshore/

Staalesen, A. (2012, April 17). Rosneft invites competitors to Russian–Norwegian waters. *BarentsObserver.* Retrieved from: http://barentsobserver.com/en

Starinskaya, G. (June 20, 2011). "Зарубежнефть" обгонит "Роснефть" в Арктике [Zarubezhneft will overtake Rosneft in the Arctic]. *RBC daily.* Retrieved from: http://rbcdaily.ru/

Stiansen, J.E., Korneev, O., Titov, O., Arneberg, P., Filin, A., Hansen, J.R., . . . Marasaev, S. (Eds.). (2009). *Joint Norwegian–Russian environmental status 2008: Report on the Barents Sea ecosystem, part II – complete report.* Retrieved from: http://idtjeneste.nb.no/URN:NBN:no-bibsys_brage_11355

Studenov, I., Larsen, L.H., Novoselov, A., Markov, V., Bambulyak, A., Jørgensen, N.M., & Camus, L. (2009). *Guidelines for coastal post oil spill damage assessment* (Akvaplan-niva report 4378.01.62). Tromsø: Akvaplan-niva.

Sydnes, A.K., & Sydnes, M. (2013). Norwegian–Russian cooperation on oil spill response in the Barents Sea. *Marine Policy, 39,* 257–264. doi: 10.1016/j.marpol.2012.12.001

Sydnes, M., Bambulyak, A., & Sydnes, A.K. (2013). *A-lex 2012: A case study. Oil spill response.* Tromsø, Norway: UiT.

Sydnes, M., & Sydnes, A.K. (2011). Oil spill emergency response in Norway: Coordinating interorganizational complexity. *Polar Geography, 34*(4), 299–329. doi: 10.1080/1088937X.2011.620721

The Fisheries Commission. (n.d.). Retrieved from: www.jointfish.com/eng/THE-FISHERIES-COMMISSION

Von Quillfeldt, C.H. (October 2012). *The integrated management plan for the Barents Sea.* Poster session presented at the Joint Norwegian–Russian Environmental Commission meeting, Tromsø, Norway.

Zemlyanov, I.V., Kochemasov, Yu. V., Zatsepa, S.N., Korshenko, A.N., Shikunova, Ye. Yu., Strokov, A.A., . . . Vorontsov, A.A. (2013). *Разработка методологии морского пространственного планирования и плана комплексного (интегрированного) управления морским природопользованием в Баренцевом море с учетом международного опыта и наилучших практик использования трансграничных ресурсов* [Elaboration of methodology for marine spatial planning and comprehensive (integrated) nature resources management plan in the Barents Sea taking into account international experience and the best practices of trans-border resources use] (Report No. 01201374149). Moscow, Russia: Zubov State Oceanographic Institute.

5   Driving forces for Norwegian–Russian petroleum B2B cooperation

Implications for the Barents Sea

Anatoli Bourmistrov, June Borge Doornich, and Andrey Krivorotov

Introduction

This chapter offers an overview of bilateral cooperation between Norwegian and Russian companies in the petroleum industry in the High North. The delimitation line dispute between Norway and Russia in the Barents Sea was unexpectedly settled in 2010, after being unresolved for many decades (Treaty on Maritime Delimitation, 2010). The borderline area is of particular interest for the Norwegian and Russian petroleum industry because of expected large deposits of oil and gas (O&G) in the Barents Sea. Joint development of trans-boundary deposits of oil and gas in the delimitation area (those that extend across the delimitation line) can give the possibility for economies of scale and positive economic effects for regional economies. This chapter focuses on business-to-business (B2B) cooperation between Norwegian and Russian oil and gas companies and companies supplying products and services to oil and gas projects, as well as on some of the regional effects of such cooperation. The aim of this chapter is twofold. It describes the history of Norwegian and Russian business-to-business cooperation in the petroleum industry in the High North, and, based on that, it provides an analysis of key driving forces and major factors that in the future can promote but also limit the scope of cooperative development in the Norwegian and Russian petroleum industry in the Barents Sea.

Cooperation between Norway and Russia and its major petroleum companies: reciprocity of interests

Business-to-business cooperation in the offshore petroleum industry between Norwegian and Russian oil and gas companies can be considered as a feasible and beneficial strategy because two major petroleum states have common interests in developing the petroleum resources in the High North. Historically, Russia and Norway have had constructive bilateral relations that demonstrated their common interest in exploring and preserving the Barents Sea. This cooperative atmosphere helped create joint fishery management regimes in the 1970s, establish dialogue on the environment in the late 80s and on energy at the beginning of the 90s (for more details, see Chapter 6). Common interests stem from both countries moving their oil and gas developments from southern provinces to those located in the High North. Cooperation in the delimitation areas in the Barents Sea can provide the advantages of economy of scale and economy of scope for business-to-business cooperation when facing similar challenges encountered in developing oil and gas fields in the High North.

The argument is advanced for the great opportunities of cooperation because of the countries' tremendous amount of already discovered and undiscovered, but expected, offshore oil and gas resources in the High North (see Chapters 8 and 9 in this book; also Zolotukhin, 2011). The significant value creation from petroleum development, which has been driven by key provinces in southern areas such as offshore oil production in the North Sea in Norway and onshore oil production in Western Siberia in Russia, is now decreasing because these provinces have entered mature phases (Rystad Energy, 2013). To compensate for the loss of energy production, both countries seem to be strategically moving towards the development of less-explored offshore petroleum provinces in the High North, and in particular the Barents Sea. With expected trans-boundary deposits of oil and gas in the delimitation areas in the Barents Sea, Norwegian and Russian companies can benefit from cooperation on joint exploration and development. Since oil and gas development in the High North presents new unique challenges for oil and gas development, such as harsh climate, fragile environment, lack of infrastructure, and feasibility for human resources, new solutions and technology are required and they will need big investments. As the countries will encounter similar challenges in developing these demanding areas, they can benefit from transferring knowledge, technology, and experience in order to make development more feasible and less costly.

Therefore, reciprocity of interest emerges as Russia holds large novel and unexplored offshore oil and gas deposits in the High North but lacks the appropriate technology and knowledge and sufficient capital for exploring and developing these provinces (Doornich, 2014; Overland, Godzimirski, Lunden, & Fjærtoft, 2013). "So far we do not possess import independence as regards offshore equipment," Mr. Valery Golubev, Deputy CEO of Gazprom, admitted in October 2014 (Shelf urges new technologies from Russia, 2014). Having focused for decades on the development of onshore resources, Russian companies have not advanced their offshore competence as far and as quickly as some Western companies. Norwegian companies with long experience and advanced technology in developing demanding offshore provinces, including experience in the High North, can therefore become important partners in developing Russia's offshore petroleum resources. The Norwegian companies' offshore competence and experience has been appreciated in Russia, where experts praise Norway as a leader in applying subsea technologies to develop oil and gas fields on the shelf as well as in establishing an appropriate national innovation system that is also part of the global system (Mirzoev, Ibragimov, & Arkhipova, 2013).

The Russian offshore market can thus become an important market for Norwegian companies to secure their own long-term survival, as activities in the mature fields on the Norwegian continental shelf (NCS) are decreasing (Overland et al., 2013). The delimitation line agreement is particularly promoting reciprocity, as large amounts of trans-boundary oil and gas resources can create conditions for great business-to-business cooperation and value creation for both countries. The question is: what we can learn about major factors promoting and/or limiting cooperative development in the delimitation line area, based on the history of previous business-to-business cooperation between Norwegian and Russian companies in the petroleum industry?

Russian and Norwegian oil and gas companies' activities across the borders

Since the early 1990s, Norwegian oil and gas companies have been actively engaged in exploring and developing oil and gas resources in the High North of Russia, where the Shtokman field in the Barents Sea has been the key project for cooperation between Norwegian and Russian companies in the Russian market of offshore projects. In recent years, Russian oil and gas companies have also increasingly participated in exploring and developing oil and gas resources on the Norwegian continental shelf, with particular interest in the Barents Sea.

The Russian natural gas monopoly, Gazprom, both directly and through its subsidiary, Rosshelf, cooperated closely with the two Norwegian oil and gas companies, Statoil and Norsk Hydro, throughout the 1990s on the exploration and development of several deposits and fields in the eastern Barents Sea and the Pechora Sea. In 2004, a trilateral memorandum of understanding (MoU) was signed by Gazprom, Rosneft, and Statoil, aiming at cooperation on the Shtokman and Snøhvit fields in, respectively, the Russian and Norwegian parts of the Barents Sea, and in Russian access to Statoil's regas facilities in North America (Gazprom, 2004). Later on, similar MoUs and cooperation agreements, covering broader areas of the High North, were signed in 2005, on joint development of hydrocarbon and design of technologies for commercial operations in the Arctic (Gazprom, 2005); these were replaced in 2009 by agreements on joint exploration, production, and infrastructure (Statoil, 2009), and later in 2010 on sci-technology cooperation (Gazprom, 2005, 2009, 2010; Statoil, 2010). Because of this business-to-business cooperation in the Russian offshore market, it came as no surprise when both Statoil and Hydro were short-listed by Gazprom in 2005 as potential partners to develop Phase 1 of the Shtokman gas and condensate field.

Case 1: Shtokman Development AG

Norwegian companies' cooperation with Shtokman Development AG represents a particular interest when looking at Norwegian oil and gas companies' representation in the Russian market. The special project vehicle (SPV) to develop Shtokman Phase 1 was set up in February 2008, originally owned by Gazprom (51%), French Total (25%), and Statoil (24%). This joint venture became the first practical attempt at Russian–Norwegian cooperation on developing a specific Barents Sea field.

The project was also groundbreaking in other respects. First of all, the field itself is rated among the top 10 global oil and gas deposits in terms of its large resources and its location much further north (73°30'N) than any producing gas fields in the world to date (Shtokman gas and condensate field, n.d.). It is also located in an area with great challenges because of seasonal heavy ice, threat of iceberg impact, polar lows, and several months without sunshine (see Chapter 10). Second, Shtokman Phase 1 was supposed to bring about the first-ever offshore gas production from the Russian Arctic seabed, the first Russian Arctic LNG plant (in Teriberka near Murmansk), and to become a trendsetter in the Russian offshore market in respect of applying cutting-edge technologies, advanced project management techniques, and the highest ethical and HSE standards. Last but not least, it was a testing ground for a new model to attract foreign investment at a time when private investors (either Russian or foreign) had been legally barred from entering the Russian Arctic shelf.

In 2008–2012, Shtokman Development AG delivered onshore and offshore surveys, Front-End Engineering Design (FEED), and technical design in accordance with Russian standards, environmental impact analyses, numerous governmental clearances, etc. The SPV ran tenders for all principal equipment packages, mapping opportunities to maximize local content within research, manufacturing, and industry education.

During this work, they also identified some important gaps in the Russian legislation on petroleum development on the Russian continental shelf. These gaps were later bridged by the Russian Duma in the new federal law on petroleum development on the Russian continental shelf in late 2013. For example, for the first time ever, the notions of "artificial islands, installations and structures", introduced by the 1982 UN Convention on the Law of the Sea, were defined clearly in Russian law. As another example, the institution of a "field operator" was introduced, allowing for foreign entities to be involved in developing offshore fields (prior to that, only license holders, which are supposed to be Russian state-owned companies, could legally develop the fields without inviting any third parties to carry out any part of the work).

The work by Shtokman Development AG and all three shareholders increased the understanding of both the challenges and opportunities of developing high-latitude oil and gas resources. On the one hand, it was proven that cooperation in, and finding technical solutions for, a sustainable production of oil and gas from such a remote field in extreme Arctic conditions is achievable. On the other hand, the economics of the project are highly dependent on the development of global prices of oil and gas. Originally targeting the US market, the project suffered dramatically from the shale gas revolution, which affected several Arctic offshore projects worldwide. This was, in addition, exacerbated by the global economic turmoil. In 2012, the shareholders stated that a final investment decision could not be made, and Statoil had to leave the project soon after. Despite this, there is still a big potential for cooperation, all the more since licensing, both in the Russian and Norwegian parts of the Barents Sea as well as in other Russian seas, has gained a huge momentum since 2012.

Case 2: cooperation between Rosneft and Statoil

Rosneft has been active in developing several bilateral agreements with Statoil. On May 5, 2012, Rosneft and Statoil signed a cooperation agreement on joint offshore operations in the Barents Sea and Sea of Okhotsk (Rosneft, 2012a). The agreement covered joint exploration of fields in the Russian part of the Barents Sea and Sea of Okhotsk, as well as Rosneft's participation in oil and gas activities on the Norwegian continental shelf. The agreement also laid the foundation for a new global partnership between companies, presenting the possibility of acquisitions by Rosneft of interests in Statoil's international projects. The agreement also included the intention to create spin-off effects for the regional supply industry by indicating an intention to place orders for ice-class vessels and drilling platforms from the Russian shipyards.

A month later, on June 21, 2012, Rosneft and Statoil signed follow-up agreements on joint bidding for licenses in the Norwegian section of the Barents Sea and on joint technical evaluation of tight oil resources in Russia (Rosneft, 2012b). On August 30, 2012, the shareholder and operating agreement was signed, which led to the establishment of a joint venture for four offshore licenses in the Barents Sea and the Sea of Okhotsk. Rosneft received 66.67% and Statoil 33.33% of stakes in the share of the project. Statoil was also supposed to fund 100% of costs in the exploration phase. Agreement has also stipulated exchange of technical personnel (Rosneft, 2012c).

On November 23, 2012, the companies announced a joint "Declaration on Protection of the Environment and Biodiversity for Oil and Gas Exploration and Development on the Russian Arctic Continental Shelf", which was supposed to lead to the development of a coordination center with the representation of the key Russian governmental agencies (e.g. Roskosmos) and ministries (Statoil, 2012). This was a joint initiative that aimed to improve coordination for safe exploration of O&G resources on the Russian side.

Case 3: entrance by Russian companies to the Norwegian Barents Sea

The Russian oil and gas companies, Lukoil and Rosneft, have made an entry onto the Norwegian continental shelf. These two were among the 29 companies that obtained licenses in the twenty-second bidding round in 2013 (Gorst, 2013). Rosneft won a 20% stake in block 713 in the Barents Sea, together with Statoil as the operator of the block and Edison and North Energy (Norway) as co-owners. Lukoil won a 20% stake in block 708, with Lundin (Sweden) as the operator and the co-owners North Energy and the Norwegian branch of Edison International (US). Lukoil also won a 30% stake in block 719 in the

Barents Sea, with Centrica Resources (UK) as the operator and North Energy as co-owner.

Russian companies are also involved in operations on the Norwegian continental shelf indirectly, e.g. through purchase and acquisition of interests in Western companies that operate in Norway. For instance, in early 2014, LetterOne Group, a consortium's investment company belonging to Alfa Group – a company founded by Mikhail Fridman – purchased interest in a German company, RWE Dea AG, which operates in Norway.

The entrance to, and the acceptance of these two Russian oil and gas companies in, the Norwegian Barents Sea indicates reciprocity of oil and gas companies' cooperation. Previously, Norwegian oil and gas companies entered the Russian offshore market for both knowledge and technology transfer in order to position themselves in the Russian offshore market, in this way securing long-term activities in a novel market. For both of these Russian companies, their participation in the exploration and development of oil and gas resources on the NCS will most likely represent valuable knowledge, the opportunity for technology transfer for offshore projects' development, and a valuable experience for Norwegian and Russian common offshore operations in the delimitation areas. Entrance to the Norwegian market is especially important for Lukoil, which, according to Russian legislation, is not allowed to be a license holder for the offshore field development in the Russian High North.[1]

Summary: reciprocity of interests, but where will it strike the delimitation areas of the Barents Sea?

The current status of Norwegian oil and gas companies' participation in developing offshore oil and gas resources in Russia demonstrates an increased cooperation over recent decades, where business-to-business cooperation was particularly focused on the Barents Sea. Although few operational experiences have occurred so far in the former delimitation area, partnerships formed can be considered as important foundations for future cooperation. A similar status seems to be also gradually evolving for Russian oil and gas companies' participation in developing offshore resources in the Norwegian part of the Barents Sea. The description above demonstrates that business-to-business cooperation between major oil and gas companies from Norway and Russia has developed as reciprocity of interests in the benefits of joint development of offshore oil and gas resources in both the Russian and Norwegian parts of the Barents Sea. In this sense, the Treaty on Maritime Delimitation and Cooperation in the Barents Sea and the Arctic Ocean, signed in 2010 in Murmansk (Treaty on Maritime Delimitation, 2010), has created a new cooperation spot, namely the opportunity for the joint development of trans-boundary oil and gas deposits in the delimitation area.

According to Article 5 and Annex II of the Treaty, a Unitization Agreement shall be signed for each of the fields developed, so that it may only be developed by Russian or Norwegian legal entities together under a "Joint Operating

Agreement". This sets the ground and requirements for Norwegian and Russian oil and gas companies to cooperate in developing resources in the delimitation areas.

Article 5, s. 2 of the treaty makes it clear, however, that "If the existence of a hydrocarbon deposit on the continental shelf of one of the Parties is established and the other Party is of the opinion that the said deposit extends to its continental shelf, the latter Party may notify the former Party and shall submit the data on which it bases its opinion." In this case, the Parties shall start respective unitization discussions. In the course of these, "the Party initiating them shall support its opinion with evidence from geophysical data and/or geological data, including any existing drilling data and both Parties shall make their best efforts to ensure that all relevant information is made available for the purposes of these discussions." This essentially means that in order to launch the unitization process, both parties shall follow a similar timetable in the geological exploration (seismic shooting and drilling) in the delimited area.

Despite that, the two nations show unequal dynamics in terms of leasing acreage and exploration. On the Norwegian side, seismic shooting started minutes after the treaty came into force, early on July 8, 2011. Licensing has been allowed in the southern part only (Barents Sea South East licensing area), and the first blocks were awarded only in 2013 (Offers for ownership interests, 2013). Russia started seismic shooting a year later, in 2012, but even before that the whole delimited area had been split into three large blocks. Licenses for all three were granted to Rosneft, which started seeking foreign partners to explore these (in a similar way as it had engaged ExxonMobil into its blocks in the Kara Sea).

The northernmost block of the delimited area, Perseevsky, became one of the principal pillars in a close cooperation between Rosneft and Statoil. However, its very remote location in the north of the Barents Sea creates massive technological and logistical challenges (see e.g. INTSOK, 2013). Drilling the first exploration well is tentatively planned for 2015 and will cost a great amount. Taking into consideration the challenges in developing such a big gas field as Shtokman because of its remote location, then it will certainly not be possible even further north, so this is a gamble on finding oil.

The larger the volume of discoveries of oil and gas resources in the Norwegian and Russian parts of the Barents Sea, the larger the incentive for cooperation, especially in the trans-boundary fields. Based on the status of exploration work and established partnerships between Russian and Norwegian oil and gas companies to date, it can be expected that, in the short term, the Norwegian continental shelf, and particularly the Norwegian southwestern and ice-free part of the Barents Sea, can be the main spot for Norwegian and Russian cooperation in the exploration and development of oil and gas resources in the High North (see also INTSOK, 2013). Potentially, in the long run, the southeast Barents Sea, e.g. the Pechora Sea with Prirazlomnoye, Dolginskoye fields, are areas for cooperation on the Russian side. These areas are more accessible and easier to develop because fewer challenges are encountered in terms of climate, logistics, and finance (INTSOK, 2013). It can be further expected that regardless of the progress in exploration and development in the delimitation area, possible joint development, especially of trans-boundary resources, are projects for the future as more experience of working in such areas is needed. The lack of such experience may result in the fact that the northern part of the delimitation area will be developed last.

Cooperation for contracts in petroleum projects between companies in supply industry: great potential but no joint experience

Oil and gas companies depend on various supply companies that offer the necessary products and services for searching for, exploring, developing, and operating petroleum fields. As the Russian offshore market is less developed, because it has been focusing for decades on the development of onshore resources, the offshore competence of Russian supply companies has not advanced as far and as fast as Norwegian supply companies. As Norwegian supply companies deliver world-class technology and complex solutions for offshore development, they offer their knowledge and expertise for developing the Russian offshore market.

Norwegian–Russian supply industry cooperation, but is it mostly on the Russian side?

The Norwegian supply industry has gained a strong international position by investing in and trading Norwegian petroleum technologies and solutions on a global scale. The Russian market has not been an exception, and Norwegian supply companies have been active in seeking access to the market for many years. Despite the fact that the size of the offshore market for supply companies is smaller in Russia compared to Norway in absolute figures (see Table 5.1), the Norwegian supply industry identifies Russia as an important market (alongside Australia, Brazil, China, UK, and the US) due to its growth potential, especially in the offshore segment (INTSOK, 2014).

Norwegian companies have already supplied critical pieces of equipment and services to key Russian offshore projects. For example, in 2006, when Gazprom needed to drill appraisal well No. 7 at the Shtokman field in the Barents Sea, it

Table 5.1 Historical and estimated volumes of spending related to investments and operational costs in the offshore industries in Norway and Russia

Country	2008	2013	2018
Norway	USD 25.3 bill	USD 38 bill	USD 45 bill
Russia	USD 3.3 bill	USD 5.8 bill	USD 6 bill

Source: Based on data from INTSOK (2014).

involved Norsk Hydro (which later merged with Statoil), who performed the job from the Deepsea Delta drilling rig owned by Odfjell Drilling. Kværner, the Norwegian leader in gravity-based structures (GBS), has been responsible for the engineering, procurement, and construction (EPC) of the GBS for the Berkut platform to be used in the Sakhalin-1 project in the Russian Far East, where both ExxonMobil and Rosneft participate. The delivery of the GBS was completed in May 2012 (The Sakhalin-1 GBS completed, n.d.), and Kværner managed to locate 90% of the production in Russia, essentially constructing a new plant in the Far East. Kongsberg-based FMC Technologies has delivered complete subsea production facilities for the Gazprom-operated Kirinskoye field offshore of Sakhalin, involving several other Norwegian companies as subcontractors (e.g. Aker Solutions supplied the umbilicals). Kirinskoye became the first offshore field in Russia to be developed with a full subsea comple-tion concept. It was put on stream in 2013, though Gazprom may revise the development scheme now, as major oil deposits were discovered in the field (Gazprom intends to increase the resource base, 2014).

Quite a few Norwegian companies have supplied equipment packages to Prirazlomnaya, the platform that, in March 2013, made the first Russian com-mercial delivery of Arctic offshore oil from the field in the eastern Barents Sea. The list of suppliers includes Aker Pusnes and Hydramarine (offshore oil ship-ment system), the Oslo branch of Siemens (all generators), Frank Mohn (fire extinguisher pumps), Øglænd systemer (cabling supports), Autronica (fire and gas alarm systems), Aker MH and Gann Mekaniske (drilling equipment). The leading Norwegian producers of offshore oilfield equipment, Aker Solutions and Kværner, ran the technical audit of the Sevmash shipyard in Severodvinsk (north of Archangelsk) where the platform was constructed. Global Maritime from Stavanger towed the platform from the shipyards in Severodvinsk to Mur-mansk and later onto the field in fall 2011. The two multifunctional icebreaking supply vessels that support the platform, Yuri Topchev and Vladislav Strizhov, were designed by Moss Maritime, and their topsides were mounted in Havyard shipyards. Altogether, Norwegians were awarded contracts worth 25% of the total value of supplies to Prirazlomnaya (Ramsdal, 2013).

At the end of July 2014, the Norwegian company, Seadrill, signed a USD 4.25 billion agreement with Rosneft for leasing six offshore rigs throughout 2022 for its offshore operations. Rosneft has also acquired shares in North Atlantic Drilling (a subsidiary of Seadrill). The deal came right before the US and EU imposed sanctions that aim to prevent the export of equipment and technologies for deepwater and Arctic production to Russian companies.

When it comes to Russian companies searching for opportunities in Nor-way, the Norwegian continental shelf is open for Russian companies to also bid. However, this requires a prequalification in a unified system "Achilles Joint Qualification System" (Learn about Achilles Group Limited, n.d.) (handling Norway and Denmark). As of today, only six Russian companies are registered in the Achilles system, and only two of those companies have production facili-ties located in the High North (see Table 5.2). For comparison, eight Russian

Table 5.2 Number of companies registered in Achilles and FPAL by country

Country	Achilles JQS	FPAL	Incl. both	Sum
Andorra	1	0	0	1
Australia	5	5	0	10
Austria	6	5	3	11
Belgium	15	16	7	31
Canada	6	12	4	18
China	19	6	4	25
Cyprus	0	5	0	5
Czech Republic	4	1	0	5
Denmark	335	19	15	354
Estonia	7	2	2	9
Faroe Islands	10	4	2	14
Finland	31	4	2	35
France	50	28	13	78
Germany	84	79	23	163
Greece	2	2	1	4
Hong Kong	0	3	0	3
India	9	12	1	21
Ireland	7	19	1	26
Israel	3	3	2	6
Italy	98	108	47	206
Japan	3	1	0	4
Lithuania	4	0	0	4
Luxembourg	3	1	1	4
Malaysia	1	3	0	4
Malta	0	4	0	4
Netherlands	140	329	64	469
Norway	2666	128	113	2794
Poland	21	11	3	32
Portugal	1	1	0	2
Romania	6	3	1	9
Russia	**6**	**8**	**2**	**14**
Singapore	15	11	2	26
South-Africa	0	4	0	4
Spain	11	23	7	34
Sweden	112	6	4	118
Switzerland	13	7	4	20
Turkey	2	4	0	6
United Arab Emirates	10	12	6	22
UK	351	2468	278	2819
US	35	33	9	68

Source: Based on Global Oil & Gas Directory (2014).

companies registered in the prequalification system for the UK (FPAL), and only two companies are registered in both systems. As seen from Table 5.2, companies from other European countries have much higher levels of presence in the Achilles system and therefore greater potential for contracts on the NCS than Russian companies. Possible reasons can be that Russian supply companies have little in general to offer on the international markets or/and that Russian companies are not interested in offering their products and services on the Norwegian continental shelf.

Another possible reason is that Russian companies prefer to focus on the domestic rather than the international market. The former Soviet Union was generally self-sufficient in terms of oil and gas equipment and oilfield services, but the economic turmoil in the 90s delivered a heavy blow to the industry. First, the domestic market collapsed. The newly established Russian oil and gas companies suffered permanently from a lack of cash and had to drastically cut all expenses, including notably exploration, field development, and partly even maintenance. Second, several Russian newly born majors (like Tyumen Oil Company, YUKOS, or Sibneft) singled out their oilfield service units into separate legal entities and sold them as noncore assets, exposing them to harsh competition. Third, foreign trade liberalization allowed the global supply industry leaders like Schlumberger or Halliburton to make a strong entry into Russia (and even more so to other former Soviet Union countries). This trend was reinforced by international oil companies, which tended to rely heavily on their worldwide suppliers, being generally reluctant to place orders within Russia. According to some estimates, foreign companies now hold about 65% of the Russian oilfield service market (Oilfield service market in import clinch, 2013).

Thus, the Russian supply industry has to tackle the same challenge nation-wide as, for instance, the Norwegian industry located in the High North faces at the regional level: to get a stronghold in the local market first. Over the past few years, the issue has enjoyed a political priority with Russian authorities, who have set the goal to increase the domestic production of offshore equipment dramatically in order to meet the challenges of developing the Arctic offshore.

The abovementioned demonstrates that the Norwegian supply industry has experience in delivering technology and solutions to key provinces in the Russian offshore market, namely the Barents Sea and Sakhalin, while the Russian supply industry focuses on the domestic market and is therefore rather absent from participation in the Norwegian offshore market. The Norwegian companies already have well-developed experience and expertise in operating in the international offshore oil and gas exploration and development market. Thus, it can be expected that the Norwegian supply industry will have a larger representation in the Russian offshore market in the long term, whereas Russian suppliers will still be absent from the Norwegian market. The main driving force for cooperation in the High North will be technology and competence transfer from Norwegian to Russian companies in the Russian market. Norwegian supply companies that are already positioned in the Russian market can be important in the future development of the Barents Sea on the Russian side, and Norwegian companies can benefit in bidding rounds for exploration and development activities, favored over other international supply companies.

Cooperation between local producers: is there room for smaller companies in the local content policies?

So far, the description above has focused on well-established supply companies engaged in exploring and developing petroleum provinces in the High North. These are mainly companies with production facilities and HQs in the southern areas, rather than originating from the High North. Although there are good potential future cooperation opportunities in the supply industry, the effects for international cooperation between particular local companies located in the High North are limited by the many barriers. Some of those barriers originate from the characteristics of northern supply companies and the characteristics of national regimes in developing petroleum resources, e.g. in terms of local content policies. One concern is that, although petroleum provinces connected to the Barents Sea will be developed, they may not create enough regional spin–off effects in northern regions of Norway and Russia. This is because regimes developed by the authorities and international oil and gas companies will not, to any considerable degree, favor the development of local suppliers.

First, an important disadvantage of supply companies located in the northern parts of Norway and Russia is that these companies are characterized in general as smaller and less-internationally experienced suppliers than companies located in the south. Thus, these companies may not be able to quickly develop adequate capacities, technological competences, track records, and financial strengths that would match the requirements of contracts related to the petroleum projects in the High North. Also those contracts are expected to be larger in terms of volumes, scope, and complexity, as well as pose exceptionally high requirements for performance standards, warrantees, and quality assurance. In this sense, the concern is that most contracts will fall into the hands of more experienced international suppliers operating from already established international hubs outside the High North and in this way result in little engagement of and contracts for suppliers located in the High North (Government of Norway, 2013).

The latest major Russian oilfield development, Vankor, located in a remote area of North Eastern Siberia, is a clear example. With 430,000 b/d of crude production in 2013, it represents some 13.5% of the gross regional product of Krasnoyarsky Kray, but less than 0.5% of employment. Neither the local workforce nor manufacturing enterprises were ready to work for the oil industry; about half the employees reside outside the region. As a result, each USD 100-worth of investment in upstream production in the region has brought only about USD 3.2 of investment in the local supply industry (Semykina, 2013), i.e. only 3.2%. In Norway, the development of the Snøhvit offshore gas field in the Barents Sea (2002–2007) was probably slightly more successful in terms of providing contracts to local suppliers and of other effects such as reversing negative population migration and employment trends, the growth of residential construction and a municipal taxation base, and improved public infrastructure. However, deliveries from the local contractor industry still represented only 5% of the total volume of deliveries in the construction phase (Nilsen, 2012).

Second, both the central, regional, and local authorities are important actors. The success of cross-border Russian–Norwegian cooperation in the High North is heavily dependent upon liberalization and harmonization of the two countries' regimes within taxation, customs, border control, etc. Tackling the administrative barriers is a heavier burden for small- and medium-sized enterprises, which as a rule lack relevant experience and possess overlimited financial resources. Some progress has been made in this regard; e.g. visa regimes have been eased sufficiently for businessmen and for citizens of both countries living in the territories adjacent to the border. However, much work still remains to be done. This factor, coupled with the major difference in the living standards on the two sides of the Russian–Norwegian border, has not allowed the implementation of the visionary Norwegian initiative of 2006 to set up a joint "Pomor Zone" of industrial cooperation, whereby entities on both sides of the border would work together to supply goods and services, especially to offshore projects (Krivorotov, 2009).

Third, oil and gas companies can in general apply various mechanisms to influence the engagement of local supply companies in petroleum projects in the High North and, in this sense, contribute to regional industrial development. One such mechanism is a local content policy that may give preference to particular kinds of suppliers. Governments can also establish particular requirements for local content policies. For instance, Shtokman Development AG has developed a local content policy that prefers Russian (especially regional) suppliers under the condition that their experience, costs, and delivery time are comparable to international supply companies. Such a policy may provide an incentive to the Norwegian supplier and an opportunity to intensify entrance to the Russian market through a close partnership with Russian companies (Bourmistrov & Mineev, 2011).

Another mechanism that petroleum companies can employ to improve the capacity of local producers to deliver products and services to large projects is through the development of regional supplier associations/networks. There are interesting examples of how the Norwegian companies, Statoil and former Norsk Hydro, have developed regional supplier associations in Norway (e.g. PetroArctic in the Norwegian High North in relation to the development and operation of the Snøhvit gas field) and in Russia (Murmanshelf in Murmansk region and Sozvezdye in Arkhangelsk region). Those associations represent platforms that can function as areas of coordination, not only between local/regional supply companies but also between local companies and national and international petroleum companies, and local and regional authorities for oil and gas project development (Mineev, 2011).

Cooperation between local producers: problems of committed cooperation?

In cases when the local content policies create openings for smaller local producers to participate in the projects and/or where local companies' engagement is secured through the work of networks of supplier organizations, there is still another important barrier to cooperation – problems of commitment to partnerships. Partnership forms of cooperation between companies, such as joint ventures, allow diversification of procurement risks and improved product and service quality to be achieved by the combination of technological competence and knowledge of local market conditions and the specifics of regional and national legislation and standards on both sides of the Norwegian–Russian border (Bourmistrov & Mineev, 2011). However, given the potential, practice shows that it is difficult for Norwegian and Russian companies in the supply industry to form committed and close partnerships. Research demonstrates that joint ventures are rarely used by Norwegian supply companies when operating in Russia (Doornich, 2014), although such ventures could be expected to be seen as a favorable partnership form, from the perspective of taking advantages and transferring market knowledge to the respective partners and of sharing investment and operational risks.

Explanations for this on the Norwegian side can be that differences in company size, in management and business cultures as well as in governmental regulation complicate cooperation (Skretting, 2011). Based on the study of Norwegian supply companies and their entrance and operation in Russia, Doornich (2014) concludes that the majority of Norwegian companies prefer to operate in the Russian market by trading their products through a local intermediary that conducts the necessary marketing and sales activities, or by establishing their own representative office. In this way, products are produced at domestic facilities in Norway and then exported to the Russian market. These companies are found to limit their supply to the Russian market through trade, in order to strategically avoid confrontation with uncertainties in the Russian market. These uncertainties are found to be dissonance in interpreting and understanding the Russian business culture, and ambiguity in interpreting red tape in Russian governmental bodies and authorities. Those few companies that invest heavily in the market prefer to establish wholly owned Norwegian ventures, without involving Russian partners because of perceived challenges in cooperating with Russian companies and because of the desire to fully control the Norwegian subsidiary in Russia.

Thus, a joint venture, where risks and commitment to business are shared between partners, is not the preferred partnership form in the supply industry. One reason can be that these Norwegian companies only offer niche products and therefore they do not desire to enter partnerships, as they want to keep the production and product details for themselves and to not be copied by other Russian companies. Another reason can be that the Norwegian supply industry is still just in the phase of discovering the Russian market, which to date has had a rather limited demand for Norwegian offshore technologies. Companies from other nations that tried to set up joint ventures in Russia have also had mixed experience. Forming joint ventures may, therefore, require more time in order to build firsthand experience operating in the market, a positive history of cooperation with local actors, and learning through the unlearning of well-institutionalized beliefs and myths about managing in the Russian context (Svishchev, 2011).

Forming a great number of committed partnerships and therefore more extensive cooperation between Norwegian and Russian local suppliers has great potential, but it is still a challenging task. Building a comprehensive cooperation strategy requires a clear understanding of what the competitive advantages of different companies are in a partnership (Skretting, 2011). In the case where a large volume of petroleum resources are discovered in the Barents Sea and conditions are right for their development, common understanding, standards, and the technological solutions needed for safe production and operation in the Barents Sea can provide an important foundation for a competitive advantage to a Norwegian–Russian industrial partnership in the supply industry. However, as the description above demonstrates, long-term partnership arrangements are not obvious choices for Russian and Norwegian companies in the supply industry.

Effects of international politics on Norwegian–Russian enterprise cooperation

So far in this chapter, we have treated the Norwegian–Russian B2B cooperation as the prerogative of Norwegian and Russian authorities and companies to make decisions on cooperation. However, another important barrier to B2B cooperation between companies is international politics and its influence on the economic cooperation climate. One example is economic sanctions against Russia that came into force in August 2014 as a result of the Ukraine crisis. The Norwegian government has decided to join the EU's sanctions against Russia, in particular the restrictions on the supply of oil and gas technologies to Arctic offshore petroleum projects in Russia (Government of Norway, 2014). Sanctions forbid the export to Russia of technologies for oil exploration and production for deepwater, Arctic, as well as shale oil projects. Any other products or technologies for the Russian petroleum industry would require prior permission from the Norwegian authorities. Any financing or service operations related to those products or technologies would also require prior approval.

The long-term effects of those sanctions on other areas of petroleum industrial cooperation, such as gas technologies or engineering, are unclear. For instance, there is some uncertainty regarding interpretations of what the concepts of "Arctic" and "deepwater" technologies mean (Ramsdal, 2014). However, institutions responsible for the introduction and following-up of sanctions have all the power to make those more targeted and specific, and in this sense provide less room for maneuver for cooperation between companies in Norway and Russia. As an example, Statoil and other Norwegian companies registered on the American stock exchanges will be forced to follow rules and American interpretations of sanctions that can be much more stringent than the sanctions of the Norwegian government (Ånestad, Riisnæs, Løvås, & Langved, 2014).

Observers differ in views on the possible impact of the sanctions. On the one hand, according to estimates by Bank of America Merrill Lynch, the Russian oil industry may lose up to USD 1,000 billion of investments. With no access to advanced upstream technologies, the oil production will soon start decreasing by 1.5% per annum due to the depletion of old fields, but this figure may well be minus 3 to 5%, bringing about a loss of between USD 27 billion and USD 65 billion by 2020.

On the other hand, Standard & Poor's (S&P) is of the opinion that most of the equipment that is hit by the sanctions may well be produced domestically or imported from countries that have not joined the sanctions, notably from China. Oil pipes are a good example. Pipes are also on the sanction list, while Russia itself is a major net exporter of pipes. As for Arctic, deep sea, and shale exploration and production, their contribution to the Russian upstream operations is to date marginal, so some of these projects may be postponed even further in time – like Shtokman, which had already been stopped well before the sanctions for other reasons, e.g. high production costs compared to expected price of gas.

A political chill towards Russia can, however, have effects that are more adverse. For instance, S&P suggests that a downgrading of the Russian sovereign ratings plus restricted access to the global capital markets may cause trouble. A further escalation of sanctions is also a possibility that may deepen restrictions placed on the Norwegian–Russian cooperation even further. For instance, the US has extended their sanctions to include not only potential future cooperative projects but also projects that had been already launched before sanctions were imposed. A good example is the Rosneft–ExxonMobil drilling agreement in the Kara Sea.

Inside Russia, also, the discussion is heavily influenced by a broader policy context. Pro-Western experts and media quote gloomy American forecasts and highlight the need for Russia to have free access to international markets and technologies. On the contrary, the government, patriotic-minded observers, and national companies tend to believe that the sanctions may be overcome and represent a good reason to modernize the industry (in the same way as Russia's own food sanctions against the US, EU, Norway, and Australia are supposed to give a boost to domestic agriculture). However, all parties in the debate view sanctions as nonproductive and harmful for both sides.

Conclusions

The aim of this chapter was to describe the status of Norwegian–Russian B2B cooperation in the petroleum industry in the High North, including major petroleum companies as well as companies in the supply industry in both countries and highlight the driving forces that can promote and limit cooperative development in the petroleum industry on the Norwegian and Russian sides. Based on the above discussions, we would like to draw some conclusions.

First, the history of cooperation described in the chapter indicates that cooperation between major Russian and Norwegian oil and gas companies was to date based on a reciprocity of interests in terms of accessing oil and gas resources in new petroleum provinces in the High North, sharing exploration and development risks as well as accessing modern petroleum technologies. This reciprocity is evidenced by Russian oil and gas companies entering the Norwegian offshore market with a particular focus on the Barents Sea, as well as Norwegian oil and gas companies extending their representation in the Russian offshore market. However, this cooperation has not yet been matched by cooperation in the Norwegian and Russian supply industries. Norwegian supply companies are much better positioned in the Russian market, while Russian companies are almost nonexistent in the Norwegian oil and gas market.

Second, it seems to be in the obvious interest of both Russia and Norway, as the only two countries sharing the Barents Sea, to cooperate in meeting the common challenges of the area, e.g. exploration and development, environmental protection, resource management, promoting regional value creation and employment. This being said, the 2010 Murmansk Treaty realistically urges both countries to proceed with exploring the delimited shelf area on their own, and cooperate only when the other party can prove that a field is trans-boundary.

Third, there is a need for more specific, down-to-earth experience, compared to what exists so far in terms of committed partnerships, to tackle formidable technological, environmental, and regulatory challenges. The bigger the discoveries made in the delimitation area of the Barents Sea, especially in relation to trans-boundary fields, the higher the incentives might be for Norwegian–Russian business cooperation.

Fourth, the international nature of the oil and gas business exposes Norwegian and Russian oil and gas and supply companies' cooperation initiatives to the risks of international politics, as sanctions that followed the Ukraine crisis indicate. Possible developments in international politics that enforce a polarization between Norway and Russia can negatively influence the nature and magnitude of Norwegian–Russian energy cooperation in the Barents Sea, by discouraging Norwegian companies from extending and widening their business in the Russian market or by preventing Russian companies from entering the Norwegian market.

Finally, as a possible result of previously mentioned factors, it may be safer for Russian and Norwegian companies to develop and operate on their own territory and for supply companies to deliver products and services in the domestic markets. Recent developments on the Norwegian continental shelf indicate that there are some promising oil and gas discoveries that could take the focus away from the delimitation areas for Norwegian companies (New oil discoveries: This could be the turning point, 2014). Economies of scope and economies of scale, indicated as one possible reason for cooperation between Norwegian and Russian companies in the Barents Sea, can be difficult to achieve. Thus, the cooperation will be dependent on how active and efficient both Russian and Norwegian authorities will be in promoting petroleum-related industrial cooperation in the Barents Sea.

Note

1 According to Russian legislation, only Russian state-owned petroleum companies that have at least five years of experience in working on the Russian continental shelf can hold the license for exploration and production of Russian Arctic offshore petroleum resources.

References

Bourmistrov, A., & Mineev, A. (2011). Differences in project management: Challenges for cooperation between Norwegian and Russian suppliers in the High North. In A. Bourmistrov, F. Mellemvik, & S.Vasiljev (Eds.), *Perspectives on Norwegian–Russian energy cooperation* (pp. 17–26). Oslo: Cappelen Akademisk Forlag.

Doornich, J.B. (2014). *Entry modes and organizational learning during internationalization: An analysis of supply companies entering and expanding in the Russian oil and gas sector* (Unpublished doctoral dissertation). Bodø Graduate School of Business, Bodø, Norway.

Gazprom. (2004, September 9). Gazprom, Rosneft, and Statoil sign memorandum of understanding [Press release]. Retrieved from www.gazprom.com/press/news/2004/september/article62894/

Gazprom. (2005, June 20). Gazprom, Statoil and Hydro seal memorandum of understanding [Press release]. Retrieved from www.gazprom.com/press/news/2005/june/article63157/

Gazprom. (2009, June 5). Газпром и StatoilHydro подписали Меморандум о взаимопонимании [Gazprom and StatoilHydro signed memorandum of understanding] [Press release]. Retrieved from www.gazprom.ru/press/news/2009/june/article57053/

Gazprom. (2010, June 18). Газпром и Statoil подписали Соглашение о научно-техническом сотрудничестве [Gazprom and Statoil signed an agreement on scientific and technical cooperation]. Retrieved from www.gazprom.ru/press/news/2010/june/article100033/

[Gazprom intends to increase the resource base of the South Kirinskoye field] Газпром намерен увеличить объем ресурсной базы Южно-Киринского месторождения. (2014, September 17). *Oilcapital.ru*. Retrieved from www.oilcapital.ru/

Global Oil & Gas Directory. (2014). Statistics retrieved from Global Oil&Gas Directory database.

Gorst, I. (2013, June 13). Norway & Russia: New oil best friends [Web blog post]. Retrieved from http://blogs.ft.com/beyond-brics/2013/06/13/norway-russia-new-oil-best-friends/#axzz2xkWMVTNI

Government of Norway. (2013). *Sluttrapport fra Nordområdeutvalget* [Final report from the Norwegian High North Commission]. Retrieved from www.regjeringen.no/nb/dep/ud/dok/rapporter_planer/rapporter/2013/sluttrapport_nord.html?id=733556

Government of Norway. (2014, August 11). Norge vil innføre nye restriktive tiltak mot Russland [Norway will implement new restrictive measures against Russia] [Press Release]. Retrieved from www.regjeringen.no/nb/dep/ud/pressesenter/pressemeldinger/2014/Norge-vil-innfore-nye-restriktive-tiltak-mot-Russland.html?id=765675

INTSOK. (2013). *Russian–Norwegian oil & gas industry cooperation in the High North. Logistics and transportation.* Retrieved from www.intsok.com/Market-info/Markets/Russia/RU-NO-Project/Focus-Areas/Logistics-and-transport/Reports2/Report-Logistics-and-Transport

INTSOK. (2014). *Annual market report (2015–2018).* Retrieved from www.intsok.com/Market-info/Annual-market-report

Krivorotov, A. (2009). "Поморская зона": взгляд теоретика и практика ["Pomor Zone" seen with the eyes of theoretician and practitioner]. In V. Chereshnev (Ed.), *Трансграничное сотрудничество России с северными странами: состояние и перспективы развития* [Russian trans-boundary cooperation with Nordic countries: Current status and prospects] (pp. 35–44). Moscow, Russia: Galeria Publishers.

Learn about Achilles Group Limited. (n.d.). Retrieved from www.achilles.com/en/about-achilles-norway/about-achilles

Mineev, A. (2011). *How has the petroleum supply industry developed in the Russian Barents Sea region? Institutional and managerial aspects* (Unpublished doctoral dissertation). Bodø Graduate School of Business, Bodø, Norway.

Mirzoev, D., Ibragimov, I., & Arkhipova, O. (2013, December 19). Инновационные технологии подводной добычи углеводородов на шельфе Арктики [Innovative technologies for subsea hydrocarbons production in the Arctic shelf]. *Neftegaz.ru.* Retrieved from http://neftegaz.ru/

[New oil discoveries:This could be the turning point] Nytt oljefunn:Dette kan være vendepunktet. (2014, October 14). *NRK Nordnytt.* Retrieved from www.nrk.no/nordnytt/storre-funn-enn-goliat-1.11984684

Nilsen,T. (2012, September). Snøhvit – Wider impacts from the LNG process plant at Hammerfest. In V. Norman (Chair), *Session 4:The geographical perspective – wider impacts:Valuing the future – public investments and social return.* Concept symposium conducted at the Concept Research Program, Losby Gods, Norway.

[Offers for ownership interests in the 22nd licensing round] Tilbud om andeler i 22. konsesjonsrunde. (2013, June 12). *Norwegian Petroleum Directorate.* Retrieved from www.npd.no/no/

[Oilfield service market in import clinch] Нефтесервисный рынок в тисках импорта. (2013,August). *Delovaya Rossiya, 8,* 32–33.

Overland, I., Godzimirski, J., Lunden, L.P., & Fjærtoft, D. (2013). Rosneft's offshore partnerships:The reopening of the Russian petroleum frontier? *Polar Record, 49*(249), 140–153. doi:10.1017/S0032247412000137

Ramsdal, R. (2013, October 23). Prirazlomnaja–Kunstig øy i Arktis spekket med norsk teknologi [Prirazlomnaja – Artificial island in the Arctic packed with Norwegian technology]. *Teknisk Ukeblad.* Retrieved from www.tu.no/

Ramsdal, R. (2014, August 12). EU-Sanksjoner. Eksportforbud for norsk oljeteknologi til Russland [EU–Sanctions. Export prohibition of Norwegian oil technology to Russia]. *Teknisk Ukeblad.* Retrieved from www.tu.no/

Rosneft. (2012a, May 5). Rosneft and Statoil agree on joint offshore operations in the Barents Sea and Sea of Okhotsk [Press release]. Retrieved from www.rosneft.com/news/pressrelease/05052012.html

Rosneft. (2012b, June 21). Rosneft and Statoil advance strategic cooperation with the signing of agreements on joint bidding for licenses in the Norwegian section of the Barents Sea and joint technical evaluation of tight oil resources in Russia [Press release]. Retrieved from www.rosneft.com/news/pressrelease/210620122.html

Rosneft. (2012c, August 30). Rosneft and Statoil sign shareholder agreements for Russian offshore exploration joint ventures [Press release]. Retrieved from www.rosneft.com/news/pressrelease/30082012.html

Rystad Energy. (2013, June 30). *INTSOK annual market report.* Retrieved from www.intsok.com/Market-info/Annual-market-report

Semykina, I. (2013). Ванкор: Эффект бабочки [Vankor: Butterfly effect]. *Expert-Sibir, 1,* 28–31.

[Shelf urges new technologies from Russia] Шельф требует от России новых технологий. (2014, October 9). *I-Mash.ru*. Retrieved from www.i-mash.ru/

Shtokman gas and condensate field. (n.d.). Retrieved from www.shtokman.ru/en/project/gasfield/

Skretting, H. (2011). How to establish cross-border business and become a part of the existing supply chain? In A. Bourmistrov, F. Mellemvik, & S. Vasiljev (Eds.), *Perspectives on Norwegian–Russian energy cooperation* (pp. 54–64). Oslo, Norway: Cappelen Akademisk Forlag.

Statoil. (2009, June 5). Gazprom and StatoilHydro sign MoU [Press release]. Retrieved from www.statoil.com/en/NewsAndMedia/News/2009/Pages/GazpromAndStatoilHydroSignMemorandumOfUnderstanding050609.aspx

Statoil. (2010, June 18). Gazprom and Statoil sign sci-tech cooperation agreement [Press release]. Retrieved from www.statoil.com/en/NewsAndMedia/News/2010/Pages/18JuneGazpromAgreement.aspx

Statoil. (2012, November 23). Rosneft and Statoil sign declaration on Russian Arctic environmental protection [Press release]. Retrieved from www.statoil.com/en/NewsAndMedia/News/2012/Pages/23Nov_Arctic.aspx

Svishchev, R. (2011). *When management control myths collide? Case study of MCSs in two Norwegian companies, operating in Russia* (Master's thesis, Bodø Graduate School of Business, Bodø, Norway). Retrieved from http://idtjeneste.nb.no/URN:NBN:no-bibsys_brage_18597

The Sakhalin-1 GBS completed. (n.d.). Retrieved from www.kvaerner.com/Products/Concrete-structures-for-offshore-platforms/The-Sakhalin-1-GBS-completed/

Treaty on Maritime Delimitation and Cooperation in the Barents Sea and the Arctic Ocean, Norway–Russia. (2010, September 15). Retrieved from www.regjeringen.no/upload/ud/vedlegg/folkerett/avtale_engelsk.pdf

Zolotukhin, A. (2011). Arctic petroleum resources: Opportunities and challenges. In A. Bourmistrov, F. Mellemvik, & S. Vasiljev (Eds.), *Perspectives on Norwegian–Russian energy cooperation* (pp. 65–77). Oslo: Cappelen Akademisk Forlag.

Ånestad, M., Riisnæs, I.G., Løvås, J., & Langved, Å. (2014, August 19). Sanksjoner skaper forvirring [Sanctions make confusion]. *Dagens Næringsliv*. Retrieved from www.dn.no/

6 Norwegian–Russian political relations and Barents oil and gas developments

Indra Overland and Andrey Krivorotov

Introduction

The political relationship between Norway and Russia will influence the development of Barents Sea oil and gas. The state plays a decisive role in both the Norwegian and Russian parts of the sea. It does so as a regulator, through taxation, and through the national oil and gas companies, Gazprom, Rosneft, and Statoil. Thus, if the two states have a good relationship characterized by mutual trust, they can coordinate, search for complementarities, and mitigate issues that arise. Furthermore, due to the rising cost of oil and gas production in the Arctic, many oil and gas fields there may deliver small returns on investments. Scale economies brought about by coordinated development, joint infrastructure, and information sharing can tip projects from being commercially unviable to viable. But this depends on the ability and willingness of the two states to actively work together.

It is commonly noted that Norway and Russia have been at peace for over 1,000 years (e.g. Støre, 2010). At the end of World War II, North Norway was liberated from Nazi occupation by Soviet forces. During the two first decades after the collapse of the Soviet Union, Russia had better relations with Norway than with many other West European countries (Jensen & Overland, 2011; Vaage & Overland, 2011). Norway has not had a highly anti-Russian foreign minister, such as Sweden's Carl Bildt, neither has it had a case such as that of Aleksander Litvinenko in the UK or Akhmed Zakayev in Denmark. Norwegian companies have invested heavily in Russia, not just in the petroleum sector but also in telecoms, the media, and breweries. Some companies have made large profits, in spite of years of continuous quarreling between Norway's Telenor and Russian co-shareholders over a hostile takeover of a Ukrainian mobile operator (Liuhto, 2007). Russian companies, Rosneft and Lukoil, have in turn been allowed onto the Norwegian continental shelf, and Russian tourists are some of the biggest spenders in Norway. Russian students and immigrants have flocked to Norway, thriving there (Bourmistrov, 2007, 2011).

Nonetheless, the bilateral political relationship between the two countries is variable and subject to risks. There are at least two main sources of concern in the relationship between the two countries: their complex direct interaction in the Barents Sea, and the broader political relationship between Russia and the West, of which Norway is a part. An accidental entanglement in the Barents Sea could lock the two countries into a negative spiral of actions and counter-actions, or a long-term cold front in Russian–Western relations over a matter such as Ukraine could cast long shadows over the bilateral relationship between the two countries.

The Barents Sea and its petroleum province are divided in two by the 1,680-km Norwegian–Russian maritime boundary (Moe, Fjærtoft, & Over-land, 2011; Norwegian Ministry of Foreign Affairs, 2011, p. 61). The length of this boundary, greater than the distance between Berlin and Moscow, means that the two countries have extensive and complex relations. The boundary crosses some of the world's richest fish stocks; Russia's only year-round, ice-free port in the Arctic is the Barents city of Murmansk; the Svalbard Archipelago on the Norwegian side of the boundary is Norwegian territory, but subject to the 1920 Svalbard Treaty, which gives other signatory states including Russia the right to engage in economic, maritime, research, and other activity on the archipelago; and, finally, the Barents Sea is the gateway to the Northern Sea Route leading to the Pacific Ocean. There are thus many opportunities for entanglement between Norwegian and Russian actors, including the joint management of fish stocks, illegal fishing, coast guards arresting fishing vessels, oil spills, nuclear accidents, and so on.

In this chapter we provide a forward-looking overview of the complexities of the relationships between the two countries. However, we start in the next section by looking back at the situation before the 2010 maritime boundary agreement. The subsequent sections deal with the reception of the boundary agreement in Norway and Russia, the place of Barents oil and gas in the broader Norwegian and Russian contexts, the linkages between Norwegian–Russian bilateral relations and broader Russian–Western relations, and implications for the future.

Before the Barents Sea maritime boundary agreement

The territorial dispute between the USSR/Russia and Norway dated back to the 1960s when the continental shelf came into the political spotlight, both as a promising petroleum province and as an emerging object of international law. The first informal Soviet–Norwegian consultations on the delimitation of the Barents Sea took place in 1970. The official negotiations were launched in 1974 and then held on a largely regular basis. Once the two countries established their 200-nm exclusive economic zones (EEZ) in 1976, the mandate of the negotiations was extented to cover fisheries as well.

The Norwegians adhered to the median line principle, while the Soviet side maintained the straight sector line established by the USSR government in 1926. The overlapping disputed area was about 175,000 square km (some 50,000 square nm) large, equivalent to over half of the Norwegian mainland territory (Moe et al., 2011).

The first 15 years of discussions resulted in virtually no progress. However, the very fact of equal bilateral negotiations between a nuclear global superpower and its small but NATO-member neighbor was of major symbolic importance during the Cold War. Moreover, as early as in 1976, the two countries signed a long-term agreement on cooperation in fisheries and established the Joint Norwegian–Russian Fisheries Commission, which among other things sets agreed catch quotas for common fish stocks in the Barents Sea (Krivorotov, 2011). Besides, in 1978, the USSR and Norway set up a temporary mechanism for regulating fisheries in the disputed area (the so-called Gray Zone agreement), which was later prolonged each year until the 2010 Murmansk Treaty was signed.

Both countries also had reasons to believe that the seabed in the area possessed large potential oil and gas resources, since Norway made numerous offshore discoveries in the North Sea and USSR in the eastern Barents Sea (Moe, 2010). In the early 1980s, a Soviet research vessel shot 2D seismic in the disputed area, which helped to identify several promising prospects, notably including the Fedynsky High. However, soon after, the two countries agreed to refrain from any further exploration in this area, and its actual reserves remain unknown.

In late 1988, the Soviet Foreign Ministry indicated for the first time that the Soviet Union might be willing to deviate from the sector line. After that, the delimitation process started making gradual progress, moving from north to south. When Mikhail Gorbachev visited Oslo as President of the USSR in June 1991, he announced that the borderline issue had already been resolved by two-thirds (Krivorotov, 2001). But in subsequent years, the talks slowed down and nearly stalled, as the negotiations moved on to the southern Barents Sea, which is the most important area for fishermen, oilmen, and navies alike.

The year 2010 finally brought about a real breakthrough in negotiations. At the end of the first visit of the Russian President, Dmitry Medvedev, to Oslo in April 2010, the foreign ministers of the two countries announced that a solution to the Barents Sea dispute had been reached and only details remained before an agreement could be signed (Bakken & Aanensen, 2010). A few months later, on September 15, the delimitation treaty was signed in Murmansk, dividing the disputed area approximately into two halves of 87,500 square km each.

The settlement, which was a surprise even to many insiders, apparently came about for several reasons. First, there had been a manifold increase in the level of bilateral relations, mutual interest, and trust over the two past decades. Russia and Norway had entered a number of agreements in various fields, exchanged numerous visits at top and high political levels, promoted mutual trade and investments, and cooperated closely in the High North, both in a bilateral format and within broader international organizations, including the Barents region and the Arctic Council. Second, it was in both countries' interest to settle the territorial dispute in light of the work they were doing to stake their claims for the continental shelf beyond the 200 nautical mile limit. An extra concern for Norway was expanding the part of its seabed available for oil and gas exploration, as its oil production had peaked in 2004 and started to decline.

Last but not least, Dmitry Medvedev, the pro-Western Russian President of that time, made a personal contribution to move ahead with the settlement. He made this clear in his joint news conference with the Norwegian Prime Minister, Jens Stoltenberg, after signing the treaty (President of the Russian Federation, 2010). This agreement was of high political value that extended far beyond the scope of the bilateral relationship. By ending a decades-old dispute at a time when many observers thought of the Arctic as the object of an intensifying geopolitical competition, two of the major Arctic states sent a clear message to the world that any disputes in the Arctic could and should be resolved peacefully based on international law.

Situation after boundary agreement

The domestic reaction to the Murmansk Treaty was starkly different in the two countries. In Norway, it was hailed by a vast majority of stakeholders, notably including the parliamentary opposition and most independent experts, as a big step forward. With it, the country had settled the last and by far the biggest territorial dispute it had with its neighbors. The North Norwegian fishermen were the only exception, as they were of the opinion that the deal could lead to a worsening of the situation for the fisheries in the area due to increased oil and gas activity and more lax fisheries protection (Fishermen fear the delimitation line, 2010).

The oil industry and northern regions praised the opportunity to develop oil and gas resources in the delimited area, reversing the negative trend in oil output, creating new jobs, and bringing income to the coastal communities. A large-scale campaign of petroleum exploration in the Arctic fits equally perfectly into the Norwegian government's strategy and rhetoric on the High North (Jensen, 2012). As soon as the Murmansk Treaty came into force, it started sponsoring seismic shooting in the previously disputed area. However, licensing in the area followed the usual path, including the issuing of environmental and social impact assessments, public hearings, etc. Exploration blocks in the southern part of the delimited area were granted for the first time in Norway's twenty-second licensing round, in 2013.

By contrast, in Russia the treaty encountered significant skepticism. Fishermen, backed strongly by the Communist faction in the Duma, came out as the strongest opponents in Russia, as they stated that they were losing access to the rich fishing grounds in the western part of the formerly disputed area, which were now Norwegian waters. Although the joint fisheries management was to remain intact for 15 more years, they feared that their catch quotas would be cut dramatically (Norway to get part of Barents Sea today from Russia, 2010). Another argument against the treaty, closely connected to the first one, was that it did not mention explicitly the special status of, and Russian rights on, Svalbard and in the adjacent waters, including notably Norway's fisheries protection zone around Svalbard, which the USSR/Russia had never acknowledged (Oreshenkov, 2010; Zilanov, 2013). The broader Russian public, which had been unaware of this dispute, also criticized the deal as a unilateral Russian concession of its traditional possessions. If it had not been for the ruling party, Unified Russia, which was chaired by then Prime Minister Vladimir Putin, the treaty would likely not have been ratified by the Duma.

Meanwhile, Rosneft, the Russian national oil company, which had for years shown an interest in the Barents Sea shelf, quickly saw the opportunities that the delimitation agreement created, all the more as the recent amendments to the Russian legislation on the continental shelf had made it possible for Rosneft to obtain Arctic shelf acreage without competitive bidding. By early 2012 the Russian part of the delimited area was split into three large blocks, and Rosneft was granted the licenses to all of these.

The Barents Sea in the broader national contexts

The Arctic in general remains high on the political agenda in both Norway and Russia, with an emphasis on maintaining a presence and leading positions in the Arctic, developing domestic northern regions, and enhancing the national Arctic identity. This may encourage both cooperation and competition, as we have seen in the Arctic since the 1960s.

Despite the high political importance to both countries of oil and gas exploration and development in the Barents Sea, any large-scale investments must be commercially viable and comply with broader national approaches to the countries' petroleum resources. In other words, it is not just a question of Norway and Russia coordinating their efforts in their respective parts of the Barents Sea, but also of how the Barents Sea fits into respectively the broader Norwegian and Russian oil and gas industries.

In this perspective, the situation is asymmetric, as Russia has more domestic alternatives to the Barents Sea than Norway does, and the political context in the two countries is different. This asymmetric situation creates a trend towards an imbalanced development of the Barents Sea: the Norwegian petroleum industry is chased away from Lofoten and towards the Barents Sea, while the Russian petroleum industry is drawn away from Europe and the Barents Sea towards East Siberia and the Far East (although the Russian geopolitical interest in the Barents Sea may only be heightened).

The domestic Norwegian context

As in northwest Siberia, the producing oil and gas fields in the North Sea are in decline and Norway needs to invest if it wants to maintain the flow of petroleum revenue. In this regard, the two countries are in a similar situation. Although Norway is a much smaller country than Russia and has much less acreage for potential petroleum exploration and extraction, Norway does also have a choice between different petroleum provinces. Three of the main options between which the Norwegians need to prioritize are investing in enhanced oil recovery (EOR) to extend the lifespan of the North Sea fields, or in greenfield areas near the Lofoten Islands, or in the Barents Sea.

The drivers and debate over priorities in Norway are, however, different from those in Russia. First, there is significantly more emphasis on EOR in Norway. The average rate of recovery in the North Sea is above 50%, whereas in Russia it is below 20% (Maugeri, 2006, p. 209). In 2014, the Norwegian government established a national center for EOR, further strengthening the emphasis on EOR (University of Stavanger, 2014).

Second, public concern over environmental issues plays a larger role in Norway. This includes both worries over local environmental issues, such as oil spills and conflicts with fisheries, and Norway's contribution to global greenhouse emissions. Sometimes these environmental agendas are debated separately; sometimes they are combined into a general environmental resistance by those lobbying against new oil developments.

One of the main ambitions of the environmentalists has been to avoid oil and gas extraction in the areas around the Lofoten Islands. Meanwhile, other local actors hope for economic benefits from increased petroleum activity in the North and actively promote it. The so-called red–green coalition government of the Center, Labor, and Socialist Left Parties that ruled Norway 2005–2013 was divided on this issue and ended up closing the area for exploration for the time being. This ensures that the matter will reappear on the political agenda during the coming years.

The Lofoten Islands have been a logical target for environmentalists because they are important spawning grounds for cod, and because their natural beauty holds an important place in Norwegian ethnic identity. The Barents Sea is probably at least as environmentally important, and significantly larger, but has still received much less attention. Propetroleum interests have thus grumblingly accepted the moratorium on petroleum exploration in the area around the Lofoten archipelago, while accelerating exploration in the Barents Sea. Thus, paradoxically, environmental resistance may have led to more rapid development of oil and gas in the Barents Sea.

While the Lofoten moratorium may have contributed to speeding up exploration in the Barents Sea, it may also be an obstacle to the development of oil and gas fields found there. This is because it would be more logical to develop the Lofoten Islands first from an infrastructure perspective, as they are located north of the last area to have already been developed, in the Norwegian Sea off central Norway. Should natural gas be found, one could then consider extending the Norwegian offshore pipeline grid northwards to the Lofoten Islands, and then later on to the Barents Sea. With the environmental moratorium on the Lofoten Islands, they become an infrastructural missing link between the undeveloped Barents Sea and the developed southern parts of the Norwegian continental shelf.

For the professional environmentalist NGOs, climate change is as important as, or more important than, local environmental protection. It is, however, more difficult to mobilize the population around climate change, especially the North Norwegian population, who can then feel that it needs to choose between the concrete benefits of jobs and rising property prices on the one hand, and the abstract concern of climate change on the other hand (Kristoffersen, 2014; Kristoffersen & Jensen, 2012).

Another way in which the Norwegian government's choices will play a role is in terms of its policy towards Russia. For Russia, Norway is a small neighbor; for Norway, Russia is its largest, and, importantly, most difficult to understand, neighbor. As mentioned, Norwegian policy towards Russia has been milder and more cooperative than that of some other European countries such as Poland, Sweden, or the UK. There has been a relatively strong, albeit implicit, consensus about this across the Norwegian political spectrum. The main exception is the Venstre Party, which has spoken out for a more critical policy towards Russia (see Borsch, 2012), but this is a small party and all the major parties have de facto supported a foreign policy towards Russia of steadily growing ties and integration. However, this could change. During the 10-year period that started with Putin's second presidential term in 2004, the attitude of Norwegian officialdom towards Russia has gradually deteriorated, especially since the events in Ukraine in 2014. Norway is also a founding member country of NATO and with strong ties to the UK and the US, potentially sources of influence for a more critical policy towards Russia. However, Norway is closer to Russia and so far the Norwegian elite have still been more cautious than those of many other Western countries in criticizing Russia.

The current coalition government of the Conservative and Progress Parties has continued the discourse on the Arctic but so far has not done much about it. Jonas Gahr Støre was quick to emphasize the High North when he was Foreign Minister under the coalition government that was led by the Labor Party. He has now been elected leader of the Labor Party and has launched climate policy (and possibly interethnic integration) as his main political cause(s). Although it is likely that the Labor Party will return to power in a 10-year perspective, there is thus little reason to expect that it will lead to a reinvigorated focus on the High North and the development of new oil and gas fields.

The domestic Russian context

There are more alternatives to the Barents Sea in Russia than in Norway. On the one hand, developing the Arctic shelf enjoys a high priority in the government's plans, as a very visible way to compensate for the falling oil and gas production of the traditional Siberian fields, to establish a presence in the politically sensitive circumpolar area, and to enhance the well-being of the country's northern territories. All the relevant government papers, like the regularly updated National Energy Strategy or the Strategy for the Russian Arctic Zone adopted in 2013 (Government of the Russian Federation, 2009; President of the Russian Federation, 2013), set the goal of creating a new upstream province on the country's Arctic continental shelf, which in the first order means the Barents Sea and eventually the Kara Sea. Russian researchers, although aware of the inherent environmental challenges, advocate strongly for intensified exploration and development of the nation's Arctic shelf, as one of the biggest remaining hydrocarbon reserves of global scale (Laverov, Dmitrievskiy, & Bogo-yavlenskiy, 2011; Tsunevskiy, 2008). Gazprom and Rosneft also highlight their Arctic profile as a part of their global market positioning. When crude oil shipments started from the Prirazlomnoye field in the eastern Barents Sea, Gazprom was happy to announce that it had opened a new Russian petroleum production center in the Arctic.

On the other hand, the above plans date back to the time when experts in and outside Russia forecasted a steady growing demand for oil and gas in the Atlantic basin, both in Europe and the United States. There has been a need to reconcile policy goals with changing market realities. First, even regardless of the current strain in Russian–Western relations over Ukraine, both Rosneft and Gazprom have to revisit their market strategies. There has been speculation for some time as to whether Gazprom had to choose between the previously undeveloped Barents Sea and the more "conventional" Yamal Peninsula (Moe, 2006, p. 393). Yamal has the advantage that, in terms of geology and natural conditions, it is nearly identical to other onshore northwestern Siberia areas where Gazprom has proven technologies and decades of experience. This dispute was, however, rather academic as long as all experts foresaw a steady increase in the global demand for fuels, justifying simultaneous on- and offshore developments. But at a time when the United States is turning into a leading global producer and a potential net exporter of gas and perhaps even oil, when natural gas prices face an increased volatility and the EU attempts to reduce its dependence on Russian energy, the priorities may need to be set more clearly. "Gazprom critically analyzes and reviews the strategies it has been following recently," its CEO, Alexey Miller, said in October 2014, addressing the global changes in the natural gas markets. "It doesn't mean that we are going to change these strategies and approaches, but it is possible" (Gazprom, 2014b).

The Ukrainian crisis has added to this strain. By June 2014, Ukraine had accumulated debt for previously delivered Russian gas worth USD 5.3 billion and Gazprom switched to deliveries against advanced payment only. This may lead to Ukraine consuming some of the transit gas delivered from Russia to the EU through its territory, something that has happened before. Both parties have sued each other in the Stockholm Court of Arbitration. Several rounds of tripartite Russia–Ukraine–EU negotiations on gas sales to Ukraine failed to produce an agreed price. Rosneft has also declared the loss of some of its oil in the Ukrainian pipeline network and in addition had to postpone the planned overhaul of its Lisichansk refinery in eastern Ukraine due to the violence in that part of the country (Rosneft plans to seek compensation, 2014). As a result, the Russian oil and gas transit through Ukraine, which had never been easy, became even more unpredictable than ever before, forcing Russia to further intensify its efforts to diversify export routes.

The second point, which is interrelated with the first, is the growing Russian focus on the expanding Eastern Asia markets (China, Japan, Korea, India, etc.). Their demand is big and growing, while natural gas prices are some periods twice as high as in Europe and the US. Besides, energy cooperation with these nations gives Russia a strong impetus to develop infrastructure in the adjacent regions of eastern Siberia and the Far East, which are vital to provide Russia with an access to the Asia–Pacific area. Problems in the European market are a secondary, still important, factor to enhance this trend.

In the past few years, Russian companies, backed strongly by the authorities, have committed to supply major quantities of both oil and gas to China. In 2009, the Russian state oil company, Rosneft, signed a deal with the China National Petroleum Corporation (CNPC) to supply 15 mt/y of oil till 2030, starting in 2012. In 2013, Rosneft signed an additional contract with CNPC for the supply of another 365 mt within 25 years, and also signed a memorandum of understanding with Sinopec to deliver another 100 mt of oil in 2014–2023 (Starinskaya, 2013). Besides their great scope and long-term nature, these contracts have the strong advantage for Rosneft of major advance payments (for example, USD 70 billion under the second Rosneft–CNPC deal alone) (Rosneft receives advance payment from China for oil, 2014). Rosneft has also recently engaged in a number of joint projects with Chinese companies on producing oil in eastern Russia and constructing an oil refinery in China (Rosneft, 2014).

In May 2014 Gazprom signed a contract worth USD 400 billion with CNPC for the delivery of 38 bcm/y of natural gas from eastern Siberia to China over 25 years starting from 2019. On September 1, 2014 Gazprom started construction of the 4,000-km-long *Sila Sibiri* [Power of Siberia] gas pipeline (Gazprom, 2014a). At the ceremony Gazprom also indicated that another contract may soon be signed with CNPC for the western route, to transport gas to China from existing fields in western Siberia, which make up the main resource base for deliveries to Europe (though Gazprom maintains that it has enough gas to supply both markets). The framework agreement on the western route was later signed by the two companies on November 9, 2014 under the Asia–Pacific Economic Cooperation Summit in Beijing (Gazprom, 2014c).

Third, as several industry experts and environmentalists have pointed out, there are promising alternatives to increasing upstream production, like enhancing oil recovery from the fields in operation, cutting associated gas flaring, and curbing nonproductive fuel and energy losses under both production and consumption. According to Russian estimates, energy efficiency may be increased by 30% in national power generation and by 40% in hot-water supply systems.

The effect of these market-driven changes, which were already well underway before the conflict in Ukraine, on Russia's interest in the Barents Sea may be exacerbated by the Norwegian government's participation in Western criticism and measures against Russia, including economic sanctions. The attempts by the US and EU to isolate Russia highlight the risks involved in close economic relations with them for a government such as that of President Putin, which is not recognized by Western governments as democratic. As predicted and theorized by Overland, Torjesen, and Kjærnet (2010, p. 93), the realization of this risk causes countries with such governments to reorient themselves towards China.

Seen with Russian eyes, the issue is more fundamental: the West has failed to establish a working global order based on a unilateral dominance, and other nations have to combine their efforts (both in political and economic terms) to construct a more balanced system of relations and protect their legitimate interests. This close interaction of economic, political, and ideological considerations makes the situation both complicated and hard to predict. However, it is rather evident that Russia lacks some key technologies to develop its Arctic shelf, and the US and EU sanctions on the transfer of Arctic and deep-sea oil and gas technologies can help make Russian companies focus more on Siberian onshore fields and Asian markets.

Another factor in the Russian domestic context is the potential changes in the country's company landscape. Novatek and Rosneft actively increase their national gas production and sales, and Gazprom could potentially lose its monopoly on pipeline exports (see e.g. Henderson, 2013; Lunden, Fjærtoft, Overland, & Prachakova, 2013). Already Novatek has been permitted to launch LNG exports from its Yamal LNG project independently of Gazprom, and Rosneft indicates a strong desire to obtain gas export rights both for LNG and pipeline gas. These changes may further enhance the Russian trend towards the East, since both Novatek and Rosneft seem to be giving high priority to cooperation with China (CNPC already has a 20% stake in Yamal LNG).

As the scenario horizon of this book is 10 years, which exceeds the constitutional term in office of President Vladimir Putin, it also raises the question of Russian policies in the longer run. The government could, for example, pursue a more liberal Western-oriented policy, or rely more on Asian partners, or become more domestically oriented. This applies to Russian behavior in the Arctic as well – different modes are possible, and the choice among these does not at all depend solely on the personality of the next Russian president. Indeed, the president possesses extensive powers, but the personal factor is often exaggerated (Overland, 2011), as the declared and especially the practical Russian policies are a product of a broader elite and government apparatus. The Arctic shelf is a good example of this. While the Russian laws ban foreign investors explicitly from the shelf resource base, this has not stopped Rosneft and Gazprom from forging offshore partnerships with foreign companies and from suggesting legislative amendments to facilitate this in September 2014 (i.e. when the Western sanctions against Russia had already been imposed). In this respect, the political developments in Russia represent an uncertainty. Russian–Norwegian political relations in the Barents Sea will be a function of, among other things, the broader Russian choices between East and West, plus the general role of the Arctic in the national political agenda.

Concluding thoughts: the broader influence of Russian–Western relations

All the factors explored above are important to understand the prospects for Norwegian–Russian cooperation. An additional and overarching factor that must be considered as we conclude is the broader relationship between Russia and the West. Relations between Russia and the West have entered a spiral of Western sanctions and Russian countermeasures over the conflict in Ukraine. As this book has a 10-year scenario horizon, it is, however, important not to become too caught up in current events – however difficult that is. The longer-term implication of the current impasse is a major break in Russian–Western relations. Even compared to previous negative incidents such as the conflict in South Ossetia, this is worse. Russia and the West appear to be locked into a negative spiral, where it is difficult for either party to offer a compromise. It will be difficult for any future Russian leader to give up or compromise on Crimea, and it will be as difficult for Western leaders to accept Crimea becoming part of the Russian Federation. Once in place, sanctions may be difficult to remove, because it puts the onus of argument on those who want to remove the sanctions. These considerations point towards a long-term worsening of Russian–Western relations.

However, it is also possible that Russia and the West will be forced to find a *modus vivendi*. Arguments pointing in this direction are a number of common challenges like fighting terrorism and reshaping the global economic order, Russia's dependence on oil and gas revenues, economic collapse of Ukraine (about which both sides may ultimately be obliged to do something), the EU's dependence on Russian energy, and Russia's fear of becoming too dependent on China.

So what then does this imply for Norwegian–Russian relations? One analysis that was carried out before the Ukraine conflict found that Russian–Western political trade had a limited impact on Norwegian–Russian trade and economic cooperation (Vaage & Overland, 2011). This analysis covered eight previous political spats between Russia and the West. However, none of these quarrels were as severe as that over Ukraine, and none involved formalized sanctions by the West against Russia. In this respect it is clear that the Ukraine crisis is different and will affect the bilateral trade relationship, although it is not possible to say how much and for how long.

What can be said with some confidence is that Norway, in spite of not being an EU member, is highly loyal to EU policy. Although Norway can choose whether or not to follow the EU's lead on Russian policy, any Norwegian government is likely to do so. This is because the main political parties in Norway – the Conservative and Labor Parties – are both firmly pro-EU, and because adhering to EU policy removes the risks involved in formulating an independent policy. As long as Norway consistently follows the EU lead, there is not so much need for the government to explain its choices, as they are made for it by the EU. As soon as Norway deviates from the EU line, the question arises whether it should be more or less lenient and why. Thus, as long as the EU is locked into a formal conflict with Russia through formalized sanctions, Norway is likely to also be so. Since the oil sector was singled out for targeted sanctions early on, this does not bode well for cooperation in the Barents Sea.

On the Russian side, the Russian–Western distrust over Ukraine is highly negative for Russian interest in the Barents Sea because the Russians are already so dependent on European gas markets. Events in Ukraine make Russia want to diversify export markets towards Asia faster, and the Barents Sea is just about as far away from Asia as one can get on the planet. At the same time, tensions with the West may strengthen Russian security and military attention regarding the Barents Sea, which might add additional negativity to the prospects for Norwegian–Russian cooperation in the area.

In the past there have been suggestions for Norwegian–Russian joint infrastructure for the transport of natural gas from the Barents Sea to markets, either in terms of extending the Norwegian offshore gas pipeline grid northwards to the Barents Sea (Barlindhaug, 2005), or in terms of building a pipeline from the Murmansk to Hammerfest so that Russia could use the Norwegian LNG capacity to export Shtokman gas when suitable and the Norwegians could pump their gas in the other direction and use the planned Murmansk–Vyborg pipeline to export gas to Europe when suitable (proposed by Karen Sund of Sund Energy, personal communication). One problem with these propositions is that they would increase Russia's dependence on transit countries, which it is generally trying to reduce (as well as increasing Norway's mutual dependency on Russia). However, in the context of a continuing standoff between the EU and Russia, such proposals might gain new currency if they helped dissipate mutual fears by mixing Russian with Norwegian gas.

References

Bakken, L.O., & Aanensen, K. (2010). Historisk løsning av delelinjen [Historical solution of boundary dispute]. *Norsk rikskringkasting.* Retrieved from www.nrk.no/

Barlindhaug, J.P. (2005). *Petroleumsvirksomhet i Barentshavet* [Petroleum activities in the Barents Sea]. Tromsø, Norway: Barlindhaug.

Borsch, R. (2012, October 25). Holdningsløs Russland-politikk [Spineless policy towards Russia]. *Norsk rikskringkasting.* Retrieved from www.nrk.no/

Bourmistrov, A. (2007). *Norwegian–Russian cooperation in business education and research: Visions and challenges in perspectives of the High North.* Oslo, Norway: Cappelen.

Bourmistrov, A. (2011). *Perspectives on Norwegian–Russian cooperation in the field of energy.* Oslo, Norway: CappelenDamm.

[Fishermen fear the delimitation line] Fiskere frykter delelinjen. (2010, June 25). *Norsk rikskringkasting.* Retrieved from www.nrk.no/

Gazprom. (2014a, September 1). Power of Siberia construction launched [Press Release]. Retrieved from www.gazprom.com/press/news/2014/september/article200026/

Gazprom. (2014b, October 7). Speech by Alexey Miller about global gas industry outlooks and problems at 4th St. Petersburg International Gas Forum [Press Release]. Retrieved from www.gazprom.com/press/miller-journal/285476/

Gazprom. (2014c, November 9). Russia and China sign framework agreement on gas supplies via western route [Press Release]. Retrieved from www.gazprom.com/press/news/2014/november/article205898/

Government of the Russian Federation. (2009). *Энергетическая стратегия России на период до 2030 года* [The energy strategy of Russia for the period until 2030]. Retrieved from http://minenergo.gov.ru/aboutminen/energostrategy/

Henderson, J. (2013). *Evolution in the Russian gas market: The competition for customers* (Report No. NG 73). Retrieved from the Oxford Institute for Energy Studies website www. oxfordenergy.org/wpcms/wp-content/uploads/2013/01/NG_73.pdf

Jensen, L.C. (2012). *Norway on a high in the North: A discourse analysis of policy framing* (Doctoral thesis, University of Tromsø, Tromsø, Norway). Retrieved from http://munin.uit. no/handle/10037/4737

Jensen, V., & Overland, I. (2011). Et blikk på Sjtokmanprosjektets blindsone: fransk-russiske relasjoner [A glance at the blind zone of the Shtokman project: French–Russian relations]. *Internasjonal Politikk, 69*(3), 387–411.

Kristoffersen, B. (2014). Securing geography: Framings, logics and strategies in the Norwegian High North. In R. Powell & K. Dodds (Eds.), *Polar geopolitics? Knowledges, resources and legal regimes* (pp. 131–148). Cheltenham and Northampton, MA: Edward Elgar.

Kristoffersen, B., & Jensen, L.C. (2012). Nordområdepolitikken: A license to drill? [The Arctic policy: A license to drill?]. *Tvergastein, 1*(2), 74–80.

Krivorotov, A. (2001). Barents Sea: Oil riches in a Cold War playground. *Oil&Gas Eurasia, 1*, 8–16.

Krivorotov, A. (2011). Неравный раздел пополам: к подписанию российско-норвежского договора о разграничении в Арктике [Partition into unequal halves: On the signing of the Russian–Norwegian treaty on maritime delimitation in the Arctic]. *Vestnik Moskovoskogo Universiteta, 25*(2), 62–91.

Laverov, N., Dmitrievskiy, A., & Bogoyavlenskiy, V. (2011). Фундаментальные аспекты освоения нефтегазовых ресурсов арктического шельфа России [Fundamental aspects of developing hydrocarbon resources of the Russian Arctic shelf]. *Arktika. Ekologia i Ekonomika, 1*, 26–37.

Liuhto, K. (2007). *A future role of foreign firms in Russia's strategic industries* (Report No. 4/2007). Retrieved from www.utu.fi/fi/yksikot/tse/yksikot/PEI/raportit-ja-tietopaketit/Documents/Liuhto04_07.pdf

Lunden, L.P., Fjærtoft, D., Overland, I., & Prachakova, A. (2013). Gazprom vs. other gas producers: Friends or foes? *Energy Policy, 61*, 663–670.

Maugeri, L. (2006). *The age of oil: The mythology, history, and future of the world's most controversial resource.* Westport, CT: Praeger.

Moe, A. (2006). Sjtokman-beslutningen: Forklaringer og implikasjoner [The Shtokman decision: Explanations and implications]. *Nordisk Østforum, 20*(4), 389–403.

Moe, A. (2010). Russian and Norwegian petroleum strategies in the Barents Sea. *Arctic Review on Law and Politics, 1*(2), 225–248.

Moe, A., Fjærtoft, D., & Overland, I. (2011). Space and timing: Why was the Barents Sea delimitation dispute resolved in 2010? *Polar Geography, 34*(3), 145–162. doi:10.1080/10 88937X.2011.597887

[Norway to get part of Barents Sea today from Russia] Сегодня Норвегия получит от России часть Баренцева моря. (2010, September 15). *REGNUM News Agency.* Retrieved from www.regnum.ru/

Norwegian Ministry of Foreign Affairs. (2011). *Nordområdene. Visjon og virkemidler* [The High North. Visions and strategies] [White Paper]. Oslo, Norway: Author.

Oreshenkov, A. (2010). Арктический квадрат возможностей. Северный полюс и шельф Шпицбергена не могут быть норвежскими [Arctic square of opportunities. North Pole and Spitsbergen shelf cannot belong to Norway]. *Rossiya v Mirovoy Politike, 8*(6), 194–202.

Overland, I. (2011). Close encounters: Russian policy-making and international oil companies. In J. Wilhelmsen & E. Wilson Rowe (Eds.), *Russia's encounter with globalization: Actors, processes and critical moments* (pp. 134–158). Basingstoke, England: Palgrave Macmillan.

Overland, I., Torjesen, S., & Kjærnet, H. (2010). China and Russia: Partners or firewalls for the Caspian petro-states? In I. Overland, H. Kjærnet, & A. Kendall–Taylor (Eds.), *Caspian energy politics: Azerbaijan, Kazakhstan and Turkmenistan* (pp. 93–100). London, England: Routledge.

President of the Russian Federation. (2010, September 15). *Совместная пресс-конференция по итогам российско-норвежских переговоров* [Joint news conference concluding Russian–Norwegian talks] [Press Release]. Retrieved from http://news.kremlin.ru/transcripts/8924

President of the Russian Federation. (2013). *Стратегия развития Арктической зоны Российской Федерации и обеспечения национальной безопасности на период до 2020 года* [Strategy for developing the Arctic zone of the Russian Federation and protecting national security for the period till 2020]. Retrieved from http://government.ru/news/432

Rosneft. (2014, November 10). Rosneft delegation took part in the APEC summit [Press Release]. Retrieved from www.rosneft.com/news/today/10112014.html

Rosneft plans to seek compensation from Ukraine for shelling of oil refinery. (2014, August 31). *ITAR-TASS News Agency*. Retrieved from http://en.itar-tass.com/

Rosneft receives advanced payment from China for oil. (2014, January 15). *RIA Novosti*. Retrieved from http://en.ria.ru/

Starinskaya, G. (2013, October 23). "Роснефть" зальет Китай нефтью [Rosneft to pour China plenty of oil]. *Vedomosti*. Retrieved from www.vedomosti.ru/

Støre, J.G. (2010). *Russland som stormakt: Åpningsforedrag ved Forsvarets Høgskole, sjefskurs nr 5, Oslo, 18. august 2010* [Russia as a great power: Opening lecture at Norwegian Defense University College, Chief Course No. 5, Oslo, August 18, 2010]. Retrieved from www.regjeringen.no/nb/dokumentarkiv/stoltenberg-ii/ud/taler-og-artikler/2010/russland_stormakt.html?id=612800

Tsunevskiy, A. (2008). Арктический шельф – будущее нефтедобычи России [Offshore Arctic Russia's oil industry future]. *Energeticheskaya politika, 1*, 1–17.

University of Stavanger. (2014, March 24). Tord Lien åpner nasjonalt senter for oljeutvinning [Tord Lien opens the National IOR Centre of Norway] [Press release]. Retrieved from www.uis.no/om-uis/nyheter-og-presserom/tord-lien-aapner-nasjonalt-senter-for-oljeutvinning-article85727-8108.html

Vaage, T., & Overland, I. (2011). Norsk-russisk handel, noe for seg selv? Nord-Norge i et globaliseringsperspektiv [Norwegian–Russian trade, a law unto oneself? Northern Norway in a globalization perspective]. In S. Jentoft, J.I. Nergård, & K.A. Røvik (Eds.), *Hvor går Nord-Norge? Tidsbilder fra en landsdel i forandring* [Where does Northern Norway go? Time pictures from a changing region] (pp. 203–212). Tromsø, Norway: Orkana forlag.

Zilanov, V. (2013). *Россия теряет Арктику?* [Is Russia losing the Arctic?]. Moscow, Russia: Algoritm.

7 Norwegian–Russian cooperation on oil and gas education

Anatoli Bourmistrov, Ove Gudmestad, Valery Salygin, and Anatoly Zolotukhin

Introduction

This chapter reviews the results of Norwegian–Russian cooperation on oil and gas education. There are many examples of Norwegian and Russian higher education institutions that started active cooperation at the beginning of the 1990s. However, what makes oil and gas education cooperation special is that it took advantage of both the political climate calling for improved energy cooperation and dialogue between Norway and Russia as well as opportunities that opened up for improved international education cooperation introduced by European harmonization in terms of the Bologna process. This chapter aims to discuss the cooperative experience between four universities in Norway and Russia that developed joint education programs in energy management and petroleum technology.

International and national contexts for Norwegian–Russian education cooperation

Before we describe the cooperation experience in setting up and running joint oil and gas education programs between two pairs of Russian and Norwegian universities, it is necessary to briefly describe the international and national frameworks in which this education cooperation has evolved. The Bologna process, launched in Europe at the end of the 1990s to create a European Higher Education Area, aimed at facilitating international cooperation in education through increased academic collaboration, mobility between academic institutions and academic recognition. Education cooperation across borders is always challenging because of differences in education systems between countries, especially in terms of degree structures, lengths of study programs, different grading systems, organization of study processes, etc. Recognizing that, the Bologna process focused especially on improving international quality assurance and transparency in order to strengthen academic collaboration in an open European area of education and training. The introduction of the European Credit Transfer and Accumulation System (ECTS) – a common tool of linking the workload of students in terms of time required to achieve specific learning outcomes – was a particular means for improving academic recognition for study abroad using commonly understood measurements (e.g. credits and grades) as well as an interpretation of national systems of higher education.

Norway and Russia have traditionally had different education systems (Bourmistrov & Mellemvik, 2007). The sections below give a brief overview of the major differences between those in terms of regulatory structure of education practices and education programs. We also describe how the education systems changed when the Bologna declaration was ratified in Norway and Russia.

National education regulation in Russia

The education regulation structure and its influence on the educational institutions have traditionally been more hierarchically arranged in Russia than in Norway (Bourmistrov & Mellemvik, 2002). In Russia, the Ministry of Education and Research was (and still is) a rather central actor in forming education policies and preparing detailed education standards and instructions as well as assuring institutional compliance. Each ministerial education standard specifies three components indicating the degree of relevance of the content and the autonomy of the local education institution to change the content: so-called federal, regional and local components. Educational institutions only have autonomy in designing subjects included in the local component; the content of courses related to the federal and regional components is usually outside the educational institution's direct influence. Each Russian education institution has to comply with those standards, as otherwise it could lose the state authorization for running particular programs.

Standards usually provide descriptions of a large number of small courses (8–10 subjects per semester as a student's workload). There are also large numbers of compulsory courses not directly related to the program specialization (such as physical culture, history, philosophy, chemistry) and defined in terms of the federal component. The Russian system has also traditionally favored a focus on class teaching as a main method of delivering the subject, with regular plenary lectures. For a two-year program, lectures could have accounted for around 2,000 class hours.

In order to join the Lisbon Recognition Convention and implement elements of the Bologna declaration, in 1999 the Russian government established the National Information Center for Academic Recognition and Mobility (NIC ARM), assuming responsibility for educational quality assurance in Russia. This center is a part of the Ministry of Education of the Russian Federation. However, it took some time to pass amendments to the legislation. In 2007, the two-cycle education system was finally introduced: bachelor (with duration of study – four years) and master (with duration of study – two years, building on the previous cycle). Later, Russia introduced new types of state education standards for higher education, orienting those more towards educational outcomes, offering a greater degree of academic freedom for educational institutions (Tempus Report, 2010).

National education regulation in Norway

Though the Ministry of Education and Research is the highest authority for education in Norway and sets the terms of the major obligations and rights of educational institutions in a national education framework, its role has been traditionally limited in terms of regulating the content of most educational programs. Other nongovernmental national standard-setting bodies that function independently of the Norwegian Ministry of Education and Research, like the Norwegian Council of Universities and the Norwegian Council of University Colleges (which, after 2000, merged into the Norwegian Association of Higher Education Institutions [UHR] [www.uhr.no]), were important in developing the educational frameworks and recommended study plans for educational institutions and study programs. In most cases, requirements from national standard-setting bodies were considered as guidelines for autonomous education institutions to take into account when designing and evaluating education programs. Contrary to the Russian system, a relatively small number of larger courses characterize the Norwegian education programs (two–five subjects per semester as a typical student load). The student workload related to class teaching is lower than in Russia (up to 500 class hours for a two-year program), but it is a requirement that students must undertake more individual self-study and group work.

Ratification of the Bologna process in Norway started with the passing of new legislation in 2002 and bringing this into practice by 2003 (The National Bologna Group, 2005). Two new independent agencies were established: 1) the Norwegian Agency for Quality Assurance in Education (NOKUT[1]) (www.nokut.no/) – to work with quality assurance, and 2) the Norwegian Centre for International Cooperation in Higher Education (SIU) to promote international cooperation in education and research (The National Bologna Group, 2005). Norway has also changed its degree structure to the 3 + 2 + 3 year model for corresponding bachelor-, master- and PhD degrees as well as transferred fully to the ECTS model.

Joint degrees: experience of cooperation between University of Nordland and MGIMO University in the field of energy management

At the beginning of 2000, inspired by the increasing political attention of the Norwegian and Russian authorities to develop energy cooperation in the High North, Bodø Graduate School of Business (HHB) at the University of Nordland established contact with the International Institute of Energy Politics and Diplomacy (MIEP) at MGIMO University. In February 2004, the partners signed an agreement to establish the Norwegian–Russian Institute of Energy Cooperation that aimed to develop joint education programs, with a special focus on the management of oil and gas resources in the High North. Particularly important was the idea of creating synergies by combining the unique strengths of MIEP (e.g. in exploring and analyzing key geopolitical, macro-economic and business related factors affecting the world energy industry) and HHB (e.g. in the management of oil and gas companies, international and cross-cultural management, innovation, logistics, environmental management) to establish new education and research programs. During 2004–2005, the partners developed two master programs: 1) a joint-degree program, Master of Science in Energy Management, and 2) a joint corporate executive MBA program, International Business in the Oil and Gas Industry, for top managers in a Russian company, Rosneft.

Energy enterprises and the authorities were active in supporting the development of those programs. On the Norwegian side, HHB involved Nordland County administration, the Norwegian Petroleum Directorate, companies, Gassco, INTSOK, Norsk Hydro, PetroArctic, Petoro, Selmer, Statoil and Total Norge, all of whom contributed differently – some secured program relevance by participating in the activities of the program boards, some provided financial resources for program development, others provided part-time faculty and teaching staff. On the Russian side, MIEP secured institutional support and active participation in the education processes by leading specialists from BP, Gasprom, Rosneft, Exxon Mobil and Transneft. The Ministries of Foreign Affairs in both countries also supported the development of such programs.

MSc in Energy Management program: learning-by-doing, the model and outcomes

This program targeted students who had completed their bachelor's degrees in the business administration/management field and who wanted to continue education at the master's level in the field of energy, specializing in management in the oil and gas business. From the start, the idea was to provide education to a joint class of 30 students (15 students enrolled in Bodø and 15 in Moscow).

Since Norway and Russia had at that time already committed to the Bologna declaration, HHB and MIEP recognized that program development would benefit from having its principles incorporated as a foundation for the development of the education programs. However, to turn ideas found in the Bologna declaration into a complete functional program was an interesting challenge, and solutions to challenges were far from clear-cut.

The work started with the formation of working groups on both the Norwegian and Russian sides with relevant formal competence in each other's education systems. However, individuals who had formal knowledge of both Norwegian and Russian systems and had previous positive formal and informal experience of Norwegian–Russian education cooperation played a crucial role in mediating the dialogue and knowledge exchange between the groups. Challenges were many, for example, differences in the requirements of programs in terms of subjects to be included in the master's program curriculum in both countries, the allocation of subjects per semester, qualifications of students to be admitted to the program and workload of students.

In this sense, the main challenge was to design a joint curriculum based on the idea of a joint degree program. The main principle was that, while some parts of the curriculum can be the subject of harmonization, it would not be possible to harmonize others, at least in the short term. The first step towards developing the common curriculum was to agree about the maximum student workload as a main point of departure. Partner universities should work from the indicator of the 30 ECTS representing the student semester load in both Norway and Russia. This helped to foster agreement about the content of the semesters, but it should not affect the teaching traditions of the respective partners. Therefore, it was possible to move towards recognition of the course content by the other partner university, with acknowledgement at the same time that the use of teaching method will certainly vary and cannot be harmonized.

Based on a constructive dialogue between the groups, it was possible to adjust the subjects' reallocation between semesters and to assign the responsibilities of HHB and MIEP for particular courses. It was important to secure transparency between the subjects the students should learn according to the Russian and Norwegian curricula, especially to ease the mutual recognition of courses and the grades received by students. Teachers provided harmonized course descriptions and the institutional administration developed routines for taking care of practical matters such as fees, incoming students' accommodation, invitations and visas, etc.

In designing the curriculum, many compromises had to be made (Bourmistrov & Sørnes, 2007). First, the challenge was to balance compulsory courses in management with specialization courses in the energy field. Second, within the specialization courses, the challenge was to balance three areas: the focus on general issues relevant for the energy field (e.g. geopolitics, energy economics); the focus on issues of natural energy resources' management that are often country-specific (e.g. licensing regimes, taxation, structure of the energy sector); and the focus on the increasingly important potential for developing petroleum resources in the High North, especially after the signing of the Delimitation Line treaty in 2010. Third, the program had also to reflect its international nature and allow for cross-cultural exchange and learning. After constructing the initial program content and adjusting the program structure to reflect the experience gained, the program structure is presented in Table 7.1.

In the model, student mobility and mutual recognition of courses taken at each other's universities represent an indispensable part of the program. The specificity of the model is that student semester exchange is a compulsory part of the program, with students spending at least one semester at each other's partner university. The program's design gathers students into a single group, allowing them to have the experience of studying together for at least one year. This represents an important networking potential during the study as well as after graduation.

During the first semester, students take compulsory business administration and management courses at their "home" institution. For the second semester, which is a joint semester in Bodø, MGIMO students stay in Bodø and study

Table 7.1 The model of the joint degree program, Master of Science in Energy Management, between MGIMO University and the University of Nordland

1st semester 30 ECTS	2nd semester 30 ECTS (BODØ)	3rd semester 30 ECTS (MOSCOW)	4th semester 30 ECTS
	Exchange semester	Exchange semester	
Compulsory courses in Business Administration and Management 30 ECTS	The Geopolitics of Petroleum and Natural Gas 10 ECTS	Energy Diplomacy and Economy of Fuel and Energy Complex 30 ECTS	
	Energy Management – Norwegian Perspectives 7.5 ECTS		Master Thesis 30 ECTS
	Research Methods 7.5 ECTS		
	Russian or Norwegian Language and Culture 5 ECTS		

specialization courses as well as courses on research methods and language. Because there is a close link between language and culture, Norwegian students learn the basics of the Russian language, while Russian students can learn the basics of Norwegian in order to facilitate the cross-cultural experience of being in a foreign country. During the third semester, Norwegian students take specialization courses at MGIMO University in Moscow together with Russian students. These are: financial management in the fuel and energy sector, international business environment for the oil and gas sector, the exchange trade in oil and oil product commodities, the economy of Russia, brand management and public relations in the fuel and energy sector, project management and investment in the energy sector, development of the Arctic energy resources, corporate finance, joint ventures and offshore zones in the energy sector, investment management in oil and gas companies, oil and gas sector business development strategies, trade policy and its main instruments, Russia and the EU: energy policy and security, and communication management. During the fourth and final semester, students have multiple opportunities for working for their master's thesis including staying at "home" institutions, taking internships in companies in each other's countries or going abroad to partner universities (e.g. the University of Texas in the US, the University of Alberta in Canada).

Upon graduation, the students receive diplomas from their "home" universities. In addition, students receive a Diploma Supplement (DS) with logos and signatures from both deans and rectors at the MGIMO and UiN, indicating that the program is a joint degree between the universities. The Diploma Supplement (DS) has been developed according to the standards of the Bologna process.

The program enrolled its first students in August 2005. In the period 2007–2014, more than 200 students graduated from the joint degree program, Master of Science in Energy Management. Work placement records from the alumni network demonstrate that, of graduates on the Norwegian side, around 50% are working in the energy-related industries (e.g. Aker Solutions, Conoco-Phillips, DNV, FMC Technologies, General Electric, Marine Aluminum, North Energy, OneSubsea, Statoil, Suncor Energy Norge, Total E&P Norge, Winter-shall), 30% in auditing and consulting business (e.g. Accenture, Deloitte, E&Y, KPMG, PricewaterhouseCoopers), 15% in the area of business analysis and research (e.g. universities, knowledge parks) and 5% in authorities and agencies (e.g. EFTA, Innovation Norway, Office of the Auditor General, Ministry of Petroleum and Energy). Graduates on the Russian side are working in companies such as Rosneft, Gazprom, Lukoil and Sakhalin Energy.

Initially, the program targeted only Norwegian and Russian students, but, with time, students from other countries enrolled in and graduated from the program (Austria, Cyprus, Czech Republic, Greece, France, Kazakhstan, Lithuania, Poland, Portugal, Romania, Nigeria, Iran, Italy, Pakistan, Swaziland and US), indicating that the program has gained international relevance.

Corporate program for Rosneft

Another interesting example is a two-year Russian–Norwegian corporate Executive MBA program, International Business in the Oil and Gas Industry, for Rosneft JSC. MIEP at MGIMO University and HHB at the University of Nordland signed an agreement with Rosneft in November 2005; the agreement has been renewed four times since then, allowing around 190 managers to complete the program.

This program targeted competence improvement in middle and top management at Rosneft JSC and its subsidiaries. The program is tailor-made for the needs of Rosneft when it comes to managing in the international oil and gas environment. It includes 12 modules, covering issues of strategic management, human resource management, public relations, technology management and innovations, international diplomacy and security, politics, ethics and environmental regulation, managing large projects in the O&G sector, as well as writing a master's thesis. Ten modules are held in Russia (responsibility of MIEP) and two are run in Norway (responsibility of HHB): one in Oslo–Stavanger and the second in Bodø–Hammerfest.

Modules organized in Norway offer particular understanding of the Norwegian system's framing and regulating of oil and gas activities on the Norwegian continental shelf. The module in Oslo–Stavanger is devoted to long-term planning of energy resources' development, state regulations on energy projects on the Norwegian shelf and how communication and dialogue take place between private companies and the state. The module in Bodø–Hammerfest focuses on aspects connected to the management of large oil and gas projects in Arctic conditions (e.g. managing practices, supply activities, environmental aspects, social responsibility, security of operations, etc.). While in Norway, program participants visit companies and organizations, where they meet with experts, e.g. Ministry of Foreign Affairs, DNV, Econ O&G, INTSOK, Statoil AS, Total E&P Norway, PETORO, Gassco, NUPI, the Russian Trade Mission, Nordland County, Petro Arctic, the local indigenous community, Rescue Coordination Center North Norway, etc.

Dual degree program, Master of Science in Offshore Field Development: experience of cooperation between University of Stavanger and Gubkin Russian State University of Oil and Gas

History of cooperation

There has been academic cooperation between the Faculty of Science and Technology at the University of Stavanger (UiS) and Gubkin Russian State University of Oil and Gas in Moscow for more than 20 years, dating back to 1991. The cooperation has involved research, the publication of textbooks in both Russian and English, participation at conferences, joint teaching and mobility of teachers, academic staff and students. Professorial exchange has been active for 18 years.

The cooperation resulted in the establishment of a double degree program, Master of Science in Offshore Field Development in 2011, financed by the Norwegian Ministry of Foreign Affairs, through the Norwegian Barents 2020 program. Funding for the project period ran from 2011 to 2013. The Russian part of the program was financed by the Russian oil and gas industry.

The program is founded on a common interest in both institutions, based on a common national priority: to prepare young graduates from both countries for the challenges of offshore developments of oil and gas fields, in particular in the Barents Sea (Zolotukhin, 2014).

Upon completion of the Barents 2020 project, the first group of students had completed their master's in 2012 (five Russian students), the second group finalized their studies in June 2013 (six Russian and two Norwegian students). In the spring of 2014, five Russian students graduated, while in the fall of 2013 another five Russian students and one Norwegian student were enrolled in the program for graduation in 2015. The status at present is that the program continues, being funded by the Russian oil and gas industry and private funds. Both universities are determined to continue the program as long as there is interest in the market for the candidates graduating from the program.

Development of common teaching material/textbooks

The cooperation between Gubkin Russian State University of Oil and Gas and the University of Stavanger has led to the preparation of textbooks for the oil and gas industry (Gudmestad et al., 1999; Gudmestad, Zolotukhin, &

Jarlsby, 2010; Zolotukhin et al., 2000; Zolotukhin & Ursin, 2000; Zolotukhin, Gudmestad, & Jarlsby, 2011).The objective has been to prepare common teaching material in English and Russian in order to align the teaching and to serve as common ground for common research activities. Joint scientific publications have also been prepared, in particular related to the development of offshore oil and gas fields in the northern region (Bulakh, Gudmestad, & Zolotukhin, 2011; Efimov, Kornishin, & Gudmestad, 2013; Efimov, Zolotukhin, Gudmestad, & Kornishin, 2014; Pribytkov, Zolotukhin, & Gudmestad, 2014). We suggest that these textbooks and publications will be useful and serve as basic reading when common Russian and Norwegian development projects take place in the future. Particular attention has been paid to attending the biannual Russian Arctic Offshore conferences held in St. Petersburg and later the Arctic and Extreme Environment conferences (2011, 2013) held in Moscow, where special sessions are organized for the presentation of student work.

The double degree Master of Science program

The double degree program, Offshore Field Development, between Gubkin Russian State University of Oil and Gas and the University of Stavanger, is organized according to a model similar to the program between MGIMO University and the University of Nordland (Table 7.1). The organization is shown in Table 7.2.

The emphasis of the program is on subjects that are general and that should help the candidate to develop a career where basic knowledge represents the cornerstone of the activities. Much emphasis is also placed on the preparation of a thesis that may be published as a contribution at a conference or in a scientific journal.

Table 7.2 The model of the double degree program, Master of Science in Offshore Field Development, between Gubkin Russian State University of Oil and Gas and the University of Stavanger

1st semester 30 ECTS (Home University)	2nd semester 30 ECTS (MOSCOW)	3rd semester 30 ECTS (Stavanger)	4th semester 30 ECTS (Home university)
	Exchange semester	Exchange semester	
Compulsory courses in Mathematics, Risk Analysis, Statistics and Offshore Field Development 30 ECTS	Specialist courses in Structural Engineering, Marine Technology, Gas Engineering and Maintenance Engineering 30 ECTS	Specialist courses in Marine Operations, Subsea Developments of Fields, Arctic Offshore Engineering and Offshore Pipeline Design 30 ECTS	Master Thesis 30 ECTS

Conclusions

What can be learned from the experience of two Norwegian and two Russian universities, cooperating for many years in the field of oil and gas education? As we can see, there are five main important points.

First, cooperation is a natural strategy when partners are able to create synergies by combining their unique strengths based on a common understanding platform. The long-term university cooperation described in this chapter has been productive possibly because university partners in Norway and Russia clearly identified those synergies and competitive advantages and worked together, based on a joint platform created by the Bologna declaration.

Second, cooperation is about respecting each other's differences and finding pragmatic ways to live with those. Increased internationalization and globalization can make cultural and regulation differences more visible but will never be able to eliminate those. The regulatory and cultural differences between the education systems in Norway and Russia experienced by the higher education institutions described in this chapter were pragmatically addressed in the unified system adopted by Russia and Norway. The European ECTS system functioned as an important "bridge" between different educational and institutional systems.

Third, cooperation is about never stopping experimenting and learning-by-doing. Cooperation based on the international principles of the Bologna process was quite new for institutions and there was no clear way of how to apply these principles in the practice. However, through discussion and dialogue, new agreements were formed and the ECTS practice established. This requires experience, will and commitment. Despite political will and governmental support, joint degrees between Norwegian and Russian institutions are still uncommon.

Furthermore, cooperation very often succeeds due to the hard work of dedicated individuals. Institutional support is important, but individuals involved at the professional science level (professors) are of most importance to be able to understand the major challenges and find the right solutions.

Finally, the cooperation should include common research and the exchange of scientific staff (mainly at PhD, post doc and professorial level) to ensure that the educational program is based on research. Research cooperation supported by the industry also ensures incentives for the preparation and quality of publications in scientific journals.

The efforts made to run these programs and to ensure that they excelled were not wasted: graduates from the joint master's programs are employed by the best companies and institutions around the world and contribute with the greatest competence to the further development of science, research and the industry.

Note

1 NOKUT stands for Norwegian Agency for Quality Assurance in Education, responsible for the quality assessment of Norwegian educational institutions (universities, university

colleges and colleges) as well as the assessment of foreign higher education in terms of requirements of the Norwegian education system.

References

Bourmistrov, A., & Mellemvik, F. (Eds.). (2002). *Norwegian–Russian cooperation in business education and research: Experiences and challenges* (HBO-report No. 11). Bodø, Norway: Bodø University College/Bodø Graduate School of Business.

Bourmistrov, A., & Mellemvik, F. (Eds.). (2007). *Norwegian–Russian cooperation in business education and research: Visions and challenges in perspectives of the High North.* Oslo, Norway: Cappelen Akademisk Forlag.

Bourmistrov, A., & Sørnes, J.O. (2007). High North cooperation between Russia and Norway – The North Western University Alliance. In G. Austin & M.A. Schellekens-Gaiffe (Eds.), *Energy and conflict prevention, Anna Lindh Program on Conflict Prevention* (pp. 222–253). Stockholm, Sweden: GIDLUNDS.

Bulakh, M., Gudmestad, O.T., & Zolotukhin, A.B. (2011, October). *Fedyn Arch – the promising zone for HC reserves in the Barents Sea following the agreement between Russia and Norway.* Paper presented at the SPE Arctic and Extreme Environments Conference & Exhibition, Moscow, Russia.

Efimov, Y., Kornishin, K., & Gudmestad, O.T. (2013, June). *Winterization needs for platforms operating in low temperature environment.* Paper presented at ASME 2013 32nd International Conference on Ocean, Offshore and Arctic Engineering, Nantes, France. Abstract retrieved from http://proceedings.asmedigitalcollection.asme.org/proceeding.aspx?articleid=1786505

Efimov, Y., Zolotukhin, A., Gudmestad, O.T., & Kornishin, K. (2014, February). *Cluster development of the Barents and Kara Seas HC Mega Basin from the Novaya Zemlya Archipelago.* Paper presented at the ATC conference, Houston, TX. Abstract retrieved from www.onepetro.org/conference-paper/OTC-24650-MS

Gudmestad, O.T., Zolotukhin, A.B., Ermakov, A.I., Jakobsen, R.A., Michtchenko, I.T., Vovk, V.A., . . . Shkhinek, K.N. (1999). *Basis of offshore petroleum engineering and development of marine facilities with emphasis on the Arctic offshore.* Moscow, Russia: Neft i Gaz, Gubkin University.

Gudmestad, O.T., Zolotukhin, A.B., & Jarlsby, E. (2010). *Petroleum resources with emphasis on offshore fields.* Southampton, England: WIT Press.

Pribytkov, E., Zolotukhin, A., & Gudmestad, O. (2014). Optimization of integrated template structures for Arctic subsea-production systems. *Oil and Gas Facilities Journal, 3*(4), 47–53.

Tempus Report. (2010). *Higher education in the Russian Federation.* Retrieved from http://eacea.ec.europa.eu/tempus/participating_countries/reviews/russia_review_of_higher_education.pdf

The National Bologna Group. (2005). *Towards the European higher education area: Bologna process, Norway National Report 2004–2005.* Retrieved from www.ehea.info/Uploads/Documents/National_Report_Norway_05.pdf

Zolotukhin, A.B. (2014, June). *Preparing specialists for the future.* Paper presented at the 21st World Petroleum Congress, Moscow, Russia.

Zolotukhin, A.B., Gudmestad, O.T., Ermakov, A.I., Jakobsen, R.A., Michtchenko, I.T., Vovk, V.A., . . . Shkhinek, K.N. (2000). *Основы разработки шельфо-вых нефтегазовых месторождений и строительство морских сооружений в Арктике* [Fundamentals of offshore petroleum engineering and development of Arctic marine facilities]. Moscow, Russia: Neft i Gaz, Gubkin University.

Zolotukhin, A.B., Gudmestad, O.T., & Jarlsby, E. (2011). *Ресурсы нефти и газа, разработка шельфовых месторождений* [Petroleum resources with emphasis on offshore fields]. Southampton, England: WIT Press.

Zolotukhin, A.B., & Ursin, J.R. (2000). *Introduction to petroleum reservoir engineering*. Kristiansand, Norway: Norwegian Academic Press.

Part III

Technology and the natural environment

8 Structure of the geological section and the main features of oil and gas content

Mark Verba, Gennady Ivanov, and Anatoly Zolotukhin

Geological zoning of oil and gas fields

Despite longstanding studies, the hydrocarbon (HC) potential of the Barents sedimentary basin has not been implicitly brought to light yet. In 1935, based on the first discoveries in Polar Urals, Novaya Zemlya and Franz Joseph Land (FJL), I.F. Pustovalov mentioned possible hydrocarbon accumulations in the eastern part of the Barents Sea shelf for the first time.

I.S. Gramberg (Gramberg, 1997) used the regional geophysical data that threw light on the Barents Sea as a basis for the first quantitative evaluation of the Arctic shelves' hydrocarbon potential, of which the Barents shelf was highlighted as the most promising.

At the same time and until recently, the prospecting was limited by the southern border of the basin and only covered its central part in patches. Since 1972 the activities have been carried out on a regular basis due to the establishment in Murmansk City of the first specialized geological and geophysical entity (MAGE JSC), which started systematic geophysical surveying, oriented on searching areas suitable for subsequent oil and gas prospecting drilling. In five years more than two dozen such areas have been found, but only after the discovery of the onshore oil deposit on the Kolguyev Island (the first area outside the continental part of the Pechora Province) did the drilling operations start. A seismic survey performed by SMNG later resulted in the discovery of several gas and gas–condensate deposits in the South Barents Basin, including the discovery of the huge Shtokman Field. An engineering survey carried out by AMIGE secured the preparation of the background for deep drilling performed later by AMNGR. The above discoveries demonstrated that practically the entire Barents shelf area is promising in terms of its oil and gas content, although to different extents. Scientific support of this study was performed by VNIIOkeangeologia, Moscow State University and VNIGNI, VSEGEI (Malyshev, Nikishin, & Drachev, 2010; Stoupakova, 2011; Stoupakova et al., 2011).

The Barents shelf geological structure key feature, which was steadily identified as a result of performed regional geophysical surveys, is the pervasive development of thick Jurassic–Cretaceous sedimentary cover that superposes older undisturbed sedimentary sequences. This allows such a shelf as to be considered as a typical coilogenic structure and to be distinguished as a unified shelf plate. Geological and geophysical data that had been acquired during recent decades by researchers from different states and entities over the Barents Sea aquatic and adjacent areas were integrated into a tectonic map 1:2,500,000, which illustrates the entire Barents–Kara Region (Khain, 1978; Verba & Ivanov, 2009, p. 20).

Together with the part of the island and mainland framing, including the Svalbard anteclise (except the Alpine dislocation zone on the island of Spitsbergen's west coast), Grumant anticline (FJL), Pechora lowland and also the Karmakul trough of the Novaya Zemlya, this plate corresponds to a large oil and gas province, whose main structural and oil and gas content features comply with common relationship. According to the viewpoint of the majority of geologists, there are two groups of areas within the Barents Province. One area includes the Pechora sineclise and the Svalbard and Central Barents anticlines, as well as the Prinovozemelskaya and Kola–Kanin margin monoclises. The structure of the above areas includes practically the full set of Phanaerozoic sedimentary formations. The other group of areas includes the West Barents, South Barents, North Barents and East Barents rift depressions, composed of Late Paleozoic–Triassic complexes of terrigenous deposits (Figure 8.1).

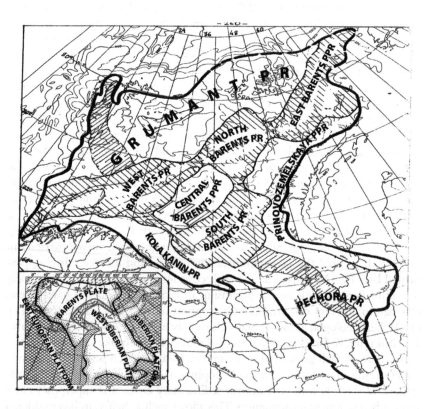

Figure 8.1 Map of the Barents Region geological zoning of oilfields.

All nine areas mentioned above (commensurable among themselves in terms of area) are subdivided into several regions. Moreover, it was suggested that one such area, the Ludlov Saddle, due to its specifics should be distinguished as a separate region, not included within any adjoining area.

Present-day ideas on the potential oil and gas content of different regions and areas of the Barents Sea, and in general on geological zoning of the shelf, are based on the results of numerous surveys. The majority of geologists share the opinion that the Barents shelf plate, as a coherent geological structure, along with the adjoining onshore areas, should be considered as a unified oil and gas province (sometimes it is suggested that it should be called a megaprovince), whose integral areas have common geological section features and commensurable specifics regarding the distribution of HC deposits and/or their attributes.[1]

Promising regions located on the Barents–North Kara megatrough framing

All five petroleum regions located on the Barents–North Kara megatrough (BNKMT) are, to some extent, determined by the normal geological and geophysical profiles, which give a rather good indication of the structure of sedimentary cover. Such geological and geophysical profiles, being comprehensive, comprise the national deep-profile and deep-well control network, and served as a base frame for the correlation of intermediate seismic profiles, previously acquired on the Barents Sea aquatic area. The availability of numerous intermediate seismic profiles allowed the interpretation of volumetric data, acquired from the reference network of profiles.

It was necessary to take into account the fact that information published over the last 15–20 years, for understandable reasons, has lost its specifics, which are necessary for the comprehensive assessment of the hydrocarbon potential of the areas under discussion. Therefore, it was necessary to use previously acquired data, which is still valid.

Pechora Petroleum Region

A general idea regarding the structure of the sedimentary deposits of the Pechora petroleum region and a general trend of gradual downwarping eastward of the Pechora plate folded basement, which sometimes is unreasonably called sineclise, can be provided by the fragment of reference profile 3-AR, acquired by the SEVMORGEO. Structures located to the west of the Pechora–Kolvin aulacogen are identified as the local West Pechora, which is traced on the Barents Sea shelf as a Kola–Kanin monoclise. The buried Bolshezemelski anticline (along the sedimentary cover – Khoreiver depression) and the Varandei–Adzva structural zone, which includes the Varandei and Medyn swells, are located to the east of the aulacogen. In terms of its structure, the Korotaikhin trough, located further to the east, is considered as a separate geological structure, although, according to the approved geological zoning of oilfields, it should be attributed to the promising region under consideration.

Oil and gas shows can be found within the Pechora lowland along practically the entire cross-section of sedimentary cover – from Vendian through Cretaceous horizons; however, the majority of valuable deposits are concentrated in a much narrower interval of the cross-section – from mid-Devonian to Lower Permian, provided that even that part of the cross-section is nonuniform in terms of its producibility. During the Pechora petroleum region study, which started in the last century, a lot of factual data was acquired and published in numerous works. This data represents the totality of the present-day vision of main trends, relating to the vertical and lateral distribution of petroleum deposits.

Hydrocarbon accumulations of different size occur within practically the entire sedimentary cover cross-section, but the oilers are mostly interested in mid-Devonian sandstones (sub-Domanik complex) and Upper Carboniferous–Lower Permian carbonates (Belonin, Prischepa, Teplov, Budanov, & Danilevsky, 2004; Borovinskikh, 2003). The lowest of horizons accumulates nearly 75% of all commercial reserves of oil, while the upper contains nearly 35% of explored gas and 20% of oil reserves. Anterior older deposits do not play a significant role in the total balance, and, all in all, their attribution to platform features is questionable.

Within the lateral series, the majority of reserves are clearly confined to the central zone of the plate, which coincides in the plan with the line structure of the Pechora–Kolvin aulacogen. Up to 62% of all HC resources in the Pechora petroleum region are accumulated in that zone. From the south to the north, the producing portion of the sequence is "rejuvenating" due to emerging pools in the Mesozoic deposits and a decreased number of pools in the mid-Paleozoic deposits, as well as due to the decreased specific gravity of oils and the replacement of oil pools with gas–oil and gas–condensate pools.

According to the estimates of V.N. Makarevich and his colleagues (Makarevich, Prischepa, Otmas, & Popov, 2000, p. 28), nearly half of the initial total in-place resources of the Timan–Pechora petroleum region (7.3 bln toe including 4.4 bln t of oil) will be found on the shelf. Highest estimates are given to areas adjoining the framing of the aulacogens and to extensions of mobile swells, such as Kolvin, Sorokin and Medynski, which are structurally different and unequally frame the Timan–Pechora petroleum region.

Vertically, as a rule, we can see the general trend, when heavy oils, down-section, are replaced with lighter ones and more saturated with gas, while the gases, on the contrary, become heavier with depth and are enriched with heavy hydrocarbons (Anischenko, Krems, & Saar, 1968; Dedeev, 1966). At depths less than 1.2 km one can find only heavy oils; below 1.2 km moderate–heavy oils dominate; at larger depths down to 4.0 km more frequently one can find light oil; and below 4 km there are gas condensates nearly everywhere, while light oils occur more rarely.

The extrapolation of trends related to oil and gas potential three-dimensional localization, which were identified in Pechora onshore, was supported by the discoveries of hydrocarbon deposits in some shelf areas, where the main structural elements of the Pechora lowland can be directly traced. The shelf extension of the Pechora–Kolvin swell is of special interest in terms of prospecting hydrocarbons; up to 40% of explored reserves of oil and 74% of gas were discovered there.

Pomor and North Pomor brachy-anticlines intersect at the extension of the Kolvin swell. The above anticlines were the first local structures prepared for exploration drilling, as far back as the early 1970s. At Pomor anticline the gas pool was penetrated by drilling the Carboniferous deposits. A distinctive feature of that pool is the extremely high content of hydrogen sulfide (up to 8.5%), which obstructs the development of the above pool.

The shelf extension of the ShapkinUryakhinski swell is not so clearly traced. It is linked to the Kolokolmor local high and possibly the Peschanoozernoye high, where the first of the Barents Sea oil pools was discovered in Triassic deposits.

The Peschanoozernoye oilfield is located on the northern coast of Kolguyev Island and is the first structure in the Barents offshore region in which a commercial oil inflow was obtained (Desiatkov, 1993, p. 70). The above structure comprises a dome-shaped fold of small size, which is well-shaped within Triassic deposits, although supposedly the structure is developed from Silurian deposits. The fullest Paleozoic sequence was accessed in the Peschanoozernoye area, with a total thickness comprising 4.5 km. A study of that sequence showed that forming of trap occurred inherently until the end of the Triassic age.

The Sorokin swell extends on the shelf area as a chain of local folds, integrated into the Gulyaev swell. The North Gulyaev, Bolshegulyaev, East Gulyaev and Prirazlomnaya local folds and a group of small domes within the Varandei area are separated within the Gulyaev swell. Oil and gas pools were penetrated by drilling within the Upper Paleozoic deposits in three areas (Varandei-More, Prirazlomnoye and North Gulyayevskaya).

In terms of its structure, the Prirazlomnoye oilfield can be attributed to the northern extension of the Sorokin swell. The trap comprises the brachy-anticline fold, well-shaped along the entire studied sequence, from Silurian to Triassic deposits. The oil pool is confined to porous Lower Carboniferous limestone, occurring at 2,370–2,487 m. The porosity of rocks decreases downward from 23% at the top of the reservoir to 5% at the base. The pool is massive, with bottom water at 2,456 m. Oil is heavy (density – 0.92 g/cm^3), resinous, with high sulfur content, and by its composition is similar to oils from other oilfields on the Sorokin swell.

The most eastern, among the prospecting structural zones of the Pechora lowland, is the Medyn swell, and it was traced on the shelf as a strip comprising a set of local highs. There are other structures on the shelf, like North Dolginskaya, Polyarnaya, Russkaya, Veltov, Sengei, Akvamarin and East Pechora, that do not have express links with II Order positive structures, mentioned above, and which have not been explored through drilling.

Kola–Kanin petroleum region

The Kola–Kanin petroleum region (PR) is the boundary region of a part of the Barents Province structure and can be traced as a long narrow strip along its entire southwest boundary from the Pechora River to Finnmarken. In terms of structure, it comprises a system of monoclines and asymmetric depressions, separating the Barents shelf plate from the slopes of the Baltic anteclise and Timan Ridge. The Kola–Kanin PR in the south includes the Izhma–Pechora depression and the Malozemelskaya monocline, which are separated by the Seduyakhinski–Korgin megaswell. The Kola–Kanin PR also includes the Kola–Kanin monocline, with the Kola swell in the north, and linking with the Finnmarken monocline in the west (Figure 8.1).

This region among other PRs of the Barents Province is characterized by better exploration status, using Common Depth Point (CDP) seismic methods. Synthesis of the above notions was performed, when plotting the tectonic map of the region (Verba & Ivanov, 2009, p. 20).

The Kola–Kanin PR is mainly formed by the Paleozoic sedimentary complexes. In lower horizons, the Tremadorian–Sedvelian and Ordovician–Nibelian series can be identified. Within the Kola shelf, the Paleozoic deposits are underlying as undisturbed upper Riphean–Vendian deposits, and they are partially overlapped by the Mesozoic sedimentary cover. The thickness of sedimentary cover rocks within the PR is rapidly increasing from hundreds of meters in the boundary zone to 6–8 km on the border with the South Barents depression. At the same time, the Upper pre-Cambrian sedimentation mass, comprising here the basement of supracrystal complex, plays an important role in the sequence. Unlike the Kanin peninsula sequences, where the entire rock mass of Neoproterozoic deposits is strongly disturbed, the deposits of that age occurring in the area, surrounding the Rybachi Island, are much less deformed and occur subhorizontally.

The composition of gas extracted from the above rocks indicates the presence of methane and heavy hydrocarbons in the proportion of 3.2:1 (Table 8.1).

Table 8.1 Composition of gases in the pre-Cambrian rocks in the northern part of Kola Peninsula

CH_4	C_2H_6	C_3H_8	C_4H_{10}	C_5H_{12}	He	Ar	Location
76.12	13.25	5.42	3.56	1.62	Not determined	Not determined	Kildin Island. Riphean time
60–70	0.5–1.2	0.005–0.1	–	–	3.8	2.54	Monchegor plutonic intrusions

Hydrocarbon gases, as a rule, accumulate in porous (porosity up to 4%) sandstones, which testifies the migration origin of the above HC.

The prospects of discovering HC deposits relate both to the old mid-Upper Paleozoic depositional complex and (to a lesser extent) to the Triassic complex. In addition, we can consider that along with a gas pool we have the same possibility of discovering the oil pool. Some hopes relate to the possible discovery of reef structures in Upper Devonian–Lower Permian carbonate rocks. The presence of such structures can be revealed based on seismostratigraphic analysis. If we assume (as was mentioned previously) that barrier reefs are positioned in parallel to the continental shelf margin and rim the edge of the deepwater rift-related basin, then one strip of reef structures can be traced along the northern border of the region under consideration, which is broken in locations, where the terrigenous material is intensively withdrawn from the paleoland, while the second strip can be anticipated on the opposite side of the rift-related trough within the limits of the Central Barents high.

Grumant petroleum region

Grumant PR, which in terms of tectonics corresponds to the Svalbard plate, is quite nonuniform: In the west it adjoins the Cenozoic collision belt of West Spitsbergen, while the entire eastern framing is represented by the Barents–North Kara structures. Grumant PR covers the area of Spitsbergen and Franz Joseph Land archipelagos, the Persei underwater high and the adjoining shelf shallow waters, extending to the south as far as Medvezhi Island and Nadezhda Island.

All stratigraphic Neogenic taxons, starting from Upper Riphean to Neogene, with total thickness comprising 7–8 km, are available in the plate sedimentary cover sequence. The sequence of sedimentation mass is separated by the series of nonconformities, and the presence of such nonconformities testifies the repeated activation of the tectonic environment (Harland & Dowdeswell, 1998, p. 122; Verba & Ivanov, 2006, p. 58). The estimation of oil generation potential of that region is nonunique.

The stage of exploration of that region is quite nonuniform. Several wells were drilled within its limits, and shows of different hydrocarbons were encountered in many wells (Table 8.2).

Ideas on the development of oil and gas-bearing deposits of the Grumant possible petroleum region are based on materials related to drilling presented in works by Russian geologists and are well described in Krasilchikov (1996) and in Russian geological studies on Spitsbergen (1962–1996, 1998). Analysis of the acquired data volume shows that oil-and-gas potential indicators were revealed, nearly continuously, in practically all the sedimentation masses of the region under consideration, starting from Late Riphean.

The Devonian terrigenous complex will be the first sedimentary complex, if we look upsection, and its generation potential is considered as regionally tangible.

Oil shows related to that complex cover a large area of the archipelago. They were described at Torell Land in 1971 by L.G. Mukashev and at Andrée

Table 8.2 Oil and gas shows in wells of the Petunia Bay area

Well No	From spud-in to total depth	HC type	HC flowrate	Sediments' age
110	280–780	combustible gas	minor shows	mid-Carboniferous
116	210–25	– " –	bleeding at surface	lower Moscovian stage (30 m from the lower boundary)
	455–470	– " –	– " –	mid-Bashkirian stage
	520–522	– " –	nearly 60 thou. m³/day	– " – (255 m from the top)
116-bis	220–230	– " –	nearly 60 thou. m³/day	lower Moscovian stage (22 m from the lower boundary)
	470–475 (?)	– " –	nearly 130 thou. m³/day	mid-Bashkirian stage (235 m from the top)
	545–550 (?)	– " –	nearly 150 thou. m³/day	mid-Bashkirian stage (305 m from the top)
	590–620	– " –	minor shows	Bashkirian stage (350 m from the top)
	631–?	gas with oil	nearly 0.2 million m³/day	Bashkirian stage (385 m from the top)
117	200–205	combustible gas	minor shows	lower Moscovian stage (22 m from the lower boundary)
	435–443.7	gas	nearly 60 thousand m³/day	Bashkirian stage (212 m from the top)

Source: Based on Verba and Ivanov (2006, p. 58).

Land by Yu. I. Mokin in 1972 (Krasilshchikov, 1996; Russian geological studies on Spitsbergen 1962–1996, 1998), and the most complete observations were performed at Dickson Land. Upper Devonian deposits, accessed here in several wells, drilled in Pyramid mine camp surroundings, are characterized by increased impregnation. So, for example, in the core samples, taken from wells #66, 68, 72, 74 and 76, sandstones saturated with oil were described. The above sandstone builds up the 5–12-m-thick beds. The total thickness of the section saturated with hydrocarbons comprises nearly 120 m. Organic matter from the enriched Devonian rocks was most likely the source of migrated fluids.

Impregnation of Carboniferous deposits was studied in detail in the Bille Fjord area, where numerous HC shows have been encountered. The above shows were encountered in wells, where a jet coring bit was used. Such wells were drilled on both sides of the fjord, in the Mimer River valley (to the west of the fjord) and also on the bank of the Petunja River (to the east of the fjord). The most valuable data was acquired from wells drilled in the area of the Ebba River (Verba & Ivanov, 2006, p. 59).

The properties of Carboniferous reservoirs based on laboratory measurements of porosity and permeability were positive, regardless of the pessimistic forecasts. We could identify four main types of porous-fractured reservoirs (Verba, 2013, p. 4).

The oil and gas generation potential of Carboniferous deposits is largely determined by the presence in the lower part of thick (up to 300 m) rocks enriched with organic matter and coal beds with reliable thickness. The catagenesis stage of organic matter is increasing from west to east, from gas stage in the area of Triungen Town up to bituminous stage in the Pyramid Mine and to coke stage in Gypsdalen. Wet gas in the carbonic rocks of the Pyramid Mine and Petunia Bay corresponds to a higher high-temperature stage of the oil and gas generation stage.

An indication of oil in the Paleogene sandstones was revealed at the Barentsburg Coal Mine in subsurface mine roadways and at Lailen, Grumant and Coalsbay sections in the coal exploration holes. Gas shows, apart from those areas mentioned above, were also identified at Sars Cape, in a deep well on the northern bank of Van Mijen Fjord and as gas seepage at Serkap Land. At Geer Cape near Barentsburg, solid, wicked lenticular kerite was encountered in Paleogene rocks.

Oil and gas shows have been observed in 15% of coal exploration wells, where a jet coring bit was used. The total number of such wells exceeded 300. Flares at wellheads sometimes burnt for several days. The most impressive oil show was observed at Well.561 at Lailen area in September 1988. The pool was penetrated at 238 m from spud-in, 56 m upsection from the bottom of the Barentsburg strata, and confined to porous sandstone interbed. The bottom of permafrost rocks could be the structural seal for the pool according to indirect data and geothermal observations in the well. Formation pressure has not been measured, but it provided a wellspring of oil, and the estimated flowrate comprised 6–8 tons/day; short-term gas bursts were also encountered.

Crude oil comprised brown (with greenish cast) liquid, which rapidly solidified in the case of a temperature drop. In terms of its composition, it was attributed to light oils, naphtheno-paraffin base crude, low tar and low paraffin. Crude oils, similar in their composition, are seeping from the Barentsburg strata in the mine driveway of Barentsburg Mine. Their flowrate comprises 30 l/day.

The composition of Paleogenic crude oil and its IR spectrum is nearly equal to crudes from Lower Triassic deposits at Kolguyev Island. Based on the results of liquid chromatography, Paleogenic crudes are equal to crudes from mid-Triassic clay rocks from Edge Island. Since the permafrost plays an important role in localizing the oil pool at Lailen area, then the migration process, which started in the Neogene period, continued nearly to the Holocene.

Summarizing the statements from above, we should highlight that deposits capable of generating HC were identified within the wide stratigraphic range – from Upper Riphean to Paleogene, while the rock masses with the greatest prospects are confined to the Upper Devonian – Lower Carboniferous, Lower Permian, Lower-mid Triassic and Upper Jurassic – Lower Cretaceous deposits. However, the contribution of those complexes differs in different parts of a region.

If we spread the above statements to the adjoining, unexplored in terms of petroleum geology, aquatic areas of the Spitsbergen shelf, then we can conclude that the most promising in terms of oil generation are the westernmost, peri-oceanic zone of PR and some central zones, like the Olgin trough, where the post-Cretaceous downwarping was as strong (based on morphological data) as in previous periods.

A special position in that part of the Svalbard "platform" is occupied by its utmost northern strip, which adjoins with the deepwater Nansen basin. A series of dome-shaped structures was identified here at suboceanic depths (up to 2,000–3,000 m) in one of the rift-related troughs of the Arctic Ocean (Brusilov Trough) by applying different geophysical methods (Verba, Astafuriva, Leonov, Mandrikov, & Khlyupin, 2004, p. 172). The above structures, based on petrophysical data, acquired at FJL, as well as geothermal data (Verba, Verba, Ivanov, & Hutorskoy, 2009, p. 30), were interpreted as diapir folds (or crypto-diapir), formed by halogenic units. The presence of structures with saline domes in that part of the region allows us to reconsider the perspective of the oil and gas potential of the entire Eurasia Continental Margin.

Prinovozemelskaya possibly petroleum region

The Prinovozemelskaya possibly petroleum region (PPR) is a heterogenous region, covering the strip of the shelf, adjacent to the Novaya Zemlya archipelago from the west, and including the geologically different Admiralteiskoye high, Sedov trough, Mezhdushar monocline and Korotaikhin trough (Figure 8.1). The length of the above PPR comprises nearly 1,200 km, and the width, less than 150 km. The region under consideration can be clearly divided into two parts: the south part (Korotaikhin) extends in a northwest direction and adjoins the Pai-Khoi–South Novozemelsky section of the strip of Early Cimmerian folds; the second, northern part (Sedov) of the PPR extends along another section of the Novozemelskaya strip of folds, which extends to the northeast and is characterized by moderate infolded deformations. The interface between the above parts of the PPR is located opposite the Karmakul trough, which is formed by the Permian deposits, even less deformed than in the northern part of Novaya Zemlya.

Paleozoic rocks of the Novaya Zemlya archipelago were studied in terms of petroleum geology as far back as the 1930s. B. A. Klubov summarized the studies (Klubov, 1983, p. 15). Within the limits of the above PPR, no oil or gas accumulations have been identified. However, the acquired data testifies to the rather high probability of their discovery in the Admiralteiski swell. On oil and gas potential maps, that region corresponds to an aquatic area with a density of predicted resources up to 30–50 thousand t/km^2 in the zones that are the most favorable for oil and gas accumulation.

The main potentially productive rock masses within the shelf's geological section under consideration are the Ludlov, Devonian and Lower Carboniferous carbonate rocks. Therefore, the identified mineral tars are mainly secondary; moreover, it is most likely that the migration occurred in at least two stages.

A high degree of metamorphism of organic matter (semianthracitous stage, apocatagenesis), most likely, is stipulated by intensive tectonic stresses that earlier accompanied the Mesozoic orogenesis. In other regions of the Barents–Kara Area there is much less organic matter maturation.

Therefore, orogenesis at the Prinovozemelsky shelf is exhibited much less, and organic matter, even in old mid-Paleozoic rocks, still keeps its oil and gas generation properties.

The above statements may be used for an approximate estimate of possible oil and gas discoveries within the Prinovozemelskaya zone of boundary structures, located on the shelf in the vicinity of the Novaya Zemlya shore. Within local structures, such as Pankratiev, Blednaya and Inostrantseva, identified in the North of Prinovozemelski shelf, most likely, the most prospective rock masses will be mid-Paleozoic deposits. The possibility of discovering petroleum deposits at such heights as Litke High, East Krestovski, Sulmenev, Martyushen, Gusinozemelski, West-Novozemelski and Mezhdusharski, located in the Sedov trough and on the Mezhdushar monocline, is estimated as more limited. Moreover, most likely, the carbonate reservoirs within the Carboniferous deposits are the most promising. Overlying terrigenous Permian deposits seem to be less promising.

On local heights, such as Krestov, Admiralteiskoye and Pakhtusov, most likely the mid- and Upper Paleozoic carbonate complex will be the most promising.

Promising regions of the Barents–North Kara megatrough

Central Barents possibly petroleum region

The region under consideration is – in terms of its geological section attitude and abyssal structure and, probably, based on the main features of its oil and gas potential (not identified yet) – close to the peripheral regions of the Barents Sea petroleum basin, which was considered above (Paleozoic terrigenous–carbonate rock masses play a key role in their structure). However, spatially, the region under consideration is fully inside the Barents–North Kara megatrough and therefore should formally be considered as a part of that subprovince.

The similarity of geological sections and abyssal structure of the Central Barents terrain and two platform blocks on both sides of the BNKMT is confirmed by the results of physical field acquisitions and previously compiled paleogeological images. Grounds for such imaging (presented earlier) are based on the assumption that there is a large oceanic geological structure in the West Arctic region and, within the limits of that structure, during the second half of the Paleozoic period, the continental crust stress and the forming of a rift-related megatrough (BNKMT) with a subcontinental or suboceanic type of Earth crust took place (Verba & Sakulina, 1999, p. 89).

Dip-corrected mapping, performed on the basis of this concept, demonstrates that, based on the magnetic field behavior, the Central Barents anticline (CBA) does not differ from regions comprising the eastern framing of the BNKMT. Based on the results of paleomagnetic studies, the position of the CBA was restored within the system of adjoining structures of the Barents Sea region and at the moment precedes the forming of the BNKMT (Verba & Sakoulina, 1999, p. 90). The importance of the above works is that (in particular) they could substantiate the infeasibility of tracing through the central part of the Barents Sea buried caledonite legs using the model, as was suggested prior to the commencement of the shelf geophysical study and repeated in 2004 by D. Gee (Gee & Pease, 2004).

For known reasons, the abovementioned area of the Barents shelf is still a frontier one. An exception to that is the regional reference seismic line 1-AR, which highlighted the structure of the eastern part of the above area (Verba et al., 2001, p. 6). On the presented portion of that seismic line, one can see that along the cross-section, together with Mesozoic rocks typical for the Barents–North Kara megatrough, there are also Paleozoic rocks, which, as previously mentioned, are common to the Timan–Pechora and Spitsbergen regions of the Barents Sea petroleum province.

In terms of structure, the abovementioned area pertains to the Central Barents block (terrain), and its structure is stipulated by the Demidov aulacogen, which is analogous to the Pechora Kolvin aulacogen (Denisov rift-related trough) on the Timan–Pechora trough and to the Andree Dickson aulacogen on Spitsbergen.

A characteristic feature of the aulacogen is the presence of large anticline highs on its western and eastern flanks in Mesozoic deposits. One high is called the Fedynsky dome, and the other, the Fersman dome. The uniformity of the common tectonic position of the Denisov, Demidov and Andree Dickson aulacogens was mentioned in several works (Verba, Daragan-Sushchova, & Pavlenkin, 1992, p. 755), thus enabling their probably similar oil and gas potentials to be mentioned.

South Barents petroleum region

The shelf of the southern part of the Barents Sea at present is an area where the most intensive petroleum exploration activities are held. By now more than three dozen local structures and four gas fields (gravitating toward the depression flanks) have been discovered in the South Barents petroleum region. Even the first well, named Sevmorgeo-1 (drilled in 1983), became a high-performance one. It was on the high and later was called the Murmanskaya Well. Subsequently, gas pools were discovered at the North Kildin and Ludlov areas, and huge gas deposits were discovered at the Shtokman area.

The potential for oil and gas generation in the South Barents PR sedimentary sequence can only be characterized based on the well logs of wells that were drilled here and penetrated the Mesozoic bodies. Underlying deposits, which may play the most important role in terms of HC accumulations in the Mesozoic strata, have not been explored yet by drilling within the limits of the depression and, therefore, the extrapolation of data from depression framing cannot be accurately fulfilled.

Data on offshore wells were published at different times. The results of the studies demonstrate that within the studied section we can see a regular increase of organic matter concentration upsection, from basis points in the Lower Triassic, up to 1.5% (and more) in the mid- and Upper Jurassic and Lower Cretaceous.

The Murmansk field comprises a flat-lying dome-shaped fold with an area of nearly 150 sq km, and the horizontal offset amplitude in the top of the Triassic deposits comprises about 110 m. Gas pools were discovered in all Triassic series and confined to beds of deltaic sandstones and siltstones, which vary strongly in the strike. Gas pools are sheet type, roof type and massive. Regarding different formation productivity: flowrates from the Upper Triassic comprise above 100 thousand m^3/day (Well #22 – 144 thousand m^3/day), from the mid-Triassic – the flowrate is nearly the same (Well #24 – 130 thousand m^3/day), and from the Lower Triassic – much more (Well #24 – up to 740 thousand m^3/day). The gas is dry.

While drilling in the Kurentsov area and penetrating the mid-Triassic deposits, increased gas indications were encountered; however, the beds, highlighted by logging, were not tested.

At the North Kildin structure, an influx of methane gas was obtained from the Lower Triassic in Well #80. Its flowrate comprised 369 thousand m^3/d.

The Shtokman gas condensate field is the largest on the Barents shelf. It was discovered in 1988. The field consists of a large dome-shaped fold within the Jurassic–Cretaceous deposits, with an area comprising nearly 800 km^2 and with amplitude of nearly 200 m.

The lateral trend of changing the oil and gas potential of the sequence is clearly visible in Table 8.3, which is compiled based on data from two neighboring regions – West Barents and Pechora. The table shows that the revealed regular "rejuvenating" of the pay zone in the Pechora PR extends further in a northwest direction up to the Shtokman field. At the same time, oil in the hydrocarbon composition is gradually replaced by the gas and gas condensate. Such a relationship allows us to suppose the possible widespread development of petroleum accumulations within the Jurassic and Lower Cretaceous sections to the north of the Barents Sea.

North Barents petroleum region

Distinguished as a separate region, the North Barents PR shares many common features with the South Barents PR and together with it represents the central,

Table 8.3 Distribution of oil and gas deposits of the Barents Province by depth of burial

Occurrence depth (m)	Pool Occurrence Probability (%)					
	Pechora PR				W. Barents PR	
	West Part		Central Part		oil	gas
	oil	gas	oil	gas		
100–500	13	11	–	–		
501–900	17	54	–	–		
901–1300	24	11	4	7		
1300–1700	11	–	16	–		
1700–2100	15	4	12	62		
2101–2500	11	4	20	31	12	23
2501–2900	9	4	4	–	62	46
2901–3300	–	11	20	–	12	–
301–3700	–	–	20	–	–	–
3701–4100	–	–	4	–	–	–
4101–4500	–	–	–	–	–	–
4501–4900	–	–	–	–	12	8
4901–5300	–	–	–	–	–	15
Number of pools	46	26	25	13	8	13

most submerged part of the BNKMT. The interface between these two regions goes across the Ludlov Saddle.

Within the North Barents depression cross-section (total thickness estimated as 14–16 km), the dominant role is played by the rocks of the Permian and Triassic periods, which build up thick (6–7 km) avandeltaic rock masses with a clear clinoform structure and which are overlapped by the less thick Jurassic–Cretaceous cover. The cover is represented by normal-shelf horizontally stratified facies.

There is a wildcat well at the Lunin area, which was suspended with a bottomhole at 1,405 m in the Upper Jurassic bituminous clay. Small gas pools in the Aptian sandstones at a depth not exceeding 1,000 m were identified in that well. This testifies that, apart from Jurassic deposits, some perspectives may be related to Lower Cretaceous sand strata.

Drilling at the Ludlov area yielded more weighty results. In 1990 a large gas condensate deposit was discovered in the mid-Callovian and Kimmerian–Oxford sandstones. The thickness of sandstones reached 85 m (pay zone is J0 analogous to the Shtokman field). As a result of testing, the gas influx was obtained with a flowrate comprising nearly 500 thousand m^3/d. The gas is methane, low nitrogen, with no sulfur.

The well has penetrated one of the abovementioned "bright" seismic horizons, which was compared with fluids from underwater discharges (Ivanov, Kholmyansky, Shkatov, Kazanin, & Pavlov, 2013, p. 255). The above comparison showed that the rock body, intersected by the well, was built up by the Irish touchstone with an amygdaloidal structure, and this smoothly corresponded with the moderate deepwater environment, where the underwater discharge of Irish touchstone took place. The age of the Irish touchstone on the basis of the K-Ar dating method comprises 131 and 159 Ma (Komarnitsky, Sapozhnikov, & Ustinov, 1993, p. 60).

Two wells were drilled in 1990–1992 in the Ledovaya area at the southern and northern domes. Hydrocarbon accumulations were penetrated in the mid-Jurassic (beds J_0, J_1 – gas, J_2 – gas condensate). As a result of J1 testing, an influx of gas was obtained with a flowrate exceeding 400 m^3/day.

The North Barents PR northeastern blocks of the northern margin are in some way similar to the Izhma Pechora structures of the Timan–Pechora area, which allows the predictive assessment of this poorly studied northern margin of the Barents Sea to improve seriously.

East Barents petroleum region

It is the furthest distance from the mainland area of the Barents Sea petroleum basin, located to the east of the Vilchevskaya saddle, and it remains the most poorly explored part of the aquatic area. Apart from regional gravimetric data, acquired as far back as the 1970s and 1980s, the PR was explored in the southern part, using a CDP seismic reflection method, and therefore appropriate seismic lines were acquired. One such line – 4-AR – is attributed to reference lines (Ivanov, Goncharov, Presolov, Gorbanko, & Krasnyuk, 2009, p. 303; Ivanov, 2011, p. 894; Ivanov et al., 2011, p. 894; Ivanov et al., 2013, p. 257), as shown in Figure 8.2. Available data suggest that structural and compositional

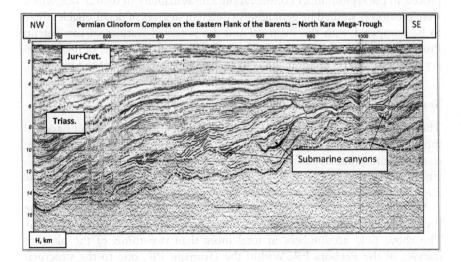

Figure 8.2 Part of geological–geophysical section of the AR-4 seismic line

complexes of sedimentary cover, identified within the North Barents PR, are extending in an easterly direction. In the case of no deep wells and the absence of key sections on the onshore part of the island, we can suppose that the sedimentary cover structure of this aquatic area will be stipulated by the Mesozoic terrigenous deposits, and their thickness based on the CDP reflection method data may comprise 6–9 km. A comparison of the available seismic sections with the cross-section of the three Mesozoic depressions, reviewed above – which together with the East Barents PR constitute the single structure of the rift-related Barents–North Kara trough – favors such a supposition.

Geochemical studies focusing on the seafloor sediments of St. Ann trench have been carried out and have revealed some indications of gaseous HC (Ivanov et al., 2011, p. 44). Geochemical data complete with geothermal data from M.D. Khutorskoi regarding the Orel trench show the activity of the present-day migration of HC gases and constitute the indirect indicator of available HC accumulations in the subsoil. Aside from that, being a part of a single geological structure means that in principle all parts of the downwarping areas of the BNKMT have similar oil and gas potential features. Based on this assumption, we can anticipate commercial HC deposits within the Jurassic- and Upper Triassic strata of the sequence.

Concluding remarks

General trends of oil and gas potential

Information regarding the oil and gas potential indications in different areas of the Barents Province (regardless of their incompleteness) allows some conclusions to be reached on the spatial–temporal trends of the oil and gas generation process in the region under consideration. The availability of such trends, which were previously studied by geologists in different degrees of detail, enables them to be compared with the main oil and gas potential features of the Barents Province and, based on that comparison, an estimate to be made of the discovery prospects of HC accumulations in as yet unexplored areas of the region.

Spatial pattern of distribution of oil and gas potential attributes

The lateral distribution of HC deposits, just as in other petroleum basins, is subject to quite clear tectonic control, which exhibits regular change of average reserves density, balance of oil and gas, oil composition and number of pools within the section (Kazanin, Shkarubo, Zayats, & Pavlov, 2014, p. 12; Kazanin, Zayats, Shkarubo, Pavlov, & Kirillova–Pokrovskaya, 2011, p. 97).

As previously mentioned, the above trend is clear through the example of the Pechora Kolvin aulacogen, along which the chain of petroleum fields is located. The above field accumulates in total more than two-thirds of the ultimate reserves of the Pechora PR. Within the Grumant PR, due to the structural heterogeneity of that region, the bilateral symmetry of the locations of oil and bitumen shows is exhibited very weakly; however, even in that case one can see their confinement to the flanks of the West Spitsbergen trough. Oil pools were not identified in the South Barents gas region, while the gas and gas condensate pools are gravitating to the peripheral zones.

The second important finding, resulting from the analysis of the deposits' lateral distribution, lies in the narrowed stratigraphic range of oil and gas potential within the axial zones of the sedimentary basins, and, at the same time, the pay deposits are "rejuvenating". This trend was analyzed above through the example of the Pechora, West Barents and Grumant PRs.

Clarification of pools' distribution by depth is quite complicated due to the different representation of the available data and due to the nonuniform exploration degree of different regions and areas. At the same time, it becomes clear at a first approximation that there is a trend of downward shift of oil and gas pools' maximum development zone within the rift-related depression compared with the adjacent stable blocks. That trend can be noticed both in the distribution of gas pools and, to a lesser extent, in those of oil pools. In all reviewed cases, oil pools could be found within a wider range of depths than gas pools. Through the example of the Pechora plate, A. Ya. Krems noted that, for the Upper Pechora River, the clear vertical zoning of the oil and gas show is indicative: higher than 1,300 m – heavy oils (very often with dry gas), 1,300–3,200 m – light oils and gas condensate, and below 3,200 m – gas condensates, very seldom with heavy residual oil. Within the West Barents region, the majority of identified pools, both gas and oil, regardless of enclosing deposits, are located within the narrow range of depths from 2,500 m to 2,900 m (see also Table 8.3).

This data testifies to a tough thermobaric environment for hydrocarbon accumulations in the rift-related downwarps, and, on the contrary, relatively soft

Table 8.4 Stratigraphic confinement of HC pools on the Barents shelf

Age of deposits (system, series)		Shtokman (1988)	Murm-ansk (1983)	Kurent-sov	Pescha-nozersk (1979)	North Gulyaev (1986)	Pomor (1935)	Priraz-lomnoye (1989)
Jurassic	Mid-Upper	gas-condensate	–	–	–	–	–	–
	Lower	–	–	–	–	–	–	–
Triassic	Upper	–	gas	–	–	–	–	–
	Mid	–	gas	gas	–	–	–	–
	Lower	–	gas	–	oil	–	–	–
Permian	Upper	–	–	–	gas	oil	–	–
	Lower	–	–	–	–	–	gas	–
Carboni-ferous	Upper	–	–	–	oil	–	condensate	–
	Mid	–	–	–	–	–	–	–
	Lower	–	–	–	–	gas-con-densate	–	oil

limitations in terms of thermal regime and pressure in the peripheral regions of the province. Since that peculiarity of HC accumulations distribution is well correlated with geothermal field parameters, one can conclude that, in the general case, the magnitude of registered heat transfer is directly linked to the depth of the main oil and gas accumulation zone, while the current geothermal gradient is inversely linked to the average (for the region) height of the oil and gas column.

Therefore, for regions where the available data allow particular judgment to be exercised, one can observe the common regular gravitation of oil pools to the regional structure periphery, while the gas pools, and specially the gas condensate pools, are gravitating to the near-axial zones. When comparing with tectonic elements, such trend looks like the confinement of gas condensate pools to zones of clear exposed rifting, while the oil pools are confined to postreef downwarps and depressions. That trend is exhibited both on the scale of 1 Order structures (sineclises, downwarps) and on the scale of the entire province.

Stages of petroleum generation

The identification of temporal trends within the oil and gas generation processes is the most complicated task, since the direct indications of migration age are small in number, while the indirect indications are not always convincing. However, the aforementioned data regarding the separate regions of the province enable us to conclude that priority in forming the most convincing indications of the oil and gas potential of its sedimentary rock masses belongs to the youngest migration stage, which in the area of consideration does not coincide in time with the Alpine epoch of tectogenesis.

We also want to add that, according to messages from Norwegian geologists, the Cenozoic uplift processes exerted the key influence on forming the oil and gas fields in the western part of the Barents Sea. Uplift means the elevation of the territory, which in our case took place in two stages. Analysis of the radioactive element decay track in apatite grains enabled the first phase to be dated as 40–60 Ma, while the second phase was dated as 5–15 Ma; moreover, to the north of the explored areas, in the direction of Spitsbergen, the above phases merged into one.

Indirect indication of the young age of migration can be found in the materials of geothermal studies. As previously mentioned, one can observe a satisfactory coincidence of present-day thermal anomalies with zones of oil and gas accumulation, which can be explained by the availability of the cause-and-effect relationship of such events.

To complete the review of general trends of the spatial–temporal distribution of direct oil and gas potential indicators, we can conclude that even the availability of such trends can strongly testify to the identification of all its structures to one integral oil- and gas-bearing province. This relates to the vertical distribution of the main oil- and gas-bearing rock mass, controlled by the sedimentation factor. It also relates to the lateral zoning of oil and gas accumulation, which is determined by the tectonic factor; in addition, it is associated with naftidogenesis staging, linked to shows of geodynamic processes, which are common to the entire region.

Note

1 In regard to the geological zoning of the Barents Sea oilfields, in general, Russian and Norwegian researchers have not yet reached a consensus; each country tries to highlight its own province, which, to some extent, is reasonable, but in this case, while surveying is taking place and HC resources are being developed, a vast area of the Barents Sea may become a conglomerate, consisting of a dozen provinces.

References

Anischenko, L.A., Krems, A. Ya., & Saar, D.A. (1968). Закономерности размещения нефтегазовых месторождений и пространственных изменений свойств нефтей на территории Тимано-Печорского бассейна [Distribution of oil and gas fields and spatial variations of oil properties in the Timan–Pechora basin]. *Geologiya Nefti i Gaza, 10*, 34–42.

Belonin, M.D., Prischepa, O.M., Teplov, E.L., Budanov, G.F., & Danilevsky, S.A. (2004). *Тимано-Печорская провинция: геологическое строение, нефтегазоносность и перспективы освоения* [Timan–Pechora province: Geology, petroleum potential and prospects of development]. St. Petersburg, Russia: Nedra.

Borovinskikh, A.P. (2003). Геодинамика и нефтегазоносность (на примере Тимано-Печорского НГБ и смежного арктического шельфа) [Geodynamics and petroleum potential (using the example of the Timan–Pechora petroleum basin and the adjacent Arctic shelf)]. In M. Belonin (Ed.), *Актуальные научно-технические проблемы раз-вития геолого-геофизических и поисковых работ на нефть и газ в республике Коми* [Current scientific and technical problems of geological, geophysical and prospecting works for oil and gas in the Komi Republic] (pp. 8–40). Ukhta, Russia: Kolskoye regionalnoye otdeleniye (RAEN).

Dedeev, V.A. (1966). *Геология и перспективы нефтегазоносности северной части Тимано-Печорской области* [Geology and petroleum potential of the northern part of the Timan–Pechora region]. Leningrad, the Soviet Union: Nedra.

Desiatkov, V.M. (1993). Историко-геологические аспекты освоения острова Колгуев [Historical and geological aspects of Kolguev Island development]. In I. Gramberg (Ed.), *Нефтегазоносность Баренцево-Карского шельфа (по материалам бурения на море и островах)* [Petroleum potential of the Barents–Kara shelf (based on the offshore and islands drilling data)] (pp. 70–74). Saint Petersburg, Russia:VNIIOkeangeologia.

Gee, D.G., & Pease, V. (Eds.). (2004). *The Neoproterozoic Timanide Orogen of Eastern Baltica.* Bath, England: Geological Society of London.

Gramberg, I.S. (1997). Баренцевоморский пермо-триасовый палеорифт и его значение для проблемы нефтегазоносности Баренцево-Карской плиты [The Barents Sea Permian-Triassic paleo-rift and its significance for the problem of Barents–Kara plate oil and gas potential]. *Doklady Akademii Nauk (DAN), Russia, 352*(6), 789–791.

Harland, W.B., & Dowdeswell, E.K. (1988). *Geological evolution of the Barents shelf region.* London, England: Graham & Trotman.

Ivanov, G.I. (2011). Комплексная геохимическая съемка для зонального прогноза нефтегазоносности Гыданской и Юрацкой губ (Карское море) [A complex geochemical survey for forecasting the oil and gas potential of the Gydanskii and Yuratskii Bays of the Kara Sea]. *Okeanologiya, 51*(5), 891–895.

Ivanov, G.I., Goncharov, A.V., Gavrilov, A.E., Krasnyuk, A.D., Rybalko, A.E., Smirnova, E.V., . . . Gorbenko, E. I. (2011). Оценка перспектив нефтегазоносности Гыданской губы по результатам комплексной геохимической съемки [Assessment of oil-gas prospecting of the Gydanskii Bay on the multidisciplinary geochemical survey results]. *Razvedka i Okhrana Nedr, 10*, 39–43.

Ivanov, G.I., Goncharov, A.V., Presolov, E.M., Gorbanko, E.I., & Krasnyuk, A.D. (2009). Региональные газогеохимические работы на арктических геотраверсах [Regional gas geochemical study on Arctic geotransacts]. In D. Mirzoev (Ed.), *Труды 9-й Международной конференции по освоению ресурсов нефти и газа Российской Арктики и континентального шельфа стран СНГ (RAO/CIS Offshore 2009)* [Proceedings of the 9th International Conference on the development of oil and gas resources of the Russian Arctic and CIS Continental Shelf (RAO / CIS Offshore 2009)], Vol. 2 (pp. 299–304). Saint Petersburg, Russia: Himizdat.

Ivanov, G.I., Kholmyansky, M.A., Shkatov, M. Yu., Kazanin, G.S., & Pavlov, S.P. (2013). Эндогенные источники поступления нефтяных углеводородов в придонную экосистему и технологии их исследования [Endogenetic sources of oil hydrocarbons entry into bottom ecosystems and technology of their study]. *Zapiski Gornogo Instituta Saint Petersburga, 201*, 253–261.

Kazanin, G.S., Shkarubo, S.I., Zayats, I.V., & Pavlov, S.P. (2014). Новые данные о геологическом строении и нефтегазоносности российского шельфа [New data on the geological structure and petroleum potential of the Russian shelf]. *Razvedka i Okhrana Nedr, 4*, 7–13.

Kazanin, G.S., Zayats, I.V., Shkarubo, S.I., Pavlov, S.P., & Kirillova-Pokrovskaya, T.A. (2011). Региональные сейсморазведочные работы в арктических морях – основные результаты нового этапа и дальнейшие перспективы [Regional seismic surveys in the Arctic seas – the main results of a new phase and the future prospects]. *Geologiya Nefti i Gaza, 6*, 90–98.

Khain, V.E. (Ed.). (1978). *Тектоника Европы и смежных областей. Древние платформы, байкалиды, каледониды. (Объяснительная записка к международной тектонической карте Европы и смежных областей масштаба 1:2500000)* [Tectonics of Europe and adjacent areas. Ancient platforms, Baikalides, Caledonides. (Explanatory note to the International Tectonic Map of Europe and adjacent areas, scale 1:2,500,000)]. Moscow, the Soviet Union: Nauka.

Klubov, B.A. (1983). *Природные битумы Севера* [Natural bitumens of the North]. Moscow, the Soviet Union: Nauka.

Komarnitsky, V.M., Sapozhnikov, E.A., & Ustinov, N.V. (1993). Трапповые тела в осадочной толще Восточно-Баренцевского мегапрогиба [Trap bodies in the sediments of the East Barents megatrough]. In V. Komarnitsky (Ed.), *Нефтегазоносность Баренцево-Карского шельфа (по материалам бурения на море и островах)* [Petroleum potential of the Barents–Kara shelf (based on the offshore and islands drilling data)] (pp. 55–63). Saint Petersburg, Russia: Roskomnedra.

Krasilshchikov, A.A. (Ed.). (1996). Soviet geological research in Svalbard 1962–1992. Extended abstracts of unpublished reports [Abstract]. *Meddelelser, 139*, 103.

Makarevich, V.N., Prischepa, O.M., Otmas, A.A., & Popov, S. Yu. (2000). Тектонические закономерности нефтегазоносности платформенных структур [Tectonic regularities of petroleum potential of platform structures]. In O. Prischepa (Ed.), *Блоковое строение земной коры и нефте-газоносность* [Block structure of the earth crust and petroleum potential] (pp. 76–81). Saint Petersburg, Russia:VNIGRI.

Malyshev, N.A., Nikishin, A.M., & Drachev, S.S. (2010). Тектоническая история осадочных бассейнов российских арктических шельфов и сопредельной суши/Тектоника и геодинамика складчатых поясов и платформ фанерозоя [Tectonic history of sedimentary basins of the Russian shelves and adjacent land/Tectonics and geodynamics of folded belts and platforms of Phanerozoic time]. *GEOS, 2,* 19–23.

[Russian geological studies on Spitsbergen 1962–1996] *Российские геологические исследования на Шпицбергене 1962–1996 годов.* (1998). Saint Petersburg, Russia: PMGRE,VNIIOkeangeologia.

Stoupakova, A.V. (2011). Структура и Нефтегазоносность Баренцево-Карского шельфа и прилегающих территории [Structure and HC potential of the Barents–Kara shelf and adjacent territories]. *Geologiya Nefti i Gaza, 6,* 99–115.

Stoupakova, A.V., Henriksen, E., Burlin, Yu. K., Larsen, G.B., Milne, J.K., Kiryukhina, T.A., … Suslova, A.A. (2011). The geological evolution and hydrocarbon potential of the Barents and Kara shelves. *Geological Society, London, Memoirs, 35*(1), 325–344. doi: 10.1144/M35.21

Verba, M.L. (2013). Коллекторные свойства пород осадочного чехла архипелага Шпицберген [Collector properties of the rocks of the sedimentary cover of the Spitsbergen archipelago]. *Neftegazovaya Geologiya. Teoriya i Praktika, 8*(1), 1–45.

Verba, M.L., Daragan-Sushchova, L.A., & Pavlenkin, A.D. (1992). Riftogenic structures of the western Arctic shelf investigated by refraction surveys. *International Geology Review, 34*(8), 753–764. doi: 10.1080/00206819209465634

Verba, M.L., & Ivanov, G.I. (2006). Есть ли нефть и газ на Шпицбергене [Is there oil and gas on Spitsbergen?]. *Neft Rossii, 11,* 56–59.

Verba, M.L., & Ivanov, G.I. (2009). Тектоническая карта Баренцево-Карского региона масштаба 1:2500 000: нефтегеологический и геоэкологический прогноз [Tectonic map of the Barents–Kara region, scale 1: 2,500,000: Oil geological and geo-ecological forecast]. Saint Petersburg: *KHIMIZDAT, 1,* 19–23.

Verba, M.L., Ivanova, N.M., Katsev, V.A., Roslov, Yu.V., Sakulina, T.S., & Telegin, A.N. (2001). Результаты сейсмических исследований по опорным профилям АР-1 и АР-2 в Баренцевом и Карском морях [The results of the seismic surveys on the AP-1 and AP-2 reference profiles in the Barents and Kara Seas]. *Razvedka i Okhrana Nedr, 10,* 3–7.

Verba, M.L., & Sakoulina, T.S. (1999). The reconstruction of the Early Paleozoic structure of the Barents Sea sedimentary basin inferred from geophysical surveys along Profile I-AR. *Polarforschung, 69,* 85–94.

Verba, V.V., Astafuriva, E.G., Leonov, V.O., Mandrikov, V.S., & Khlyupin, N.I. (2004). Строение северной континентальной окраины Баренцевского шельфа в районе Земли Франца Иосифа [The structure of the northern continental margin of the Barents shelf in the area of Franz Josef Land]. In V. Ivanov (Ed.), *Геолого-геофизическая характеристика литосферы Арктического региона вып. 5 (труды ВНИИОкеангеология, т. 204)* [Geological and geophysical characteristics of the lithosphere in the Arctic region, issue 5 (VNIIOkeangeologia proceedings, vol. 204)] (pp. 169–176). Saint Petersburg, Russia: VNIIOkeangeologia.

Verba, V.V., Verba, M.L., Ivanov, G.I., & Hutorskoy, M.D. (2009). Галогенные толщи в разрезе рифто-генных прогибов Арктических морей по геофизическим и геотермическим данным [Halogen strata in the profile of rift troughs of Arctic seas, using geophysical and geothermal data]. In D. Mirzoev (Ed.), *Труды 9-й Международной конференции и выставки по освоению ресурсов нефти и газа Российской Арктики и континентального шельфа стран СНГ (RAO-CIS Offshore 2009)* [Proceedings of the 9th International Conference and Exhibition for the Development of Oil and Gas Resources of the Russian Arctic and CIS Continental Shelf, 2009] (pp. 33–36). Saint Petersburg, Russia: KHIMIZDAT.

9 Barents Sea hydrocarbon resource base and production potential

Anatoly Zolotukhin, Anton Sungurov, and
Vlada Streletskaya

Introduction

The Arctic continental shelf is believed to be the area with the highest unexplored potential for oil and gas as well as for unconventional hydrocarbon resources such as gas hydrates. The region has potential as a future energy supply base.

The Russian part is recognized to be the largest among the oil and gas resources owned by Arctic nations. However, scarce information and available geological data create uncertainty regarding the Russian Arctic's future role as a main base for energy supply in the second part of the twenty-first century. A further uncertainty is the pace at which production from northern areas, including the Arctic, will be brought on stream – either because of national policy, infrastructure development, or investment by the state and the oil companies. These areas embrace those where development has already begun (offshore Sakhalin, Pechora Sea, Yamal Peninsula) and those awaiting future involvement, like the Barents and Pechora Seas, Kara Sea, East Siberia, near Yamal shelf, and Far East (Zolotukhin, 2014, p. 69).

Challenges associated with the development of Arctic oil and gas resources (severe climate, presence of ice, high cost, undeveloped infrastructure, low exploration status, often lack of technology and appropriate equipment, shortage of qualified personnel, environmental issues, logistics, etc.) together with geopolitical issues present real and potential threats to the development of the oil and gas fields located in the Arctic.

However, future tremendous opportunities to extract, transport, and consume vast Arctic petroleum resources are driving forces to stimulate the development of domestic and international petroleum industries and their active collaboration.

Active involvement of the Russian Arctic resources in the global energy supply process needs a clear understanding of the market potential for Russian gas and oil (required volumes, time frame, transportation routes) and requires the government's close attention to the most important issues that should be in place.

The future role of the Arctic region should be further understood, and its resources should be further explored and assessed. There is no doubt that, in the second part of the twenty-first century, production of hydrocarbons (HC) in the Arctic petroleum megabasin will be as important for energy supply as the Persian Gulf and West Siberia basins are today.

This chapter gives an overview on hydrocarbon resources allocated in the Russian and Norwegian part of the Barents Sea and shows existing opportunities for a joint development of one of the richest petroleum megabasins in the world.

Petroleum resources of the Great Barents Sea

There is a common view that the shelves of the Barents, Kara, and Pechora Seas are considered as the most prospective areas for offshore oil and gas field development. With nearly 31 billion tons of oil equivalent (btoe) of oil and gas resources (see Figure 9.1) (ca. 223 billion barrels of oil equivalent [Bboe]), the Barents and Pechora Seas represent one of the most attractive areas for petroleum resources development.

Figure 9.1 Barents Sea fields and some of the prospective structures

Source: Based on Storvik & Co AS (2013).

So far, two gas-condensate fields – Shtokman and Ledovoye – and three gas fields – Ludlovskoye, Murmanskoye, and Severo–Kildinskoye – have been discovered in the Barents Sea. Potentially interesting structures have been detected in the Fersman–Demidov shoulder, the Shatsky and Vernadsky swells, and also in the area of the Medvezhy and Admiralteisky swells (Zolotukhin & Gavrilov, 2011).

The former disputed area, which was a point of disagreement between Norway and Russia, has high potential in the area of the Fedynsky swell and East-Barents foredeep, where quite a number of structures show great prospects for both gas and oil.

Up to the present time, oil has not been discovered in Russian Arctic seas, except the Pechora Sea; therefore these locations, including the Admiralteisky swell, are of particular interest.

It has already been anticipated that development of the Barents Sea will start from the Shtokman field, which later will be accompanied by the satellite fields of Ledovoye, Ludlovskoye, and Terskoye and subsequently by the fields of the Fersman and Demidov swells. This concept would enable utilization of the available infrastructure so as to reduce investment costs.

The 2010 Norwegian–Russian agreement on the delimitation of the Barents Sea has opened a new round of cooperation between the two countries on the development of Arctic resources. The new agreement opens new opportunities for active cooperation in developing this strategically important region. Possible large accumulations of petroleum resources in the former disputed area are located closer to the shoreline than the Shtokman field, and this may facilitate a new concept for the development of the whole Barents region, as is further discussed in Chapter 10.

The shelf of the Pechora Sea is the only one among all the Russian Arctic shelves where oil has been discovered. The main fields of this region are the Prirazlomnoye, Dolginskoye, Medyn-more, Varandey-more and Kolokomorskoye oilfields, the Severo–Gulyaevskoye oil-gas-condensate field, and the Pomorskoye gas-condensate field. Besides these fields, there are several large and prospective structures located in the southeastern part of the Pechora Sea: Yuzhno–Russkaya, Pakhanchevskaya, Sakhaninskaya, and Papaninskaya. According to the estimates, the total resources of the Medyn–Varandey and Kolokomorsky structures amount to 410 million tons of oil with a recoverable volume of 80 million tons. It is planned that the Prirazlomnoye field, which has started oil production in the Pechora Sea, will be followed by the development of other fields.

It should be briefly noted here that development of the Barents Sea may be more cost-effective if its resource base is united with the resources of the Kara Sea, and the Novaya Zemlya archipelago is used as a cluster base for the development of the whole region. In this case the "unitization principle" can be implemented, which might improve the economics of field development due to less overall investment in the common infrastructure (Efimov, Zolotukhin, Gudmestad, & Kornishin, 2014, p. 1).

Hydrocarbon resources of the Barents Sea[1]

This section is devoted to a new outlook on the Barents Sea petroleum resources, generated with the assistance of the modern Internet-based methodology, namely UCube, designed by Rystad Energy, a private Norwegian company.

Figure 9.2 gives an outlook on the oil and gas resources of the Barents Sea, which for convenience are split into Norwegian and Russian parts.

A similar evaluation has been made recently and published by the Norwegian Petroleum Directorate (Norwegian Petroleum Directorate, 2014). However, in this chapter we would like to use the UCube approach, which, for the purposes of forecasting production from both Norwegian and Russian parts of the Barents Sea, seems to be more convenient.

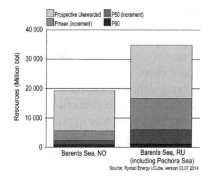
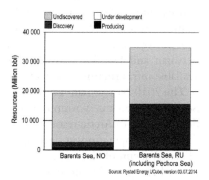

Figure 9.2 Expected ultimate recovery (EUR) resources of the Barents Sea, Norwegian and Russian (including the Pechora Sea) parts. Left: split by probability (P90, P50, Pmean, Prospective); Right: split by life cycle

Source: Rystad Energy AS (2014).

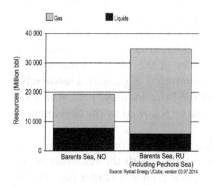
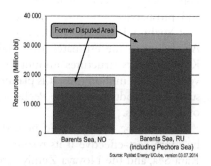

Figure 9.3 EUR resources of the Barents Sea, Norwegian and Russian (including the Pechora Sea) parts. Left: split by liquid/gas; Right: split by the area (note the former disputed area)

Source: Rystad Energy AS (2014).

Figure 9.3 indicates that both Russian and Norwegian parts of the Barents Sea are at nearly the same development stage. As follows from the left-hand side plot of Figure 9.3, the larger resource base of the Russian part is mostly gas prone (ca. 80% of resources is gas), while the gas/liquid ratio in the Norwegian part is close to 60/40. The right-hand side of Figure 9.3 shows that the former disputed area makes a high contribution to the resources base of both Norwegian and Russian parts of the Barents Sea, which indicates great potential for international collaboration in this area.

As follows from Table 9.1, the overall expected ultimate recovery (EUR) potential of the largest 10 fields and potential structures located in the Russian part of the Barents Sea exceeds by nearly 3.5 times that of the Norwegian part. Undiscovered potential in the Norwegian area accounts for almost 83% of EUR, while the Russian yet-to-find resources, due to the Shtokman discovery, are slightly below 55% of EUR.

Table 9.1 Top 10 largest fields and structures by EUR resources in Norwegian and Russian parts (including the Pechora Sea) of the Barents Sea

Province	Project	Asset Type	Life Cycle Category	Resources (Million bbl)	Resources (Million toe)
Barents Sea, NO	Snøhvit, NO	Field	Producing	964.6	131.6
			Discovery	599.5	81.8
			Sum	**1564.2**	**213.4**
	Bjarmeland Platform Offshore Barents Sea, NO	Open	Undiscovered	1117.6	152.5
	Barents Sea Edgeøya Platform, NO	Open	Undiscovered	1100.9	150.2
	Barents Sea Kvitoya Basin, NO	Open	Undiscovered	883.6	120.5
	Barents Sea Hjalmar Johansen High, NO	Open	Undiscovered	870.1	118.7
	Finnmark Platform Offshore Barents Sea, NO	Open	Undiscovered	842.9	115.0
	Barents Sea Kong Karl Platform, NO	Open	Undiscovered	811.5	110.7
	North Barents Platform Offshore Barents Sea, NO	Open	Undiscovered	788.3	107.5
	Barents Sea Hornsund Fault Complex, NO	Open	Undiscovered	718.3	98.0
	Barents Sea Moffenflaket Ny, NO	Open	Undiscovered	666.0	90.9
	Sum			**9363.4**	**1277.4**

(*Continued*)

Table 9.1 (Continued)

Province	Project	Asset Type	Life Cycle Category	Resources (Million bbl)	Resources (Million toe)
Barents Sea, RU (including Pechora Sea)	Shtokman, RU	Field	Discovery	15162.4	2068.5
		License	Undiscovered	5.2	0.7
		Sum		**15167.5**	**2069.2**
	South Barents Sea Basin East Offshore Barents Sea, RU	Open	Undiscovered	8747.6	1193.4
	Barents Sea Hjalmar Johansen High, RU	Open	Undiscovered	2588.5	353.1
	South Barents Sea Basin Offshore Murmansk, RU	Open	Undiscovered	2564.5	349.9
	Barents Sea Polarrev High, RU	Open	Undiscovered	1385.8	189.1
	Barents Sea Tiddly-banken Basin, RU	Open	Undiscovered	1040.5	141.9
	Prirazlomnoye, RU	Field	Producing	511.1	69.7
	South Barents Sea Basin East Offshore Komi, RU	Open	Undiscovered	495.2	67.6
	Barents Sea Finnmark Platform, RU	Open	Undiscovered	434.8	59.3
	Barents Sea Kong Karl Platform, RU	Open	Undiscovered	262.1	35.8
	Sum			**33197.7**	**4529.0**
Grand total				**42561.1**	**5806.4**

Source: Rystad Energy AS (2014).

It should be noted here that the contribution of the Pechora Sea to the hydrocarbon resources of the 10 largest fields and structures of the Barents Sea is very moderate. From all discovered fields and identified prospective structures, which total close to 30 (see Figure 9.4) only the Prirazlomnoye field, with its EUR of nearly 70 million toe (in the Russian estimates – ca. 72 million toe), is included in the table.

This is explained by a concept used in UCube software: only assets believed to be commercially viable are included in EUR resources. Thus, an estimate made by using UCube software may (and certainly will) disagree with the Russian evaluation of the resources of the Pechora Sea, which is primarily based on the concept of initial geological resources (STOOIP) multiplied by the average ORF (oil recovery factor), available at this stage of estimates and typical for the region of study.

There is no debate regarding analysis of the strong and weak points of both approaches. What is important is that they are based on different concepts and thus, rather complement than contradict one another.

Our rough assessment, based on the STOOIP and ORF evaluation concept, indicates that the Pechora Sea alone has in place volumes amounting to ca. 20 billion boe (2.7 btoe).[2] This quantity is enough to secure produced volumes in the forecasted period (2014–2040) close to 3,360 million boe (758 million

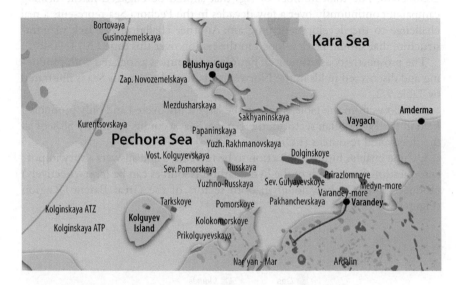

Figure 9.4 Discovered fields and prospective structures of the Pechora Sea

Source: Based on Storvik & Co AS (2013).

Table 9.2 EUR resources of top 10 producing and discovered fields in the Norwegian part of the Barents Sea

Province	Project	Asset Type	Life Cycle Category	Resources (Million bbl)	Resources (Million toe)
Barents Sea, NO	Snøhvit, NO	Field	Producing	964.6	131.6
			Discovery	599.5	81.8
			Sum	**1564.2**	**213.4**
	Johan Castberg, NO	Field	Discovery	597.0	81.4
	Goliat, NO	Field	Under development	247.3	33.7
	7324/8–1 (Wisting Central), NO	Field	Discovery	118.0	16.1
	Alke South, NO	Field	Discovery	80.9	11.0
	Nucula, NO	Field	Discovery	28.0	3.8
	Tornerose, NO	Field	Discovery	24.3	3.3
	Dumbo, NO	Field	Discovery	18.0	2.5
	Alka, NO	Field	Discovery	17.8	2.4
	7124/3–1, NO	Field	Discovery	12.1	1.6
	Sum			**2707.5**	**369.4**

Source: Rystad Energy AS (2014).

toe). In order to maintain this production, approximately 500 production and injection wells should be drilled in the region in this period, starting with 5–8 wells drilled annually during 2014–2018 and then gradually increasing the number to 25 by 2030 and remaining at this level in the following decade, 2030–2040. The total number of rigs that should be engaged in the drilling campaign continuously over a few decades in the Pechora Sea represents a real challenge to the development program. Another challenge is a lack of infrastructure that should be developed in the region over this time (2014–2040).

The prospectivity assessment of petroleum resources associated with producing and discovered fields in the Norwegian part of the Barents Sea is illustrated by Table 9.2.

As follows from the table, Snøhvit, the largest discovered and only producing field in the Norwegian sector of the Barents Sea, accounts for nearly 58% of all the discovered resources (EUR) in the area.

UCube enables future production to be forecasted and answers a very important question: how much of the hydrocarbon resources can be (cost-effectively) produced (and for how long) in both sectors of the Great Barents Region (Figures 9.5–9.7).

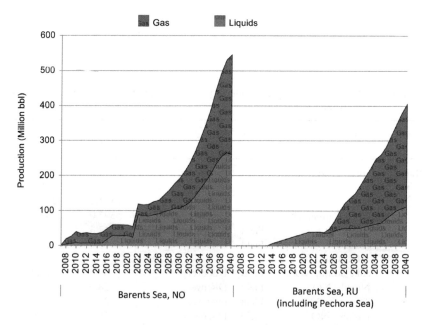

Figure 9.5 Liquid and gas production from Norwegian and Russian (including the Pechora Sea) parts of the Barents Sea, million boe/year

Source: Rystad Energy AS (2014).

As follows from Figure 9.5, the Norwegian sector of the Barents Sea has higher chances of being developed faster with a higher annual production than its Russian counterpart. By 2040 the overall annual production from the Norwegian sector could reach 550 million boe, with the average gas/liquid ratio nearly 50/50 value. Starting with the Prirazlomnoye field in 2014, production from the Russian part of the Barents Sea is expected to reach 400 million boe by 2040, of which gas contributes nearly 72%.

The shape of the forecasted production indicates a steep production growth in the period from 2030 to 2040 which will, most likely, remain valid for a few decades beyond 2040. Obviously, the production potential of the Great Barents Region is so high that it could supply the world with oil and gas at the annual rate that could be reached by 2040 (950 million boe or 130 million toe) for more than 100 years.

In conclusion, we would like to note again that future tremendous opportunities to extract, transport, and consume the vast Arctic petroleum resources of the Great Barents Region are driving forces to stimulate the development of domestic and international petroleum industries and their active collaboration.

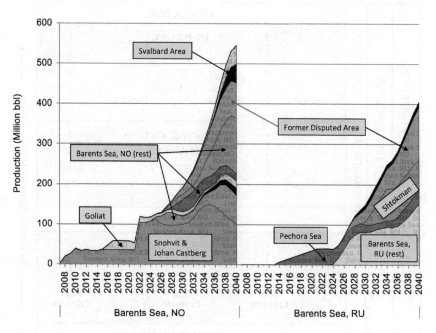

Figure 9.6 Production profiles for the Barents Sea: Norwegian and Russian (including the Pechora Sea) parts, million boe/year

Source: Rystad Energy AS (2014).

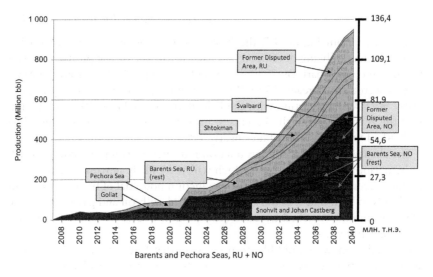

Figure 9.7 Contribution of the Norwegian and Russian (including the Pechora Sea) sectors in overall production from the Barents Sea, million boe/year

Source: Rystad Energy AS (2014).

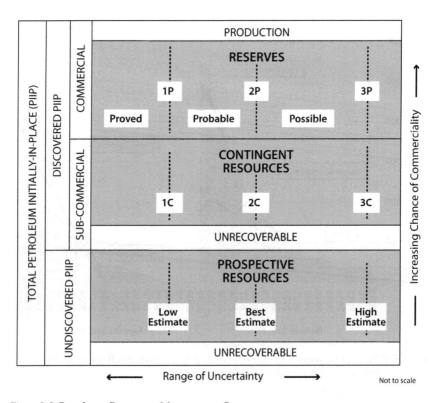

Figure 9.8 Petroleum Resources Management System

Source: Society of Petroleum Engineers (2007).

Specifics of the UCube evaluation of resources and recoverable volumes

The resources estimated by UCube do not correspond directly with company-reported 1P (Proven/Proved Reserves) or 2P (Proven + Probable Resources) numbers. To reduce confusion, the term "resources", not "reserves" is used in UCube. The resources in UCube correspond to the expected ulti-mate recovery of the fields. The EUR number is based on reported 1P and 2P numbers, as well as empirical studies and case-by-case judgment. Whereas real fields may have both 1P, 2P, and 3P (Proven + Probable + Possible) reserves, 1C, 2C, and 3C contingent reserves, as well as low, best, and high estimate prospec-tive resources, each UCube asset is assigned only the EUR, which is assumed to include all the above contributions. Similarly, UCube assets have only one life cycle, whereas real fields may have resources of different maturity.

Petroleum resources are best classified by the Petroleum Resources Manage-ment System (PRMS), as described by Society of Petroleum Engineers (2007) and illustrated by Figure 9.8 (Society of Petroleum Engineers, 2007, 2011).

The resources variable in UCube is identical to the sum of future produc-tion; thus resources and production variables are internally consistent (with the exception that other liquids are not included in resources). For one asset, the resources value for a year is identical to the remaining reserves on January 1 that year, i.e. the sum of production for this and the following years (see Figure 9.9).

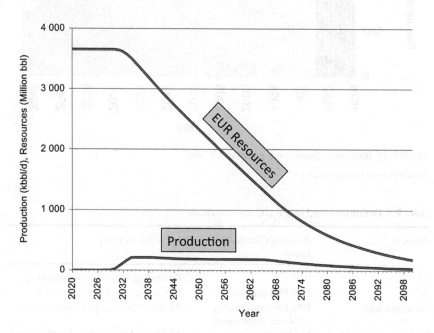

Figure 9.9 Internal consistency of the resourced and production variables in UCube

Source: Rystad Energy AS (2014).

Resource classification proxy

The resources variable can be split by the resource classification proxy (see Table 9.3). This split is modeled, and the purpose is to simulate the process of maturing the resources at asset level. This is shown for one asset in Figure 9.10. Before the license is awarded, the resources are "prospective unawarded".

Through seismic interpretation, exploration, appraisal, and field development, the resources gradually mature to P50 and P90 resources, and the remaining resources shrink as resources are produced. Note that since P50 includes P90, and Pmean includes P50, the system displays the additive "P50 (increment)" and "Pmean (increment)". Thus, P50=P90+P50 (increment). The resource classification proxy can be used to analyze how companies mature their portfolios, and to estimate 1P and 2P values at portfolio level.

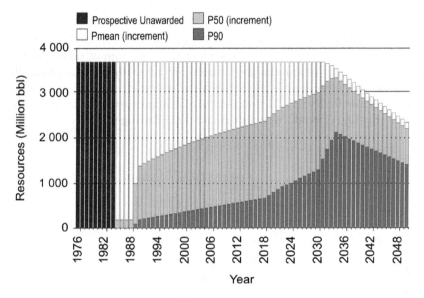

Figure 9.10 Resource classification proxy in UCube

Source: Rystad Energy AS (2014).

Table 9.3 Definitions used in the UCube evaluation

Estimate	Resources Classification Proxy	Life Cycle Category
1P	P90	Producing, Under development
2P	P90, P50 (increment)	Producing, Under development
Resource base	P90, P50 (increment), Pmean (increment)	All life cycles except Undiscovered
Resource potential	No filtering	All life cycles including Undiscovered

Source: Rystad Energy AS (2014).

Table 9.4 Correspondence between UCube and PRMS definitions

	Proved Reserved (1P)			2P Reserves			Resource Base			Resource Potential		
	P90	*P50*	*P10*	*P90*	*P50*	*P10*	*P90*	*P50*	*P10*	*P90*	*P50*	*P10*
Sanctioned												
Discovered												
Prospective												

Source: Rystad Energy AS (2014).

Based on resources, the resource classification proxy (horizontal dimension in the SPE classification chart) and the life cycle category (vertical dimension) of this approach enable 1P and 2P estimates to be worked out at portfolio (company, region, country . . .) level (Table 9.4).

Conclusion

Active involvement of the Great Barents hydrocarbon resources in the global energy supply process needs a clear understanding of the market potential for Arctic gas and oil (required volumes, time frame, transportation routes). The future role of the region should be further understood, and its resources should be further explored and assessed. There is no doubt that international collaboration in the Great Barents area between Norway and Russia, with the active participation of all the nations interested in the development of this region, could make production of HC in this region a world-class project.

Notes

1 All the estimates referred to in this section and the following parts of the chapter are based on the use of the UCube software developed by Rystad Energy, an Internet-based company specializing in hydrocarbon resource evaluation and production forecasts. A short description of the specifics of the UCube evaluations is given at the end of this section.
2 This quantity is somewhat moderate as compared with 4.9 btoe given in Belonin & Prischepa (2006).

References

Belonin, M.D., & Prischepa, O.M. (2006). *Нефтегазовые ресурсы сееро-западного региона России и перспективы их освоения* [Oil and gas resources of the northwest region of Russia and prospects for their development]. Moscow, Russia: Oil and Gas Publishing House.
Efimov, Y., Zolotukhin, A., Gudmestad, O.T., & Kornishin, K. (2014, February). *Cluster development of the Barents and Kara Seas HC Mega Basin from the Novaya Zemlya Archipelago.* Paper presented at the ATC conference, Houston, TX. Abstract retrieved from www.onepetro.org/conference-paper/OTC-24650-MS

Norwegian Petroleum Directorate. (2014). *The petroleum resources on the Norwegian continental shelf 2014. Fields and discoveries.* Retrieved from www.npd.no/Global/Engelsk/3-Publications/Resource-report/Resource-report-2014/Resources-2014-nett.pdf

Rystad Energy AS. (2014). Statistics retrieved from Rystad Energy UCube database.

Society of Petroleum Engineers. (2007). *Petroleum resources management system.* Retrieved from www.spe.org/industry/docs/Petroleum_Resources_Management_System_2007.pdf

Society of Petroleum Engineers. (2011). *Guidelines for application of the petroleum resources management system.* Retrieved from www.spe.org/industry/docs/PRMS_Guidelines_Nov2011.pdf

Storvik & Co AS (Cartographer). (2013). Arctic Europe petroleum resources and infrastructure [Resource map]. Retrieved from Arctic Europe Petroleum Activities website: www.arctic-europe.com/images/Kart_noytralt_2013.pdf

Zolotukhin, A. (2014). Russian Arctic resources. In S. Eriksen, H. Haflidason, O. Olesen, H. Schiellerup, & A.M. Husås (Eds.), *NGF abstracts and proceedings, No. 2, 2014* (p. 69). Trondheim, Norway: Norsk Geologisk Forening.

Zolotukhin, A., & Gavrilov, V. (2011). Russian Arctic petroleum resources. *Oil & Gas Science and Technology–Revue d'IFP Energies Nouvelles, 66*(6), 899–910. doi: 10.2516/ogst/2011141

10 Development of hydrocarbon fields in the newly delineated border area of Norway and Russia with emphasis on subsea development schemes

Maria Bulakh, Ove Gudmestad, and Anatoly Zolotukhin

Introduction

The Barents Sea is the most western among the Arctic seas off the coasts of Western Russia and Northern Norway and is located between the northern European coasts and the islands of Vaigach, Novaya Zemlya, Franz Josef Land, Svalbard, and Bear Island. The sea communicates with the warmer Norwegian Sea, the cold Arctic Basin, and also with the Kara and White Seas.

The area of the Barents Sea is 1.4 million square kilometers with an average water depth of 230 m. The water volume is estimated at 322,000 km³. Typically, three-quarters of its surface is covered by ice during the winter, and it never freezes completely due to the influx of warm Atlantic waters, preventing the cooling of the surface layer to freezing point.

The bottom is not uniform, having crossed seamounts, valleys, and gutters. The hydrological conditions of the sea are affected by the river flow in its south-eastern part. In general, however, the flow is relatively small (annually 163 km³) and therefore has little effect on the salinity and chemical composition of the Barents Sea water, which is close to the characteristics of ocean water (Dodrovolskii & Zalogin, 1982). The Barents Sea water masses represent a combination of influence of energy exchange with the atmosphere and water circulation. The inrush of water from other basins and underwater uneven terrain creates a very complex system of surface and deep currents, in which the numerous branches of the Norwegian current and cold water coming out of the Arctic Basin and the Kara Sea play the leading role. Periodic tidal currents are superimposed on a system of permanent currents; periodic tidal currents in the surface layer may reach 150 cm/s and this rate exceeds the rate of constant currents (Terziev, 1990).

Major deposits discovered so far in the Barents Sea outside the former disputed area include the Norwegian Snøhvit gas field and Goliat oilfield, the Johan Castberg field (formerly termed the Skrugard field), the Russian Shtokman gas field and the Russian oil fields in the Pechora Sea.

We should note that future developments of fields in the region should be viewed in an area perspective in order to obtain the best possible economy for the development. This relates in particular to development of the gas offtake solution from the region, where gas from several fields must be collected to obtain a satisfactory solution. This will require open and thorough cooperation between Norway and Russia, on both technical and economic matters. North Sea developments across borderlines with the unitization of fields crossing the borders could serve as models for the required cooperation needed to obtain optimal development solutions.

Physical environmental conditions in the area of the Fedynsky High area

Climate

The climatic conditions of the Barents Sea in the Fedynsky High area are determined by its proximity to the warm Norwegian Sea and to the cold Arctic Basin areas. Through the Barents Sea, the greater part of the warm North Atlantic cyclones take their course, coming to the east and northeast of the Arctic region. Often this transfer of warm air masses is suspended by powerful polar anticyclones, accompanied by the penetration of cold Arctic air masses far to the south (Terziev, 1990). This is one of the most troubled aspects of working in the region and might cause a number of challenges while conducting surveys or exploration activities. That is why, before starting drilling and production works, we should collect a database about the physical conditions in the region and present forecasts for the long term, establishing exceedance probabilities of waves, winds, polar low effects, etc. for operational and design conditions (Gudmestad, 2013).

As mentioned above, compared to all other Arctic seas, the climate of the Barents Sea is characterized by relatively high air temperatures, mild winters, and high rainfall. The average temperatures in the coldest months in the eastern part are equal to −10°C to −15°C along the coast and up to −20°C to −22°C further north. In July the average temperature in the sea area of the Fedynsky High ranges from +1°C to +7°C. Under the influence of incoming masses of warm water and air from the Atlantic Ocean and the cold air from the Arctic Basin, the climate in the Barents Sea, especially in the eastern part, is very heterogeneous.

Some areas are subject to physical conditions that differ significantly from those found in the Norwegian Sea. The most significant criterion is the presence of sea ice, for which borders can be illustrated, as proposed by DNV in the Barents 2020 project; see Figure 10.1.

The sub-Arctic area ii of Figure 10.1: Barents Sea offshore (the coast of Norway and Murmansk) is generally ice-free. The former disputed area (marked with a dotted line) is located in this region and considered to be a predominantly ice-free area, with local first-year ice sheets in the wintertime and with occasional icebergs (Abramov, 1996).

Hydrological regime

The hydrological regime of the former disputed area of the Barents Sea has a great diversity and develops as a result of the circulation of waters with different origins and different properties:

Figure 10.1 Barents Sea regions

i) Spitsbergen/usually ice every winter, ii) Barents Sea/generally ice free, iii) Franz Josef Land/usually ice every winter, iv) North East Barents Sea/usually ice every winter, v) Novozemelsky/in between, vi) Kola/in between, vii) Pechora/usually ice every winter, viii) White Sea/usually ice every winter

Source: Based on Storvik & Co AS (2013).

- Warm water coming from the North Atlantic Ocean,
- Warm and fresh waters with low density from the rivers,
- Relatively cold local waters,
- Cold polar waters.

Water temperature

In the Barents Sea, the water temperature has a much greater influence than in other Arctic seas on all processes associated with the density structure of the water (convection, the formation of layers, etc.). In addition, in the Barents Sea and in the former disputed area particularly, the water temperature is a key indicator of the distribution of warm Atlantic waters, which determine the ice conditions.

Sea level and tidal waves

Wind-surge level fluctuations reaching the coastal sea areas are at a level of 1–2 m (in the southeastern part of the sea, even 3–4 meters). The tidal wave moves eastward in the Barents Sea to the Fedynsky High destination and the value of the major tidal component (M2) in Vadsø in the eastern part of Finnmark is 1.09 m. It is known that the combined storm surge and the tide can cause considerable flooding as was the case in the Varandey area on July 24, 2010 when the oil treatment and storage terminal, located kilometers inland, was flooded and the air runway close to the coast was damaged.

Currents

The former disputed area has a complex system of surface and deep currents due to its location, the most common feature of which is the movement of water in a counterclockwise direction; see Figure 10.2. Formed by large-scale processes in the North Atlantic ocean–atmosphere system, it is responsive to

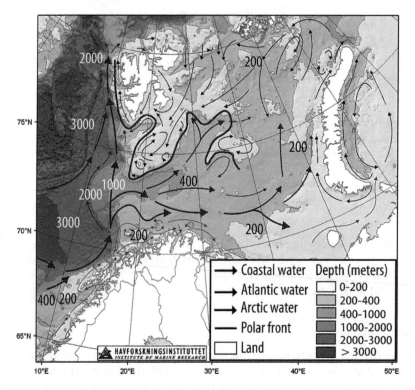

Figure 10.2 Currents in the Barents Sea

Source: Institute of Marine Research (2014).

the variability of the synoptic conditions directly above the Barents Sea. The spread of the tidal wave from the Atlantic and the Arctic Basin and the variability of the density structure of sea waters also influence the current pattern. One of the main features of the Barents Sea dynamics in the former disputed area is the tidal currents. Caused by tidal level fluctuations, the current has the same frequency, but the direction change of tidal currents is not the same in different regions. The speed of tidal currents is usually higher than the rate of the constant tide, especially in the surface layer; the mean velocity of this current is $0.10–0.12$ ms^{-1} (Terziev, 1990) (Figure 10.2).

Waves

Most storms and hurricanes in the Barents Sea are dominated by weather from the southwest, which is the sector with the longest wave-generating fetches. From NORSOK Standard N-003 (Standards Norway, 2007), it can be seen that the significant wave height H_{m0} and related maximum peak period T_P with an annual probability of exceedance of 10^{-2} for sea states of three hours' duration in the Western Barents Sea are comparable with the other areas on the Norwegian continental shelf; however, peak wave periods are longer than in the North Sea and comparable to those in the Norwegian Sea. Iso-curves for wave heights are indicated with solid lines, while wave period lines are dotted; see Figure 10.3 for reference.

While the design conditions are well established, the main challenge for construction work in the Barents Sea is the lack of predictability of the weather during the early and late construction season, mainly due to the unpredictability of the polar low pressures. This might lead to long periods of "waiting on weather" (Gudmestad & Karunakaran, 2012).

It is also important to mention the ice edge's influence on the wave climate, especially in the northern and eastern areas. At a given location in summer, the fetch length from sectors subject to winter icing will increase. Therefore, the resultant wave heights of waves from this direction will be greater in summer than during the winter. In the marginal ice zone itself, the presence of ice will dampen out and reflect energy arriving from the off-ice sector such that the wave height will decrease somewhat away from the ice edge.

Winds and polar low pressures

The wind in the middle and eastern areas (which include the former disputed area) is dominated by cyclones that form in the North Atlantic and move into the Barents Sea. According to the climate specifics of this area, in the summer period the pressure gradients are weaker and the wind direction is more equally distributed between the main wind axes, along southwest-northeast, in the Barents Sea. One more challenge we might meet in this area is that low pressures, which occur over northern Scandinavia during the summer, lead to the more frequent occurrence of northeasterly to easterly winds.

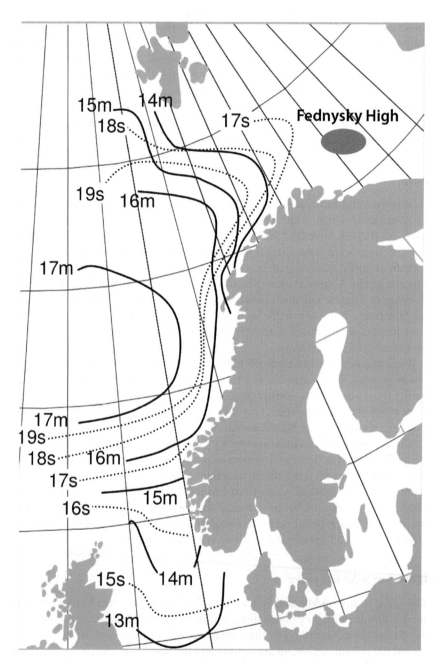

Figure 10.3 Wave heights and periods in the Western Barents Sea compared to other areas on the Norwegian continental shelf

Source: Standards Norway (2007).

Great attention must be paid to the phenomena of polar low pressures, which are the most specific phenomena of this area and occur from early fall to late spring. A polar low is a small, but fairly intense atmospheric low pressure system found in maritime regions, considerably north of the polar front. The typical diameter is 100–500 km and the average lifespan is 18 hours. The polar low gives strong and rapidly changing winds and dense showers of snow or hail; it is generally more unpredictable than the larger and more common synoptic lows (Polar low pressure area, 2010). For 15–18 hours' duration the average maximum wind speed is 46 knots, which is a severe gale. Of these lows, 35–50% have storm force winds of 50 knots or more, and the strongest recorded since 2000 had a wind speed of 70 knots. Polar lows are mostly found in the Norwegian and Barents Seas (see Figure 10.4), with the majority being between 65°N and 74°N. The season is from October to the end of May, with most polar lows occurring in the months of December to March. Typically, 10 to 20 fully developed polar lows are seen in the Norwegian and Barents Seas during the season.

Formation of polar lows

A polar low forms when unstable air in the lower atmosphere interacts with cold air above. A typical precursor to its development is cold Arctic air at low

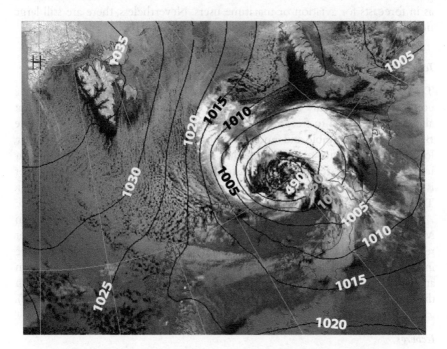

Figure 10.4 Polar low pressure in the Barents Sea, east of the former disputed area

Source: Polar low pressure area (2010).

levels moving southwards over the Gulf Stream off the Norwegian coast. Stability then decreases due to the heat from the sea and large convective shower clouds form. These have a strong vertical motion of air, and an influx of air occurs under the base of the cloud. In areas of strong convection, the shower clouds are organized in lines (troughs) with surface winds of 30–40 knots associated with the influx. When the convection interacts with cold Arctic air at heights of 5–8 km, the influx at the surface grows strong enough for a vortex to form and a polar low is born.

Due to their violent and sudden nature, the polar lows have been the cause of many losses at sea. In the past, polar lows were extremely challenging to forecast. Their small size meant that they hid easily between observation points in the Arctic, and they did not have sufficiently high visibility in the weather prediction models. Also, the physical processes were not well enough described in the models. This led to poor model performance and often false or absent indications in the numerical prognoses, as well as a general lack of confidence among forecasters. Subsequently, the lows were often omitted in forecasts to the public. In recent years, the availability of satellite data (images of cloud structures) and wind data from the sea surface has greatly improved. Satellite data are now assimilated in the numerical models, and, together with a finer resolution, this has led to a higher quality of short-range forecasting. Forecasts of potential polar lows are now routinely included in text forecasts of gale warnings, as well as in forecasts for aviation or maritime users. Nevertheless, there are still large uncertainties in these weather forecasts (Wilcken, 2012).

Ice conditions

The Barents Sea is linked to the Arctic seas, but it is never covered with ice completely. This occurs due to the influx of Atlantic waters, which does not allow water to cool to freezing temperatures. Because the ice exchange in the Barents Sea is negligible and amounts to just about 3% of the ice in late winter, locally originating ice mainly dominates. Only in some years is there multiyear ice in the northwestern and northeastern parts of the sea. The largest ice cover is usually observed in mid-April, the lowest, in late August and early September. The remaining part of the Barents Sea is usually ice-free south of 75°N.

The southeastern and middle parts of the sea are usually cleared from ice in May, but sometimes ice remains until August. The thickness of ice cover in winter reaches 70–75 cm (Terziev, 1990). The central areas of the sea are cleared from ice in June and July. By this time the ice has reached a thickness of 1 m. The minimum amount of ice in the north part of the sea is observed in August. The ice cover in the open sea has a high degree of continuity all throughout winter (Terziev, 1990).

Icebergs

Icebergs drifting in the Barents Sea originate from the glaciers at Svalbard and Franz Josef Land. They are usually rather smooth, less than 100 m thick and with a horizontal extension of maximum 300–400 m (DNV GL, 2008).

A number of giant icebergs have, however, been observed. In 1881 one iceberg was observed close to the Norwegian coast as far south as 70°N, and in 1929 20 icebergs were observed off the east coast of Finnmark (Dodrovolskii & Zalogin, 1982). Apart from these reports, no icebergs have been observed south of 72.5°N and west of 32°E. This former disputed area is liable to iceberg appearances, first and foremost because of the climate conditions and effects such as polar low pressures. The probability of finding icebergs within an area of 100 x 100 km is shown in Figure 10.5. The construction contractors will, however, by all means try to keep away from floating ice features and there will be warnings in case ice floats into the construction area (Gudmestad & Karunakaran, 2012).

Spray icing

Another challenge for the Barents Sea (and the Fedynsky High region) is the sea spray icing. Wind speed and air temperature are the most important parameters

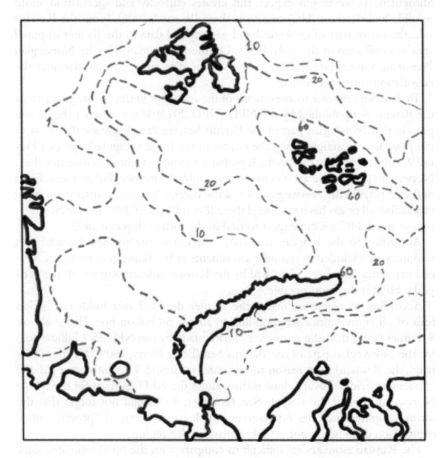

Figure 10.5 Annual probability of occurrence of icebergs

Source: Based on Abramov (1996).

affecting sea spray icing intensity. The wind speed has an obvious effect on the generation of sea spray. In addition, it influences the cooling rate of the airborne droplets. The intensity of icing will steadily increase with decreasing air temperature from about −2°C and down to the lowest temperature to be anticipated during offshore operations. The influence of sea surface temperature on the icing intensity is less than for wind speed and air temperature. It is of importance in the initial stage of icing, i.e. at moderate wind speeds and air temperature down to −5°C, but has a marginal influence at high icing intensities. This factor should be considered very carefully while any kind of topside works is ongoing on site.

Potential resources in the former disputed area

The former disputed area has the size of the Norwegian North Sea with large identifiable structures not too far from several large gas fields, like Snøhvit and Shtokman. As we would expect, this creates curiosity and speculation about possible hydrocarbon (HC) resources there (Ræstad, 2006). From the Russian side, the major part of geological and geophysical data in the former disputed area was collected in the early 1990s. On the Norwegian side, the Norwegian Petroleum Directorate (NPD) started seismic data collection the day after the negotiations were concluded.

To date, we can refer to assessments of the resources in the Norwegian part of the Barents Sea published by the NPD (NPD, 2013). If we consider the proven plays in that Norwegian part of the Barents Sea, we can clearly see that most of the plays are cut straight along the border of the former disputed area (see Figure 9.1 in Chapter 9 of this book). It probably would be right to assume that these Norwegian prospective areas continue even into the former disputed area. Eight of the 23 plays in the Norwegian part of the Barents Sea are confirmed, meaning producible oil or gas has been found there (Econ Pöyry, 2009). The question then is: how much HC we can expect to find in the former disputed area?

According to the Russian database, estimates of the former disputed area resources are included in resource assessments of the Russian Barents Sea. Several structures have been identified by the Russian side, among which the Fedynsky High is the most notable.

According to recent estimates, the former disputed area holds 6.8 billion tons of oil equivalents, corresponding to almost 50 billion boe. This is almost 8.6 times larger than the resource estimate made by the NPD (5.7 billion boe) for the Norwegian part of the Barents Sea (Econ Pöyry, 2009). On the other hand, the Russians have reason to be more optimistic. The Shtokman gas and condensate field discovery alone is three times the NPD estimate for the whole Norwegian part of the Barents Sea. However, we should not forget that the former disputed area has no reserves which can be termed "proven", since exploration drilling has not yet taken place in this region.

The Russian estimates are difficult to compare with the NPD estimates, since the two are of such different magnitudes. However, the Severo–Kildinskoye is a proven gas discovery right next to the border of the former disputed area.This implies that there is knowledge of the geology in the west. From 1978, regular seismic surveys were conducted in the border areas by the Soviet Union. Four wells have been drilled in the vicinity of the former disputed area on the Fersmanovskoye and Severo–Kildinskoye structures. Russia resumed seismic activities in 1999.

The main structural elements in the former disputed area are, from south to north: the Finnmark Platform, the Tiddly Bank Basin, the Fedynsky High, the Nordkapp Basin, the Bjarmeland Platform, the Central Bank High, and the Hopen/Persey High. To the east lie the hydrocarbon-prolific South and North Barents Basins, while to the west the Hammerfest Basin has finally proven its commerciality. However, it is ambitious to suggest that huge Russian gas discoveries in the Jurassic to the east can be duplicated in the former disputed area based on its propinquity. The reason is the presence of a marked transition from the Jurassic-aged gas fields in the Barents Basins up onto the platforms where the Jurassic-aged sediment cover is thin and lying at a shallow depth. Paleozoic- and Mesozoic-aged rocks subcrop below the Quaternary in the former disputed area with no Tertiary-aged sediments present. In the Nordkapp and Tiddly Bank Basins, Triassic sands trapped against salt pillows are the main prospects. Triassic fluvial sands trapped against salt have been found to be gas-bearing in the Pandora discovery in the southern Nordkapp Basin. By this we can claim the next three main period formations which are most likely to have the prospect of HC presence; these are: Triassic, Paleozoic, and pre-Jurassic source rocks. A key well drilled by Statoil in 2005 on the Finnmark Platform close to the former disputed area, targeting a huge stratigraphic trap, was, however, abandoned as a dry well probably because of lack of a good migration pathway and/or poor seal (Ræstad, 2006).

With regard to pre-Jurassic sources, with respect to source rock, the prolific Jurassic Hekkingen Formation has barely reached maturity in the South Barents Basin to the east. However, shales in the Upper Permian Tempelfjorden Group are in the oil window along the platform margin and on the Fedynsky High and are gas-prone in the deeper northern parts of the former disputed area. The recently discovered deeper oil-bearing formations in the Goliat oilfield to the west are important evidence for the presence of a pre-Jurassic source rock of probable Middle Triassic age (Ræstad, 2006).

The Barents shelf, however, has a challenge that is the Cenozoic deep erosion that has breached earlier oil reservoirs, either by fault-induced leakages or by gas expansions due to uplift. Erosion has been in the order of 1,000–2,000 meters in the former disputed area and is a negative factor in the prospective evaluation. From a structural point of view, the Fedynsky High is a huge basement-induced uplift some 130 km in diameter. The Russians have indicated and named five potential prospects in the vicinity of the high. The deepest targets in the Paleozoic region are within acceptable depths for reservoir preservation. This high and the eastern end of the Nordkapp Basin are potentially the two most attractive areas for future exploration. Mapping over these structures has been based on a fairly dense seismic grid.

Since surveys have begun in the nearby areas of the former disputed area, data collected indicate that factors necessary for hydrocarbon generation, migration, and preservation are present. Structures forming large potential traps have already been identified. However, more extensive and better quality seismic data are required in order to properly evaluate the reservoir potential. Drilling must be carried out to assess the quality of the source and reservoir rocks, thereby potentially confirming the commerciality of a discovery.

Development schemes, main challenges for the Fedynsky High

The main purpose of this chapter is to determine the possible development schemes for prospects on the Fedynsky High in the Barents Sea. Field development constitutes the process/activities necessary to design, construct, and install all the facilities needed to enable the petroleum to be brought from the source rock to the refinery or land terminal. The design criteria for the field development concept choice are given by:

- Oceanographic and meteorological data
- Reservoir and fluid properties
- Well completion data
- Process and operation data
- Host facilities data
- Transport to market
- Safety and hazard requirements

Operating according to these factors, we can present a table of possible schemes regarding Fedynsky High's physical environmental conditions, and we give a recommendation regarding the most promising development solution, Table 10.1, provided that the well stream product is mainly dry gas.

Subsea systems

By preparing this concept screening table, we can see the advantages of using a subsea system with a production pipeline to shore with multiphase flow, which will require relatively dry gas (Minikeeva & Gudmestad, 2013). With the development of subsea processing technologies, the subsea-to-shore solution will be even more attractive as water can be taken out from the well stream using offshore processing equipment located on the sea floor. Worldwide experience from sub-Arctic offshore oil and gas fields' development thus gives us a recommended development scheme for the Fedynsky High region.

In the North Sea, the oil companies have previously often built large production platforms standing on the sea floor, equipped with process facilities separating gas/oil and water. The gas is sent to market via a pipeline, while the oil is shipped directly or sent to shore in another pipeline. Today, the operators

Table 10.1 Comparison analysis of developing schemes for the Fedynsky High

Physical condition in the Fedynsky High region	Subsea to shore with multiphase flow line	Possible development solutions				
		Subsea system and topside processing	Jacket platform	Semi-submersible platform	FPSO solution	Floating LNG
Water depth, 300 m	+	+	–	+	+	+
Distance to shore, 320 km	–	+	+	+	+	+
Sea ice cover	+	+	–	–	+/–	–
Sea spray icing	+	+/–	+	+	+/–	–
Waves, H, 9–12 M	+	+/–	+	+	+	–
Polar lows effect	+	+/–	+	+	+/–	–

often choose subsea developments where the untreated well stream is sent directly from a subsea template to an existing platform or to shore in one multiphase pipeline. In cases where a subsea development with multiphase transport is feasible, billions may be saved by dispensing with costly platforms.

Subsea to shore

The remoteness of many huge oil and gas deposits, combined with the harsh environmental and ice conditions, means that a subsea-to-shore development can offer significant benefits over any kind of platform. In some cases, tie-back to shore might even be a strict necessity for the technical and economic feasibility of the field development. For instance, this scheme was successfully applied and is currently on stream in the High North offshore (Norway and UK) at the Snøhvit field in the Barents Sea (146 km offshore), the Ormen Lange in the Norwegian Sea (120 km offshore), and at the Laggan Tormore project in the UK part of the North Sea (143 km offshore, closer to the North Atlantic).

In the case of the Fedynsky High, the most challenging task is how to provide sustainable multiphase flow management over ultralong distances (about 320 km offshore) and how to deliver electrical power to subsea from shore. We will try to identify the major long-distance subsea tie-back issues, and clarify which are the limiting factors and the related technology barriers appropriate to this region. The main purpose of this discussion is to see whether the step-out distances would be technically feasible based on the existing technologies.

All-subsea production systems

We will state that the most probable development solution for the Fedynsky High prospect (in the case of a gas find) will be based on an all-subsea production system, controlled remotely from shore through electro-hydraulic umbilicals, with a multiphase flow pipeline to an LNG plant onshore. Alternatively, pipeline transport to the market will be discussed.

For the Fedynsky High all-subsea development scheme with a long step-out distance, a subsea high voltage power distribution system may be required in order to provide sufficient power. Hence, support subsea gas compression units will most likely be considered for this area. For the time being, the required power levels and transmission distance exceed the current capabilities of the industry in this regard.

It is proposed that the subsea wells are tied back to a cluster manifold. Each manifold and XMT (Christmas tree) template should include a "fishing-friendly" integrated protection structure that deflects trawl boards, so that fishing activities can take place across the seabed where the subsea facilities are located, if deemed necessary. The subsea trees should have remotely operated valves that are used to control the well stream. Providing a large bore diameter will help to avoid significant pressure drops and accommodate large gas volumes. As required, subsea trees will be equipped with a variety of instrumentation for monitoring operational performance, for instance high resolution pressure and temperature transmitters and wet gas flow meters, etc. All these necessitate high data transmission rates. A central distribution unit (CDU) is one of the main pieces of equipment in a full subsea complex.

The CDU carries hydraulic control fluid, a high voltage electric power supply and a fiber optic modem for communication between electrical and optical signals, and a high-speed communication system. A high voltage supply is necessary in order to limit the electrical transmission losses over the long umbilical. All in all, the CDU distributes incoming electrical power, the control signals, antifreeze chemicals, and hydraulics out to the templates/manifolds and XMT trees by means of infield umbilicals. There are, however, a number of outstanding engineering solutions required to provide sustainable development of such a complex field: large bore subsea connection systems for diver-less connections of the export and infield pipelines, subsea pig launcher systems for intelligent pigging of the pipeline, and a new subsea transformer system for high voltage (typical 3,000 volts).

The development of this cold climate region requires the minimization of all risks with regard to offshore operations, exploration, and production as well as transportation. For example, if the primary fiber optic communication system through the main umbilical could fail, a secondary back-up communication system based on superimposing control signals on the high-voltage power cables in the umbilical should be considered. A thorough risk analysis needs to be done in the early concept selection stages.

By giving this brief overview of the existing challenges, we can conclude that the following areas would need to be examined:

- Multiphase flow regime (flow assurance)
- Electric power supply
- Hydraulic system

- Communication system and electrical signals
- Umbilical system

Although this scheme of development is quite well known in the North Sea for shorter distances, in the case of the former disputed area we met a number of challenges – how to manage multiphase flow over an ultralong distance (about 320 km) offshore; how to deliver electrical power to subsea processing systems from shore; and how a subsea processing system might influence the main production and economic parameters in comparison with a multiphase flow solution.

Case study: comparison of solutions for the Fedynsky High

We will try to clarify the limiting factors and the associated technological barriers relating to this region. Moreover, the main purpose of this discussion is to present a case to conduct comparative analysis of two proposed scenarios for development of the Fedynsky High, Figure 10.6:

- Subsea production system (SPS) with subsea processing (separation, compressing/boosting) depends on fuel composition;
- SPS with multiphase flow to shore.

To start this case study research, we should first assume the reservoir properties and fuel composition. As there is no detailed information regarding the properties of possible prospects, we are not able to conclude on one particular

Figure 10.6 Artistic view, principal scheme of subsea-to-shore development

scenario. Therefore, we suggest several geological models with different reservoir characteristics.

There are three main reservoir characteristics that are of consequence to production: the character of the reservoir rock, the composition and purity of the hydrocarbons, and the strength and nature of the drive mechanism, all of which influence the flow rate and ultimately the productivity of a reservoir. According to the proposed development schemes and fluid type, which will be discussed below, we will also check how these reservoir parameters change over the field-life.

Regarding reservoir type, geological data are discussed in previous chapters; from that we can conclude some facts about oil and gas prospects in the Barents Sea. The Barents region is generally represented by oil provinces in the High North and southern part of the sea; meanwhile the central and eastern areas appear promising for gas and condensate prospects. For instance, the giant oil resources in Pechora Basin belong to the southern part of the Barents Sea, and there is a unique gas and condensate field in the east of Barents – Shtokman. A reserve of gas is located in the southwest of Barents – the Snøhvit, Albatross, and Askeladden reservoirs. The northwestern area is represented by the newly discovered Johan Castberg and Alta oilfields. So far, the former disputed area is assumed to be a gas-dominated region, although oil has also been encountered.

One geological model with particular reservoir characteristics could have four different types of fluid composition:

- wet gas,
- natural gas with condensate,
- natural gas with some amount of oil or volatile oil,
- oilfield with some amount of dissolved natural gas or black oil.

Wet gas/gas with condensate to volatile oil is the most likely scenario for development solutions.

These four hypothetical fluid composition models will also contain various amounts of water in the mixture; so, from that, we can draw a conclusion regarding the possibility of a multiphase flow regime in these cases. Based on scenarios for the distribution of geological formations in the Barents Basin, and the experience of developing similar reservoirs, we can claim that the most likely HC prospects could be found in the Triassic–Jurassic region, which consists primarily of shallow marine sandstone. Reservoir characteristics could be presented by the following:

- Porosity and permeability might be distributed such that the porosity (Φ) values vary between 10% and 25%, with a wide range of permeability values from 0.1 mD to 1,000 mD;
- Water saturation is considered in our geological model.

Depending on the reservoir fluid composition, the design of the SPS will vary with subsea processing modules. Subsea processing can take several forms, comprising a wide range of subsea separation and boosting scenarios. Table 10.2 shows a classification of subsea processing systems that might be used, as well as being a basic reference for most common subsea processing scenarios. Strategic technologies that are believed to be essential for the successful implementation of subsea processing include multiphase pumping, compact separation, and multiphase metering, which are all in varying stages of maturity.

Multiphase pumping usually represents the only commercial form of subsea processing. Multiphase pumping can be classified as a "Type 1" subsea processing system. It directly handles the multiphase mixture with a minimum of equipment. A multiphase pump is essentially a hybrid of a pump and a compressor. The gases are compressed toward the discharge end. This leads to a

Table 10.2 Classification of subsea processing systems

Classification	Characteristic of the subsea processing scheme	Equipment	Water disposal	Sand disposal
Type 1	Multiphase Well stream is handled without processing	Multiphase pump	Water is pumped with the well stream. Hydrate inhibitor needed to provide flow assurance	No sand disposal. The sand is pumped with the fluid. Beware of erosion
Type 2	Partial separation Partial separation of the water in the well stream	Separator and multiphase pump. Wet-gas compressor to be considered	The processed water to be re-injected. Hydrate inhibitor needed to provide flow assurance	No sand disposal. The sand is pumped with the fluid. Beware of erosion
Type 3	Complete separation of the well stream at or near the subsea production location	Separator and scrubber Single or multiphase pump. Wet-gas compressor to be considered	Re-injection of majority of water produced. Hydrate inhibitor needed to provide flow assurance	Sand control needed. Beware of erosion
Type 4	Export pipeline Oil & gas qualities	Multistage separator and fluid treatment. Single-phase pumps and compressors	Re-injection of the produced water	Sand control needed. Beware of erosion

Source: Based on Scott, Devegowda, & Martin (2004).

significant reduction in the gas volume fraction, the GVF, and the volumetric rate, as well as an increase in the mixture density.

Subsea processing demonstrates a number of advantages:

- Accelerating production
- Extending subsea tie-back distance
- Reducing well-intervention costs
- Reducing subsea-development costs
- Permitting oil and gas developments in harsh environments

Pumping multiphase production streams, however, still faces many challenges yet to be overcome, for instance:

- *Changes in flow condition during the life of the asset.* Over time actual production may deviate from the initial expectations, so the multiphase pump should be designed to have a wide range of operating parameters to cope with changing flow conditions
- *Gas volume fraction (GVF) variation.* In extreme cases, this variation can be 100% liquid followed by 100% gas (i.e. GVF from 0 to 100%), which will cause sharp fluctuations in the pumped-mixture density. As a result, the pump load, and, thus, the torque of the shaft, may undergo abrupt variations that could result in serious mechanical problems in the pump. Multiphase pumps can also be used in conjunction with other types of subsea processing schemes. For example, the Type 2 subsea processing system makes use of partial separation of the produced fluids. In this case a multiphase pump will still represent the best option for pumping a liquid stream that will contain some associated gas. A multiphase pump (Type 1) or wet-gas compressor will also represent the best choice for the gas stream. If the gas stream is not left to flow under its own pressure, a multiphase pump or wet-gas compressor can boost the pressure of the gas stream, even when it contains several percent of liquid by volume.

A number of separation options are being considered for Type 3 and Type 4 subsea systems. Subsea processing will avoid lifting large volumes of water to the surface for processing and disposal. This can reduce lifting costs and allow economies in topside water processing and handling capacities and could extend the economic life of deep water projects and reduce development risks. However, a safety systems consideration for subsea processing is an area where little work has been done to date. While the remote subsea location reduces the risks to personnel, environmental risks still remain.

Technical challenges for subsea processing of well stream from the Fedynsky High

Subsea processing technologies are becoming preferable options for improving technical and economic performance, improving the reserves recovery and operation strategy, and even for reducing the associated development CAPEX. Even though the benefits of subsea processing on the bottom are difficult to underestimate, there are still challenges that remain in the key pieces of the "SPS to shore" development concept.

The required power supply to subsea compressors typically would be in the range of 6 to 12 MW per compressor. It is hard to say for sure whether subsea compressors will be needed for the Fedynsky High because of the lack of exact information about reservoir conditions (pressure, temperature) and the component mixture of the HC. If the technology is required for the Fedynsky High, the system will most likely work on the Åsgard field compressor station principle: flows through the existing pipelines into the manifold station, which distributes it into compressor trains located at the subsea compression station. In each compressor train, the multiphase stream is first cooled down in a specially designed heat exchanger and then it enters the scrubber where the gas and liquid (condensate and water mainly) are separated. The gas stream out of the scrubber is then routed to a 12 MW centrifugal compressor and the liquid steam to a 700–800 kW centrifugal pump. At the compressor discharge, a recycle line with a fast-acting valve takes the gas back to upstream of the inlet cooler in case the operating conditions get close to the compressor surge curve. Yet, at the compressor high pressure side, a discharge cooler lowers the gas temperature to below the limit dictated by the existing pipelines before it is comingled with the liquid from the pump. At last, the multiphase stream flows back to the manifold station and further to shore.

As for flow management, electrical power issues are no less important and require outstanding solutions for long step-out subsea fields using subsea processing. Alternating current (AC) power at standard 50 Hz grid frequency (higher supply voltage) works sustainably, but it is very sensitive to distance, as power transmission losses will inherently limit offshore location to about 250 km. The limiting factors relate to capacity loading current, voltage variation, and inductive losses. One of the solutions proposed is to use a lower supply AC frequency; with this approach even ultralong step-outs are achievable (for example Stokmanovskoe field – 600 km offshore).

Hence, if we consider subsea compressors for the Fedynsky High subsea system, due to sufficient pressure drops on the well head and all over the pipeline, the power supply will be in the megawatts range, such as for a wet-gas compressor (12 MW). This means that the longer the step-out distance, the greater the benefits gained from a subsea compressor, but, at the same time, it requires a more difficult power supply at a sufficient level.

With increasing distance, it is evident that the response time will also be increased, i.e. the time elapsed between pressing the button in the onshore control module and when the subsea piece of equipment actually responds on that command/signal. The same solution is found for hydraulic system issues. It is proposed to use subsea accumulators on the wells, assisted by the accumulation effect provided by the umbilical itself. For communication and data transmission requirements for step-out fields, we should take the example of transmitting massive signal rates over transatlantic distance by using fiber optic technology. This technology has shown itself to be a reliable and sustainable solution, so an ultralong distance for the communication systems should not be a problem.

Currently, umbilical systems used for subsea fields are rather complicated, both in terms of cost and technical complexity. For example, the main umbilical for Snøhvit is 144,267 m long and weighs about 2,000 tons; and in May 2012 Oceaneering received an order from Petrobras for the supply of approximately 200 kilometers, or 125 miles, of thermoplastic production control umbilical for field development projects offshore of Brazil in the Santos Basin. So, ultralong distances can be accommodated by manufacturing the umbilical in several sections, which then are spliced together into one continuous length during installation. Such splices would offer a natural opportunity to insert optical isolating amplifiers or repeaters into the umbilical, thereby improving signal fidelity.

Flow assurance

Much attention is to be paid to the design and operation of multiphase transportation systems (flow assurance). Multiphase transportation implies many new challenges:

*   Under unfavorable conditions, oil and water may flow in large batches (slug flow), which can disturb the receiving facilities
*   Oil and water may form emulsions that give high pressure losses and reduced production
*   Wax and hydrates (ice-like substances) may precipitate and block the pipe
*   Unfavorable water chemistry may lead to fatal corrosion attacks piercing the pipe

Before commissioning a field, it is important to be able to predict possible problems and to predict flow patterns and pressure losses as accurately as possible so that pipelines and process plants may be designed optimally (Minikeeva & Gudmestad, 2013).

Transport to market: LNG and/or pipeline

LNG

The exploration and production of natural gas in the sub-Arctic region create a challenge for shipping gas in such extreme conditions. In this chapter, we mainly explore available alternative transportation options via LNG or pipelines and do not investigate the natural gas market at all.

Energy demands are increasing steadily throughout the world, and concern for the environment and the greenhouse effects of fossil fuel is growing. This development has contributed to the growing attractiveness of more environmentally friendly alternatives to oil and coal.

Natural gas is projected to be a growing fuel source through 2030 because it is clean-burning, reliable, and abundant. Additionally, advances in technology have made it economical to ship natural gas all over the world, making it a truly global resource.

To deliver the fuel to the customers as well as to the local market, it is necessary to make a choice of transportation route and method. For the Barents Sea area, there are two ways: LNG and pipeline transport. A discussion on the more suitable method of transportation will be given below.

Transforming gas from its natural state into liquefied natural gas (LNG) means that the gas can be delivered via tankers from distant production areas to markets that need it. Given its flexibility, environmental benefits, and large resource base, LNG is a natural choice to help meet the world's growing energy needs.

It is easy to overlook the fact that LNG is not a new energy source. LNG technology and infrastructure provide a means of monetizing otherwise stranded gas reserves and bringing them to market. For the LNG industry, a growing long-term gas demand drives major investment in global LNG facilities. Furthermore, there is the prospect of further demand for natural gas as the world considers the future of nuclear energy.

Pipeline transport

Transportation to the markets is not a challenge for conventional LNG tankers. In Figure 10.7 the main transportation export routes are shown. The European market might be seen as the main region for importing LNG from the Barents Sea area. With LNG terminals onshore in Norway or Russia, LNG transportation could be the most promising scheme for the Barents region. International markets will be located in Asia and the US, where there is still a discussion on shale gas rates; and in this case, LNG must be delivered by vessels.

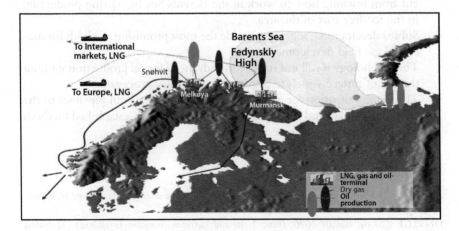

Figure 10.7 Possible High North development layouts (LNG transport and/or pipelines)

Regarding natural gas consumption in Europe, we can also consider pipeline transport along the Norwegian coast or by pipeline net through the Russian Federation, for instance, using the "Nord Stream" pipeline to the European market; see Figure 10.7.

Development schemes for oilfields

With reference to Table 10.2, it must be noted that wet-gas developments, gas-condensate developments, and oil developments require the use of off-shore processing schemes. Thus there will be a need to place surface facilities with process equipment at the field offshore. Associated with this, the need to ensure safety during the entire lifetime of the production raises important issues, such as:

- Will there be a need to disconnect the production facilities should ice drift or icebergs threaten (Gudmestad, 2011)?
- Winterization will be necessary for all equipment (DNV GL, 2013), personnel, and evacuation methods (Jacobsen & Gudmestad, 2012).
- Oil-spill pollution equipment must be developed to function in cold climates, possibly in icy waters. This remains a large challenge and should be discussed separately before a decision to develop a field is taken.

Conclusions

From the above information and discussions, we present the following conclusions:

- The Barents Sea area has large potential for oil and gas development, as there are very interesting prospects that could contain large volumes of oil and gas;
- The physical conditions of the area are very challenging, and one will benefit from learning how to work in the Barents Sea by starting production in the ice-free part of the area;
- Subsea development schemes provide the most promising methods for successful gas field developments;
- The technology is still not sufficiently advanced for oil production without the use of surface vessels to provide the necessary processing;
- The market situation for gas is challenging; however, both pipelines to the European market and LNG production represent well-established methods for safe delivery to customers.

References

Abramov, V. (1996). *AARI, Arctic and Antarctic Research Centre atlas of Arctic icebergs*. St Petersburg, Russia: Blackbone Publishing.

DNV GL. (2008). *Barents 2020. Phase 1. Ice and metocean (maritime & offshore)* (Technical report No. 2008–0664). Oslo, Norway: DNV.

DNV GL. (2013). *Winterization for cold climate* (DNV-OS-A201). Oslo, Norway: DNV GL.

Dodrovolskii, A.D., & Zalogin, B.S. (1982). *Моря СССР* [Seas of the USSR]. Moscow, Russia: Moscow State University.

Econ Pöyry. (2009, December). What if an agreement was reached with Russia over the area of overlapping claims? *Norwegian Continental Shelf Quarterly, 4*, 34–39.

Gudmestad, O.T. (2011). Criteria for disconnection of a moored floater in ice. In A. Bourmistrov, F. Mellemvik, & S. Vasiliev (Eds.), *Perspectives on Norwegian–Russian energy cooperation* (pp. 184–201). Oslo: Cappelen Akademisk Forlag.

Gudmestad, O.T. (2013). Marine construction and operation challenges in the Barents Sea. *International Journal of Ship Research Technology, 60*(3), 128–137.

Gudmestad, O.T., & Karunakaran, D. (2012, July). *Planning for construction work in cold climate regions.* Paper presented at the ASME 31st International Conference on Ocean, Offshore and Arctic Engineering OMAE2012, Rio de Janeiro, Brazil. Abstract retrieved from http://proceedings.asmedigitalcollection.asme.org/proceeding.aspx?articleid=1733054

Institute of Marine Research. (2014). Statistics retrieved from Institute of Marine Research database.

Jacobsen, S.R., & Gudmestad, O.T. (2012, July). *Evacuation from petroleum facilities operating in the Barents Sea.* Paper presented at the ASME 2012 31st International Conference on Ocean, Offshore and Arctic Engineering OMAE2012, Rio de Janeiro, Brazil. Abstract retrieved from http://proceedings.asmedigitalcollection.asme.org/proceeding.aspx?articleid=1733055

Minikeeva, A., & Gudmestad, O.T. (2013). Parametric study of multiphase flow in potential Barents Sea pipelines from Fedyn Arch to shore. In C.A. Brebbia & P. Vorobieff (Eds.), *Computational methods in multiphase flow VII: Vol. 79* (pp. 157–180). Southampton, England: WIT Press.

Norwegian Petroleum Directorate. (2013*). The petroleum resources on the Norwegian continental shelf. Exploration.* Retrieved from http://npd.no/Global/Engelsk/3-Publications/Resource-report/Resource-report-2013/Ressursrapport-2013-eng.pdf

[Polar low pressure area off the coast of Eastern Finnmark] Polart lavtrykk utenfor Øst-Finnmark. (2010, November 22). Retrieved from http://met.no/Polart+lavtrykk+utenfor+%C3%98st-Finnmark.b7C_w7vK3T.ips

Ræstad, N. (2006, March). Barents Sea "nondiscussed" area. *Geo ExPro, 3*(2), 46–47. Retrieved from www.geoexpro.com/

Scott, S.L., Devegowda, D., & Martin A.M. (2004). *Assessment of subsea production & well systems* (Project No. 424). Retrieved from Bureau of Safety and Environmental Enforcement website: www.bsee.gov/Research-and-Training/Technology-Assessment-and-Research/tarprojects/400-499/424AA/

Standards Norway. (2007). *Actions and actions effects* (NORSOK Standard N-003). Retrieved from www.standard.no/en/PDF/FileDownload/?redir=true&filetype=Pdf&preview=true&item=132376&category=5

Storvik & Co AS (Cartographer). (2013). Arctic Europe petroleum resources and infrastructure [Resource map]. Retrieved from Arctic Europe Petroleum Activities website: www.arctic-europe.com/images/Kart_noytralt_2013.pdf

Terziev, F.S. (Ed.). (1990). *Гидрометеорология и гидрохимия морей СССР. Том 1. Баренцево море. Выпуск 1. Гидрометеорологические условия, Проект "Моря СССР"* [Hydrometeorology and hydrochemistry of the USSR. The Barents Sea. Hydrometeorological conditions (Vol. 1, Issue 1)]. Leningrad, the Soviet Union: Gidrometeoizdat.

Wilcken, S. (2012). *Alpha factors for the calculation of forecasted operational limits for marine operations in the Barents Sea.* (Master's thesis, the University of Stavanger, Stavanger, Norway). Retrieved from www.nb.no/idtjeneste/URN:NBN:no-bibsys_brage_33806

11 Petroleum production facilities in Arctic operational environments

Tore Markeset, Anette Sæland, Ove Gudmestad, and Javad Barabady

Introduction

The Arctic is said to have a harsh and cold environment; most of it has a remote location and a sensitive environment. However, one should be aware that there is a large variation in the degree of coldness of the climate, harshness of the weather and remoteness of the location. The southwestern part of the Barents Sea, north of Norway, has, for example, a relatively mild sub-Arctic climate due to the warm waters of the Gulf Stream, which is an Atlantic Ocean current originating from the warm Mexican Gulf. The possibility of icebergs and drifting ice in this region is small. This region is also relatively close to the northern cities of Tromsø, Norway and Murmansk, Russia. However, an industrial production facility in this region will still experience low temperatures, large temperature variations and long periods of darkness during the winter. Other Arctic areas relevant for oil and gas (O&G) production (such as the west coast of Greenland, north coasts of Alaska, Canada and Siberia, etc.) do have a much colder climate, more severe weather and even further distances from populated areas with good infrastructure, larger population and competitive markets for products, supplies, services and qualified personnel (Gudmestad et al., 2007).

The unpredictable weather and harsh Arctic climate found in most of the Arctic include cold temperature, wind, Arctic hurricanes (polar lows), icing, snowdrift, etc., which will affect exposed equipment and personnel. The performance of the operating and maintenance personnel and work processes in general will also be influenced by the cold climate conditions, in particular by low temperatures and icing. The cold climate conditions will influence the functional performance of the equipment/machines/systems as well as the reliability. The remote geographic location, sparse population and poorly developed infrastructure will also cause increased demands on operational and maintenance logistics and industrial support services. To reduce risks, the functional capabilities need to be suited to the production strategies, the manning and logistics need to assure health and safety, the environmental requirements must be met and costs and other requirements must be satisfied.

To be economically viable, any industrial production facility needs to have an acceptable level of performance. We may summarize that a production facility's performance is dependent on the technology (technical systems, equipment, machinery, processes, etc.), the organization (organization, facilities, support tools, external support, infrastructure, etc.) and the humans involved in all phases of the life cycle; all must produce acceptable performance. For example, an O&G production facility should be running when needed at a predefined acceptable operational state. For an O&G production facility, this is 24 hours a day, seven days a week, all year round, and this may be more difficult to achieve in an Arctic climate with harsh weather conditions in a remote location.

The adaption of a production facility's design to the cold climate conditions and harsh weather may result in a more complex design through the integration of hardware, software, sensors, controls, information technology, etc. However, this may also result in the systems having more complex failure modes, which are more difficult to diagnose and repair, and in becoming more complex to operate and maintain. Reliability, maintainability and supportability will be affected and may result in reduced availability performance, increased costs and, thus, reduced profitability over time.

Most maintenance activities should, in general, be proactive and planned. However, due to the harsh and unfamiliar environment, an increased number of unplanned failures (often occurring suddenly) may be expected, resulting in unplanned and expensive corrective maintenance and unplanned downtime with no production – especially at the beginning of the life cycle. Even if the production facility is designed to meet the climatic and weather challenges, its operation and maintenance strategies need to be developed to suit the localization and environmental conditions as well.

It is not difficult to imagine how a cold Arctic climate and daily Arctic weather might affect a production facility, as most have experienced cold temperatures and bad weather and felt how it affects our physical and mental state and our activities. However, in order to discuss the consequences of the particularities of an Arctic operational environment, we will first take a look on the general goals of production facility operations. Thereafter we will discuss how the Arctic climate and locations affect these goals and finally what can be done to overcome the operational challenges in an Arctic environment.

This chapter mainly focuses on the offshore oil and gas production in the southwestern Barents Sea, north of Norway, where the current oil and gas activities are focused (Gudmestad, 2013). However, most of the discussion is general and relevant for other industrial operations as well. Furthermore, we limit ourselves to discussing how the climate and weather influence an industrial production facility design, operation, maintenance and support.

Operational goals

To develop O&G fields in remote Arctic areas, the production facility needs to be designed in such a way that the operations performance and maintenance activity ensure the fulfillment of health, safety, environmental and quality (HSEQ) requirements. Due to environmental concerns, a strict policy of zero release of waste and chemicals to the sea has been decided upon and will also be enforced. The Goliat field is located relatively close to shore and close to sensitive fishing grounds. Potential spills or leakage to the sea, therefore, will need to be dealt with at the design stage to reduce and/or mitigate risks. The design and operational concepts must include measures to protect water, vegetation and wildlife. Furthermore, the climate will be more extreme than in the Norwegian Sea and the North Sea further south. The normal weather conditions may not be worse than experienced further south in Norway, but one will expect increased frequency of storms with increased severity, and thereby increased risks.

Modern industrial offshore production facilities are advanced, complex and integrated systems that are designed to safely, economically and continuously facilitate the transportation and processing of the oil, gas and water from the reservoir and the transformation into energy used by society.

The mechanical, hydraulic, pneumatic, electrical, etc. systems consist of dynamic machinery (with moving parts, e.g. motors, pumps, turbines, compressors) and static equipment (no moving parts, e.g. tanks, separators, pipes, pipelines, etc.), in combination with automation and control systems, consisting of sensors, switches, cables, controllers, electronics, electric circuitry and software, placed on top of an offshore structure (e.g. a platform or ship).

The most important operational goals for such advanced, complex and integrated production facilities are normally specified with respect to the:

- Health and safety of the plant personnel and the surrounding society
- Pollution of the environment in which the facility is operated
- Plant availability over time
- Plant operational quality (effectiveness, efficiency, productivity, etc.)
- Quality of the plant output
- Life cycle costs and profits

Health

Health goals relate to the long-term effects on the plant personnel's physical and psychological health caused by the technical plant, the operational, maintenance, etc. activities and the surrounding environment (e.g. local climate and daily weather variations). Furthermore, the plant and its operations should not affect the society and people living nearby. For example, pollution, noise, traffic, etc. should not make people living near the plant sick. Furthermore, psychological health may be affected by location effects, such as darkness, long distance from home, work-related stress, etc., and may affect the quality and speed of work.

Safety

Safety relates to accidents and incidents that have an immediate negative effect on the plant personnel and people in the surrounding society (e.g. although smoking is a health issue, as it has no immediate negative effect on the smoker it is not a safety issue, whilst a falling hammer is a safety issue as it may have an immediate effect if it hits someone). We will discuss further the safety of the plant.

Environment

Environmental consequences can consist of either pollution to the surrounding environment (air, water, earth, etc.) or wasteful energy usage. Animals, fish, birds, insects, etc. should not be affected by pollution from the plant or by the plant's activities. If energy-inefficient machinery is used, pollution is created in producing the extra energy. For example, a machine often degrades and wears over time due to usage. This may result in increased energy consumption to produce the same output as when it was new. In this case, preventive maintenance of the machinery to bring it back to the original condition may be costly, but it may also remove the pollution related to producing the extra energy and also reduce the energy consumption and thereby the costs.

Plant availability over time

Plant output is dependent on the plant being built to accommodate the production volumes anticipated and being available to be run when needed. This production capability and capacity also need to be consistently reliable over time to be competitive. The customers are interested in and paying for safe, secure and timely delivery of the output (the product) of the right quality from the production facility. To ensure timely delivery, one may build in buffers in the production system in case an unplanned shutdown delays delivery to the customer.

For example, for a typical offshore oil and gas production facility, the goal is that the plant should be running continuously without any interruption at all. However, things do not always go as planned, and sometimes systems degrade/fail and cause interruptions to oil and gas production. To minimize such interruptions, some production facilities have, for example, built in storage tanks that can be used to store oil in case the oil tanker hired in to transport the oil to the customer is delayed. Similarly, a tanker may load its cargo from the tank if the production facility is having problems.

Another example of a buffer system that may increase the availability for shorter periods is the pipelines built to transport gas to the customers. As the pipelines have a large diameter and the gas is under great pressure, they contain a large volume of gas. If the production facility is facing problems and stops delivering gas into the pipeline, the customers may still get uninterrupted gas delivery from the gas already enclosed in the pipeline until the pressure becomes too low. This solution buys some time, and the customers do not see and experience the effect of a production problem. However, most often this is a solution that may be costly and that only will buy some time.

The assurance of the production availability is dependent on the reliability, maintainability and supportability of the plant machinery, equipment, components, etc.

Reliability

The main goal of reliability is to avoid failures causing stoppages of the system function or reducing system function performance. To achieve high reliability, the components should be manufactured to tolerate the internal and external loads and wear and tear over time. Reliability is also dependent on the assembly, integration with other components, machinery and structure being carried out properly and on the correct installation, commissioning and testing processes. In addition, operations should be within specifications and intentions (i.e. the machine should be used for the purpose it is designed for without overloading it). Furthermore, high reliability does not mean that machinery is maintenance-free – often high reliability is achieved as a result of excellent preventive maintenance performed before the degradation is allowed to develop into the occurrence of a failure event where the performance is less than specified or completely absent and, in the worst case, causing a hazard for people and for the plant itself. Reliability is a design parameter – after the design phase reliability can only reduce. Improvement in reliability after the design phase requires a redesign of the technical function solution, an upgrading in the material selected or a change in how the function solution is implemented in manufacturing, assembly, testing and integration with surrounding systems.

Maintainability

The term "maintainability" refers to deciding how easily and fast one is able to perform preventive maintenance (before a failure event) and to perform restoration and repairs after a failure event. The maintainability parameters include enough space to conduct maintenance activities, components that are not too heavy (built-in lifting arrangements if the components are too heavy), usage of standard tools in maintenance activities, modular design that enables easy and fast exchange of deteriorated or failed modules, etc. The main maintainability goal is to reduce the downtime and to enable fast, safe, effective and efficient preventive and corrective maintenance activities.

Supportability

All systems need support services that are delivered by internal and external providers during the various life cycle phases. The support during maintenance activities may, for example, seriously affect the quality of the maintenance and the time it takes. If a spare part or a specialist needed for a maintenance activity is delayed, the consequences are extended downtime with no production and no income to cover the costs that are running, even though production is not.

Examples of support services needed during operations include spare parts and field engineers from an original equipment manufacturer (OEM), planning, scheduling and execution of maintenance activities, training of operators and maintainers, operational performance analysis, engineering during plant modifications, etc. The output of a supportability analysis decides how effectively and efficiently support services can be delivered to the system when needed. This requires an organization to be in place with the ability and means to plan, organize, administrate and deliver the support when needed. This also requires an infrastructure that has the required capacity and capability and that is also reliable.

One also should realize that reliability, maintainability and supportability are design parameters that should be thought about as early as possible in the design process to enable effective and efficient systems.

Plant operational quality (effectiveness, efficiency, productivity, output quality, etc.)

The operational quality is dependent on the plant technology being designed such that technical processes are able to meet the production goals (quantity, volume, quality) effectively, efficiently and continuously when called upon. This requires that there should be no bottlenecks in the technical process and that the technical systems function as intended within specifications and without failure. The plant output should be of such quality that the customers are satisfied and are willing to pay full price. However, the operational quality is also dependent on being operated by qualified and skilled personnel and on there being an effective and efficient organization in place to organize and administrate, plan and schedule, etc. the plant's activities according to needs.

Maintenance needs

The maintenance needs are decided by the 1) unreliability of components due to insufficient or wrong quality of materials or manufacturing and assembly processes; 2) human errors due to insufficient training or poor operational and maintenance procedures; 3) statutory requirements which may vary depending on physical location, country, etc.; 4) accidents, etc. Maintenance is a compensating work process carried out to prevent system failure (preventive maintenance) or to restore the system function after a failure occurs (corrective maintenance).

Even simple systems are almost impossible to design so they are maintenance-free, due to costs and technological considerations. Most advanced and complex systems are not 100% reliable and experience occasional failures followed by corrective maintenance. Systems that are 100% reliable are often due to the preventive maintenance designed to keep the systems running. Furthermore, even though components, equipment, systems and machines have become much more reliable than before, the use of advanced, complex and integrated systems has resulted in the fact that failures may be difficult to diagnose, repair and/or restore and may also increase the downtime and thereby reduce the production output and increase the downtime costs.

Life cycle costs

For a production facility to be profitable, it needs to be able to produce the output at sufficient and agreed upon quality, and to deliver it at the right time and at the right costs to customer satisfaction over time. The income from the output should support operational inputs (e.g. raw materials, organization, personnel, external support, etc.) needed to produce the output, the payment of the bank loans needed to build the plant, the insurance, etc. To be competitive, the costs should be as low as possible and the quality as good as defined in the agreement with the customers.

Next we will discuss what is special about the Arctic climate, weather and location and how the plant goals are affected.

The Arctic operational environment: key aspects of importance for production and maintenance

When considering industrial activities in Arctic locations, one obviously needs to consider the local climate and weather. Climate and weather both refer to how the atmosphere is behaving and its effect upon human life and activities (What's the difference between weather and climate?, 2005). "Climate" describes the average long-term weather over time and space, whilst "weather" refers to short-term (minutes to months) changes in the atmosphere. An easily remembered phrase, expressed by Robert Heinlein (1973) in a science fiction novel, states that, "climate is what you expect, weather is what you get." Even though the climate data shows the average long-term weather behavior, one needs to use the extreme weather data for worst-case scenario predictions for production facilities' design dimensioning, as well as for the planning of any operational and logistic activities.

Weather may be described in terms of temperature, humidity, precipitation, cloudiness, brightness, visibility, wind and atmospheric pressure (high/low) (What's the difference between weather and climate?, 2005). In addition, one must consider the winter darkness that increases in duration the further north one is from the polar circle.

The most important parameter is the temperature – it strongly affects the materials used and the human capability and capacity for cognitive and physical abilities. However, the other parameters should not be dismissed – often it is the combination of several factors that creates the most severe weather effects.

The humidity and precipitation in combination with wind may cause atmospheric icing, which may cause the accumulation of ice on facility structures. The cloudiness may cause stoppages in helicopter activities, important for the logistics of people and materials. The long periods of darkness during winter may cause human depression; the period of brightness during the summer may cause sleep problems. It is well known that humans make more errors if depressed or tired. Visibility is reduced when it is snowing, raining, foggy or dark. Strong winds in combination with precipitation in the form of snow or rain may reduce all kinds of operational activities as well as causing stoppage and delays in logistical operations.

As mentioned briefly in the introduction, the Arctic is a large area with a huge variation in the climate and weather. For example, the Arctic climate in Alaska, Canada and Russia is a "stable" cold climate, whilst the climate in the southwestern Barents Sea is cold with frequent changes in temperature. These temperature variations may create additional challenges. The sub-Arctic climate in the Barents Sea is strongly influenced by the warm Gulf Stream originating from the Gulf of Mexico. The possibility for icebergs is quite remote, even though there is a small possibility of drift ice in the northern part of this area. The geographical area is sparsely populated but rich in wildlife and fishing resources. This demands an additional focus on requirements that need to be considered in the design phase regarding operations, maintenance and support.

Temperature

A temperature of 0°C has been cited as the key element in the definition of what should be considered a "cold region". Materials such as metals, plastic and lubricants begin to show the effect of cold temperature on their properties well below 0°C temperature (Freitag & McFadden, 1997). Temperatures vary according to location and season. In the Arctic, the coldest months are often January or February (−30°C to −40°C) and the warmest month is July.

For sub-Arctic areas, the equipment and facilities not only have to be resistant to low temperatures, but also to large variations in temperature during short periods of time.

Wind

In the Barents Sea, the phenomenon of "polar low pressure" may occur. The so-called "polar low" storm or "Arctic hurricane" is a shallow, short-lived low pressure center, causing severe weather with heavy snow and strong surface winds that appear suddenly, forming over polar seas (Polar low – The Arctic hurricane, n.d.). They may be identified using satellites but are not easy to forecast and may therefore create huge problems for industrial activities in the Arctic (Gudmestad, 2013).

Icing

Ice on structures/equipment may cause enormous challenges if maintenance is needed. Depositions of ice glaze and accumulations of wet snow on the surface of facilities, communications and power transmission lines, and white frost formations are often observed.

When designing a plant and a production facility, it would be an advantage to know how the weather affects the location (e.g. the probability of rain, freezing rain and wet snow, wind direction, frequency of winds stronger than 10 m/s for different air temperatures). This type of information may tell us in which direction and at which temperature different precipitation events are most likely to occur (Drage & Mølmann, 2003). In addition, the wave height in combination with strong winds will have an influence on the degree of sea-spray. The design should therefore protect the production facility against the direction in which it is most likely to grow ice (see also American Bureau of Shipping [ABS], 2006).

In the early winter of 2006, the production facility at Melkøya experienced icing of the equipment due to the storm named "Narve". For pictures, see www.finnmarkdagblad.no/bildeserier_fd/article1920428.ece. The production was closed down for four to five days, and it took nearly one month before operation of the facility was back to normal (Isaksen, 2006).

Snowdrift

Snowdrift is another climate factor to consider during the design, construction, maintenance and operation of a production plant. Snow is relatively easily suspended and transported by wind and creates a variety of problems in cold regions. Snow that remains will metamorphose over time into an assemblage of roughly spherical ice grains. Even if the temperature remains well below freezing point, the snow/ice crystals grow due to vapor diffusion and freezing at contact points.

The concentration of snow in the air increases rapidly with wind speed. Snow accumulation at production facilities may be problematic for maintenance and operation work. Wind-blown snow can restrict the access to equipment, instruments and ventilation outlets, and can block doors, rails, stairs, etc.

In situations with snow precipitation and strong wind, the snow crystals will accumulate in low-velocity areas near obstacles and create snow depositions. The process is often self-intensifying. Especially during the design and construction of an onshore production facility, possible snow accumulation should be considered thoroughly. A possible efficient solution could be the construction of snow fences (Drage & Mølmann, 2003; Freitag & McFadden, 1997).

Weather forecasting

The northern region has a poor coverage of weather observation stations (S. Wergeland, personal communication, November 20, 2006). Experience from the weather stations in the north of Norway shows that the weather forecasting abilities are inadequate. The forecast may indicate that a low pressure is building up, but the size, location and strength are hard to predict (Torrissen & Johansen, 2006).

Effects of the Arctic environment on operations

The severe Arctic climate and remote locations may seriously influence the production goals. The cold temperatures may affect the performance of the materials used in the technical systems, and the performance of the operation, maintenance and support personnel. Furthermore, the remote location with less-developed infrastructure, smaller populations and fewer markets may affect the organization of operational and maintenance activities and support processes.

Materials

A number of materials such as iron and steel, polymers and plastics, concrete and composite materials experience embrittlement at low temperatures (ABS, 2006; Freitag & McFadden, 1997). This may cause failures at loads that are routinely imposed without damage in warmer climates. When the brittle transition range falls within the material service temperature, brittle fractures are a paramount concern. Steel and alloys of iron that have been treated to change the crystal structure tend to lose the benefit of treatment when the service temperature is below −10°C. During cold-weather welding, preheating has to be included in welding procedures and careful postheating is necessary to avoid the rapid cooling of the heat-affected welding zone, which often creates a zone of very strong but also extremely brittle metal.

Seals and gaskets are primarily made of elastomers that can be fabricated for low-temperature service (Freitag & McFadden, 1997). However, when some polymers are cooled slowly enough, the resulting crystallization will affect the mechanical properties and sealing capabilities. The consequences may be serious leakages of lubricants, coolants, etc. Highly crystallized plastics are rigid and brittle, making them poor candidates for cold temperature service. Cold temperatures also cause the generation of static electricity that can destroy electronic components in computers, control circuitry, etc.

A simple approach for winter concreting is to avoid exposing concrete to freezing temperatures (Freitag & McFadden, 1997). New additives for antifreeze and quick set, new materials for high strength, and new techniques for placement promise to extend the range of conditions under which good quality concrete can be produced.

Engines and equipment operating during cold weather are subject to higher wear and increased breakage (Freitag & McFadden, 1997). Lubricants are used to reduce friction and thereby wear rates between moving components in dynamic machinery. Their secondary function includes removing particles between moving surfaces and cooling components heated by friction or combustion. Oil becomes more viscous as the temperature falls, thus making it more difficult to supply lubricant to renew the protective oil film.

If the lubricant fails to perform, one will experience increased energy usage, increased wear rates and thereby earlier failures, as well as an increased amount of unplanned corrective maintenance and extended downtime. Routine operations such as steering, starting, braking and operation of controls will require increased energy usage due to inadequate lubrication performance and thereby increased friction. Also the rolling friction in bearings, for example, will be higher and require increased energy usage in the form of higher fuel consumption and richer air/fuel mixture. Slow uniform warming of the entire engine is desirable during cold weather and of critical importance during extremely cold weather.

A hydraulic system will cease to perform when the temperature drops to a few degrees above the pour point (Freitag & McFadden, 1997). Arctic-grade hydraulic fluids should be used and hydraulic hoses must be rated for cold weather use. Some synthetic materials that are acceptable for hot-weather work become brittle and fail under pressure during cold-weather operations.

To avoid freezing and the rupture of liquid cooling systems, one should use freeze protection for any vehicle that is exposed to temperatures below 0°C.

Human factors – "Man in the Arctic"

Wind, snowfall and darkness, in combination with low temperatures, will reduce the operational effectiveness drastically in a cold climate. Humans were "designed" to operate in a very narrow temperature range, and, when we push the limits of that range, we are subject to increasing physiological stressing (see also ABS, 2006). At low temperatures during the performance of manual tasks, humans have reduced cognitive/reasoning abilities and cognitive errors are more likely to occur. In general, as the ambient temperature falls below freezing, the effectiveness of workers declines significantly (Perkins, 1996).

More energy is needed to keep the body operating and it tires more quickly. Coordination suffers, the body moves more slowly and productivity decreases. The possibility of making mistakes or being inaccurate will also increase. Extra time must be allowed for all operations when the temperature drops (Freitag & McFadden, 1997; Påsche, Holand, & Myrseth, 1990).

Wind chill

When exposed to cold temperatures, the rate of cooling and heat loss for an exposed surface, such as skin, depends not only on the temperature but also on the speed of the wind (Freitag & McFadden, 1997). When the wind speed rises, heat generation must also increase or more clothes must be worn to prevent the body's temperature from dropping.

In 2001, the National Weather Service implemented a new wind-chill formula to provide a more accurate understanding and useful formula for calculating the dangers from winds and freezing temperatures. The new formula estimates a significant reduction in the wind-chill effect (National Oceanic and Atmospheric Administration [NOAA], 2014). When dealing with exposure conditions, an unheated shelter of any kind is better than being exposed to even the slightest wind. A tent or a tent-like structure around the worksite can improve conditions significantly. If it is impossible to enclose the work area, frequent breaks in a warm location help to slow performance deterioration. Long, infrequent breaks are not as good as frequent, short breaks in maintaining performance and worker contentment (Freitag & McFadden, 1997).

Clothing

Heavy clothing is necessary for protection as humans are fairly vulnerable in cold temperatures. Heavy clothes impede motion, and more energy is required for even the most routine chores when dressed in cold weather gear. In a cold climate a person is totally dependent on his/her personal protective equipment. The establishment of proper work procedures and work task training is necessary to perform the work within specific safety and efficiency limits. Even with these preparations, an extremely cold environment represents a work environment that may be hazardous for people's health. For work requiring a high degree of activity, it is important that the clothing has as good ventilation as possible to reduce the perspiration effect resulting in damp inner clothing and cold injuries (Påsche et al., 1990).

Food intake

One physiological aspect that does not slow down is the appetite. After a full day of work in the cold, the body compensates for the increased energy use and heat loss by increasing the metabolism and the result is a much greater appetite than normal. When supplying rations for outdoor winter activity, the normal amount of food supplies should be increased by factors from 1.5 times to twice the normal. Warm liquids also help to avoid dehydration, which is a frequent problem when working in extremely dry, cold air (ABS, 2006; Freitag & McFadden, 1997).

Darkness

Winter in latitudes north of the polar circle is characterized by periods of complete absence of daylight. The darkness reduces the efficiency of workers. The length of periods when the sun is above the horizon at a site is determined by the relative position of the sun, the earth and the location (Freitag & McFadden, 1997). At worksites, artificial light is necessary in periods when most of the day is dark. However, it has been a challenge to make light bulbs that have a long, efficient life and at the same time are resistant to long, cold periods (S. Dragsund, personal communication, November 15, 2006).

Effects caused by the remote location

Transportation and communication are vital to the growth and prosperity in any region. In general the cold regions in the north are not as populated as further south, and the development of roads and railroads is limited. Even where roads exist, winter conditions of ice and snow seriously degrade the effectiveness of transport. The number of adequate airports in these areas is limited, and airplane communication is not as frequent as in other regions in the country. In the sub-Arctic areas in Norway the situation is better, but the railroad is not developed. Helicopters can be used regularly, but weather conditions may restrict the frequency.

Transportation

In the Arctic region it is only in Russia that there are shipyards capable of taking on the large-scale construction projects needed to build large-scale production facilities. Fabricated modules will most likely be built in yards far away from the development site. Transportation from the yard to the site has to be taken into serious consideration. Most heavy transportation is carried out using ships and barges. The cost of transportation of the modules will be high and requires careful planning. The capacity to perform repair work is, however, available in Norway and Russia. The physical environment may be rough and unpredictable, and it is important to be familiar with the differences in seasons. Ice must be avoided, but wave heights, wind strength/direction, as well as icing in harbors and open water also have to be considered. The weather window for transportation is less than elsewhere.

Competence

O&G production facility development and construction requires a lot of equipment and labor. In the Arctic regions, getting enough competence to the area may be challenging. Most likely, there is no one (or very few) in the area that has expertise or experience with such technology. One solution may be to educate and train local inhabitants, if there are any, in the necessary skills. However, most often skilled labor has to be hired in for periods or moved to the development area.

Onshore development in remote areas, such as for example constructing/operating process facilities or terminals, will also need a large workforce. Establishing a new society in a remote area will take time, not only to get people to settle down for longer periods, but also to get people to flourish and to keep them there. For extremely remote areas, it may be advantageous to let the personnel work in shifts and rotations (e.g. four-week rotation).

Communication

Modern communication systems have proven to be very important to the development of the cold regions. A radio-telephone system with microwave and satellite linkage has, for the most part, removed the isolation from even the smallest communities. Telecommunication systems not only permit direct conversation on matters of daily concern but also carry educational programs and furnish specialized technical advice and remote support to supplement the knowledge of the resident personnel. In the case of an accident, medical advice from the closest hospital could easily be given with today's telecommunication technology.

With the aid of web cameras and the possibility to transfer medical data directly to experts at the hospital, it is feasible to give medical advice and treatment to offshore installations and to other remote areas. With a similar technique, information and communication technology (ICT), telecommunication systems may be used to provide technical advice and problem-solving during the development period and operation stage. The work processes are improved at the same time as the operational expenses are reduced. Advancement in ICT has made it possible to inspect, supervise and control processes 24/7 remotely and away from the production or operation site. ICT also enables access to experts located in different parts of the world.

Furthermore, companies can use emerging technology to improve performance and develop smarter operations, maintenance and support processes (Kumar, 2005; Kumar, Markeset, & Kumar, 2006).

Support services

Support is a wide concept, and includes logistics, inventory and infrastructure, information and communication, as well as competence and skills. When aiming for cost-efficiency, these factors are essential throughout the service life of any production facility. In the Arctic region, one should expect the costs of support to be higher. The population is often much smaller and the infrastructure less developed. In addition, lack of competence, and needs with regard to the transportation of equipment/modules/people, spare-parts and inventory management will demand more time and planning.

Inventory

One of the most important tasks, during development and operation, is to maintain sufficient equipment, tools and parts inventories. Supporting a field development project of a large magnitude in a remote location requires careful planning and flexibility.

The geographical distribution of customers is becoming a critical factor in decision-making concerning service delivery strategies, spare parts logistics and inventory management. The distance of the user from the manufacturer, distributor/supplier can bring an additional influence on spare parts management. For remote areas, due to increased delivery time, the inventory has to contain a larger number of spare parts and also critical parts that normally could be delivered from the supplier at short notice. To optimize product support, these issues also need to be considered in the design phase by the manufacturer, supplier and customer (Ghodrati, 2005; Ghodrati & Kumar, 2005; Markeset, 2003).

Offshore and subsea activities

During the installation and commissioning of an offshore facility one will be dependent on the weather being suitable for the activities planned. Critical activities may have to be performed during the short summer season to avoid the risk of job delay or cancellation due to storms or bad weather. However, even during the summer months, one faces the risk of fog and thereby reduced visibility. Subsea installations are not so affected by the cold Arctic climate as the subsea water temperature is not so different from at other locations. However, the installation, maintenance and inspection of subsea systems are critical operations that are affected by the cold temperature and the weather as they are performed from ships or from platforms and often by using remotely operated vehicles (Gudmestad, 2013; Markeset, Moreno-Trejo, & Kumar, 2013).

Design for the Arctic operational environment

The physical environment, geographical location and regulatory requirements present different challenges regarding the choice of materials, equipment and support strategies. Technology should be suitable for the specific environment, and safety measures should be kept at a satisfactory level as the requirements may be higher than elsewhere (Samarakoon & Gudmestad, 2011).

It is the operator's responsibility to include economic as well as technical considerations in recommending a production facility design solution, taking into consideration the operational environment and geographic location. The economic evaluation will include all aspects related to the costs of development and will consider in particular investment costs, operation costs and maintenance costs. Important in this analysis is the selection of equipment based on a production availability analysis (Gudmestad et al., 1999). The aim is to optimize the design in relation to:

- Requirements regarding design or operations given by authority regulations
- Requirements given in various international standards and statutory bodies
- Requirements regarding health, safety and environment
- Requirements regarding safety equipment based on risk analysis and overall safety acceptance criteria
- Project constraints such as budget, realization time, national and international agreements
- Conditions in sales contracts
- Requirements regarding market performance

Reliability is one of the most important aspects to consider for reducing costs. The lower the reliability, the higher is the probability of failure, accidents, environmental pollution, etc. Due to the severe climate and harsh weather, one may expect that it is not possible to predict and design out all possible failures. Furthermore, one may expect that failure may have more severe consequences with a higher possibility of negative HSE effects and longer downtime. More frequent failures will increase the safety and health risk of personnel as well as the risk of polluting the environment. In addition, the personnel are also affected by being exposed to the cold environment and may err more in the performance of activities.

To increase the overall failure resistance, a strengthening of some components may be needed, which would lead to increased costs. Thus, from an economic point of view, one would try to make a design robust enough, considering the time duration and the operational environment, to obtain a reasonable level of reliability.

When designing the maintenance strategies one would like to see that all failures of critical equipment can be predicted so that all failures can be prevented using compensating maintenance activities before the failure event. The failures can, for example, be predicted using statistical estimates based on experience and historical data. However, one of the problems is that one may lack the historical data of how particular machinery behaves in the harsh Arctic climate. As an alternative, one may try to observe the real-time system condition using modern condition monitoring techniques. However, this may not be possible if the failure develops fast or if there is no method of observing parameters usable for predicting failures, or lack of proper sensors.

Through creating excellently designed systems with respect to reliability and maintainability (Markeset, 2008; Markeset & Kumar, 2003a, 2003b), as well as increasing the use of automation and remote operations, one may be able to reduce the requirements with respect to the workforce and logistics. The identification of factors that may have an effect on the production facility performance may also facilitate a more accurate prediction of operational, maintenance and support needs in the design phase (Gao & Markeset, 2007; Ghodrati, 2005; Jardine, Banjevic, Wiseman, Buck, & Joseph, 2001; Kumar, 1990; Kumar, 1996, Kumar, Klefsjö, & Kumar, 1992).

In general, the life cycle cost (LCC) is defined as the total costs associated with the product or system over a defined life cycle. LCC-analysis is an engineering and economic optimizing technique, where the main goal is to identify and choose alternatives that generate the highest revenue over lifetime or, in other words, generate the lower life cycle cost (Markeset & Kumar, 2000). Some of the factors that may influence LCC in the Arctic regions include:

- Winterization of equipment. This depends on the duration of time the temperatures are below zero
- Functional and ergonomic design of the equipment. It is important to bear in mind that both the equipment and the operator move more slowly in cold temperatures
- Zero environmental spill policy. Produced water from the reservoir should not contain more than 10 ppm oil if released to the sea in the Barents Sea, compared to the 30 ppm oil content requirement in the North Sea
- The production facility end-of-life/disposal. Higher cost in remote areas. Less possibility of reusing winterized equipment

Evacuation and rescue

Due to the harsh conditions of the physical environment, it may be difficult to ensure that the evacuation means are available when needed. Of particular concern are snow and icing that could cause blockage of access to lifeboats; therefore lifeboats in these areas may have to be kept in heated shelters.

Furthermore, there has been an effort in Norway to improve the quality of survival suits to ensure that the Arctic immersion suits are self-righting and that they maintain the temperature over a period of six hours even if the sea water is at near freezing condition.

Means to ensure evacuation and survival suits for frozen waters are under development; however, the equipment must be qualified for each area under consideration as the requirements will vary in the cold climate regions.

Following evacuation, rescue must be ensured. The helicopters used for rescue operations on the Norwegian shelf will have to be upgraded to extend to the licenses where exploration drilling is planned on the Norwegian shelf. Furthermore, emergency landing sites must be identified. The protective area of Bear Island, midway between Norway and Spitzbergen, as well as the drilling rigs or stand-by vessels operating in the area could serve such a purpose (Jacobsen & Gudmestad, 2013).

Discussion and concluding remarks

The Norwegian offshore industry has little experience in the design of O&G production facilities in the cold and harsh environment of the Arctic region. Exploration/drilling rigs have been operative in the Barents Sea for several years, but only the Snøhvit onshore LNG terminal at Melkøya in Hammerfest has been built and operated for some years. The Goliat platform is being built but has not yet come into operation. Both are located in a sub-Arctic environment.

One drilling rig that does have experience in the Barents Sea is the Polar Pioneer, owned by TransOcean. The rig is a mobile semisub, and has been through substantial reconstruction to resist the cold and harsh environment expected in the Barents Sea. The deck is built-in, and the area where the equipment is located is insulated. In addition, the rig has equipment for de-icing by the use of steaming equipment (Torrissen & Johansen, 2006). However, the building-in of the deck area creates several restrictions such as crane operations, storage, inspection, etc. In the case of gas leakage, the ventilation has to be good to avoid the increased risk of inhalation and explosion. Explosion panels, opening at low overpressure, are often installed to avoid the buildup of high explosion pressure in confined modules.

The Polar Pioneer rig has a double hull, and all pipes are laid inside a heated area between the outer and inner skin to avoid icing (Steensen, 2006). Outside pipes are installed with heating cables and insulation. In addition, machines, equipment and sensitive instruments, etc. are built in enclosures with extra insulation. This makes it much easier to both maintain and work in the area. All

the escape openings are electrically heated, the recreational rooms are additionally insulated and the instrumentation is certified to resist the low temperatures.
Both columns and pontoons hold equipment and tanks for storage.

Placing the equipment inside heated areas to avoid icing may be a requirement for all future offshore installations, but it may be more challenging to
achieve for onshore installations. However, one needs to consider whether all
the equipment inside the heated area still needs to be designed to resist extreme
temperatures.

When deciding upon the design for maintenance, operation and support in
an Arctic climate, there are three main factors to be taken into account, namely:

- The physical environment at the particular geographical location
- The component/system at the location
- The human being who works at the facility at the particular location

Operation, maintenance and support in cold and harsh environments will
require a different strategy than that used in more temperate climates and less
remote locations. Some periods of the year may, for example, not be suitable
for work outdoors due to the fact that systems/components may not be accessible because of snow/ice or because the management has decided that workers
are not allowed to go outside when the temperature is too low. One solution
would be to delay major maintenance to the warmer summer months. However, if something unexpected happens one should be able to resolve the problem to avoid downtime.

The choice of the optimum design of an offshore structure is important
because it often determines the price, robustness and reliability of the structure.
It is, however, impossible to recommend a generic optimum structural form for
a region since each region has its own specific environment with related challenges. In the early phase of the development, studies and observations should
be carried out to define the dominating factors for these locations.

The goal is a business that is as profitable as possible, while at the same
time prioritizing HSEQ issues. A properly designed working environment is a
cost-effective investment in the operation of a production facility and improves
efficiency by reducing the time needed for operation and maintenance.

Finally, the operators will always have to deal with other actors such as nongovernmental organizations and indigenous people, who may not support the
development of the northern region. Political and environmental issues related
to the Arctic region will most likely continue to be contentious.

References

American Bureau of Shipping. (2006). *Guide for vessels operating in low temperature environments*.
Houston, TX: Author.
Drage, M.A., & Mølmann, T. (2003). Arctic coastal climate impact on design construction
and operation of Hammerfest LNG plant. In A. Collins, S. Løset, J. Dempsey, G. Timco, &

202   Tore Markeset et al.

I. Kubat (Eds.), *Proceedings of the 17th International Conference on Port and Ocean Engineering under Arctic Conditions, POAC'03, Trondheim, Norway* (pp. 421–429). Trondheim, Norway: Norwegian University of Science and Technology.

Freitag, D.R., & McFadden, T. (1997). *Introduction to cold region engineering.* New York, NY: ASCE Press.

Gao, X., & Markeset, T. (2007). Design for production assurance considering influence factors. In T. Aven, J.E. Vinnem, & C. Guedes Soares (Eds.), *Proceedings of the European Safety and Reliability Conference (ESREL2007), Stavanger, Norway* (pp. 519–525). Stavanger, Norway: University of Stavanger.

Ghodrati, B. (2005). *Reliability and operating environment based spare parts planning* (Doctoral thesis, Luleå University of Technology, Luleå, Sweden). Retrieved from http://epubl.ltu. se/1402-1544/2005/51/LTU-DT-0551-SE.pdf

Ghodrati, B., & Kumar, U. (2005). Operating environment-based spare part forecasting and logistics: A case study. *International Journal of Logistics: Research and Applications, 8*(2), 95–105. doi: 10.1080/13675560512331338189

Gudmestad, O.T. (2013). Marine construction and operation challenges in the Barents Sea. *International Journal of Ship Research Technology, 60*(3), 128–137.

Gudmestad, O.T., Alhimenko, A.I., Løset, S., Shkhinek, K.N., Tørum, A., & Jensen, A. (2007). *Engineering aspects related to Arctic offshore developments.* St Petersburg, Russia: LAN Publishing House.

Gudmestad, O.T., Zolothukhin, A.B., Ermakov, A.I., Jacobsen, R.A., Michtchenko, I.T., Vovk, V.S., & Shkinek, K.N. (1999). *Basics of offshore petroleum engineering and development of marine facilities: With emphasis on the Arctic offshore.* Moscow, Russia: Neft i Gaz.

Heinlein, R.A. (1973). *Time enough for love.* New York, NY: Berkley Publishing Group.

Isaksen, O. (2006, March 28). Melkøya kan stoppe opp [Melkøya can stop]. *Finnmark Dagbladet.* Retrieved from www.finnmarkdagblad.no/

Jacobsen, S.J., & Gudmestad, O.T. (2013, June). *Long-range rescue capability for operations in the Barents Sea.* Paper presented at the 32nd International Conference on Ocean, Offshore and Arctic Engineering, OMAE 2013, Nantes, France. Abstract retrieved from http://proceedings.asmedigitalcollection.asme.org/proceeding.aspx?articleid=1786515

Jardine, A.K.S., Banjevic, D., Wiseman, M., Buck, S., & Joseph, T. (2001). Optimizing mine haul truck wheel motors' condition monitoring program: Use of proportional hazards modeling. *Journal of Quality in Maintenance, 7*(4), 286–301.

Kumar, D. (1996). *Reliability analysis and maintenance scheduling considering operating considerations.* Unpublished doctoral dissertation, Luleå University of Technology, Luleå, Sweden.

Kumar, D., Klefsjö, B., & Kumar, U. (1992). Reliability analysis of power transmission cables of electric mine loaders using the proportional hazard model. *Reliability Engineering & System Safety, 37*(3), 217–222. doi: 10.1016/0951-8320(92)90126-6

Kumar, R. (2005). *Industrial service strategy: Development, implementation and execution.* Unpublished doctoral dissertation, University of Stavanger, Stavanger, Norway.

Kumar, R., Markeset, T., & Kumar, U. (2006). Implementation and execution of industrial service strategy: A case study from the oil and gas industry. *Journal of Quality in Maintenance Engineering, 12*(2), 105–117.

Kumar, U. (1990). *Reliability analysis of load-haul-dump machine.* Unpublished doctoral dissertation, Luleå University of Technology, Luleå, Sweden.

Markeset, T. (2003). *Dimensioning of product support: Issues, challenges and opportunities.* Unpublished doctoral dissertation, Stavanger University College, Stavanger, Norway.

Markeset, T. (2008). Design for high performance assurance for offshore production facilities in remote harsh and sensitive environment. *Quarterly Journal of the Operational Research Society of India, OPSEARCH, 45*(3), 275–290.

Markeset, T., & Kumar, U. (2000). Application of LCC techniques in selection of mining equipment and technology. In T.N. Michalakopoulos & G.N. Panagiotou (Eds.), *Proceedings of the 9th International Symposium of Mine Planning and Equipment Selection, Athens, Greece* (pp. 635–640). Rotterdam: A. A. Balkema.

Markeset, T., & Kumar, U. (2003a). Design and development of product support and maintenance concepts for industrial systems. *Journal of Quality in Maintenance Engineering, 9*(4), 376–392. doi: 10.1108/13552510310503231

Markeset, T., & Kumar, U. (2003b). Integration of RAMS and risk analysis in product design and development: A case study. *Journal of Quality in Maintenance Engineering, 9*(4), 393–410. doi: 10.1108/13552510310503240

Markeset, T., Moreno-Trejo, J., & Kumar, R. (2013). Maintenance of subsea petroleum production systems: A case study. *Journal of Quality in Maintenance Engineering, 19*(2), 128–143. doi: 10.1108/13552511311315940

National Oceanic and Atmospheric Administration. (2014). *Wind chill temperature index.* Retrieved from www.nws.noaa.gov/os/windchill/wind-chill-brochure.pdf

Perkins, R.A. (1996). Risk assessment of vapor in cold regions, cold region engineering. In R.F. Carlson (Ed.), *Cold regions engineering: The cold regions infrastructure – an international imperative for the 21st century: Proceedings of the Eighth International Conference on the Cold Regions Engineering, University of Alaska, Fairbanks, Alaska* (pp. 360–369). New York, NY: American Society of Civil Engineers.

Polar low – The Arctic hurricane. (n.d.). Retrieved from www.weatheronline.co.uk/reports/wxfacts/The-Polar-low – the-arctic-hurricane.htm

Påsche, A., Holand, B., & Myrseth, E. (1990). Cold climate work clothing. In *Proceedings of The Polartech '90 International Conference on Development and Commercial Utilization of Technologies in Polar Regions* (pp. 325–334). Hørshelm, Denmark: Danish Hydraulic Institute.

Samarakoon, S.M.S.M.K., & Gudmestad, O.T. (2011). Qualification of offshore facilities prior to application in a new field. *Journal of Cleaner Production, 19*, 13–20. doi: 10.2495/RAV090081

Steensen, A.J. (2006, May 2). Rigges opp for arktiske strøk [Rigged for Arctic regions]. *Teknisk Ukeblad.* Retrieved from www.tu.no/

Torrissen, T., & Johansen, A. (2006). *Operasjonsbetingelser og mulige utfordringer for petroleumsoperatører i Barentshavet* [Operating conditions and possible challenges for petroleum operators in the Barents Sea]. Unpublished bachelor's thesis, Tromsø University College, Tromsø, Norway.

What's the difference between weather and climate? (2005, February 1). Retrieved from www.nasa.gov/mission_pages/noaa-n/climate/climate_weather.html

12 Crisis management considerations and designs in cold climate areas

Ove Njå and Ove Gudmestad

Introduction

"Great events have small beginnings" (Perrow, 1984, p. 9). Traditionally, crisis investigations have provided analyses that address critical malfunctions of equipment and systems, founded in simple linear causal explanations. During the last 20 years the trend has been towards system approaches, where tight couplings and complex interactions between subsystems, units and components have been seen as contributing factors to crises. This has triggered researchers to develop new accident models (for example Hollnagel, Nemeth, & Dekker, 2008; Hollnagel, Woods, & Leveson, 2006; Leveson, 2004, 2011). Modern crisis investigations reveal circumstances that normally function but, in unfortunate combinations, the crisis has emerged and attained its magnitude. Working with crisis management in cold climates needs to reflect the complex systemic characteristics.

The natural resources in the Arctic areas are valuable; for example, fish, meat, oil and gas, minerals and coal deposits, the tourist industries and economically viable transport routes attract commercial interests. At present the Arctic is being exposed to pressures not seen before, indicated in Laurence Smith's futuristic assessment of the North (Smith, 2011). The international agreement on the exploration and government of Spitsbergen (Svalbard Treaty, 1920) is an example of the international community's respect for vulnerable areas in the polar region. Furthermore, Norway and Russia have recently (2010) signed an agreement on the boundary (Delimitation Line) in the Barents region. This agreement increases the pressure on exploring these areas for oil and gas resources. The potential for major disasters has been addressed by stakeholders over a long period. However, to date the data material on Arctic offshore crises is scarce and fragmented, which corresponds with the restricted exploration and operations seen in the area. That does not mean that risk is low, but we need to draw on experience that somehow could be relevant, crises occurring in onshore cold regions.

In this chapter we discuss the contextual premises for characterizing Arctic and cold climate areas. These premises are further connected with industrial and other commercial activities with possibilities for major crises. We analyze past reported major accidents and incidents with the potential for becoming major crises in order to illuminate the need to address the performance of the crisis response systems. The concept "crisis response systems" comprises all efforts made by the activity/systems at the sharp end (Arctic), the apparatus provided by other organizations and the society, also at the sharp end, and all related efforts at the blunt end (regulatory bodies, enterprise management, crisis operation centers, etc.). Thus, the emergency preparedness definition: "All technical, operational, organizational measures which prevent a dangerous situation that has occurred from developing into an accidental event, or which prevent or reduce the harmful effects of accidental events that have occurred" is relevant as a starting point. Hence, the responsible decision maker must identify which situations should be labeled "dangerous" and which situations should be interpreted as accidents.

We interpret the notion "crisis management design" by adopting Donald Schön's (1991, p. 79) claim that "design is a reflective conversation with the situation." Thus, the situation is characterized by cold climate hazard characteristics assessed against the activities subjected to purposes such as oil and gas explorations, tourism or transport. Crisis is understood as "a serious threat to the basic structures or the fundamental values and norms of a system, which under time, pressure and highly uncertain circumstances necessitates making critical decisions" (Rosenthal, Charles, & 't Hart, 1989, p. 10), to which the output artifacts, the systems, whether they are dominated by technology or not, are the answer to the reflective conversation. We intend to provide a tool that enables a reflective process to develop crisis management designs in cold climates.

What is meant by Arctic areas? Most people intuitively think of the areas close to the North Pole, which is covered by ice. Some define "Arctic" by the maximum limit of floating ice. However, the exact borders of the Arctic are not definite. Often the concept of "Arctic areas" is contextual and contingent on the issues that are addressed; for example, when discussing Arctic oil and gas activities, the content is related to identified basins which inter alia include areas as far south as the Faroese Shelf and Bering Sea (US Outer Continental Shelf) (Arctic Monitoring and Assessment Programme [AMAP], 2007). Another definition is related to climate, for example the 10-degree isotherm for July, or some define "Arctic" as the southern border of the permafrost (Bernes, 1996). ISO 19906 (International Organization for Standardization [ISO], 2010) concerning Arctic and cold region areas defined "Arctic" as where sea ice may occur. Geographically, one could also think of Arctic as defined by the Polar Circle. The are many options, but in general the Arctic is characterized by harsh cold climate, large uncertainties of environmental phenomena, scattered human populations and far fewer human activities than further south.

The complexity and numerous considerations to be made in designing crisis response could be exemplified by the Vassdalen accident on March 5, 1986, when a snow avalanche killed 16 soldiers as they were building a winter road for tanks in Norway's Troms County (Norwegian Official Report, 1986, p. 20). The preparation troop approached an area of the valley with heavy tracked vehicles without proficient knowledge about avalanche hazards; neither precautions nor responses had been consulted in the planning phase or in the execution phase. All weather conditions developed very negatively the week before the exercise (heavy snowfall and strong winds occuring a short time before the accident). The signs were numerous; troop commanders were worried and threatened to ignore orders to enter the area; avalanche experts were consulted very late in the proceedings without a real opportunity to do their job; and communications were impeded and information lost on the way. In the period before the exercise there were many signs and messages about the avalanche hazards, but the responsibility for acting upon them was not taken. The commanding officers were concerned about the ongoing exercise scenario, and, at the top-level command (for the exercise and the brigade), reflections about snow avalanche hazards were underestimated. The organizational complexity in this case is obvious, but the predictability of avalanches and their physical preconditions is also challenging (Kleemayr, 2004). The avalanche was huge, and 31 persons and two belt wagons were transported 100–150 m downhill in bad weather (snowfall, −10°C and strong winds). Of the 17 victims buried deep (1–3m), only one survived (he sat close to a belt wagon and had an air pocket). The search and rescue work was extremely complex (Rostrup & Gilbert, 1993; Rostrup, Gilbert, & Stalsberg, 1989; Stalsberg et al., 1989). The ongoing NATO exercise was stopped and the Norwegian Army has since put in place new procedures to avoid hazardous training events during wintertime. The subsequent investigations were also criticized for not appropriately addressing responsibilities.

The Norwegian Army has also lost soldiers due to drowning when they have been crossing unsafe lakes covered with ice (the latest incident was on December 1, 2003). In this respect it is necessary to be aware that the ice on a lake may not be homogeneous but will vary in thickness over the lake. In particular, near river outlets strong currents may reduce the thickness of ice so bandwagons must avoid these areas and not cross.

This means that emergency preparedness is inherent at all levels, presented by individual attitudes and competence together with organizational, technical and operational arrangements in the harsh working environment the sector and society involved. Emergency preparedness is every precaution made in order to ensure that any situation is handled in a controlled way and the risk is reduced accordingly. Hence, emergency preparedness covers all consequence-reducing arrangements. This wide definition implies that all arrangements with multiple functions also have functions related to emergency response activities. A pipeline in the Arctic areas accommodating a gas flow serves as a containment of gas flow, but it must also be designed to resist extreme external and/or internal loads, and, combined with its maintenance/inspection program, it must ensure that the normal operation function is maintained.

Challenges for crisis management in cold climate – characteristics and past events

The climatic conditions in the Arctic areas comprise large uncertainties with respect to the exceedance probabilities of waves, winds, polar low effects, etc. for operational and design conditions (Gudmestad, 2013).

The related challenges that must be taken into consideration are:

- Insufficient data for accurate weather prediction
- Rapid variations in weather conditions
- Harsh weather conditions for long periods at a time
- Harsh weather combined with darkness and low visibility
- Potential for icing and difficult operational conditions for all equipment
- Freezing temperatures making equipment unsuitable, as for example hydraulic equipment and firefighting systems
- Cold polar waters

Past accidents

Some examples of accidental situations in harsh weather will be discussed in the following in order to illustrate the magnitude of forces and ill-designed response systems seen in Arctic areas.

Accidents caused by wave conditions and storm surges

The Norwegian Coastal Steamer (Hurtigruten) has been an important institution, linking the communities along the Norwegian coast from Bergen to Kirkenes, since 1893. Accidents have happened, generally in large storms. Over its 118 years, 15 ships have been lost. Here it should, however, be noted that the ships sail in almost any weather along the partly open coast of Norway ("Many accidents," 2011). When Sanct Svithun went down on October 21, 1962, 41 persons were lost. The reported cause was a navigation error during strong gale winds and heavy rain. Rescue operations were particularly difficult as the ship was off course.

The loss of the fishing vessels, the British trawler Gaul (near Bear Island, February 8, 1974, 36 fatalities, see Marine Accident Investigation Branch [MAIB], 1999) and the Norwegian trawler Utvik Senior (February 17, 1978, nine fatalities, see Norwegian Official Report, 2004, p. 9) have not been fully explained. The most likely causes seem to be large waves, potentially combined with low freeboard and icing, causing flooding and loss of vessel intact stability.

It is known that the combined storm surge and tide can cause considerable flooding, as was the case in the Varandey area in northern Russia on July 24, 2010, when the oil treatment and storage terminal located kilometers inland was flooded and the air runway close to the coast was damaged.

Accidents caused by polar low pressures

An important challenge is the lack of weather predictability during some parts of the seasons, mainly due to the unpredictability of the polar low pressures, which again is partly due to the lack of sufficient information to establish reliable forecasts. This might lead to long periods of "waiting on weather"

(Gudmestad & Karunakaran, 2012). In northern Norway stories are told about sudden winds that have taken many lives at sea. Fishermen could go to sea in calm weather and be surprised by strong winds and snow, and there are stories from certain communities where the main part of the male population was lost at sea during these large winds. The famous priest and poet, Petter Dass (1647–1707), was working in northern Norway and tells about fishing settlements losing too many men.

During an incident in February 1848, up to 500 men drowned when fishing off the Lofoten Islands while being surprised by the outbreak of a polar low (Kolstad, 2007). According to Kari Wilhelmsen (interviewed by Grønås & Skeie, 1999), 56 vessels were lost and 342 people lost their lives in accidents in Norwegian waters in the twentieth century. Many of these losses were related to polar low pressures, sudden outbreaks of strong winds, often with heavy snow and large waves.

Due to their violent and sudden nature, the polar lows have been the cause of many losses at sea. In the past, polar lows were extremely challenging to forecast. Their small size meant that they easily were hidden between observation points in the Arctic, and they did not have a sufficiently high visibility in the weather prediction models. Also, the physical processes were not well enough described in the models. This led to poor model performance and often false or absent indications in the numerical prognoses, as well as a general lack of confidence among forecasters. Subsequently, the lows were often omitted in forecasts to the public. In recent years, the availability of satellite data (images of cloud structures) and wind data from the sea surface has greatly improved. Satellite data are now assimilated in the numerical models, and, together with a finer resolution, this has led to a higher quality of short-range forecasts. Forecasts of potential polar lows are now routinely included in text forecasts of gale warnings, as well as in forecasts for aviation or maritime users. Nevertheless, there are still large uncertainties in these weather forecasts (Wilcken, 2012).

An earlier episode that received much attention in Norway was the storm in which seven ships went down off the coast of Eastern Greenland (Vestisen) on April 5, 1952, killing 78. There were 53 vessels in the area for fishing and seal hunting. Five of these were never found (Alme, 2009). Økland (1998) has suggested that an Arctic front led to strong amplification of the winds parallel to the ice edge. In this area the ice conditions vary greatly, and unstable weather conditions with strong winds, fog and snow also make crisis response very difficult.

Accidents caused by ice conditions

The 1952 accident in Vestisen is just one of very many accidents with loss of vessels and loss of lives associated with fisheries and seal hunting near the ice edge in northern waters (Alme, 2009). In general, the older type of wooden sealers were not built for large ice load pressure (Aristova & Gudmestad, 2014), and the remote locations made rescue operations very difficult. The crews were dependent on their pals on other vessels. On April 7 to 9, 1917, six vessels disappeared with 84 men during a fierce storm. In 1933 (April 9 to 10) seven ships with 13 men were lost, and in April 1939 two vessels with 28 men disappeared.

The most dangerous situations were caused by ice pressure in northeasterly winds when open leads in the ice cover closed and by multiyear ice floes drifting in waves. With the introduction of steel hulls, only one vessel, Veslekari, was lost in Vestisen in 1988. The improved performance was also due to less activity and better weather forecasting.

In Russian Arctic seas a number of vessels have been lost over the years in heavy ice conditions. During Soviet times, many of the records were classified. Recently, Marchenko (2012) has been given access to old archives and has prepared a monograph, summarizing all known events from the Kara Sea to the Chukchi Sea. Steel vessels have also been lost, and the danger of a floating multiyear ice floe should not be underestimated. Furthermore, parts of the North Eastern Passage are unchartered and sandbanks are shifting location, so full attention must be kept when navigating in these waters. The communication system and the possibility for rescue in these distant waters are of concern and it is understandable that Russian authorities require icebreaker assistance for navigating this passage during periods of dangerous ice conditions.

On September 16, 1989, at 23:05, the cruise vessel, Maksim Gorkiy, ran into an ice floe at full speed 60 nm west of Isfjorden, Svalbard. There were 953 persons onboard; of these, 575 were passengers, many of them elders with reduced mobility. The Norwegian Coast Guard vessel, KV Senja, was called at 00:40 and arrived at 4:00 after having travelled at a speed of 22 knots. The passengers went into lifeboats at 01:30. Then the ship started to take in water and was listing (Kvamstad, 2013). Eventually all were rescued due to the fortunate situation that the Coast Guard vessel was that close, the weather situation was calm and the rescue was carried out in a professional manner (Hovden, 2012). There was great potential for the loss of many lives. It may be impossible to rescue everyone from a cruise vessel in the case of an accident in northern waters far from available emergency equipment. A cruise vessel in northern areas might represent the ultimate challenge and also the highest risk in terms of personnel loss.

Particularly challenging conditions for crisis management

Water temperature

The low temperature of the seawater in cold climate areas for large parts of the year means that survival in the cold sea is less probable than in more temperate seas. The expected time before exhaustion or unconsciousness sets in decreases sharply when the temperature drops below 4°C and the expected time of survival is in the order of an hour or less. It is therefore necessary to provide the workers on facilities and vessels in cold climate offshore areas with the best possible survival suits. Work has been initiated to provide improved suits and these have proved very useful, allowing the rescue team some added time to reach the location. It should be noted that the distance from facilities to shore in northern waters quite often is large, stretching the efficiency of the crisis management team to the limit.

Water temperature and cold exposure during immersion can be life-threatening and are often the direct cause of fatalities in accidents. Immersion accidents often consist of four life-threatening phases – cold shock response, inhibited muscular function/coordination, hypothermia and post-immersion (Thelma AS, 2010).

Spray icing

When a vessel is moving in waves and wind, spray icing, caused by water freezing to ice when hitting the vessel, could cause a large accumulation of ice on the vessel. This large amount of ice can lead to loss of buoyancy, in particular in the case where a vessel is overloaded (as may be the case for heavily loaded fishing vessels where the freeboard is low). Furthermore, accumulation of ice on a vessel will lift the center of gravity and lower the GM, the value of the metacenter height, which is a measure of the stability of the vessel. Smaller vessels with equipment located high up from the waterline (like fishing vessels) are particularly exposed to dangerous icing situations. If combined with waves, the vessel stability can be threatened. It is thought that icing was involved in the sinking of Gaul (see above). Furthermore, as an example, the Lady of Grace, a fishing vessel in Nantucket Sound, sank on January 26, 2007, due to ice buildup on the decks (United States Coast Guard [USCG], 2008).

Another incident is the loss of the Kolskaya jackup during tow in the Okhotsk Sea. The jackup listed and took in water and spray ice lodged on the legs and deck. Eventually the jackup capsized, leading to the loss of 53 crew members (Aristova & Gudmestad, 2014).

Design principles for crisis management

Safety has traditionally been managed by adopting recognized standards and codes. Standards and codes often prescribe how to develop arrangements or directly present those arrangements that should be chosen in safety and emergency management, implicitly providing an acceptable safety level. In using this approach, no attempt is made to express (calculate) the performance of the systems. In many sectors, performance assessments are part of the technical, operational and organizational safety and emergency management, through the employment of functional requirements. Functional requirements describe what to achieve instead of what arrangements are to be selected. The important question is then how to develop requirements, assess performance and choose emergency preparedness and response arrangements for systems and activities operating in Arctic areas. Ghoneim (2011) favors applying recognized standards in the Arctic but has also revealed inconsistencies in the prevailing standards. Lack of experience and novel activities combined with mature knowledge in some relevant fields call for tailor-made solutions adapted to actual enterprises or the sectors involved. However, performance analyses must be carefully considered with respect to, for example, relevance of data, modeling and validation.

For all cases with sudden strong winds, possibly combined with snow, immediate crisis response activities would be very difficult. To reduce the risk, the authorities have emphasized the need for improvements in the weather forecasts. During a cold break in the winter of 2012, fishing vessels were not allowed to leave harbors in Finnmark County as the combination of winds, temperatures and waves made vessel icing highly probable with the high potential for ships to lose stability.

Specific challenges in the cold regions can be exemplified by discussing the Vnukovo Airline crash in 1996. On August 29, 1996, a plane from Vnukovo Airlines in Moscow crashed into the Opera Mountain on Svalbard during an attempted instrument landing at Longyearbyen airport. The crash resulted in 141 persons losing their lives upon impact. The cause was deemed to be incorrect navigation in low skies (Aircraft Accident Investigation Board/Norway [AAIB/N], 1999). Communication between the tower and the plane was also very difficult due to language problems. As a consequence, approaches to the airport from the eastern direction are in general restricted.

Below are three approaches presented to express and interpret situations for use in crisis response planning. These approaches represent practices from the Norwegian oil and gas industry (Njå, 1998).

Defined situations of hazard and accident (DSHA)

DSHA relates to a selection of possible events to be dealt with by the emergency preparedness of the activity in question. These situations are partly defined by means of risk analysis based on experience and qualified evaluations. DSHA includes the dimensioning (a reference) of accidental events, less extensive accidental events and situations connected with a temporary increase of risk.

Worst case

The worst-case approach puts the focus on extreme conditions connected to emergency situations. This could be, for example, extreme weather conditions simultaneously occurring with a fire in a specific area. The risk picture obtained from the risk analysis is given less attention, and it will only serve as initial guidance for the development of the extreme situations. These situations could also be directly developed as scenarios or accidental loads, without a risk analysis.

A cluster of specific situations denoted as situation classes

As opposed to the other two approaches, this approach does not focus on detailed described situations but on classes of situations, for example fire or types of fires such as liquid fires or jet fires. Flexibility is sought by focusing on the crisis response arrangements and their functionality. The flexibility of the crisis response arrangements to perform tasks in building crises should be investigated through performance analyses.

The situation class approach contains assessments of the crisis response arrangements' flexibility to function in the class. A class of situations represents a cluster of single situations identified through a variety of descriptions; for example, the scenarios could be included in risk analyses as a branch in the event tree. Of course, situations more likely to occur than others are not indifferent in the choice of crisis response arrangements. Risk analysis could be used to provide information about the proneness to hazards and accidents, but such analyses could also be replaced by scenario identification without associating probabilities. It is the continuous analysis of the flexibility of the proposed crisis response arrangements that is important, how the acting and reacting "forces" communicate, not how probable those novel situations might be. The variability, for example of the situations or load parameters within the situations, could be described by uncertainty distributions. In this case, the performance requirements could be gradually developed through performance analyses, particularly focusing on consequences to be avoided. A proper crisis response system is dependent on a conscious and active use of performance requirements. There is a need for systematic approaches when dealing with performance measures/quantities such as reliability (will the systems be there when needed?), effectiveness (capacity and execution time regarding the systems' expected functions) and survivability (systems' vulnerabilities to the crisis scenario). *Capacity* could be related to the ability of the evacuation means to evacuate injured people, and the *execution time* could be the related time for carrying out this activity. In a planning process the analyses have to be futuristic; thus it includes uncertainties associated with the performance measures. It is the crisis response arrangements that are the starting point and the issue for the assessments.

As seen in crisis response planning today, the focus has to a large degree been placed on the accuracy and complexity of DSHA descriptions. Requirements, often with an unclear background, are aimed at tasks in these specific situations. This process should be reconsidered by moving towards a flexible class of situations approach, in which a systematic development of requirements is included. This method of interpreting situations for use in crisis planning is adopted for the approach to optimize the performance requirements using phase models.

How to approach and assess performance of emergency response systems

The Emergency Prevention, Preparedness and Response Working Group concludes that "Infrastructure inadequate for response operations, coupled with the unique environmental difficulties present in polar environment, provide real challenges to risk assessment and mitigation" (Emergency Prevention, Preparedness and Response Working Group [EPPR], 2011, p. 15). There are major uncertainties about fundamental crisis response issues regarding capabilities in Arctic environments, which calls for careful consideration about systems expected to operate in emergencies and their interrelations.

A classification scheme – a model describing the stages from perception of danger to the possible responses to dangerous situations – has been developed in order to comply with the emergency preparedness definition. Thus, the model is split into two coherent sub models: (1) preaccident model, and (2) postaccident model. Using this model (classification) as a basis, revisions can be made to represent the total crisis response system/organization.

Preaccident model

The preaccident model focuses on all accident preventive preparations. At this stage, the design principles, technology achievements, motivational and competence philosophies related to the personnel, organizational development, etc. are important arrangements. The harsh climatic conditions, time spans, ecological vulnerabilities, etc. must be seen in light of the planned activities, such as oil and gas exploration, tourism or transport. The communication systems have limited availability in the High North (Kvamstad, 2013), which is another type of vulnerability together with physical availability and tracks to reach the facility (Spring & Hansen, 2011).

Level of danger

The level of danger could, for instance, be communicated on the basis of risk analyses, safety meetings, safety audits, statistics and experience data, or signs/indicators critical for the activity execution, cf. the Vassdalen case above. A conscious practice of danger contemplation characterizes an organization focusing on high reliability. A suitable contingency design will provide necessary signs to responsible persons sufficiently in advance to allow corrective actions to be taken. The presentation of the crisis response phases below is partially descriptive, including examples to illuminate the concept followed by important issues to consider when designing each phase. Currently Dawson, Johnston and Stewart (2014) are concerned that there is no central authority to govern the growth of the Arctic expedition cruise industry, in order to supervise and control the level of danger. The need for better weather forecasting has been a major concern in the ship traffic emergency system in the Barents Sea, as illustrated by the deployment of Wavescan metocean buoys (Mathisen & Bidlot, 2011). In general, an enhanced focus on weather forecasting tools in the Arctic is a prerequisite for crisis management systems designed for the Barents Sea (Barabadi, Gudmestad, & Barabadi, 2014).

Inspection and preventive maintenance are arrangements that heavily intervene in this process, in the way that hazards will be systematically searched for and removed. However, these measures are not necessarily appropriate since they could mislead the focus onto areas of minor importance. The challenge is therefore to critically examine whether the inspection is performed in areas with potential hazards and whether maintenance is carried out on the basis of the criticality and reliability aspects of important components. This is part of the objectives of hazard seeking.

- Is the system oriented at danger contemplation, e.g. detection systems, report systems, etc.?
- What inspection schedule is planned?
- What maintenance philosophy is laid down?
- Are the employees trained to seek hazards?

As a summary of an analysis of Arctic cruise activity, based on Canadian data, concerns about aging and insufficient infrastructure and capacity are raised. There is an aging ship fleet, but also major limitations in search and rescue (SAR) resources, salvage and clean-up contingencies (Dawson et al., 2014). A further assessment of their study, addressing rapid changes and major uncertainties in the industry, shows the industry as extremely vulnerable if the tourist service providers are not concerned with hazard-seeking activities.

Managing safety requires a conscious attitude regarding the level and type of competence needed, either appreciating a flexible and cognitive understanding of systems or accepting a superficial understanding, focusing on error signs as sufficient. Hazard recognition is closely related to hazard seeking. Behind hazard recognition there is a requirement to understand the cause-and-effect relations that lead from those signs and symptoms to the occurrence of the potential disease, accident or disaster. The skills of searching and inspection systems therefore need to be combined with the cognitive, diagnostic function of putting those indicators together and making sense of them.

- Which signs of danger should be expected?
- Are inspection methods capable?
- Are employees trained at fault diagnosis – cause and consequence evaluation?

Very often, even when hazards are well known, they are still not recognized as such. Prior to the fatal avalanche in the Vassdalen in March 1986, the day before there had been another significant avalanche in the area. However, no one recognized the hazard as being relevant for the troop working in the valley preparing the path for belt wagons.

Assessment of priority

Assessment of the priority and importance of the danger lies in the cognitive and affective area, in the sense that motivational factors are as important as the knowledge base. The use of technical safety device systems, such as detectors and activating systems that need to be responded to or deactivated, pushes motivational factors aside. However, every system needs to be carefully considered due to its coupling with other systems or activities. Lord Cullen (Cullen, 1990) reports that the crew on Piper Alpha knew that many sprinkler heads were defective, but nobody found it important to repair them. In this case, lack of knowledge about potential consequences dominated, but of course the motivational level of the responsible people was not perfect either.

- What causes a situation to be labelled as dangerous?
- Who will communicate the need for action and who will appreciate it?
- What systems assess the priority and importance of specific actions?

Wave-ice interactions (Dumont, Bertino, Sandven, & Kohout, 2011) are pressing issues in Arctic activities, for example in the tourism business. A thorough understanding of these effects is of utter importance for the shipping industry challenging interesting spots and areas. The Maksim Gorkiy incident and rescue could have been an extreme case with slightly different wave-ice conditions; however, there was no evidence that the shipowner had paid much attention to this prior to the incident (Hovden, 2012).

Allocation of responsibility

Allocation of responsibility covers the correct acceptance of the responsibility for action by an individual or a technical device. Hale (1984) refers to a questionnaire directed towards supervisors regarding the responsibility for taking action when hazards occur. For 64% of the hazards present, action was regarded by the supervisors as being the responsibility of someone else. This was despite the fact that the supervisors were, according to their enterprises, responsible for everything that happened on the sites that were being inspected.

- Who or what system is responsible for taking action?
- How is this responsibility communicated?
- What kind of decision must be made?

Sydnes and Sydnes (2013) have studied the bilateral oil response regime between Norway and Russia. They claim that shared understanding and common interests increase the reliability that a situation will be handled efficiently in the Barents Sea. The basis for their policy analysis is interviews and evaluation reports from exercises, from which they conclude that the involved parties show commitment and operational responsibilities.

Deciding and acting

When a hazard has been recognized and the responsibility for action has been accepted, it is quite obvious that the knowledge of courses of action must be present. Human knowledge and skills, effectively interacting with the functionality of equipment, is the fundamental key to obtaining an optimal crisis response system. Appropriate training is needed, with a focus on analytical ability, i.e. cause and consequence consideration, to enhance the knowledge-based behavior of responsible personnel.

- What action is needed?
- Is the time horizon critical?
- Is sufficient flexibility provided in the training of humans and/or system designs to identify appropriate actions?

The decision to act is the final part of the cognitive behavior or the system activation. Again, designs of automatic devices could replace the high motivation pressure upon personnel to actually carry out the decision to act. Automation implies standardized courses of action, which does not allow for a weighing of competing courses of action. In many cases weighing is necessary, and in such cases individual cognitive behavior would be preferable.

- What triggers action?
- What consequences are to be expected from lapses and mistakes?
- How are decisions communicated and instructed?

The final barrier to ensuring an incident does not develop into an accident, is the action sequence, which covers the skills necessary to carry out the incident recovery work. This includes performance of maintenance work, response to suddenly arising incidents and the removal of technological, organizational and operational aspects that increase the risks.

- Is sufficient skill provided to ensure that the incident does not develop into an accident?
- What equipment is needed?
- Is feedback of the action sequence given to check that the hazard is removed?

Eik and Gudmestad (2010) discussed iceberg management, addressing whether an iceberg would be detected, actions considered and proper towing arrangement set up, and towing successfully executed prior to collision with an offshore facility. The assessment depended on many quantities such as the distance, shape and size of target, sea state, and personnel and tug master's competence. The complexity of including and simulating the iceberg collision situation, for example in the Shtokman area, needs to be carefully considered as part of the crisis management action sequence.

The preaccident model is coherently connected by the critical development of the situation. The remaining dangerous situation will (dependent of time) shift from being a dangerous situation to an accidental situation if no or inappropriate corrective actions are taken. Even though the distinction or limitations between the descriptions of the situations are not clear, an accidental situation should be characterized by the compelling actions to be taken.

The departure from the preaccident model to the postaccident model is characterized by the occurrence of an accidental situation. An accidental situation implies a certain level of harm done. The body or system that perceives the harm must evidently become the focus.

Postaccident model

When a situation has developed from being dangerous into an actual accident, the question is whether the crisis response organization is prepared and able to bring the situation under control. This is a critical transition, which has often revealed substantial deficiencies in the crisis response systems (cf. Piper Alpha accident). As with any prediction of the future, one major problem is to describe the events accurately.

Responsibility and knowledge

There is no doubt that an accident requires action, and thus the *responsibilities of action* must be clear. The emergency organization should be designed to be sufficiently robust to deal with some extent of variability.

- What damage is to be expected?
- Is adapting to the crisis response organization carried out smoothly?
- How is the crisis response organization structured, e.g. with respect to responsibility?

As the accident situation has occurred and the responsibility for action is clear, the knowledge of an appropriate course of action must be present. Human knowledge and skills effectively interacting with functionality of emergency equipment are necessary for dealing with situations where time factors and accurate performance are a matter of life and death.

- What action is needed?
- Is the time horizon critical?
- Is sufficient flexibility provided in the training of humans and/or system designs for the appropriate actions?

Deciding and acting

The decision to act is the final part of the cognitive behavior or the emergency system activation. Designs of automatic devices could replace the high motivation pressure upon personnel to actually carry out the decision to act.

- What triggers action?
- What consequences are to be expected of mistakes?
- How are decisions to be communicated and instructed?

Even though the Vassdalen avalanche might be seen as a disaster, the victims in the area partly covered by snow made a heroic effort to release their friends. This is the most effective rescue arrangement in all avalanches, and this case was no exception. Seven partly buried victims were rescued by their mates (Stalsberg et al., 1989).

Components of an action plan

Upon the decision to act, the "regular" crisis response activities are to be performed. Usually an action plan is established in order to describe the arrangements for alert, danger limitation, rescue, evacuation and normalization. To meet the goals for these phases:

- The alert shall be carried out to ensure a totally effective mobilization of all relevant emergency preparedness resources.

  ○ Who is to be alerted?
  ○ Is the alarm equipment designed properly to alert all humans and counteracting resources?
  ○ Is a system provided to ensure/check that the alert is successfully carried out?

Alarm systems encompass all efforts to scramble the dedicated crisis response systems. Whether such systems need to be designed with special precautions has not been the subject for critical reflection in the research literature. However, for every activity, whether in oil and gas, fisheries, shipping, tourism or other, society is organized with joint rescue coordination centers. "Alert" is a major response phase influencing the performance of the combat and rescue arrangements; thus, special concerns are needed.

- Measures for danger limitation shall be implemented to reduce the consequences of an accident that has occurred, such that rescue and evacuation can take place in a safe and organized manner, damage from pollution is prevented and financial loss is kept within defined limits.

  ○ Is the area of the accident sufficiently limited with physical barriers?
  ○ Are active danger limitation resources (external and internal) available in time, and have they sufficient capacity?
  ○ What is the escalation potential?
  ○ Are critical conditions identified, e.g. environmental, terrorist, public interference, etc.?

There has been extensive research and analyses on how to mitigate oil responses in ice conditions (Ghoneim, 2011). In situ burning (Fritt-Rasmussen, 2010) and various types of skimming and encapsulating methods have been tested for their efficiencies (Dickins, 2011). This is an area that has been given an extreme political focus; thus, the societal credibility regarding recommended solutions is of major importance.

- Rescue measures shall ensure that missing persons are found and injured persons are given necessary first aid and are brought to a safe area for treatment by the health service.
    - ○ How are missing persons to be notified and located?
    - ○ Is the rescue equipment sufficient, and is the accident area open for access?
    - ○ Where are safe shelters and first aid locations to be sited?
    - ○ How are the injured personnel to be prepared for transportation to hospital?

In his study of available search and rescue arrangements for the petroleum industry in the Barents Sea, Jacobsen (2012) concludes that it is not advocated in the present state to facilitate "all year petroleum activity everywhere in the Barents Sea" (p. 141). The distances are too large and the capacity of helicopters and vessels combined with the harsh environment would not be sufficiently safe.

- Evacuation on and from the plant (installation) shall be carried out in a safe and organized manner in order that all personnel are brought to a safe area.
    - ○ Are all evacuation routes available?
    - ○ Are necessary evacuation means available in time?
    - ○ Is sufficient training given to access and maneuver evacuation means?
    - ○ Are personnel able to assess the prevailing situation, and are they familiar with alternative evacuation possibilities?

Over the years, evacuation means have been subject to technological developments adapted for the geographical climate conditions; see for example Hall and Seligman (2011), Jacobsen (2012), Marsden, Totten, and Spring (2011), Ré (2011) and Ré and Veitch (2013). Marsden et al. (2011) recommend multiple types of crafts to provide options for vastly different conditions and more integrated approaches that seek to balance the weaker components.

- Normalization shall ensure that injured personnel are given treatment and care, the environment is restored to its normal condition and damage to the plant (installation) is stabilized/repaired.
    - ○ How are people involved in the accident followed up?
    - ○ How are relatives taken care of?
    - ○ What is the strategy for informing the public?
    - ○ How is the damage to be repaired?
    - ○ What impact on future activity is expected?
    - ○ How is damage compensation organized and settled?

When an accidental situation has occurred, the consequence mitigation work is not chronologically structured in the indicated phases. Phases could be parallel, due to prioritizing of the actions needed. The phases are seldom accomplished in an effective manner, and accident investigations often reveal culpable conditions related to the performance of the crisis response arrangements in these phases. The situations were, for example, either totally unexpected (no emergency preparedness at all), different to what was expected or the mental, emotional and physical reactions to the accident disturbed performance. Should measures that improve the preaccident behavior be selected in priority to measures that improve the postaccident behavior? This is a matter for the analysis process and in particular in defining acceptance criteria and performance requirements. The phase models include all crisis response aspects: competence and organizations as well as technical systems for direct emergency actions.

Dimensioning of emergency management in cold climates

The issue of emergency response, evacuation and rescue in the northern areas is important, though problematic. The distance to hubs makes it difficult to reach targets within a reasonable time, and the weather conditions are, on many days, very problematic. In addition, the dark winter comes without daylight. Jacobsen (2012) offers a discussion about evacuation and rescue in the Barents Sea in Norwegian waters. The discussion covers the area south of Bear Island at 74.5° N and east to 19° E toward the border with Russia. This is the area where Norwegian authorities presently are issuing licenses to the oil and gas industry to explore for oil and gas. Of particular concern is the need to station search and rescue helicopters at locations where offshore facilities can be reached and at the offshore facilities. This might also involve the stationing of vessels halfway between land base and offshore facilities so that fuel can be ensured for the flight to the facilities and the return flight to base.

The organization of search and rescue operations in the case of disasters in Arctic areas is based on the ability of Joint Rescue Coordination Centers to provide sufficient situation awareness and management of scarce resources. One major concern is the mass rescue of passenger vessels, similar to the case of Maksim Gorkiy. Today there is no prepared emergency response system that is ready to perform under the probable harsh weather conditions seen in the north, taking the criterion of the survival of passengers as a design criterion. Work is going on within the International Maritime Organization (IMO), but this is long term without any conclusion on regulations and guidelines. Since 2010, the International Maritime Rescue Federation (IMRF) has organized conferences on mass rescue topics (International Maritime Rescue Federation [IMRF], 2010).

What should govern the design of the emergency response systems in the northern areas is yet to be clarified, and worst cases might not be so relevant.

However, safety considerations must be part of all design phases as well as the operational procedures, such as during all navigation.

Another potential problem in northern waters could arise, even if the greatest care is taken: in the case of navigation taking place in unchartered waters. This calls for chartering all waters where vessels might traverse. Of potential concern are submerged rocks that may need a very dense chartering net to be detected.

It should also be mentioned that radio communication in northern waters is not reliable, and this situation poses a threat to all navigation in the northern waters. The communication system is therefore being further developed for this region.

Conclusions

We conclude that while most industrial activities in populated areas in the south are accessible and well known, this is not the case in the northern cold climate. As a starting point, the known unknowns, which are the well-known risks, need to be sufficiently explored. However, this is not enough. Efforts should be made to reveal possible totally unexpected issues ("Black Swans"/ unknown unknowns) that might challenge the short- and long-term consequences for humans and the environment, but to what extent is it possible to reveal "Black Swans" before they occur? Annerløv (2012) has developed an approach to assess Black Swans. We will further recommend that potential disasters in the cold climates of the north should be classified into 't Hart and Boin's (2001) crisis typology framework, addressing the speed of development and the speed of termination. Such assessments of the Arctic systems involved will reveal uncertainties related to the performance of systems and their phenomenological knowledge. This is vital for a proper regulation of the northern assets and for all stakeholders involved in the Arctic.

References

't Hart, P., & Boin, R.A. (2001). Between crisis and normalcy: The long shadow of post-crisis politics. In U. Rosenthal, R.A. Boin, & L.K. Comfort (Eds.), *Managing crises: Threats, dilemmas, opportunities* (pp. 28–46). Springfield, IL: Charles C. Thomas.

Aircraft Accident Investigation Board/Norway. (1999). *Report on the accident to Vnukovo Airline's Tupolev TU-154M RA 85621 near Svalbard Airport Longyear, Norway on 29 August 1996* (Report No. 07/99). Retrieved from www.aibn.no/Aviation/Reports/1999-07

Alme, J.B. (2009). *Ishavsfolk si erfaring: Boka om is, isens menn, storm og forlis* [Experiences from the people of the icy oceans: The book on ice, men, storms and losses]. Trondheim, Norway: Tapir akademisk forl.

Annerløv, G. (2012). *Risikostyring – "the black swans". En studie av det ukjente* [Risk management – the black swans. A study of the unknown]. Master's thesis, University of Stavanger, Stavanger, Norway. Retrieved from www.nb.no/idtjeneste/URN:NBN:no-bibsys_brage_34119

Arctic Monitoring and Assessment Programme. (2007). *Arctic oil and gas 2007*. Retrieved from www.amap.no/documents/doc/arctic-oil-and-gas-2007/71

Aristova, A., & Gudmestad, O.T. (2014, July). *Kolskaya and Kulluk. A disaster and a near disaster.* Paper presented at the ICETECH 2014: International Conference and Exhibition on Performance of Ships and Structures in Ice, Banff, Canada.

Barabadi, A., Gudmestad, O.T., & Barabadi, J. (2014). RAMS data collection under Arctic conditions. Manuscript submitted for publication in *Reliability Engineering and System Safety*.

Bernes, C. (1996). *Arktisk miljø i Norden: urørt, overutnyttet, forurenset?* [Arctic environment in the Nordic countries: Untouched, over-exploited, contaminated?]. Copenhagen, Denmark: Nordisk Ministerråd.

Cullen, W.D.L. (1990). *The public inquiry into the Piper Alpha disaster*. London, England: HMSO.

Dawson, J., Johnston, M.E., & Stewart, E.J. (2014). Governance of Arctic expedition cruise ships in a time of rapid environmental and economic change. *Ocean & Coastal Management, 89*, 88–99. doi: 10.1016/j.ocecoaman.2013.12.005

Dickins, D. (2011, February). *Behavior of oil spills in ice and implications for Arctic spill response*. Paper presented at the Arctic Technology Conference, Houston, Texas.

Dumont, D., Bertino, L., Sandven, S., & Kohout, A.L. (2011, February). *A model for wave-in-ice and sea ice dynamics in the marginal ice zone*. Paper presented at the Arctic Technology Conference, Houston, Texas.

Eik, K., & Gudmestad, O.T. (2010). Iceberg management and impact on design of offshore structures. *Cold Regions Science and Technology, 63*(1–2), 15–28. doi: 10.1016/j.cold regions.2010.04.008

Emergency Prevention, Preparedness and Response Working Group. (2011). *Arctic emergencies: Current and future risks, mitigation, and response cooperation*. Retrieved from www.arctic-council.org/eppr/wp-content/uploads/2011/03/EPPR_ARCTIC_EMER GENCIES-22SEP20111.pdf

Fritt-Rasmussen, J. (2010). *In situ burning of Arctic marine oil spills. Ignitability of various oil types weathered at different ice conditions. A combined laboratory and field study*. Copenhagen, Denmark: DTU Civil Engineering.

Ghoneim, G.A. (2011, February). *Arctic standards – A comparison and gap study*. Paper presented at the Arctic Technology Conference, Houston, TX. Abstract retrieved from www.onepetro.org/conference-paper/OTC-22039-MS

Grønås, S., & Skeie, P. (1999). A case study of strong winds at an Arctic front. *Tellus A, 51*(5), 865–879. doi: 10.1034/j.1600-0870.1999.00022.x

Gudmestad, O.T. (2013). Marine construction and operation challenges in the Barents Sea. *International Journal of Ship Research Technology, 60*(3), 128–137.

Gudmestad, O.T., & Karunakaran, D. (2012, December). *Challenges faced by the marine contractors working in Western and Southern Barents Sea*. Paper presented at the Arctic Technology Conference, Houston, TX. Abstract retrieved from www.onepetro.org/conference-paper/OTC-23842-MS

Hale, A.R. (1984). Is safety training worthwhile? *Journal of Occupational Accidents, 6*(1–3), 17–33. doi: 10.1016/0376-6349(84)90026-9

Hall, T.A., & Seligman, B.H.J.W. (2011, February). *ARKTOS shear zone evacuation craft design development*. Paper presented at the Arctic Technology Conference, Houston, TX. Abstract retrieved from www.onepetro.org/conference-paper/OTC-22058-MS

Hollnagel, E., Nemeth, C.P., & Dekker, S. (2008). *Resilience engineering perspectives*. Farnham, England: Ashgate.

Hollnagel, E., Woods, D.D., & Leveson, N. (Eds.). (2006). *Resilience engineering: Concepts and precepts*. Aldershot, England: Ashgate.

Hovden, S.T. (2012). *Redningsdåden: om Maksim Gorkiy-havariet utenfor Svalbard i 1989* [The Rescue: About the Maksim Gorkiy-accident outside Spitsbergen in 1989]. Sandnes, Norway: Commentum Forlag.

International Maritime Rescue Federation. (2010). *International Maritime Rescue Federation conference on mass rescue at sea, Gothenburg 7–8 June 2010: Conference report*. Retrieved from

www.international-maritime-rescue.org/phocadownloadpap/G3conference/g1%20
mass%20rescue%20conference%20report.pdf

International Organization for Standardization. (2010). *Petroleum and natural gas industries: Arctic offshore structures (ISO:19906).* Geneva, Switzerland: Author.

Jacobsen, S.R. (2012). *Evacuation and rescue in the Barents Sea, critical issues for safe petroleum activity.* Master's thesis, University of Stavanger, Stavanger, Norway. Retrieved from www.nb.no/idtjeneste/URN:NBN:no-bibsys_brage_33271

Kleemayr, K. (2004). Modelling and simulation in snow science. *Mathematics and Computers in Simulation, 66*(2–3), 129–153. doi: 10.1016/j.matcom.2003.11.009

Kolstad, E.W. (2007). *Extreme winds in the Nordic seas: Polar lows and Arctic fronts in a changing climate.* Doctoral thesis, University of Bergen, Bergen, Norway. Retrieved from http://hdl.handle.net/1956/2329

Kvamstad, B. (2013, June). *Communication in the high north – supporting safe maritime operations.* Paper presented at the 32nd International Conference on Ocean, Offshore and Arctic Engineering, OMAE 2013, Nantes, France. Abstract retrieved from www.sintef.no/home/Publications/Publication/?pubid=CRIStin+1074189

Leveson, N. (2004). A new accident model for engineering safer systems. *Safety Science, 42*(4), 237–270. doi: 10.1016/S0925-7535(03)00047-X

Leveson, N. (2011). *Engineering a safer world: Systems thinking applied to safety.* Cambridge, MA: MIT Press.

[Many accidents with "Hurtigruten" during the years] Mange ulykker med Hurtigruten gjennom årene. (2011, September 19). *Skipsrevyen.* Retrieved from www.skipsrevyen.no/

Marchenko, N. (2012). *Russian Arctic seas: Navigational conditions and accidents.* Heidelberg, Germany: Springer.

Marine Accident Investigation Branch. (1999). *Report on the underwater survey of the Stern Trawler GAUL H. 243 and the supporting model experiments, August 1998–January 1999.* London, England: Author.

Marsden, A., Totten, M., & Spring, W. (2011, February). *Feasibility of escape, evacuation and rescue for facilities in Arctic shear zone environments.* Paper presented at the Arctic Technology Conference, Houston, TX. Abstract retrieved from www.onepetro.org/conference-paper/OTC-22055-MS

Mathisen, J.P., & Bidlot, J.R. (2011, February). *Application of the buoy network in the Barents Sea.* Paper presented at the Arctic Technology Conference, Houston, TX. Abstract retrieved from www.onepetro.org/conference-paper/OTC-22051-MS

Njå, O. (1998). *Approach for assessing the performance of emergency response arrangements.* Stavanger, Norway: Aalborg University/Stavanger University College.

Norwegian Official Report. (1986). 20. *Skredulykken i Vassdalen 5. mars 1986* [The snow avalanche in Vassdalen March 5, 1986]. Oslo, Norway: Statens forvaltningstjeneste, Informasjonsforvaltning.

Norwegian Official Report. (2004). *Fiskefartøyet "Utvik Seniors" forlis 17. februar 1978* [The loss of the fishing vessel "Utvik Senior" February 17,1978]. Oslo, Norway: Statens forvaltningstjeneste, Informasjonsforvaltning.

Perrow, C. (1984). *Normal accidents: Living with high-risk technologies.* New York, NY: Basic Books.

Ré, A.J.S. (2011, February). *Criteria for the next generation of cold regions evacuation systems.* Paper presented at the Arctic Technology Conference, Houston, TX.

Ré, A.J.S., & Veitch, B. (2013, June). *Evacuation in ice: Ice loads on a lifeboat during field trials.* Paper presented at the 32nd International Conference on Ocean, Offshore and Arctic Engineering, OMAE 2013, Nantes, France. Abstract retrieved from http://proceedings.asmedigitalcollection.asme.org/proceeding.aspx?articleid=1786517

Rosenthal, U., Charles, M.T., & 't Hart, P. (Eds.). (1989). *Coping with crises: The management of disasters, riots, and terrorism.* Springfield, IL: C. C. Thomas.

Rostrup, M., & Gilbert, M. (1993). Snøskredulykker [Snow avalanche accidents]. *Tidsskrift for Den norske legeforening, 113*(9), 1100–1103.

Rostrup, M., Gilbert, M., & Stalsberg, H. (1989). Skredulykken i Vassdalen [The snow avalanche in Vassdalen]. *Tidsskrift for Den norske legeforening, 109*(7–8), 807–813.

Schön, D.A. (1991). *The reflective practitioner: How professionals think in action.* Aldershot, England: Avebury.

Smith, L.C. (2011). *The new north: The world in 2050.* London, England: Profile Books.

Spring, W., & Hansen, M. (2011, February). *Stereographic analysis of aerial photographic imagery for Arctic development and technology planning.* Paper presented at the Arctic Technology Conference, Houston, TX. Abstract retrieved from www.onepetro.org/conference-paper/OTC-22059-MS

Stalsberg, H., Albertsen, C., Gilbert, M., Kearney, M., Moestue, E., Nordrum, I., . . . Ørbo, A. (1989). Mechanism of death in avalanche victims. *Virchows Archiv A Pathological Anatomy and Histopathology, 414*(5), 415–422.

Svalbard Treaty, February, 9, 1920. Retrieved from www.sysselmannen.no/Documents/Sys selmannen_dok/English/Legacy/The_Svalbard_Treaty_9ssFy.pdf?epslanguage=en

Sydnes, A.K., & Sydnes, M. (2013). Norwegian–Russian cooperation on oil-spill response in the Barents Sea. *Marine Policy, 39*, 257–264. doi: 10.1016/j.marpol.2012.12.001

Thelma AS. (2010). Kalde utfordringer. Helse-og arbeidsmiljø på innretning i nordområdene [Cold challenges. Health and working environment on installations in the High North] (Report No. 10–31). Retrieved from Petroleum Safety Authority Norway website: www.ptil.no/getfile.php/PDF/Kalde%20utfordringer%20-%20helse%20og%20 arbeidsmilj%C3%B8%20p%C3%A5%20innretning%20i%20Nordomr%C3%A5dene_ Thelma%20juni%202010.pdf

United States Coast Guard. (2008). *Report of investigation into the sinking and loss of four crewmembers aboard the commercial fishing vessel Lady of Grace.* Retrieved from www.uscg.mil/hq/cg5/cg545/docs/documents/LadyOfGrace.pdf

Wilcken, S. (2012). *Alpha factors for the calculation of forecasted operational limits for marine operations in the Barents Sea.* Master's thesis, University of Stavanger, Stavanger, Norway. Retrieved from www.nb.no/idtjeneste/URN:NBN:no-bibsys_brage_33806

Økland, H. (1998). Modification of frontal circulations by surface heat flux. *Tellus A, 50*(2), 211–218. doi: 10.1034/j.1600-0870.1998.t01-1-00004.x

13 Environmental effects of oil and gas exploration and production in the Barents Sea

Roald Kommedal, Andrea Bagi, and Tor Hemmingsen

Introduction

Environmental impacts are normally classified according to the environmental compartment affected (air, water and soil), and/or oil and gas industry location (on- or offshore). Northeast Atlantic oil and gas exploration and production, mainly in the Barents Sea, represents a combined consortia of on- and offshore activities, with likely impacts on all three compartments. In addition to permanent and temporary exploration and production facilities, service activities like refining, transport and storage of crude and refined petroleum, production chemicals and technical equipment, as well as solid and liquid wastes, should all be included when attempting to describe the total environmental risk posed by the industry.

Table 13.1 presents an overall list of the main risk parameters, pollution sources and environmental subcompartments negatively affected by oil and gas exploration and production.

In this chapter we will limit our focus to offshore discharges to the marine environment posing immediate detrimental environmental effects. Furthermore, we also limit our attention to crude oil and refined petroleum products, leaving inorganic ions (heavy metals and inorganic salts), radioactive sources, gases and solid waste products out of our scope. While this restricted view excludes important hydrocarbon inputs to the marine environment from onshore oil and gas activities, the marine fate and effects of those inputs can be considered similar to offshore discharges, as transport and conversion mechanisms are source-independent.

Sources of petroleum in the marine environment

Hydrocarbons enter the marine environment by the release of petroleum oil or gas. Offshore sources include natural seeps, accidental oil spills, blow outs, leakages from production-, transport- and storage facilities, hydrocarbons in produced water, drill cuttings and muds, noncombusted hydrocarbon in flaring and mud burning, and from drainage and ballast water. Environmental concerns are to a large extent limited to the liquid and dissolved petroleum fraction, as

Table 13.1 Risk parameters, pollution sources and environmental subcompartments negatively affected by oil and gas activities

Risk parameter	Source, cause	Effects	Compartment
Crude oil	Accidental spills, produced water, leakages, flares, cuttings and mud	Acute toxicity, ecotoxicity, bioaccumulation, carcinogenicity	Pelagic, Sediment, Intertidal, Soil, Atmosphere
Dissolved hydrocarbons	Produced water, ballast water	Acute toxicity, ecotoxicity, bioaccumulation, carcinogenicity	Pelagic
Refined petroleum products	Spills, drainage water, slop oil, drilling mud	Ecotoxicity, bioaccumulation, carcinogenicity	Pelagic, Sediment, Intertidal, Soil
Priority organic pollutants	Production chemicals, drilling mud, solvents, detergents, solid wastes	Acute toxicity, ecotoxicity, bioaccumulation, carcinogenicity	Pelagic, Sediment, Intertidal, Soil
Combustion gases (CO_2, SO_2, NO_x)	Power generation	Global warming, acid rain	Atmosphere
Volatile organic carbons (VOC)	Storage, transport, process leakages, venting and flares	Toxicity, carcinogenicity	Atmosphere
Low radioactive wastes	Scale deposits, solid waste, drill cuttings, produced water	Carcinogenicity	Pelagic, Sediments
Heavy metals	Drill cuttings, produced water, paints, structural degradation, solid wastes, decommissioning	Ecotoxicity, bioaccumulation, carcinogenicity	Pelagic, Sediments
Inorganic salts	Produced water, production chemicals, household wastewater	Eutrophication, saprobiation (hypoxia), ecotoxicity	Pelagic, Sediment
Non-native species	Ballast water	Biodiversity	Pelagic, Sediments
Slop water	Emulsions, drainage slop, cleaning operations	Acute toxicity, ecotoxicity, bioaccumulation, carcinogenicity	Pelagic, Sediments

the gaseous components are volatile and escape to the atmosphere. Our current knowledge on worldwide releases is based on probability estimations combining some basic assumptions, like natural seepage rates, unregistered spill frequency and leakage rates, and quantifications limited to case areas (Schmidt-Etkin, 2011; Wilson, Monaghan, Osanik, Price, & Rogers, 1974). Natural oil seeps have been known since ancient times (Levorson, 1954) and do account for a significant fraction of hydrocarbons released to the environment (Kvenvolden & Cooper, 2003; Smith, 1968). In a recent review by Schmidt-Etkin (2011), the annual worldwide release of oil has been estimated at about 2.10^6 tons/year, of which about 30% is due to natural seepages, 6–8% originates from municipal and industrial land runoff, 21–49% from transportation (including operational and accidental spills) and 2–3% from atmospheric precipitation. Offshore exploration and production amounted to 1–2% in the same study; however, a single accident like the Macondo, Gulf of Mexico, spill, which happened just after this was published, would change that to 35%, indicating the uncertainty and variability of these estimates.

Wilson et al. (1974) estimated the annual oil release to the Arctic environment to be about 450–1,700 tons of the total marine input of $200–600 \star 10^3$ tons. Hence, a relatively small operational or accidental input in this region would significantly change the overall inputs. In order to assess the environmental impact of such events, it is essential to understand the fate of oil in the marine environment. Therefore, in the following paragraphs we focus on describing the mechanisms involved in shaping the fate and effect of accidental oil spills. The fate and effects of the alternative sources listed above would normally imply the same, or a subset of the same, mechanisms.

Environmental fate of oil in the environment

News of marine oil spills first reached the public through the media attention following the Torrey Canyon accident on March 18, 1967, in which about 130,000 tons of crude were released into the English Channel, killing more than 15,000 seabirds and smearing close to 300 km of shoreline (Smith, 1968). While most spills are very small (70% < involve releases of less than 30 kg oil), the rare but larger spills account for the bulk of inputs to the marine environment (60% <) and represent the environmental risk of immediate concern (Schmidt-Etkin, 2011). Spills may occur from various activities related to exploration and production, shipping and land-based transport, pipeline transport, storage and refining. Environmental risk assessment of oil spills involves an evaluation of the probability and environmental consequences imposed by the spill. While the former is outside the scope of this text (see International Maritime Organization [IMO] [2010] for details), environmental consequences, primarily linked to the fate and effect of the individual constituents and the oil phase itself, are discussed in detail. Figure 13.1 shows the major mechanisms involved in oil phase transport and conversion in marine environments.

Evaporation of volatile and semivolatile compounds from the surface oil slick is a major mechanism, transferring hydrocarbons from the sea to the atmosphere (Fingas, 2011a). Volatile compounds, like short chain alkanes, alkenes and cyclo-alkanes, along with monoaromatics will evaporate within hours depending on their volumetric fraction, sea and air temperature, and wind conditions. About 80% of all volatiles disappear within days (Fingas, 2011b). Even though

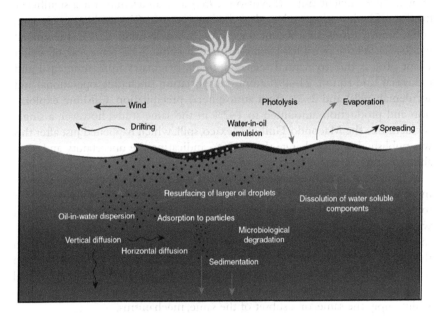

Figure 13.1 Main conversion and spreading mechanisms affecting the fate and effect of oil
spills in the marine environment

Source: With permission from SINTEF, Odd Gunnar Brakstad.

evaporation models exist for a large range of crude oils, the process may lead
to the formation of solid or tar-like "skins" at the surface of spills due to the
accumulation of resin and heavy constituents, resulting in retarded evaporation
that is difficult to predict. As the temperature in the Arctic is significantly lower
than that in temperate seas, evaporation under Arctic spill conditions is likely to
deviate significantly from more temperate experiences, as both evaporation and
skin formation will be more pronounced.

A secondary effect of volatilization causes the remaining slick properties,
like viscosity, flash point and density, to change significantly, altering their
physico-chemical fate and biological effects.

Another surface-linked conversion mechanism is the photo-oxidation (pho-
tolysis) of hydrocarbons by radiation-dependent formation of reactive oxygen species, which converts hydrocarbons to short chain fatty acids, alcohols,
ketones and aldehydes (Payne, Phillips, & Hom, 1987). Photo-oxidation of certain polyaromatic hydrocarbons (PAHs) and thiophenes causes the formation
of degradation products with significantly higher toxicity compared to their
hydrocarbon origin, while also generally increasing biodegradation (Lee, 2003;
Maki, Sasaki, & Harayama, 2001; Plata, Sharpless, & Reddy, 2008). Under Arctic
summer conditions, photo-oxidation may therefore be significant, due to light
intensity and radiation time.

Depending on the chemical composition of oil, wave and mixing conditions, oil and water will mix and form discontinuous but relatively homogenous mixtures called emulsions (in the case of water droplets in the oil phase) or dispersions (oil droplets in a continuous water phase). Unstable emulsions are formed by the entrapment of water droplets retained by viscosity forces. Semistable emulsions form when asphaltenes and resins in the oil interact with weak chemical surface forces in addition to viscosity retainment. If sufficient polar resins and asphaltenes are present, stable emulsions may form (Fingas & Fieldhouse, 2009). Emulsions are often named according to their physical similarity to chocolate mousse, either as oil mousse or just mousse. Emulsions increase in volume (due to water entrainment) and viscosity, making cleanup operations difficult and limited (Fingas, 2011b). In addition, degradation processes and evaporation are in general reduced (Fingas, 2011c). Models for the prediction of emulsion formation and behavior have been proposed, taking oil composition, viscosity and density as input data (Fingas, 2014). It is thought that this is sufficient for predictions, and that special Arctic factors are implicit. The dispersion of fine droplets of oil into water is caused by wave action or turbulent currents, and the smaller fractions < 20 μm are stable for relatively long residence times. Surface active compounds originating from the oil, released by marine organisms or actively sprayed onto the slick as a means of oil spill cleanup strategy, will stabilize and promote the formation of stable dispersions. As dispersion will enhance the surface-to-volume ratio (oil–water interphase), surface-dependent processes, like biodegradation, particle adsorption and dissolution, will proceed faster and increase the rate of observed removal of surface oil. Also, dispersion stimulates the transport of spilled oil into the water column, reducing exposure to surface organisms.

The water accommodated fraction (WAF) of oil in water is constituted of fairly soluble compounds such as C1 to C8 alkanes, lower cyclo-alkanes and aromatic compounds, phenols and acids. Solubility is limited (WAFs typically account for < 1% of total hydrocarbons in crude oil in water tests) (Faksness, Brandvik, Daae, Leirvik, & Børseth, 2011; Southworth, Herbes, & Allen, 1983), and even though single compounds have considerable solubility, much lower concentrations are found in the presence of crude oil phases, typically 0.1–0.5 ppm (Baker, Clark, Kingston, & Jenkins, 1990; Grahl-Nielson, 1987). However, soluble hydrocarbons represent the bioavailable fraction of hydrocarbons in crude oil water mixtures and also represent the fraction acutely toxic to meio- and microfauna in seawater (Patin, 1999). Hence, even though dissolved hydrocarbons do not represent the major fraction in an oil spill, the role of marine water systems in conversion and effects is of uttermost importance. Similar to evaporation, dissolution also contributes to changing the continuous oil phase physico-chemical properties, aging the oil into a more viscous and dense oil with implications for cleanup strategies.

Sedimentation by high density aged crude oil residuals or oil sorbed to suspended particulates represents a process of deposition of spilled oil to bottom waters and sediments. Sorption to suspended particles occurs close to shorelines and coastal regions and may occur during any stage of the oil-spill aging process. Sedimentation due to aging is the result of all processes leaching volatile light fractions, leaving the heavy fractions to accumulate until the specific gravity of the residual becomes higher than seawater.

Wind-driven drift, tidal and oceanic currents represent the major horizontal spreading mechanisms of surface slicks. In calm waters, spreading due to buoyant pressure and interfacial tension forces drives horizontal transport into a thin surface slick. The thickness of the final slick depends on the oil characteristics, wind and wave pattern as well as aging and mixing of oil and water. Normally, slicks are thinner towards the edges, leading to a characteristic "fried egg" shape. While the surfaces of oil slicks move about 1–3% of wind speeds up to 10 km/h, the deeper layers drift slightly to the right due to the Coriolis effect (typically 10° to 20° at 1 to 1.5% of the wind speed) (Fingas, 2011b; Reed et al., 1990). During strong winds, wave mixing intensity causes slicks to be entrained into mixed waters and follow the Ekman drift. A range of spill drift and spreading models has been developed for trajectory forecasting by implementing wind drift, surface currents and tidal currents, along with vertical dispersion and advection (Galt, 1997; Marta-Almeida et al., 2013; Liu & Peter Sheng, 2014), providing adequate tools for oil-spill contingency decision makers (Galt, 1997; Reed et al., 1999). Models for short-term trajectory predictions have also been adapted to ice conditions (Drozdowski et al., 2011).

Uptake, conversion and mineralization by living organisms are commonly known as biodegradation. By and large, the major group of organisms responsible for biodegradation in most environments (including the marine) are the bacteria (Atlas & Bartha, 1998). Normally not regarded as biodegradation, uptake and conversion by higher organisms, mainly through detoxification metabolism, also contribute to the overall removal of hydrocarbons. Potentially, all components in crude oil are biodegradable (alkanes, alkenes, cyclic aliphatics, aromatics, PAHs, resins, etc.); however, their biodegradability is limited by bioavailability and kinetics (Head, Jones, & Röling, 2006). Bacterial uptake of hydrocarbons is directly linked to the bacterial growth process, whereby hydrocarbons serve as primary substrate. The growth process is stoichiometrically linked to the uptake of nutrients and an electron acceptor, which, under aerobic conditions, is molecular oxygen. Generally, hydrocarbons used for growth are restricted to the dissolved fraction (Harms, Smith, & Wick, 2010; Parales & Ditty, 2010), but bacteria has been shown to develop aggregates, known as biofilms, at surfaces of oil droplets (Grimaud, 2010). This latter mode of growth reduces transport limitations but does not involve direct oil-phase uptake. Stimulation of bacterial growth by the addition of limiting nutrients, especially nitrogen and phosphorous, is a known strategy for enhanced biodegradation of oil spills, first tried out in large-scale field applications during the Exxon Valdez accident in 1989 (Pritchard & Costa, 1991; Atlas & Hazen, 2011). Biodegradation rates increased to up to 1.5% reductions per day (mass) but reduced as the easily biodegradable fractions were depleted and slow bacterial growth on the more insoluble heavier fractions took over (Bragg, Prince, Harner, & Atlas, 1994).

This is a general pattern seen in natural biodegradation and bioremediation studies, and it contributes to the aging process described for evaporation and dissolution, and subsequently for remediation and cleanup strategies. Biodegradation is an important process for removing oil spill by complete mineralization. In extreme environments, like the low temperature Arctic and deep sea, biodegradation is thought to be the main process controlling environmental fate (Bragg et al., 1994). Hence, adequate knowledge of this process is of uttermost importance in order to predict environmental risk and actively remediate hydrocarbon pollution.

As mentioned above, the fate and effects of other sources of marine discharges of hydrocarbons are controlled by the same mechanisms influencing the oil spills. Leakages and release of drainage and slop water follow the same transport and conversion pattern, while release of produced water and ballast water from hydrocarbon storage installations introduce mainly dissolved and dispersed hydrocarbons prone to water column transport, evaporation and biodegradation conversions. The fate and effects of oil sorbed to drill cuttings, or present in mud, is subjected to immediate sedimentation. Slowly, dissolution and biodegradation convert these hydrocarbons, or they get buried in the sediment strata.

Marine effects of hydrocarbons

Up till now we have focused on the environmental fate of hydrocarbons released to the marine environment and limited our discussion on effects. In addition to the effects caused by hydrocarbons, the additional environmental effects of offshore oil and gas exploration and production must be recognized, ranging from inorganic chemical discharges and chemical leaching from structural components to seismic habitat disturbances. Our scope limits this section to environmental effects caused by hydrocarbon releases.

Biological (at organism level) and ecological (at community level) effects form a large research field and we will summarize current knowledge on the importance of sound environmental management and policymakers. The common perception of oil in the physical environment is oiled and dead macrofauna, including sea birds, fish and marine mammals. The media and social effects of oil spills (especially) are also outside the scope of this short review, but should not be forgotten. In fact, several authors including industrial interest organizations claim the social and public perception of oil spills to be more dramatic than the actual environmental effects. This is speculative and tendentious but should still be considered in environmental management.

Extensive literature exists on the toxicological effects of hydrocarbons on marine organisms. It is not easy to extract conclusions upon concentration and effect levels from the overall literature, as some studies report no effects at considerable hydrocarbon concentrations, while others report significant metabolic and/or ecological disturbances at even trace levels. Some of this variability can be related to vast differences in methodologies, experimental and environmental factors and sampling conditions. It also reflects the very large possible response range of complex marine organisms and communities. Patin (1999) proposed using a combination of concentration-response curves, median LC_{50} and EC_{50} concentrations (lethal and ecologically effective concentrations, respectively), for standardized tests and risk assessment evaluation. In a summary of literature data looking at bacterio- and phytoplankton, macrophytes, crustaceans, fish and bivalves, the same author concludes that LC_{50} of early development stages are significantly lower than mature organisms, with WAF ranging from 10–100 μg/l for early stages, and 0.1–10 mg/l for developed organisms. No observable effect concentration (NOEC) of dissolved hydrocarbons was found in the range 0.1–1 μg/l (Patin, 1999). Details regarding different organisms and specific hydro-carbon compounds and production chemicals are now available, giving more specific and precise information on effects and effect concentrations (Holdway, 2002). Linking toxicity to specific hydrocarbon groups, Bakke, Klungsøyr, and Sanni (2013) recently linked the effects of produced water discharges to the concentration of alkylated phenols and PAHs. Taking into account dilution and body burden exposure, they concluded physiological effects on cod and edible mussels to be limited to 1–2 km from produced water discharges of North Sea conditions. Sensitive stages are not, however, restricted to early life stages but also include periods of metamorphic changes, reproduction and periods of metabolic stress like starvation (Anderson, 1985). Environmental factors also affect threshold and lethal dose concentrations, and temperature seems to be an especially important factor (Anderson, 1985; Robertson, 1998). When it comes to ecosystem-level responses, linking hydrocarbon discharges to observ-able effects on, for instance, fish stocks or sea mammal distribution, it becomes extremely difficult (Bakke et al., 2013; Holdway, 2002; Shigenaka, 2010). The problem is partly linked to experimental or observational methodologies and data analysis uncertainty. In addition, extrapolation to community-level effects is very difficult as alternative factors explaining observed responses cannot be ruled out (Hjermann et al., 2007). A possible route towards a population- and/ or community-level environmental-effect management strategy is the appli-cation of molecular biomarker responses and proteomic, metabolomics and/ or genomic methodologies (Jager & Hansen 2013; Hansen, Altin, Øverjordet, Jager, & Nordtug, 2013).

Management of operational and accidental hydrocarbon discharges

The primary decision in oil-spill management is whether to actively remediate or leave the fate of spills to natural degradation processes as described above. For active fighting, technologies for the remediation of oil spills are numerous and have been recently reviewed in Fingas (2011d). These include physical meas-ures, such as booms, skimmers, sorbents, in situ burning, sprinkling and flushing, suction and manual removal. The application of chemicals is another option for the treatment of oil spills. Often combined with physical and/or biological measures, these are: dispersants and washing agents, emulsion breakers and inhibitors, solidifiers, sinking/ballast agents, adhesive skimming enhancers, bacterial cosubstrates and fertilizers. Finally, the addition of biologically active phases for stimulated biodegradation (bioremediation) includes: addition of sewage sludge, wastewater treatment plant activated sludge, pure or enhancement cultures, genetically modified microorganisms and freeze-dried powders of bioactive potential (unknown composition). The selection of oil-spill cleanup method is often dictated by parameters of the local environment, governmental regulations and public perception, as well as crude oil characteristics, degree of aging (the time window), accessibility and secondary safety, human health and ecological risk. Choosing among the many available alternatives should follow from a thorough analysis, a net environmental benefit analysis (NEBA), as outlined in several framework documents (e.g. Efroymson, Nicolette, & Suter, 2003).

For nonaccidental discharges, such as produced water, slop water and drill cuttings including muds, technologies for on- and off-site treatment have been developed and adopted by the oil and gas industry from other industries already using those technologies. Produced water treatment includes hydro-cyclones, centrifugation, filtration, flotation, adsorption and absorption techniques (Fakhru'l-Razi et al., 2009). Novel technologies are still being considered; however, new developments are now moving towards zero emission management involving 100% reinjection (Garland & Hjelde, 2003). Reinjection techniques have also been developed for drill cuttings and drilling mud, and they are thought to be the only environmentally sound disposal option on the Norwegian continental shelf (Nagel & McLennan, 2010). Therefore, most likely these techniques will have relevance in the Arctic region, including the Barents Sea in the future.

Environmental issues related to oil and gas activities in the Arctic

The Arctic marine ecosystem plays an important role in the regulation of the global climate and it is also an important source of economic and cultural value. Due to climate change, the sea's ice extent has been reaching minimums within the last decade (in 2007 and again in 2012), and sea surface temperature on the ice edges has been measured to exceed the long-term average. As a result, the Arctic has become a rapidly changing environment, challenging its inhabitants (Arctic Monitoring and Assessment Programme [AMAP], 2010b; Protection of the Arctic Marine Environment [PAME], 2013). Future prospects of increasing Arctic offshore oil and gas activities bring further stressors, as previously introduced. Additionally, the increase in temperature will likely enable an ice-free transportation route to be established in the North-East Passage throughout the whole year, allowing for both oil and gas transportation and other transportation of goods by ship on the Arctic continental shelf (Arctic Climate Impact Assessment [ACIA], 2004). This implies that the level of pollution arising from shipping traffic will increase, together with the risk of an oil spill. Levels of oil transportation from ports and terminals in northwestern Russia had already reached 13 million tons by 2009 and exceeded 15 million tons by 2010. Predictions suggest this capacity will reach up to 100 million tons per year during the next 5–10 years (Bambulyak & Frantzen, 2011).

The major concern regarding hydrocarbon releases originates from their well-known toxic effects, as mentioned in the previous part of this chapter. Species in the vicinity of accidental spills are directly exposed to this hazard, and humans may experience indirect effects through food obtained from polluted areas. In those parts of the Arctic region where large fish resources are being exploited by the fishing industry, environmental protection and food safety become closely related issues. The Barents Sea is an excellent example of such an area (Stiansen et al., 2009). Besides focusing attention on highly valuable regions, it is important to keep in mind that the marine environment is very dynamic. The transportation of large water masses over great distances (e.g. through currents) and other mixing mechanisms takes place continuously, making it easy for even point source pollutions to be carried over large distances (Schlosser, Swift, Lewis, & Pfirman, 1995). Pollution can also become dispersed as contaminants are transferred through the marine food web, between ecosystem members at different trophic levels. In this context, for example, migrating species of the Arctic represent a risk for carrying persistent organic pollutants (including also persistent oil components) to and from the area. In recent decades, the Arctic nations have recognized the importance of establishing thorough knowledge about the current functioning of the Arctic ecosystem, including geographical, oceanographical, chemical and biological features. Although the ecosystem of the Arctic Ocean is still the least explored of all the oceans due to its limited accessibility, challenging climate and logistic difficulties, Arctic Council working groups have compiled extensive data about its status in recent years (AMAP, 2010a).

The Barents Sea ecosystem as an example

The Barents Sea is considered as a moderately productive ecosystem, which is capable of producing substantial fish stocks due to its size. The foundation of the ecosystem consists of microscopic phytoplankton (algae) that utilize the energy from the sunlight and assimilate inorganic carbon (i.e. carbon dioxide) into cell material. Just like trees in terrestrial environments, algae are the most important primary producers in the Barents Sea and in other parts of the Arctic Ocean (Arneberg, Titov, Filin, & Stiansen, 2013; Stiansen et al., 2009; Word, Pinza, & Gardiner, 2008). As light is essential for their growth, algae blooms are limited to spring and summer seasons and relatively shallow water depths. Although algae blooms have been recently observed under sea ice, the increase of ice-free open water surfaces favors enhanced phytoplankton growth. As Figure 13.2 shows, major consumers of these microscopic organisms are tiny zooplanktons, which create a link with higher-level organisms, such as different fish species. The arrows represent the direction of the energy flow. Zooplankton members are called "keystone" species in the Arctic marine food webs. Without them the ecosystem would collapse, as energy cannot be transferred further up from the primary producer level. Hence zooplankton (and algae) must be considered in environmental monitoring of the Arctic in order to spot potential dangers that can affect valuable fish populations. Figure 13.2 can be used to detect the many interdependent relationships characterizing the Arctic ecosystem. As all species are directly or indirectly connected, Ecosystem Based Management (EBM) has been recognized as the most useful framework for risk assessment and decision making in the fishing industry (Arneberg et al., 2013; Stiansen et al., 2009).

Status of the environment and sensitivity of Arctic species

There have already been substantial amounts of oil and gas produced in the Arctic region. With technological developments, better understanding of pollutant fate and effect, and stricter regulations, current activities are far less dangerous than at the beginning of the Arctic oil era (AMAP, 2010a). As a result, hydrocarbon levels in the Arctic Ocean are low, except for areas where natural petroleum sources are present (AMAP, 2007). Ecotoxicological assessments of prior activities are rare; the majority of ecotoxicological studies assessing the effect of oil industry related chemicals originate from temperate areas (Bakke et al., 2013). A number of studies used native Arctic species to elucidate ecotoxicological effects, and some set out to establish the sensitivity of Arctic species in comparison to temperate ones (Bechmann et al., 2010; Hansen et al., 2011; Skadsheim et al., 2009). Their conclusions suggest that Arctic species are

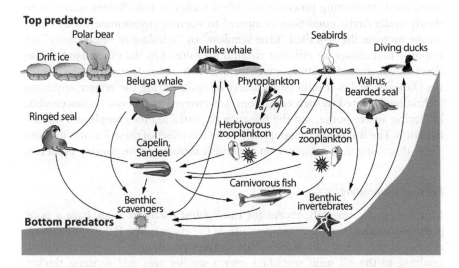

Figure 13.2 Simplified Barents Sea food web

Source: AMAP (2007).

sometimes more, sometimes less, sensitive to tested pollutants under labora-tory conditions, compared to temperate ones (Camus & Olsen, 2008; Hatlen, Camus, Berge, Olsen, & Baussant, 2009). The obtained data is not yet substantial enough for solid conclusions. Moreover, it is not yet clear whether the observed moderate toxicity levels are a result of Arctic-specific environmental features or unique adaptation of the species; hence, overall it is too early to conclude about the sensitivity of Arctic species (Hjermann et al., 2007). Most likely, the response mechanisms of individual organisms, such as metabolism of pollutants, can be expected to be mostly the same in Arctic species. The real vulnerabil-ity of the Arctic ecosystem to even localized oil spills comes from biological features, such as: (1) extreme seasonality of biological production (most pro-duction occurs in summer when there is daylight), (2) seasonal aggregation of marine animals (locally high diversity and abundance at certain times of the year), (3) short food chains and (4) migration of species from and to the Arctic.

Fate of oil spills in the Arctic environment

Currently, hydrocarbon levels in the Arctic are low, and over half of the existing hydrocarbons originate from natural seepages (for example, nearshore Beaufort Sea, along the coast of Baffin Island at Scott Inlet, at Buchan Gulf). As zero pro-duction emission policies seem to be implemented in the Barents region, the largest threats to the Arctic Ocean environment are considered to be accidental oil spills.

Unique characteristics, i.e. permanently cold temperature, extreme seasonal light/dark cycle and the presence of seasonal and permanent sea ice, affect oil-weathering processes in the Arctic region. In general, due to low tempera-tures, most weathering processes described earlier in this chapter occur more slowly under Arctic conditions compared to warmer environments. This could ideally increase the so-called "time window" or "window of opportunity" for response that allows for efficient cleanup measures. On the other hand, it also slows down natural recovery mechanisms, such as biodegradation by bacte-ria. Darkness makes it difficult to detect oil spills during the winter, requiring technology adapted to such conditions. Ice-covered waters can be inaccessible, hindering any response, and the presence of partial sea ice complicates oil dis-tribution. The following paragraphs describe the effect of these features in more detail, discussing their influence on previously introduced weathering processes.

Effect of temperature

Most types of crude oils, except for the lightest paraffinic ones, have a pour point higher than the mean temperature of the Barents Sea. Below pour point, oils begin to solidify. This implies that surface spreading will become limited, resulting in the oil spills spreading over a smaller area and forming thicker slicks than under warm conditions (Potter, Buist, Trudel, Dickins, & Owens, 2012). Consequently, surface-dependent fate processes are less pronounced.

The decreased evaporation rate reduces the transfer of small molecular weight alkanes and aromatics (e.g. BTEX) into the atmosphere, thereby making it more likely for these components to be dissolved and enhance potential toxicity (Fingas, 2011a). Dissolution rates and the solubility of hydrocarbons are reduced at lower temperatures. Equivalently, dispersion rates also reduce with temperature, most likely due to increased viscosity (Li, Lee, King, Boufadel, & Venosa, 2010). Srinivasan, Lu, Sorial, Venosa, and Mullin (2007) found that dispersant efficiency was almost two times lower at 5 °C compared to 16 °C, provided there was sufficient mixing energy. The metabolic processes of all living organisms tend to occur more slowly at reduced temperatures, including biodegradation. Nevertheless, cold-adapted hydrocarbon degraders have been shown to be able to degrade oil under Arctic conditions, even in sea ice (Brakstad, 2008; Brakstad & Bonaunet, 2006; Brakstad, Booth, & Faksness, 2009; Brakstad, Nonstad, Faksness, & Brandvik, 2008; Lo Giudice, Bruni, De Domenico, & Michaud, 2010). In a recent study, microorganisms from the Chukchi Sea were found to degrade both fresh and weathered crude oil in the presence and absence of chemical dispersants at −1 °C with oil losses ranging from 46–61% and up to 11% mineralization over a 60-day test period (McFarlin, Prince, Perkins, & Leigh, 2014). As shown by Bagi, Pampanin, Lanzén, Bilstad, and Kommedal (2013), cold-adapted seawater communities have the capacity to consume a biologically available single hydrocarbon, naphthalene, as fast as temperate counterparts, when compared at their in situ temperatures. However, biodegradation of the complex mixture, the whole oil, under Arctic conditions, is still expected to occur with rates below those experienced under temperate conditions due to factors other than the capacity of hydrocarbon-degrading bacteria. The authors proposed that the reduced bioavailability of oil components, lack of sufficient amounts of nutrients and possibly the low numbers of hydrocarbon degraders present will cause oil to degrade more slowly in the Barents Sea.

Effect of darkness

Darkness mainly represents difficulties for tracing and tackling the spilled oil. Regarding oil weathering, only photo-oxidation is directly affected. No or limited photo-oxidation implies that the formation of water-soluble and toxic compounds is retarded and the oxidized "skin" on the surface of the slick will likely not build up. In the summer season, the opposite effect can be expected (Barron, Carls, Short, & Rice, 2003).

Effect of ice

As Figure 13.3 illustrates, oil can be distributed in several different ways on, under, among and in ice. The accessibility of oil for recovery under different ice concentrations and coverage is limited. Ice sheets (or pancakes) can also behave as booms that collect and contain the oil, in which case the contingency might

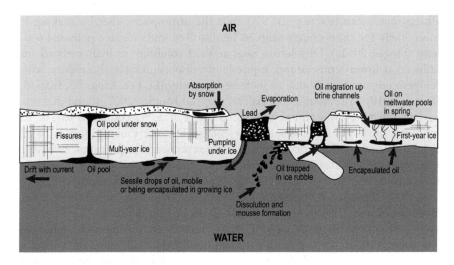

Figure 13.3 How oil interacts with sea ice

Source: AMAP (1998).

become easier (Brandvik, Sørheim, Singsaas, & Reed, 2006). This effect of sea ice can be utilized for in situ burning; a substantially thick oil layer must be developed to reach ignitability.

Oil in pack ice evaporates even more slowly than from cold open water due to thick film formation. Ice coverage (as in % of surface occupied by ice) in particular appears to significantly influence the extent of evaporative loss of hydrocarbons (Brandvik & Faksness, 2009). Oil encapsulated in ice will not evaporate at all (Potter et al., 2012). Emulsification and dispersion are generally retarded under icy conditions, as brash or pack ice dampens wave action, which would provide the mixing energy necessary for these processes. Oil encapsulated in ice was shown to diffuse down to the bottom of the ice sheet to a very low extent, which means that water-soluble components are not likely to be leaching out from the ice (Faksness et al., 2011).

Strategies to tackle oil spills in the Arctic

The Arctic is one of the most challenging environments when it comes to oil-spill response; therefore, prevention becomes even more important (Rossi, 2013). The remoteness and harsh climate makes it extremely difficult to respond to disaster quickly. Oil-spill cleanup can be a particularly great challenge during the winter months when sea ice may cover transportation routes and there is no daylight. Detailed planning and extreme preparedness are therefore essential (PAME, 2009; The PEW Charitable Trusts, 2013). Equipment needs to be stored on site when distances are too great to get the necessary cleanup measures to the area quickly, and personnel need to be trained to be able to use the equipment. So far, no major oil spills have occurred in the Arctic offshore. Experience from spills in more temperate climates and a number of small-scale field studies carried out in Arctic waters serve as a knowledge base for oil-spill contingency and response (Brandvik et al., 2006). The remaining area for development is to improve the ability to deal with oil spills in ice and in complete darkness in the case of winter operations.

All response strategies require an understanding of the location, mass balance and movement of the spilled oil. In poor light conditions and in poor weather, remote sensing tools, such as vessel-based or airborne remote sensing systems, are necessary. Monitoring the fate of oil after an incident usually includes the usage of advanced modeling tools and sampling of the area (Singsaas & Lewis, 2011). As concluded earlier, oil is expected to undergo slower weathering in ice, which can be an advantage for certain types of oil-spill scenarios. Yet, the "window of opportunity" is limited, and rapid decision making is required to make use of it. Oil fate models serve as an aid for such decision making. Examples of such models are OSCAR (Reed, Aamo, & Daling, 1995), OILMAP (Spaulding, Odulo, & Kolluru, 1992), ADIOS (Lehr, Jones, Evans, Simecek-Beatty, & Overstreet, 2002), OSIS (Walker, 1995), OILTRANS (Berry, Dabrowski, & Lyons, 2012), Seatrack Web (Ambjørn, 2007), a hybrid model by Guo and Wang (2009) and OILPOL, a specific model developed for the Arabian Gulf (Al-Rabeh, Lardner, Gunay, & Hossain, 1995). The most widely used model in the Norwegian sector is the Oil Spill Contingency and Response (OSCAR) model.

The three major response strategies that have already been assessed for their efficiency under Arctic conditions during the Oil in Ice Joint Industry Program (JIP) were: (1) mechanical recovery, (2) dispersant use and (3) in situ burning. Research developments regarding this area are described in detail in the JIP report published by research center SINTEF (Brandvik et al., 2006) and also discussed extensively in "Spill response in the Arctic offshore" by Potter et al. (2012). The latest developments, guidelines and research findings related to response strategies under Arctic conditions can also be found on the Arctic Response Technology Oil Spill Preparedness (2012) website. Here we include a selection of interesting conclusions from these works.

The efficiency of mechanical recovery using traditional booms proved to be limited under icy conditions. Instead, new prototypes of skimmers have been developed specifically for working under partial ice cover, and test results have been promising. Dispersant use has been shown to have an increased "window of opportunity" for application at higher ice coverage (approximately 1.5 day compared to maximum 12 hours without ice); however, this time window is still shorter than that of more temperate scenarios (Brandvik & Faksness, 2009). In situ burning has also been suggested as a viable alternative; in fact, it is considered the response strategy with the highest potential under Arctic conditions. The ignitability of oil slicks depends mainly on the concentration of light and volatile components in the residual oil and the water content emulsified into the oil. High ice coverage, which enables retention of volatiles and blocks emulsification, appears to be suitable for the application of in situ burning as it facilitates a thick slick with a high concentration of volatiles remaining (Fritt-Rasmussen & Brandvik, 2011). Oil trapped under ice for the winter season can still be ignitable when it surfaces during spring melting and hence can be burned. The major drawback of this strategy is the massive soot production and release of partially oxidized hydrocarbons into the air. Risk assessments must balance the negative effects of air pollution from in situ burning with the achievable ecological benefits to the marine ecosystem.

Need for harmonized standards of operation

As the Barents Sea is an area of common interest for Norwegian, Russian and other parties, both with respect to fish resources and oil and gas resources, it is of great importance to agree on rules for operation and to harmonize standards for oil-spill preparedness and response. There are several activities centered on developing guidelines and regulations for this purpose in the Arctic under the work of the Emergency Prevention, Preparedness and Response (EPPR) and Protection of the Arctic Marine Environment (PAME) working groups of the Arctic Council. A recently established Arctic Council Task Force appears to be a good way to begin addressing the challenge of Arctic marine oil pollution prevention on an international level, by providing an arena for extensive and direct communication and collaboration between the Arctic nations. A more "local" forum in the Barents region for discussion and cooperation, the Barents Euro–Arctic Council (BEAC), was established in 1993. Its major aim is to "provide impetus to existing cooperation and consider new initiatives and proposals" (Barents Euro–Arctic Council [BEAC], n.d.)

Industrial parties are generally very optimistic and trust modern technology to prevent disasters. The scientific opinion is more pessimistic and does not trust the human factor involved in the process. Most of the oil spills in history have been induced by human error. Under the tough conditions of the Arctic, workers are under even more stress compared to other offshore platforms due to difficult weather conditions, which makes them more prone to mistakes. Hence, Arctic offshore facilities and working conditions have to be designed accordingly after careful evaluation of health and safety parameters as discussed in the following part of this chapter.

Health and safety in the Arctic

Health, safety and environment (HSE) is a focus area for offshore activities and is paid special attention regarding work in the harsh and cold environments of the North. HSE work includes health and environmental protection, working environment and safety. The work should be proactive in order to avoid incidents that may be serious or fatal in these regions. Important climatic factors have to be taken into consideration, such as temperatures, wind, icing, polar low, uncertain weather forecasts and dark polar nights. Some focus areas for offshore work in Arctic regions are paid special attention, such as the number of working hours and rest periods on the installations, preparedness for long transportation distances with helicopters in case of injuries (Jacobsen & Gudmestad, 2013), effect of darkness with respect to work processes and ability to sleep, low temperatures – which affect physical and concentration problems, handling of equipment in cold environments and aspects of use of chemicals under these conditions.

As a prerequisite for offshore oil and gas field development in the Barents Sea, a common set of internationally recognized safety standards needed to be adapted to Barents Sea specific conditions. A four-year-long project, Barents 2020, has been carried out in order to meet these aims. This undertaking, which involved the cooperation of Norwegian and Russian partners, resulted in harmonized HSE standards and guidelines summarized in the Barents 2020 report (DNV GL, 2012). Other international guidelines are given in an International Association of Oil & Gas Producers (OGP) report (International Association of Oil & Gas Producers [OGP], 2008), and challenges for work in extreme climates with respect to health are provided in other reports (Dahl-Hansen et al., 2000; Knardahl, Medbø, Strøm, & Jebens, 2010; Thelma AS, 2010).

The development of offshore oil and gas fields in the Barents Sea represents major financial and technical undertakings, which require international cooperation and risk sharing between several partners. A common set of internationally recognized safety standards adapted to Barents Sea conditions, to which all parties can agree, was, and is, seen as a prerequisite for such projects to be developed.

Work in both elevated and lowered temperatures gives a higher risk of accidents, as the outside temperature moves away from the optimal temperature of 17 °C. Normally, the heat produced by doing physical activities is removed by wind chill. Thus, both the temperature and wind are important factors for cooling the body. For colder regions, a too-high wind chill index (WCI) will cause problems (Canadian Network for the Detection of Atmospheric Change [CANDAC] 2014). A frostbite guide gives the following consequences based on the efficient temperature:

> −27 °C: Low risk of frostbite for most people
< −28 °C: Increasing risk of frostbite for most people within 30 minutes of exposure
< −36 °C: High risk for most people in 5 to 10 minutes of exposure
< −44 °C: High risk for most people in 2 to 5 minutes of exposure
< −55 °C: High risk for most people in 2 minutes of exposure or less

In addition, the humidity is important. Clothes should therefore have the ability to transport sweat from the skin to outer layers of the clothes. An inner layer of nonabsorbent, moisture-transporting material, such as polypropylene filaments and wool as a moisture-absorbent but still insulating material, is therefore preferred. The outer material should be able to protect against wind and water.

New technology has provided smarter clothes. The materials used could be phase change materials (PCM), which can regulate heat transport through the clothes; these are heat-conducting materials with an energy resource and materials with sensors measuring temperature, humidity and heart rate. In addition to good insulation for the feet, arms and body, it is very important to protect the head and neck region with a scarf and face mask to avoid substantial heat loss. Insulation of tools reduces the heat loss directly to the metal from the hands, and power tools, cranes and other support will help in reducing the need for individual work. A lower temperature will affect the ability to work properly, which will increase the risk of accidents. The optimal skin temperature for hands and fingers is 32–36 °C, and below that the function is slower and less precise. Overall, it is extremely important to have adequate clothes, and to keep the hands and feet warm. Under cold conditions the extremities will swell and become painful. Freezing may be divided into three phases (OGP, 2008):

1. degree: freezing without peeling and blistering, but with color change of the skin
2. degree: blistering and peeling of the skin with pain and a violet color of the skin
3. degree: freezing with blackening and death of skin tissues, which gives pain and numbness

If body temperature drops below 35 °C, the situation is defined as hypothermia. Bodily responses to cold are included in Table 13.2. A report prepared for

Table 13.2 The response to hypothermia

Body temperature	Effects on body
37	Normal body temperature.
36	Judgment may be affected.
35	Definition of hypothermia threshold. Feels cold, looks cold, uncontrollable shivering.
34	Change of personality (usually withdrawn – 'switches off'). Stumbling, falling, confused. Inappropriate behavior e.g. sheds clothing. Lack of appreciation – 'doesn't care'.
33	Consciousness clouded. Shivering stops. Incoherent.
32	Heart stoppage now very much a risk. Heat loss will continue unless protected. Limbs stiffen.
31	Moves into unconsciousness.
30	Unlikely to detect breathing or pulse.
28	Fixed dilated pupils (no constriction to light).
24	Survival unusual if any colder.
18	Lowest temperature of accidental hypothermia with recovery.
9	Lowest temperature of deliberate hypothermia with recovery.

Source: International Association of Oil & Gas Producers (2008).

the Petroleum Safety Authority, Norway, relates to work in cold environments (Thelma AS, 2010), and a report with an extensive literature review was compiled by Stami for similar conditions on land (Knardahl et al., 2010). The most extreme situation on a platform is an immersion accident, where a person falls in the water.

A series of medical papers related to the petroleum industry and health was published in Norway in 2004. It was reported that a very limited number of papers had been published related to offshore petroleum work, and thus medical doctors had very limited knowledge in this area. A focus was placed on shift-work and accidents (Bjørkum, Pallesen, Holsten, & Bjorvatn, 2004). An increase in the number of accidents was reported due to shiftwork and especially due to work on the night shift. Shiftwork disturbs the body's natural rhythm; hence, regular rest periods need to be organized. Sleep disorders are frequently registered as a result of shiftwork, especially for the night and early morning shifts (Pallesen, Holsten, Bjorkum, & Bjorvatn, 2004). The risk of failures is highest in the period from 3:00 to 4:00 am during the night, and it becomes even higher with longer working periods and as the working period gets further from the last rest period (Folkard & Tucker, 2003; Tucker, Folkard, & Macdonald, 2003). The melatonin metabolite is a good indicator of a sound day rhythm. The acro-phase of the melatonin metabolite did not change for day shifts. For night shifts, the acro-phase of the melatonin metabolite was delayed, returning to normal after four to seven days. For lighter periods, i.e. in spring, the adaption period from night to day was much shorter. Artificial light exposure also had a positive effect with respect to adaption time to the day shift. In order to obtain a good sleep, other stimuli such as physical activity, noise, light and coffee should be avoided. Regular 12-hour night shifts for 14 days, for example, are better than having a swing shift, as the awake period improves with longer night periods (Parkes, 1994; Barnes, Deacon, Forbes, & Arendt, 1998; Bjorvatn, Kecklund, & Åkerstedt, 1998, 1999; Gibbs, Hampton, Morgan, & Arendt, 2002).

Conclusions

Environmental and human safety considerations in the Barents Sea region require extraordinary prudence from industrial parties due to the extreme conditions of the area. Potential oil spills represent the largest threats to the Barents Sea. Therefore, this chapter focused on the environmental fate and effects of such events and introduced some of the most common contingency strategies.

Understanding the principal mechanisms that govern oil spreading and distribution is crucial for the evaluation of environmental risk and contingency planning. Remediation technologies are numerous, and an increasing number of new technologies are being developed for Arctic conditions. Hydrocarbons are of concern as they have well-known toxic effects to biota. It is, however, difficult to conclude upon concentrations and effect levels from the overall literature due to the large variability in reported values. Currently existing data is also not yet sufficient to establish the sensitivity of Arctic species in comparison to temperate ones. Besides the immediate risk to biota, the indirect exposure of humans to oil hydrocarbons through food obtained from polluted areas is also an important issue. Especially in the Barents Sea, where large fish stocks are harvested, environmental protection and food safety are closely linked matters.

The permanently cold temperature and extreme seasonal light/dark cycle affects not only oil-weathering processes but also workers' ability to cope with everyday challenges and emergency situations. In the challenging conditions of the Arctic, personnel are under exceeding stress compared to more temperate regions, leading to increased risk of human errors. Hence, Arctic offshore facilities and working conditions have to be designed accordingly. Overall, the remoteness and harsh climate of the Barents Sea makes it difficult to respond to disaster quickly. Therefore, the most important goal is to achieve the state of extreme preparedness necessary to minimize response time.

References

Al-Rabeh, A.H., Lardner, R.W., Gunay, N., & Hossain, M. (1995, November). *OILPOL—An oil fate and transport model for the Arabian Gulf.* Paper presented at the 4th Saudi Engineering Conference, Jeddah, Saudi Arabia.

Ambjørn, C. (2007). Seatrack web, forecasts of oil spills, a new version. *Environmental Research, Engineering and Management, 3*(41), 60–66.

Anderson, W. (1985) Oil pollution: Effects and retention in the coastal zone. In N.L. Chao & W. Kirby-Smith (Eds.), *Proceedings of the International Symposium on Utilization of Coastal Ecosystems, Planning, Pollution, Productivity, 22–27 November 1982, Rio Grande, Brazil, Vol. I* (pp. 197–214). Beaufort, NC: Fundacao Universidade do Rio Grande and Duke University Marine Laboratory.

Arctic Climate Impact Assessment. (2004). *Impacts of a warming Arctic: Arctic Climate Impact Assessment (ACIA).* Retrieved from www.amap.no/documents/doc/impacts-of-a-warming-arctic-2004/786

Arctic Monitoring and Assessment Programme. (1998). *AMAP assessment report: Arctic pollution issues.* Retrieved from www.amap.no/documents/doc/amap-assessment-report-arctic-pollution-issues/68

Arctic Monitoring and Assessment Programme. (2007). *Arctic oil and gas 2007.* Retrieved from www.amap.no/documents/doc/arctic-oil-and-gas-2007/71

Arctic Monitoring and Assessment Programme. (2010a). *Assessment 2007: Oil and gas activities in the Arctic – Effects and potential effects* (Vol. 1). Retrieved from www.amap.no/documents/doc/assessment-2007-oil-and-gas-activities-in-the-arctic-effects-and-potential-effects.-volume-1/776

Arctic Monitoring and Assessment Programme. (2010b). *Assessment 2007: Oil and gas activities in the Arctic – Effects and potential effects* (Vol. 2). Retrieved from www.amap.no/documents/doc/assessment-2007-oil-and-gas-activities-in-the-arctic-effects-and-potential-effects.-volume-2/100

Arctic Response Technology Oil Spill Preparedness. (2012). *Spill response in the Arctic offshore.* Retrieved from www.arcticresponsetechnology.org/wp-content/uploads/2012/11/FINAL-printed-brochure-for-ATC.pdf

Arneberg, P., Titov, O., Filin, A., & Stiansen, J.E. (Eds.). (2013). *Joint Norwegian–Russian environmental status report on the Barents Sea ecosystem. Update for current situation for climate, phytoplankton, zooplankton, fish and fisheries in 2011*. Retrieved from Institute of Marine Research website: www.imr.no/filarkiv/2013/09/imr-pinro_3–2013_web.pdf/nb-no

Atlas, R.M., & Bartha, R. (1998). *Microbial ecology: Fundamentals and applications*. New York, NY: Pearson Education.

Atlas, R.M., & Hazen, T.C. (2011). Oil biodegradation and bioremediation: A tale of the two worst spills in US history. *Environmental Science & Technology, 45*(16), 6709–6715. doi: 10.1021/es2013227

Bagi, A., Pampanin, D.M., Lanzén, A., Bilstad, T., & Kommedal, R. (2013). Naphthalene biodegradation in temperate and Arctic marine microcosms. *Biodegradation, 25*(1), 111–25. doi: 10.1007/s10532-013-9644-3.

Baker, J.M., Clark, R.B., Kingston, P.F., & Jenkins, R.H. (1990, June). *Natural recovery of cold water marine environments after an oil spill*. Paper presented at the 13th AMOP Seminar, Edmonton, Canada.

Bakke, T., Klungsøyr, J., & Sanni, S. (2013). Environmental impacts of produced water and drilling waste discharges from the Norwegian offshore petroleum industry. *Marine Environmental Research, 92*, 154–169. doi: 10.1016/j.marenvres.2013.09.012

Bambulyak, A., & Frantzen, B. (2011). *Oil transport from the Russian part of the Barents region. Status per January 2011*. Retrieved from www.barents.no/Filnedlasting.aspx?MId1=2504&FilId=1717

Barents Euro–Arctic Council. (n.d.). Retrieved from www.beac.st/in-English/Barents-Euro-Arctic-Council

Barnes, R.G., Deacon, S.J., Forbes, M.J., & Arendt, J. (1998). Adaptation of the 6-sulphatoxymelatonin rhythm in shiftworkers on offshore oil installations during a 2-week 12-h night shift. *Neuroscience Letters, 241*(1), 9–12. doi: 10.1016/S0304-3940(97)00965-8

Barron, M.G., Carls, M.G., Short, J.W., & Rice, S.D. (2003). Photo-enhanced toxicity of aqueous phase and chemically dispersed weathered Alaska North Slope crude oil to Pacific herring eggs and larvae. *Environmental Toxicology and Chemistry, 22*(3), 650–660.

Bechmann, R.K., Larsen, B.K., Taban, I.C., Hellgren, L.I., Moller, P., & Sanni, S. (2010). Chronic exposure of adults and embryos of *Pandalus borealis* to oil causes PAH accumulation, initiation of biomarker responses and an increase in larval mortality. *Marine Pollution Bulletin, 60*(11), 2087–2098. doi: 10.1016/j.marpolbul.2010.07.010

Berry, A., Dabrowski, T., & Lyons, K. (2012). The oil spill model OILTRANS and its application to the Celtic Sea. *Marine Pollution Bulletin, 64*(11), 2489–2501. doi: 10.1016/j.marpolbul.2012.07.036

Bjorvatn, B., Kecklund, G., & Åkerstedt, V. (1998). Rapid adaptation to night work at an oil platform, but slow readaptation after returning home. *Journal of Sleep Research, 40*, 601–608.

Bjorvatn, B., Kecklund, G., & Åkerstedt, V. (1999). Bright light treatment used for adaptation to night work and readaptation back to day life. A field study at an oil platform in the North Sea. *Journal of Sleep Research, 8*, 105–112.

Bjørkum, A.A., Pallesen, S., Holsten, F., & Bjorvatn, B. (2004). Skiftarbeid og ulykker – relevans for offshoreindustrien [Shiftwork and accidents – relevance for the offshore industry]. *Tidsskrift Norsk Lægeforening, 124*, 2773–2775.

Bragg, J.R., Prince, R.C., Harner, E.J., & Atlas, R.M. (1994). Effectiveness of bioremediation for the Exxon Valdez oil spill. *Nature, 368*(6470), 413–418.

Brakstad, O.G. (2008). Natural and stimulated biodegradation of petroleum in cold marine environments. In R. Margesin, F. Schinner, J.C. Marx, & C. Gerday (Eds.), *Psychrophiles: From biodiversity to biotechnology* (pp. 389–407). Berlin, Germany: Springer–Verlag.

Brakstad, O.G., & Bonaunet, K. (2006). Biodegradation of petroleum hydrocarbons in seawater at low temperatures (0–5 °C) and bacterial communities associated with degradation. *Biodegradation, 17*(1), 71–82. doi: 10.1007/s10532-005-3342-8

Brakstad, O.G., Booth, A.M., & Faksness, L.G. (2009). Microbial degradation of petroleum compounds in cold marine water and ice. In A.K. Bej, J. Aislabie, & R.M. Atlas (Eds.), *Polar microbiology – The ecology, biodiversity and bioremediation potential of microorganisms in extremely cold environments* (pp. 231–253). London, England: Taylor & Francis.

Brakstad, O.G., Nonstad, I., Faksness, L.G., & Brandvik, P.J. (2008). Responses of microbial communities in Arctic Sea ice after contamination by crude petroleum oil. *Microbial Ecology, 55*(3), 540–552. doi: 10.1007/s00248-007-9299-x

Brandvik, P.J., & Faksness, L.G. (2009). Weathering processes in Arctic oil spills: Meso-scale experiments with different ice conditions. *Cold Regions Science and Technology, 55*(1), 160–166. doi: 10.1016/j.coldregions.2008.06.006

Brandvik, P.J., Sørheim, K.R., Singsaas, I., & Reed, M. (2006). *Short state-of-the-art report on oil spills in ice-infested waters* (Report No. 1). Retrieved from www.sintef.no/project/JIP_Oil_In_Ice/Dokumenter/publications/JIP-rep-no-1-State-of-the-art-2006-oil-in-ice.pdf

Camus, L., & Olsen, G.H. (2008). Embryo aberrations in sea ice amphipod *Gammarus wilkitzkii* exposed to water soluble fraction of oil. *Marine Environmental Research, 66*, 223–224. doi: 10.1016/j.marenvres.2008.02.074

Canadian Network for the Detection of Atmospheric Change. (2014). *Environment Canada wind chill chart.* Retrieved from www.candac.ca/candac/Outreach/Teacher_Resources_Index/tri/31.pdf

Dahl-Hansen, E., Barbey, A., Arnulf, L., Covil, M., de Jong, G., Dugelay, F., ... Ross, J. (2000, June). *Health aspects of work in extreme climates within the E&P industry: The heat.* Paper presented at the SPE International Conference on Health, Safety and Environment in Oil and Gas Exploration and Production, Stavanger, Norway. Abstract retrieved from www.onepetro.org/conference-paper/SPE-61018-MS

DNV GL. (2012). *Assessment of international standards for safe exploration, production and transportation of oil and gas in the Barents Sea. Final report. Phase 4.* Retrieved from www.dnv.com/resources/reports/barents2020.asp

Drozdowski, A., Nudds, S., Hannah, C.G., Niu, H., Peterson, I.K., & Perrie, W.A. (2011). *Review of oil spill trajectory modelling in the presence of ice.* Retrieved from the Government of Canada Publications website: http://publications.gc.ca/collections/collection_2012/mpo-dfo/Fs97-18-274-eng.pdf

Efroymson, R.A., Nicolette, J.P., & Suter II, G.W. (2003). *A framework for net environmental benefit analysis for remediation or restoration of petroleum-contaminated sites.* Retrieved from Environmental Sciences Division website: www.esd.ornl.gov/programs/ecorisk/documents/NEBA-petrol-s-report-RE.pdf

Fakhru'l-Razi, A., Pendashteh, A., Abdullah, L.C., Biak, D.R.A., Madaeni, S.S., & Abidin, Z.Z. (2009). Review of technologies for oil and gas produced water treatment. *Journal of Hazardous Materials, 170*(2), 530–551. doi: 10.1016/j.jhazmat.2009.05.044

Faksness, L.G., Brandvik, P.J., Daae, R.L., Leirvik, F., & Børseth, J.F. (2011). Large-scale oil-in-ice experiment in the Barents Sea: Monitoring of oil in water and MetOcean interactions. *Marine Pollution Bulletin, 62*(5), 976–984. doi: 10.1016/j.marpolbul.2011.02.039

Fingas, M. (2011a). Evaporation modeling. In M. Fingas (Ed.), *Oil spill science and technology* (pp. 201–242). Oxford, England: Elsevier.

Fingas, M. (2011b). Introduction to spill modeling. In M. Fingas (Ed.), *Oil spill science and technology* (pp. 187–200). Oxford, England: Elsevier.

Fingas, M. (2011c). Models for water-in-oil emulsion formation. In M. Fingas (Ed.), *Oil spill science and technology* (pp. 243–273). Oxford, England: Elsevier.

Fingas, M. (Ed.). (2011d). *Oil spill science and technology*. Oxford, England: Elsevier.

Fingas, M. (2014). Water-in-oil emulsions: Formation and predictions. *Journal of Petroleum Science Research, 3*(1), 38–49. doi: 10.14355/jpsr.2014.0301.04

Fingas, M., & Fieldhouse, B. (2009). Studies on crude oil and petroleum product emulsions: Water resolution and rheology. *Colloids and Surfaces A: Physicochemical and Engineering Aspects, 333*(1), 67–81. doi: 10.1016/j.colsurfa.2008.09.029

Folkard, S., & Tucker, P. (2003). Shift work, safety and productivity. *Occupational Medicine, 53*(2), 95–101.

Fritt-Rasmussen, J., & Brandvik, P.J. (2011). Measuring ignitability for in situ burning of oil spills weathered under Arctic conditions: From laboratory studies to large-scale field experiments. *Marine Pollution Bulletin, 62*(8), 1780–1785. doi: 10.1016/j.marpolbul.2011. 05.020

Galt, J.A. (1997). The integration of trajectory models and analysis of spill response information systems. *Spill Science & Technology Bulletin, 4*(2), 123–129.

Garland, E., & Hjelde, E. (2003, March). *Discharge of produced water: New challenges in Europe*. Paper presented at the 2003 SPE/EPA/DOE Exploration Production Environmental Conference, San Antonio, TX. Abstract retrieved from www.onepetro.org/conference-paper/SPE-80585-MS

Gibbs, M., Hampton, S., Morgan, L., & Arendt, J. (2002). Adaptation of the circadian rhythm of 6-sulphatoxymelatonin to a shift schedule of seven nights followed by seven days in offshore oil installation workers. *Neuroscience Letters, 325*(2), 91–94. doi: 10.1016/S0304-3940(02)00247-1

Grahl-Nielson, O. (1987). Hydrocarbons and phenols in discharge water from offshore operations. Fate of the hydrocarbons in the recipient. *Sarsia, 72*(3–4), 375–382. doi: 10.1080/00364827.1987.10419741

Grimaud, R. (2010). Biofilm development at interphases between hydrophobic organic compounds and water. In K.N. Timmis (Ed.), *Handbook of hydrocarbon and lipid microbiology* (Vol. 1, pp. 1492–1497). Berlin, Germany: Springer.

Guo, W.J., & Wang, Y.X. (2009). A numerical oil spill model based on a hybrid method. *Marine Pollution Bulletin, 58*(5), 726–734. doi: 10.1016/j.marpolbul.2008.12.015

Hansen, B.H., Altin, D., Rørvik, S.F., Øverjordet, I.B., Olsen, A.J., & Nordtug, T. (2011). Comparative study on acute effects of water accommodated fractions of an artificially weathered crude oil on *Calanus finmarchicus* and *Calanus glacialis* (Crustacea: Copepoda). *Science of the Total Environment, 409*(4), 704–709. doi: 10.1016/j.scitotenv.2010.10.035

Hansen, B.H., Altin, D., Øverjordet, I.B., Jager, T., & Nordtug, T. (2013). Acute exposure of water soluble fractions of marine diesel on Arctic *Calanus glacialis* and boreal *Calanus finmarchicus*: Effects on survival and biomarker response. *Science of the Total Environment, 449*, 276–284. doi: 10.1016/j.scitotenv.2013.01.020

Harms, H., Smith, K.E.C., & Wick, L.Y. (2010). Introduction: The problem of hydrophobicity/bioavailability. In K.N. Timmis (Ed.), *Handbook of hydrocarbon and lipid microbiology* (Vol. 1, pp. 1480–1490). Berlin, Germany: Springer.

Hatlen, K., Camus, L., Berge, J., Olsen, G.H., & Baussant, T. (2009). Biological effects of water soluble fraction of crude oil on the Arctic sea ice amphipod *Gammarus wilkitzkii*. *Chemistry and Ecology, 25*(3), 151–162. doi:10.1080/02757540902964978

Head, I.M., Jones, D.M., & Röling, W.F.M. (2006). Marine microorganisms make a meal of oil. *Nature Reviews Microbiology, 4*(3), 173–182. doi:10.1038/nrmicro1348

Hjermann, D.Ø., Melsom, A., Dingsør, G.E., Durant, J.M., Eikeset, A.M., Røed, L.P., . . . Stenseth, N.C. (2007). Fish and oil in the Lofoten–Barents Sea ecosystem: Synoptic review of the effect of oil spills on fish populations. *Marine Ecology Progress Series, 339,* 283–299.

Holdway, D.A. (2002). The acute and chronic effects of wastes associated with offshore oil and gas production on temperate and tropical marine ecological processes. *Marine Pollution Bulletin, 44*(3), 185–203. doi: 10.1016/S0025-326X(01)00197-7

International Association of Oil & Gas Producers. (2008). *Health aspects of work in extreme climates. A guide for oil and gas industry managers and supervisors* (Report No. 398). Retrieved from www.ogp.org.uk/pubs/398.pdf

International Maritime Organization. (2010). *Manual on oil spill risk evaluation and assessment of response preparedness.* London, England: IMO Publishing

Jacobsen, S.R., & Gudmestad, O.T. (2013, June). *Long-range rescue capability for operations in the Barents Sea.* Paper presented at the ASME 2013 32nd International Conference on Ocean, Offshore and Arctic Engineering, Nantes, France. Abstract retrieved from http://proceedings.asmedigitalcollection.asme.org/proceeding.aspx?articleid=1786515

Jager, T., & Hansen, B.H. (2013). Linking survival and biomarker responses over time. *Environmental Toxicology and Chemistry, 32*(8), 1842–1845. doi: 10.1002/etc.2258

Knardahl, V., Medbø, J.I., Strøm, V., & Jebens, E. (2010). *Utredning om virkninger av arbeid i kalde omgivelser* [Study on effects of working in cold environments] (Report No. 8). Retrieved from the Norwegian National Institute of Occupational Health website: www.stami.no/arbeid-i-kalde-omgivelser?lcid=1033

Kvenvolden, K.A., & Cooper, C.K. (2003). Natural seepage of crude oil into the marine environment. *Geo-Marine Letters, 23*(3–4), 140–146. doi: 10.1007/s00367-003-0135-0

Lee, R.F. (2003). Photo-oxidation and photo-toxicity of crude and refined oils. *Spill Science & Technology Bulletin, 8*(2), 157–162. doi: 10.1016/S1353-2561(03)00015-X

Lehr, W., Jones, R., Evans, M., Simecek-Beatty, D., & Overstreet, R. (2002). Revisions of the ADIOS oil spill model. *Environmental Modelling & Software, 17*(2), 191–199. doi: 10.1016/S1364-8152(01)00064-0

Levorson, A.I. (1954). *Geology of petroleum.* San Francisco, CA: Freeman Press.

Li, Z., Lee, K., King, T., Boufadel, M.C., & Venosa, A.D. (2010). Effects of temperature and wave conditions on chemical dispersion efficacy of heavy fuel oil in an experimental flow-through wave tank. *Marine Pollution Bulletin, 60*(9), 1550–1559. doi: 10.1016/j.marpolbul.2010.04.012

Liu, T., & Peter Sheng, Y. (2014). Three dimensional simulation of transport and fate of oil spill under wave induced circulation. *Marine Pollution Bulletin, 80*(1–2), 148–159. doi: 10.1016/j.marpolbul.2014.01.026

Lo Giudice, A., Bruni, V., De Domenico, M., & Michaud, L. (2010). Psychrophiles – Cold-adapted hydrocarbon-degrading microorganisms. In K.N. Timmis (Ed.), *Handbook of hydrocarbon and lipid microbiology* (Vol. 3, pp. 1898–1921). Berlin, Germany: Springer.

Maki, H., Sasaki, T., & Harayama, S. (2001). Photo-oxidation of biodegraded crude oil and toxicity of the photo-oxidized products. *Chemosphere, 44*(5), 1145–1151. doi: 10.1016/S0045-6535(00)00292-7

Marta-Almeida, M., Ruiz-Villarreal, M., Pereira, J., Otero, P., Cirano, M., Zhang, X., & Hetland, R.D. (2013). Efficient tools for marine operational forecast and oil spill tracking. *Marine Pollution Bulletin, 71*(1–2), 139–151. doi: 10.1016/j.marpolbul.2013.03.022

McFarlin, K.M., Prince, R.C., Perkins, R., & Leigh, M.B. (2014). Biodegradation of dispersed oil in Arctic seawater at − 1°C. *PLoS One, 9*(1):e84297. doi: 10.1371/journal.pone.0084297.

Nagel, N.B., & McLennan, J.D. (Eds.). (2010). *Solids injection*. Richardson, TX: Society of Petroleum Engineers.

Pallesen, S., Holsten, F., Bjorkum, A.A., & Bjorvatn, B. (2004). Er søvnvansker ved nattarbeid et problem for offshoreindustrien? [Are sleep difficulties in night work a problem for the offshore industry?]. *Tidsskrift Norsk Lægeforening, 124*, 2770–2772.

Parales, R.E., & Ditty, J.L. (2010). Substrate transport. In K.N. Timmis (Ed.), *Handbook of hydrocarbon and lipid microbiology* (Vol. 1, pp. 1546–1553). Berlin, Germany: Springer.

Parkes, K.R. (1994). Sleep patterns, shiftwork, and individual differences: A comparison of onshore and offshore control-room operators. *Ergonomics, 37*(5), 827–844. doi: 10.1080/00140139408963692

Patin, S. (1999). *Environmental impacts of the offshore oil and gas industry*. New York, NY: Eco-Monitor Publishing.

Payne, J.R., Phillips, C.R., & Hom, W. (1987). Transport and transformation: Water column processes. In D.F. Boesch & N.N. Rabalais (Eds.), *Long-term environmental effects of offshore oil and gas development* (pp. 176–218). New York, NY: Elsevier.

Plata, D.L., Sharpless, C.M., & Reddy, C.M. (2008). Photochemical degradation of polycyclic aromatic hydrocarbons in oil films. *Environmental Science and Technology, 42*(7), 2432–2438. doi: 10.1021/es702384f

Potter, S., Buist, I., Trudel, K., Dickins, D., & Owens, E. (2012). *Spill response in the Arctic offshore*. Retrieved from the American Petroleum Institute website: www.api.org/~/media/Files/EHS/Clean_Water/Oil_Spill_Prevention/Spill-Response-in-the-Arctic-Offshore.pdf

Pritchard, P.H., & Costa, C.F. (1991). EPA's Alaskan oil spill bioremediation project. Part 5. *Environmental Science and Technology, 25*(3), 372–379. doi: 10.1021/es00015a002

Protection of the Arctic Marine Environment. (2009). *Arctic offshore oil and gas guidelines*. Retrieved from www.pame.is/images/03_Projects/Offshore_Oil_and_Gas/Offshore_Oil_and_Gas/Arctic-Guidelines-2009-13th-Mar2009.pdf

Protection of the Arctic Marine Environment. (2013). *The Arctic Ocean review project. Final report. (Phase II 2011–2013)*. Retrieved from www.pame.is/images/03_Projects/AOR/Reports/126082_pame_sept_2.pdf

Reed, M., Aamo, O.M., & Daling, P. (1995). Quantitative analysis of alternate oil spill response strategies using OSCAR. *Spill Science & Technology Bulletin, 2*(1), 67–74. doi: 10.1016/1353-2561(95)00020-5

Reed, M., Johansen, Ø., Brandvik, P.J., Daling, P., Lewis, A., Fiocco, R., … Prentki, R. (1999). Oil spill modeling towards the close of the 20th century: Overview of the state of the art. *Spill Science & Technology Bulletin, 5*(1), 3–16. doi: 10.1016/S1353-2561(98)00029-2

Reed, M., Turner, C., Odulo, A., Isaji, T., Sørstrøm, S.E., & Mathisen, J.P. (1990). *Field evaluation of satellite tracked surface drifting buoys in simulating the movement of spilled oil in the marine environment*. Narragansett, RI: Applied Science Associates Inc.

Robertson, A. (Ed.). (1998). Petroleum hydrocarbons. In S.J. Wilson, J.L. Murray, D.J. Gregor, H. Loeng, L. Barrie, H.P. Huntington, . . . J.C. Hansen (Eds.), *AMAP assessment report: Arctic pollution issues* (pp. 661–701). Retrieved from www.amap.no/documents/doc/amap-assessment-report-arctic-pollution-issues/68

Rossi, B. (2013). *Summary report and recommendations on the prevention of marine oil pollution in the Arctic*. Retrieved from Emergency Prevention, Preparedness and Response working group website: www.arctic-council.org/eppr/recommended-practices-rp3-report/

Schlosser, P., Swift, J.H., Lewis, D., & Pfirman, S.L. (1995). The role of the large-scale Arctic Ocean circulation in the transport of contaminants. *Deep Sea Research Part II: Topical Studies in Oceanography, 42*(6), 1341–1367. doi: 10.1016/0967-0645(95)00045-3

Schmidt-Etkin, D. (2011). Spill occurrences: A world overview. In M. Fingas (Ed.), *Oil spill science and technology* (pp. 7–48). Oxford, England: Elsevier.

Shigenaka, G. (2010). Effects of oil in the environment. In M. Fingas (Ed.), *Oil spill science and technology* (pp. 985–1024). Oxford, England: Elsevier.

Singsaas, I., & Lewis, A. (2011). *Behavior of oil and other hazardous and noxious substances (HNS) spilled in Arctic waters (BoHaSA)* (SINTEF Report No. A18116). Retrieved from Emergency Prevention, Preparedness and Response working group website: www.arctic-council. org/eppr/wp-content/uploads/2012/07/Final-Report-BoHaSA_23–02–20111.pdf

Skadsheim, A., Sanni, S., Pinturier, L., Moltu, U.E., Buffagni, M., & Bracco, L. (2009). Assessing and monitoring local and long-range-transported hydrocarbons as potential stressors to fish stocks. *Deep-Sea Research Part II: Topical Studies in Oceanography, 56*(21–22), 2037–2043. doi: 10.1016/j.dsr2.2008.11.014

Smith, J.E. (Ed.). (1968). *"Torrey Canyon" pollution and marine life. A report by the Plymouth Laboratory of the Marine Biological Association of the United Kingdom*. Cambridge, England: Cambridge University Press.

Southworth, G.R., Herbes, S.E., & Allen C.P. (1983). Evaluating a mass transfer model for the dissolution of organics from oil films into water. *Water Research, 17*(11), 1647–1651. doi: 10.1016/0043-1354(83)90024-6

Spaulding, M.L., Odulo, A., & Kolluru, V.S. (1992, June). *A hybrid model to predict the entrainment and subsurface transport of oil*. Paper presented at the 15th Arctic and Marine Oil Spill Program Technical Seminar, Environment Canada, Edmonton, Canada. Abstract retrieved from https://inis.iaea.org/search/search.aspx?orig_q=RN:25009592

Srinivasan, R., Lu, Q., Sorial, G.A., Venosa, A.D., & Mullin, J. (2007). Dispersant effectiveness of heavy fuel oils using baffled flask test. *Environmental Engineering Science, 24*(9), 1307–1320. doi:10.1089/ees.2006.0251

Stiansen, J.E., Korneev, O., Titov, O., Arneberg, P. (Eds.), Filin, A., Hansen, J.R., Marasaev, S. (Co-eds.). (2009). *Joint Norwegian–Russian environmental status 2008. Report on the Barents Sea ecosystem. Part II—Complete report*. Retrieved from Norwegian Institute of Marine Research publication base website: http://brage.bibsys.no/xmlui/handle/11250/117006

The PEW Charitable Trusts. (2013). *Arctic standards. Recommendations on oil spill prevention, response, and safety in the US Arctic Ocean*. Retrieved from www.pewtrusts.org/~/media/Assets/2013/09/23/ArcticStandardsFinal.pdf

Thelma AS. (2010). Kalde utfordringer. Helse-og arbeidsmiljø på innretning i nordområdene [Cold challenges. Health and working environment on installations in the High North] (Report No. 10–31). Retrieved from Petroleum Safety Authority Norway website: www.ptil.no/getfile.php/PDF/Kalde%20utfordringer%20-%20helse%20og%20arbeidsmilj%C3%B8%20p%C3%A5%20innretning%20i%20Nordomr%C3%A5dene_Thelma%20juni%202010.pdf

Tucker, P., Folkard, S., & Macdonald, I. (2003). Rest breaks and accident risk. *The Lancet, 361*(9358), 680. doi: 10.1016/S0140-6736(03)12566-4

Walker, M.I. (1995, November). *The Oil Spill Information System (OSIS) and Eurospill models: Background documentation*. Paper presented at the AMSO International Workshop on the Modelling of Accidental Oil spills and other Calamities at Sea, the Hague, the Netherlands.

Wilson, R.D., Monaghan, P.H., Osanik, A., Price, L.C., & Rogers, M.A. (1974). Natural marine oil seepage. *Science, 184*(4139), 857–865.

Word, J.Q., Pinza, M., & Gardiner, W. (2008). *Literature review of the effects of dispersed oil with emphasis on cold water environments of the Beaufort and Chukchi Seas*. Retrieved from New Fields website: www.newfields.com/dl/alaskaworkgroup/Anchorage%20Workshop%202008/NewFields%20Literature%20Review-%202008/Literature%20Review%20Final.pdf

14 Winterization of onshore facilities and outdoor work areas

Per-Arne Sundsbø

Introduction

The onshore development in Arctic and cold regions is challenged by severe climatic conditions characterized by strong winds, low temperature, drifting snow, precipitation, etc. In such a climate, a strong blizzard is capable of more or less paralyzing a region by blocking most of the traffic and outdoor activity on land, at sea and in the air. Most critical for the operability and maintainability of onshore facilities in the Arctic climate is the cold environment's impact on outdoor activity, i.e. outdoor operations, emergency response and evacuation, transportation, etc. Processing facilities and plant infrastructure are often affected by strong winds and severe drifting snow conditions. Exposure to cold stress and the combined effects of precipitation and icing affect comfort and human health. Snowdrifts, icing and low visibility may physically hinder or block outdoor activity and the functionality of equipment. Special considerations are often necessary during the design and fabrication of onshore facilities and infrastructure in cold regions. Winterization includes all design, layout and operational measures made with respect to safe operability and maintainability in a cold climate.

This chapter offers a review and principal description of winterization measures and design guidelines for wind and snow control on Arctic onshore facilities and the appurtenant outdoor activity areas. The basic functionality found in traditional cold climate design and state-of-the-art wind, snow and ice management provides the basis for sustainable winterized onshore solutions.

Most snow-related problems are caused by blowing snow

Snow accumulations affect most outdoor activities and the regularity of all kinds of land traffic. Snow loads may directly damage or destroy buildings, structures, power lines, etc. and drift formations are often the main cause of avalanches. In general, snowdrift, whether directly or indirectly, is a major cause of accidents, structural damage, injuries and loss of lives. Blowing snow and reduced visibility affect most outdoor activity and the regularity of land, sea and air traffic and cause accidents that lead to structural damage, injuries and loss of lives. The financial implications are large.

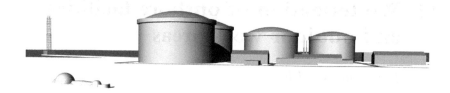

Figure 14.1 Modern onshore O&G production facilities are considerably larger than traditional settlements in the Arctic

Airborne snow may entrain into structures and ventilation systems. Snow entrainment into mechanical and natural ventilation systems, naturally ventilated building sections, machines/mechanical systems and ventilated enclosed constructions/vessels may cause damage. Enclosing larger constructions and vessels for the rough Arctic conditions may create problems related to snow entrainment. This represents considerable challenges in the development as well as the operational phase (Gudmestad & Quale, 2011).

Similar to offshore constructions, onshore waterfront areas with on- and offloading facilities may be exposed to heavy sea spray and combinations of atmospheric types of icing, which requires comprehensive protection efforts. Wet airborne snow contributes to several types of icing, causing rapid growth of ice and considerable ice loads. Ice accretion and clogging of weather panels, louvers, ventilation openings, gratings, doors, equipment, etc. is a problem offshore and onshore.

Onshore, snow-drift related problems may appear immediately after the Arctic shoreline (Sundsbø & Bang, 2000). In general, most snow-related problems are caused by blowing snow and drifting-snow transport. Blowing snow is usually defined as snow that has been relocated or eroded from the snow surface by wind, and most of the following snow-mass transport occurs centimeters above the surface. Tabler estimated that, during wind speeds lower than 20 m/s, most of the blowing snow is transported within centimeters above the surface (Tabler, 1994). For most drift control purposes, transport above 5 m can be ignored. Even if the mass concentration of blowing snow above 5 m in height is negligible, the high number of small suspended snow particles may contribute to reduced visibility. Blowing snow causes low visibility and snowdrifts that may be many times higher than the average snow depth on flat ground. In a rather simplified characterization, snow will be eroded in zones where the wind is sufficiently strong, and transported downstream until the wind or wind transport efficiency decreases. Typically the drift forms leeward of buildings, structures and terrain formations. Drifts formed by accumulated snow tend to be several times larger than the average snowfall on ground. The snow transport is mainly driven by this interaction between wind, topography and vegetation, and the interactions between moving snow particles, humidity, temperature, etc. affect the overall transport (Pomeroy & Gray, 1995).

This chapter is based on research and the development of winterized solutions for the Snøhvit process plant at Melkøya, land development on Sakhalin, offshore development on Goliat and Shtokman and residential, road and railroad projects in Norway.

The principal winterization measures, designing methods and considerations presented in this chapter apply to the design of new installations and the modification or upgrading of existing installations for the onshore drilling, production and pipeline transportation of petroleum, including accommodation units for such activities. The relevance of the methodology and the conceptual winterization measures also applies to the design and development of roads, railroads, airports, and residential and industrial areas.

The functionality in traditional cold climate design

In order to survive by simple means, the indigenous people living in cold regions had to develop a unique accommodating capacity, as they adjusted their lifestyle to the severe climate and seasonal changes. Outdoor activity in the High North has traditionally been conditioned by the weather, and, during the coldest and darkest periods, people simply stay indoors (Figure 14.1). Shelter was of supreme importance to the indigenous people, which is reflected in the traditional requirements for siting and building form. To reduce the impact from strong winds and blowing snow, they primarily settled in favorable and less windy locations. Their dwellings were designed to be low in height and streamlined in order for the wind and drifting snow to pass as undisturbed as possible. This approach creates minimum surrounding wind and drift problems and has for thousands of years been the predominant winterization principle.

The early traditional Arctic dwellings, such as the Inuit igloo and the Sami/ Inuit turf hut and lavvo, are characterized by simplicity in design and extreme functionality with respect to strong winds from more than one direction (Figure 14.2). The Inuit igloo is a unique adaptation to the rough Arctic conditions and close to an optimal solution with respect to design and functionality. This low-lying, semi–underground and aerodynamic design has practically no significant wind capturing details. Being highly streamlined and oriented parallel to the prevailing wind means that the surrounding snow accumulations are reduced to a minimum (Børve, 1989).

The traditional Viking longhouse is a streamlined-rectangular building, with a low-lying volumetric centerline. When built on a ridge, the longitudinal profile could be slightly curved with the terrain (Figure 14.3). The characteristic shape of the longhouse resembles the hull of a ship turned upside down, which obviously is a highly streamlined solution. For longitudinal winds, the outward curved lateral walls reduce potential lateral wind vortice and give a smooth airflow along the building. This minimizes surrounding snowdrift formations and provides maximal access to the building. All doors are naturally located on the long sides, parallel to the wind and away from potential drifts. In general, longhouses were often built sufficiently large to accommodate several functions

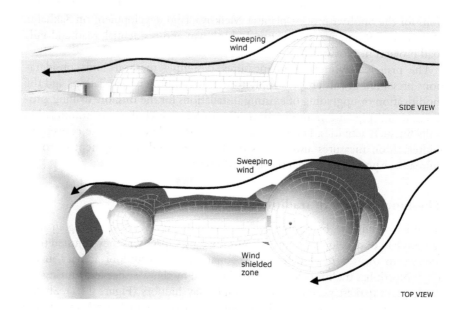

Figure 14.2 The Inuit igloo

in one building. Nordlandshuset is a traditional rectangular-shaped dwelling from the northern part of Norway that was designed, and until the beginning of last century used, as a longhouse. In windy locations Nordlandshuset was without exception weather oriented, with the longitudinal axis aligned with the prevailing wind and snowdrift direction.

The principle of raising buildings on piles, allowing for undergoing scouring winds, is a traditional Norwegian design solution, particularly applicable to deep snow conditions. The encounter with the windward wall deflects portions of the airflow under the structure, clearing the area beneath from snow. When properly designed, the scour zone covers an area wider than the building. This was in particular a favorable design solution for unoccupied and unheated storehouses, since the undergoing winds have a drying effect that keeps the indoor humidity at an acceptable level. Buret is an old traditional Norwegian storehouse based on a log design on pillars. The elevated building has an additional favorable design detail: inwardly inclined walls deflect the wind downwards and thereby increase the undergoing airflow and create rather strong surrounding wind vortices. This minimizes the surrounding snow accumulations.

Along with the industrial development, man became more and more dependent on transportation, and regularity became a matter of necessity. To enable year-round safe and operational infrastructure in a cold climate, more winterized designs were developed and systematic snow-controlling measures had to be applied. In an early written description, G.D.B. Johnson (1852) analyzed the

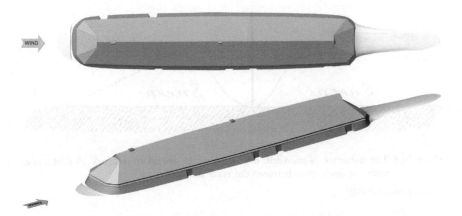

Figure 14.3 Snowdrift around the streamlined-rectangular Viking longhouse design. All doors are located on the long sides, parallel to the wind

Figure 14.4 Traditional Norwegian grain barn on pillars located at Bardu rural museum

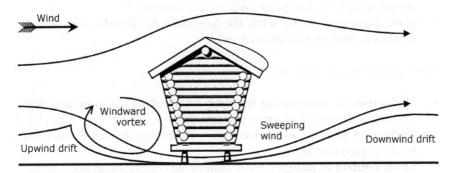

Figure 14.5 Snowdrift and sweeping winds around a traditional Norwegian storehouse on pillars

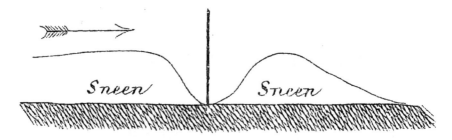

Figure 14.6 The influence of snowdrift over flat ground around an ordinary 10-foot fence, with one-inch space between the vertical boards

Source: Johnson (1852).

effect and consequences of snowdrift around structures and terrain formations. Johnson gave a remarkably good description of snowdrift around porous fences, walls, buildings and road cuts. He even studied the effect of snow fences used in combination, and his work is probably one of the first written scientific studies within the field of snow engineering.

Even though primitive dwellings such as the igloo, the lavoo, etc. have no direct application to modern building design, the basic cost-effective, wind- and snow-controlling functionality still applies.

The control of blowing snow

Snow-controlling designs are based on:

- reducing the near ground wind speeds below the threshold value for deposition in order to capture the blowing snow in drifts upwind of the area to be protected or
- maintaining wind speeds above the threshold value for deposition in order for the snow to be transported further downstream or
- maintaining wind speeds below the threshold value for relocation of snow in order to prevent relocation of snow.

Snow-controlling methods are:

- **Collection of snow using barriers** – controlling the snow into drifts upwind of the area to be protected.
- **Deflection of snow using barriers** – controlling the snow around and from the protected area.
- **Snow control in design** – snow-controlling designs (streamlined, deflective, collective, elevated, protective, weather panels, etc.) including collective

snow-controlling arrangements considering sections (cluster, etc.) or the entire facility as one.

- Snow control in design includes favorable site selection (naturally sheltered from wind and/or incoming drifting snow) and site planning/ facility layout.

- **Snow management – snow removal** – mechanical removal, heat tracing, chemical (salt, etc.), on-site snow-melting units (trucks with melt water storage capacity). Safe, efficient and minimum-time snow clearing by specialized high-capacity snow-removal equipment.

Collection of snow using barriers

Topographic and mechanical barriers, such as snow fences, shelterbelts and terrain modifications, may successfully be used to collect snow in drifts in order to prevent snow from drifting into an area to be protected. Snow-collecting measures are usually barriers arranged perpendicular to the prevailing wind direction.

A snow-collector fence may be installed upwind of the facility, road section or residential area to protect from the incoming near terrain drifting snow. The main collecting mechanism is simply that the wind velocities are decreased behind or near the fence, so that the snow settles. Wind speed reduction and drift formation is highly affected by the porosity (Figure 14.7), height, aperture size/ geometry and orientation of the fence, so fence design and localization must be carefully planned in order to obtain the requested efficiency of snow trapping and collecting. The leeward drift must not, under any circumstances, extend into the area to be protected. Snow-collector fences that are 40 to 50% porous (open area fraction) have the highest storage capacity and are probably the most commonly applied type of snow fence (Tabler, 2003). For fences of equal porosity, variations in aperture geometry may result in varying shielding and collection capabilities. In general, smaller aperture size increases the wind resistance.

Snow-collector fences typically vary in height from 2–6 m and may be designed in a multiple-row system. For many purposes, a single row of tall fences seems to be preferable.

Snow walls may be designed as stand-alone structures with solid cladding or solid cladding bolted to an existing rack structure. A stand-alone snow wall is in reality a solid fence and may be similar in construction to the snow fences, the main difference to the porous snow fence being the use of solid cladding instead of boards. Solid fences have significantly lower storage capacity than porous fences. However, solid walls have the advantage of collecting most of the snow upwind of the barrier, totally protecting the leeward side until the upwind drift has reached the top of the barrier. In the early drift stages, downwind accumulation is a result of snow being swept back by the circulating wind, cleaning the downwind area.

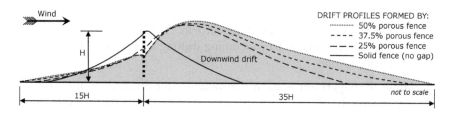

Figure 14.7 Effect of snow-fence porosity on drifts formed by snow-collector fence located on flat terrain

Source: Based on Tabler (2003).

Snow walls may successfully be located close to the area to be protected. Depending on the application, snow walls are typically 4–7 meters high and may be designed for combined snow-collecting and -deflecting purposes.

Snow-collecting terrain modifications may be used to increase the collection capacity and are usually applied when the conditions allow. A snow-collecting ditch may favorably be used to increase the collection capacity down-wind of a porous snow fence or the collection upwind of a snow wall. The upwind-facing step applies in the situation of rising terrain, providing an additional snow-collecting effect.

Deflection of snow using barriers

Deflectors are designed in order to accelerate and increase the near terrain airflow, forcing the snow to deposit further downwind (Sundsbø, 1998). In this way the incoming drifting snow is carried past the area to be protected.

Vertical deflectors may be successfully applied as a local measure to clear road sections, entrance regions, emergency exits and other prioritized locations (provided there are predictable local wind conditions). Architectural issues have resulted in the limited application of deflectors on buildings. However, vertical deflectors may be highly functional and applicable to the petroleum industry. It should be noted that wind chill in the wind-swept area might be higher than acceptable for an outdoor workplace.

Lateral deflectors may be efficient to deflect the incoming blowing snow away from buildings, clusters of structures, etc.; ref. case study.

Snow control in design – basic building concepts

The basic building concepts found in the traditional northern–Arctic building design are most applicable to modern onshore facilities. Elevating buildings on pillars is a favorable solution for areas of heavy snowdrift. For buildings on pile foundations in permafrost, the ground clearance also prevents (Figure 14.8) heat from the building impacting on the thermal equilibrium of the permafrost. Elevation heights required for efficient snow deflection vary with building dimensions and the local drifting-snow conditions. In moderate snowdrift areas in Norway, an elevation of one meter seems to be effective. For severe drifting-snow conditions in Antarctica, buildings are elevated several meters. Precautions must be taken with respect to the leeward snow accumulation that tends to form downstream from the elevated structure.

A non-heated storage building may be successfully elevated in order to create the best possible indoor climate.

There are several advantages of inwardly inclined wall designs to control the potential impact from heavy drift formation. The increase in surrounding wind vortices deflects more snow from the walls, and the inclination reduces the possibility of the drift leaning towards the walls, creating potential strong horizontal snow creep forces. The design solution is commonly used for snow-drift cover, protecting the railroad in the Norwegian high mountains. Inwardly inclined designs are highly applicable for deep drift areas/sections.

Design guidelines for snow-controlling buildings (building winterization) (Figure 14.9):

- the building design should be streamlined – rectangular and oriented with the prevailing snow-drifting wind
- leeward and windward sides of the building should be designated to drift formation and walls could favorably be inwardly inclined
- all doors should be located on the drift-free, long sides, parallel to the wind
- buildings' doors should be elevated from the ground to allow for time to remove accumulated snow
- extended passageways may provide free access through drift blockage near buildings and enable efficient and minimum-time snow clearing by specialized high-capacity snow-removal equipment
- avoid low-lying windows where drifts may form

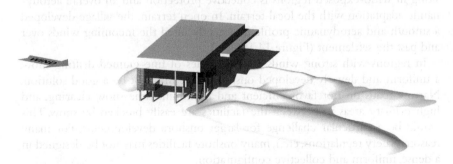

Figure 14.8 Modeling of snowdrift around a building elevated 1.45 m above the terrain (Sakhalin II Phase 2 project)

Basic snow-controlling principles, as presented for single-building designs, also apply for collective arrangements, considering sections of structures, clusters, etc. or the entire facility as one.

If the building is to be located as a single unit without adjacent structures, it should be designed relatively low to the ground. In the presence of neighboring structures, the building heights should be equal or follow a collective ridge profile. At no point should the height of the building be substantially higher than neighboring buildings.

Snow may accumulate in roof steps and in leeward pitched roof areas, see Figure 14.5. Consequently, snow-collecting roof steps designs should be avoided and roof pitch must be carefully selected with respect to the prevailing snow-drifting wind. In windy locations, the snow tends to be blown off and not to accumulate on moderate-sized flat roofed or relatively low roof pitch designs. However, most failure in roof constructions because of high snow loads generally occurs on larger flat roofed, steel buildings.

Site selection – for wind and snow control

Favorable site selection forms the basis for all traditional settlements. The Inuit carefully selected sites that were naturally sheltered or least exposed to strong winds and blowing snow. Traditional villages in the cold and windy parts of Norway were always located in naturally sheltered zones. There are many critical factors related to onshore site selection in the northern regions, which usually leaves us with few optional sites. However, the most exposed areas should be avoided (analysis/site assessments, etc.).

Site planning/site development – for wind and snow control

In traditional settlements in areas exposed to wind, buildings were often located close to their neighbors, arranged in a dense village structure, providing collective weather protection. Efforts were put into minimizing the impact from penetrating wind corridors and down-current winds. The basis for traditional siting in wind-exposed regions is collective protection and an overall aerodynamic adaptation with the local terrain. In open terrain, the village developed a smooth and aerodynamic profile that gently lifted the incoming winds over and past the settlement (Figure 14.10).

In regions with strong winds and quantities of fine-grained drifting snow, a uniform and densely developed onshore plant may not be a good solution. Narrow roads do not favor efficient and minimum-time snow clearing, and high priority areas in-between the facilities are easily blocked by snow. This would be a particular challenge for larger onshore developments. For many reasons (safety regulations, etc.), many onshore facilities may not be designed in a dense, uniform and collective configuration.

However, structures and buildings may be arranged in groups or sections as one, based on snow-controlling design concepts, such as those of the traditional

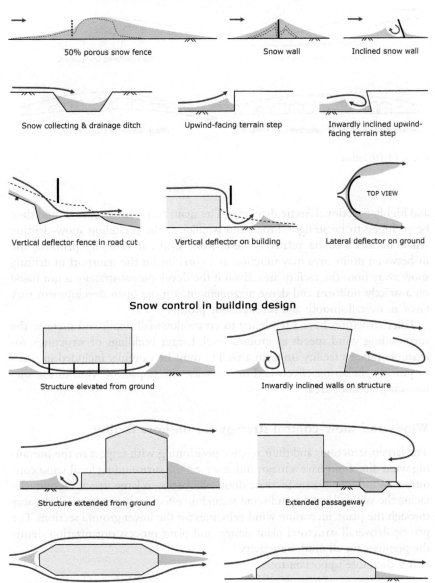

Collection and deflection of snow using barriers

50% porous snow fence

Snow wall

Inclined snow wall

Snow collecting & drainage ditch

Upwind-facing terrain step

Inwardly inclined upwind-facing terrain step

Vertical deflector fence in road cut

Vertical deflector on building

Lateral deflector on ground

TOP VIEW

Snow control in building design

Structure elevated from ground

Inwardly inclined walls on structure

Structure extended from ground

Extended passageway

Streamlined structure (plan view)

Streamlined structure (profile)

Figure 14.9 Measures for collection and deflection of snow using barriers and snow-controlling designs

Siting

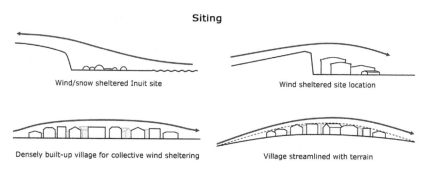

Wind/snow sheltered Inuit site   Wind sheltered site location

Densely built-up village for collective wind sheltering   Village streamlined with terrain

Figure 14.10 Siting

and highly functional Arctic dwellings. The main connecting roads should then be arranged to be straight, broad and parallel to the prevailing snow-drifting wind, in order to be relatively clear from drifts. If carefully planned, the in-between utility area may function as a corridor for the transport of drifting snow away from the facility area. Even if the development strategy is not based on a strictly uniform and dense arrangement, a more open development may favor an overall smooth and aerodynamic profile.

Taller structures have a tendency to create downfall winds and increase the surrounding wind speeds at ground level. Larger buildings or structures, for example process facility units, in a facility must be carefully included in order to provide sheltering effects and not increase the impact of wind in the surrounding outdoor area.

Wind- and snow-control strategy for onshore facility

The largest structures and their relative positioning with respect to the prevailing wind directions have a major influence on the surrounding local wind conditions. Wind speeds may increase drastically between large structural obstacles facing the wind direction, and wind tunneling effects may penetrate all the way through the plant, increasing wind velocities for the lower ground sections. The principal/overall structural plant design and plant process organization define the premises for all outdoor activity.

It is therefore important to:

1. Collect and analyze all available climate data
2. Reduce possible undesirable local climatic effects caused by the larger structures' arrangement
3. Utilize the inherent opportunities of possibly creating sheltering effects from the larger dominant structures and the collective effects of favorable arrangements

4. Create the best possible local climatic solutions within the framework with respect to choice of technology, technological solutions, process planning, etc.

In Arctic regions, the prevailing snow-drifting wind direction(s) should be regarded as one of the most important design parameters. Control of blowing snow includes wind control.

All winterization planning must be based on a common and well-defined strategy. Control of wind and blowing snow on an onshore facility, as for a residential development area, is often best achieved by utilizing a combination of several winterization measures or a wind- and snow-control strategy:

1. Favorable site selection (if possible)
2. Conceptual design
    – Favorable arrangement of facilities in order to promote collective wind- and snow-controlling effects
3. Outer shielding measures
    – Reducing drift into plant area
4. Inner shielding measures
    – Reducing unwanted drift inside plant area
5. Winterization of respective plant functions
    – Wind and snow control in design, individual adaptation, local wind shielding, etc.
6. Snow management
    – Include the concept of safe, efficient and minimum-time snow clearing by specialized high-capacity snow-removal equipment

Outer shielding measures

The main objective of the outer shielding measures is to reduce wind and snow drifting into the plant area or an area to be protected. Aside from suitable site selection, this is usually the most important and most cost-efficient snow-controlling measure.

The outer wind and drift shielding may include several combined snow-collecting measures, forming a snow-shielding system consisting of combinations of snow fences, vegetation and snow-collecting terrain modifications, such as embankments and ditches. Snow-collecting ditches may also be combined with the surface water drainage system. Outer shielding measures should be located as close as possible to the facility to allow for the minimum re-entrainment of snow, see see Figures 14.11 and 14.12.

Outer shielding measure – snow-collector fence

Snow-collector fence(s) could be located outside the plant area with the main objective of reducing the drifting snow into the plant area. A large amount of

Figure 14.11 Outer shielding snow fence for onshore facility (designed by Sundsbø for company)

Outer shielding system for onshore facility

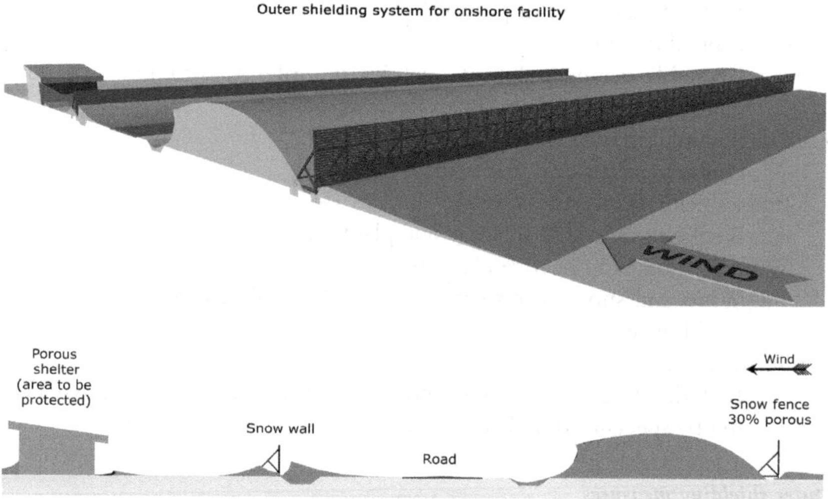

Figure 14.12 Outer shielding system for onshore facility (designed by Sundsbø for company)

snowdrift will usually occur after snowfall or during no-snowfall conditions. A snow-collector fence will be most efficient under such conditions.

Considering how leeward snow accumulations form behind a fence, it is possible to use a larger fence than strictly necessary for collecting the incoming amount of drifting snow. By locating a trench leeward of the fence, the storage capacity and drainage will be increased. In this case, the leeward drift is not intended to reach the road quickly or within a single snowstorm period. Snow accumulations behind the fence can be removed if or before it reaches the road. Snow may also accumulate on the windward side of the fence.

Inner shielding measures

The main objectives for inner shielding measures are to reduce redistribution and blowing snow inside the facility area and to provide local protection with respect to drift and blowing-snow entrainment.

Snow walls may be used for snow collecting and deflecting purposes close to the area to be protected. The design should prepare for efficient removal of the collected snow, see Figure 14.13.

Vertical deflectors may be used for clearing selected prioritized locations and lateral deflectors to deflect the incoming blowing snow away from buildings, clusters of structures, etc.

Some general remarks

- All analysis and dimensioning of the presented wind- and snow-controlling measures must be based on verified meteorological data.
- The prevailing snow-drifting wind direction(s) should be regarded as one of the most important design parameters. However, snow storms/blizzards may appear from directions other than the prevailing direction.

Snow fences and deflectors are usually made of wood. For onshore developments, flammable fencing materials or vegetation such as trees are normally not acceptable near petroleum facilities or in the surrounding firebreak zone. Metal for porous fence designs must be carefully selected due to the potential of wind-generated noise.

It should be noted that snow-controlling measures, such as those described in this chapter, will not eliminate local drifting snow and snowdrift, but, with a proper design, the impact from blowing snow will be reduced to fulfill the design requirements given in NORSOK Standard S-002 (Standards Norway, 2004).

Weather protection of outdoor working environment

The general need for weather protection

Analysis of the overall exposure to temperature, wind, icing and precipitation is a basis for the identification of the need for weather protection and the selection of shielding measures for open- and semi-open work areas. Working environment analysis shall be performed early in the design/layout development and shall be updated when design changes are made that will affect the

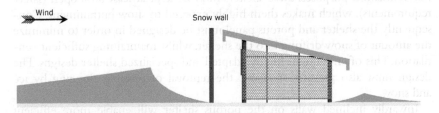

Figure 14.13 Snow wall protecting from blowing snow entrainment into semi-open shelter on onshore processing facility (designed by Sundsbø for company)

exposure of personnel to cold stress (Standards Norway, 2004, para. 4.4). On all installations that are planned for use in areas with an Arctic climate, outdoor operations are to be identified and reduced to a minimum (Standards Norway, 2004, para. 5.8.0–3). However, onshore activity is associated with the minimum of outdoor activity required for maintenance, inspections, snow/ ice-management, etc.

In cold regions with strong winds, the overall exposure to cold stress/wind chill in open areas may in general be above what is accepted for a workplace where there is frequent work with a duration of 10 min or more. In practice this means that if not shielded by larger buildings or structures, weather protection of workplaces is necessary to comply with the wind chill index (WCI) and other functional requirements. Measures to avoid exposed workplaces or reduce the exposure to wind and/or precipitation include redesign/ relocation of equipment and local weather protection using weather panels/ windbreaks.

Weather protection methods

- **Semi-open protections** – porous weather panels, porous natural vented shelters and half climatic zones, etc.
- **Enclosure** – work area is fully protected against exposure to the open air and ambient conditions
- **Shielding in design** – suitably located workplaces, redesign/relocation of equipment, collective wind-controlling arrangements, etc.

Shielding in design includes favorable site selection (naturally sheltered from wind and/or incoming drifting snow) and site planning/facility layout.

Semi-open protections

To protect from the impact of wind chill, blowing snow, lashing rain and sleet, porous weather panels may be applied on shelters, stair towers, buildings, etc., or as stand-alone structures to protect exposed workplaces.

Porous weather panels or perforated screens are installed on naturally ventilated shelters for weather protection and to maintain the required ventilation. For ventilation purposes, these shelters must be kept at least 50% open (safety requirements), which makes them highly exposed to snow entrainment. Consequently, the shelter and porous panel must be designed in order to minimize the amount of snow drifting into the shelter, whilst maintaining sufficient ventilation. This often requires highly adapted and specialized shelter designs. The design must also prevent or enable the removal of possible clogging by ice and snow.

Inwardly inclined walls on the porous shelter will enable more efficient removal of potential snow and ice (clogging); see Figure 14.14.

Porous & natural ventilated shelters

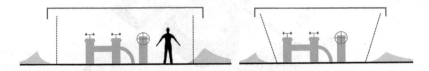

Figure 14.14 Naturally ventilated shelters

Company strategy – open work areas versus enclosure

As a starting point, a given work area may be defined as an open work area. The working environment analysis should further clarify whether the actual open work area needs weather shielding, subsequently with semi-open protection (panels, etc.) or totally enclosed protection.

The big question within onshore petroleum activity in cold climates is to enclose or not. Due to wind chill and precipitation, outdoor work areas that in warmer climates would have been designed as open have to be weather-protected and classified as semi-open or enclosed work areas in the cold climate conditions. In enclosed areas with the potential for hydrocarbon leakages, ventilation requirements could be considerable. This raises challenges due to:

- The consequences related to safety precautions/measures, etc.
- Company requirements, different Russian, Norwegian and American design policies.

Case study: conceptual design for onshore facilities and outdoor work areas

A representative selection of characteristic onshore structures from Melkøya is selected as a design proposal to be rearranged/redesigned in order to create favorable conditions for outdoor operations (Figure 14.15). The selection includes storage and some additional buildings. The design proposal is arranged in a rather open and non-streamlined design configuration that allows for penetrating winds in-between the structures. The site is considered to be on flat terrain with no surrounding obstacles.

As regards the redesign, the main objective is creating favorable conditions for outdoor activities at ground level in open surroundings. This is achieved by reducing the impact of wind chill and snowdrift on the outdoor working environment. The redesign is based on rearrangement of buildings/structures into groups or sections based on the wind- and snow-controlling design concepts, such as those for the traditional Arctic dwellings. The redesign does not

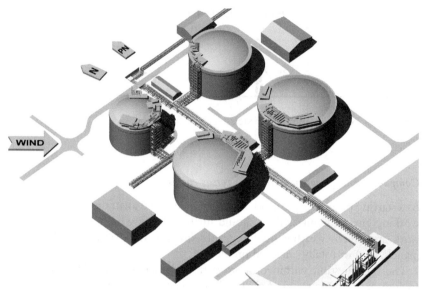

LNG storage package selected as **design proposal** for working environment analysis.

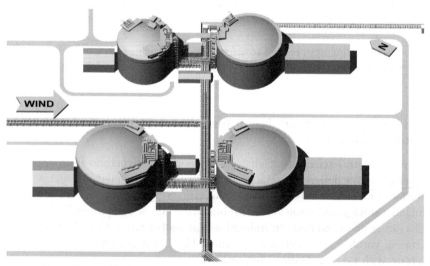

Streamlined **redesign** of design proposal for working environment analysis.

Figure 14.15 Selected design proposal and redesign for case study

include any considerations related to potential restrictions or safety requirements related to relative localization of the storage units etc.

Wind is simulated using Flow3D from Flow Science Inc. (Flow Science Inc.,
n.d.). The WCI is calculated from the simulated wind speed based on the formula in ISO/TR 11079, Annex D.

Working environment requirements – outdoor operations (Standards Norway, 2004, para. 5.8.0–2).

For evaluations of the acceptability of a WCI above 1,000 W/m^2, the following operational restrictions should be assumed to prevent harmful effects of
wind chill on unprotected skin:

WCI > 1,600 W/m^2:   No outdoor work to be performed;
1,600 W/m^2 > WCI > 1,500 W/m^2:   The available working time per hour
                                        and person increases from 0% to 33%
                                        linearly;

1,500 W/m^2 > WCI > 1,000 W/m^2:   The available working time per hour
                                        and person increases from 33% to 100%
                                        linearly.

The wind speed is set to u(10)= 10 m/s and the ambient air temperature,
t_a = −13°C. This corresponds to WCI= 1,644 W/m^2 at the height of 1.75 m in
open ground.

Results from numerical simulation of wind around design proposal

The selected design proposal allows for penetrating wind corridors that increase
the impact from wind and blowing snow, see Figure 14.15. Shelter from wind
is mostly found in the fluctuating and snow-accumulating leeward side of the
structures. The situation is vulnerable to minor changes in wind direction.

Results from numerical simulation of wind around redesign

The streamlined redesign reduces the impact from prevailing wind(s) and
controls the sheltered effect into designated areas between the structures, see
Figure 14.16.

A minimum amount of blowing snow will entrain into the wind-sheltered
zone, because of collective snow-ploughing effects from the sections, and generally more snow will be transported away from the area.

The in-between utility corridor with roads, etc. will be snow-free and works
as a corridor for the transport of drifting snow further downstream.

The solution is less sensitive with respect to changes in wind direction and
stable with respect to two prevailing wind sectors.

The principle of arranging plant structures in two streamlined sections with
the prevailing wind works favorably with respect to wind and snow control.

WIND & WIND CHILL IN OUTDOOR WORK AREAS

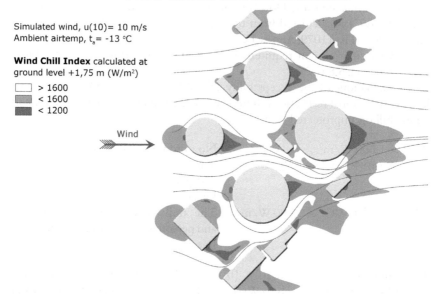

Simulated wind, u(10)= 10 m/s
Ambient airtemp, t_a= -13 °C

Wind Chill Index calculated at
ground level +1,75 m (W/m²)

☐ > 1600
▨ < 1600
■ < 1200

Wind →

Selected design proposal allows for penetrating wind corridors that increases the impact
from wind and blowing snow. Shelter from wind is mostly found in the fluctuating and snow
accumulating leeward side of the structures.

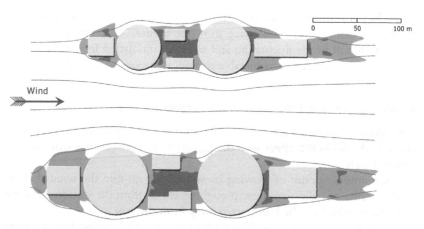

0   50   100 m

Wind →

Redesign of proposal into two streamlined sections, controls and reduces the impact from
prevailing wind(s). A snow ploughing effect allows for most of the blowing snow to pass,
reducing possible drifts in between the tanks.

Figure 14.16 Wind chill and airflow around design proposal and redesign for case study

The fine-grained Arctic snow

Immediately after settling, wind-transported snow particles start to form inter-particle bonds. In a few hours these bonds may be quite strong and resistant towards further wind erosion. In general, removal of snowdrifts is usually much harder than removal of newly fallen snow (Tabler, 1994). Driven by cold and strong winds, the blowing snow on land and ice is characterized by fine-grained and dense particles, which makes the particle bonding in deposition even stronger. Consequently, the onshore Arctic drift formations may be extremely compact and considerably harder to remove than drifts formed in a milder climate. Another important aspect is that the fine-grained snow particles tend to penetrate more easily into openings, ventilation systems and in-between processing equipment. The "Arctic" type of snow represents one of the key challenges with respect to the winterization of onshore facilities, and the basis for the snow-management strategy is:

- Safe, efficient and minimum-time snow clearing by specialized high-capacity snow-removal equipment
- Snow removal by hand must be reduced to an absolute minimum (man-power is limited)
- The facility layout must above all focus on avoiding snowdrifts in high-priority locations
- Local temporary snow deposits may provide a time buffer for snow removal in extreme weather situations
- Ensure sufficient snow-removal capacity for extreme snowstorm situations

Conclusions

In cold regions the wind increases the heat loss (wind chill) and represents the primary cause of drifting snow and several types of atmospheric icing. Since we cannot change the outdoor temperature, wind is generally considered as the controlling design parameter for creating favorable conditions for onshore outdoor operations. The reduction of local wind speeds and drifting snow into the developed area is therefore the principal challenge and must be given the highest priority.

1. The largest structures and their relative positioning with respect to the prevailing wind directions have a major impact on the local wind conditions. A conceptual onshore design proposal should aim at promoting the shielding potential of the larger dominating structures or form clusters or sections of the structures.
2. Outer shielding measures reduce snow drifting into the facility area (plant), and a high snow-collector fence located on the perimeter may also contribute to wind reduction.
3. Outdoor work areas and important infrastructure are primarily to be located in wind-sheltered locations in which snowdrifts do not form.

This also includes the outdoor area locations likely to be identified as workplaces.

4. Special attention must be paid to preventing the snow blockage of emergency exits, site emergency evacuation routes, HSE critical equipment, high-priority transport routes and facility areas, etc.
5. Further winterization measures are generally required and include local shielding, sheltering and design adaptations with respect to wind and snowdrift.

The fine-grained Arctic snow penetrates more easily into structures and is generally harder to remove. The facility layout must enable safe, efficient and minimum-time snow clearing by large and specialized high-capacity snow-removal equipment. Snowdrifts in high-priority locations must by all means be avoided.

For petroleum activity development projects in an Arctic climate, it is most important to include the concept of "systematic management of working environment in design and fabrication" (Standards Norway, 2004). Adopting basic wind- and snow-control strategies and design principles at all levels and in all phases of the development planning reduces possible cold climate related problems and is the very premise for successful winterization and for onshore operability and maintainability.

Existing technical solutions and best practice from traditional wind and snow engineering is sufficient to provide sustainable winterized solutions for further onshore development in Arctic environments. However, there is still a lack of experience in the application and implementation of winterization measures in the petroleum industry.

References

Børve, A.B. (1989). *The design and function of single buildings and building clusters in harsh, cold climates*. The Oslo School of Architecture and Design (AHO), ISBN 82 5470 068 0.

Flow Science Inc. (n.d.). Retrieved from www.flow3d.com.

Gudmestad, O.T., & Quale, C. (2011). *Technology and operational challenges for the High North* (Report IRIS-2011/166). Retrieved from the Petroleum Safety Authority Norway website: www.ptil.no/getfile.php/PDF/high-north.pdf

Johnson, G.D.B. (1852). *Nogle Ord om Snedreev, Snefog og Snefonner* [Some words about drifting snow, snow storm, and snowdrifts]. Christiania, Norway: P.T. Mallings Forlags Boghandel.

Pomeroy, J.W., & Gray, D.M. (1995). Snowcover – Accumulation, relocation and management. *Hydrological Sciences Journal, 41*(3), 422–423. doi: 10.1080/02626669609491514

Standards Norway. (2004). *Working environment* (NORSOK Standard S-002). Retrieved from www.standard.no/en/PDF/FileDownload/?redir=true&filetype=Pdf&preview=true&item=132389&category=5

Sundsbø, P.A. (1998). Numerical simulations of wind deflection fins to control snow accumulation in building steps. *Journal of Wind Engineering and Industrial Aerodynamics, 74–76*, 543–552. doi: 10.1016/S0167-6105(98)00049-X

Sundsbø, P.A., & Bang, B. (2000, June). *Snow drift control in residential areas – Field measurements and numerical simulations.* Paper presented at the 4th International Conference on Snow Engineering, Trondheim, Norway. Abstract retrieved from http://trid.trb.org/view.aspx?id=671769

Tabler, R.D. (1994). *Design guidelines for the control of blowing and drifting snow* (Report SHR P-H-381). Retrieved from http://onlinepubs.trb.org/onlinepubs/shrp/SHRP-H-381.pdf

Tabler, R.D. (2003). *Controlling blowing and drifting snow with snow fences and road design* (Report NCHRP Project 20–7,147). Retrieved from http://sicop.transportation.org/Documents/Tabler.pdf

Index

absorption techniques 233
Accenture 117
Achilles Group Limited 85
Achilles Joint Qualification 85–6
acute toxicity 60
ADIOS 239
Admiralteiskoye high/height 134, 135
Admiralteisky (Admiralteiski) swell 134,
    149
adsorption techniques 233
Agreement on Cooperation on Marine Oil
    Pollution Preparedness and Response in
    the Arctic 68
Agreement on Maritime Safety and
    Environmental Protection Against Oil
    Pollution 67
air pollution 38, 61; from in situ burning
    240
Aker MH 85
Aker Pusnes 85
Aker Solutions 85, 117
Akvamarin 129
Alaskan oil and gas production 184
Albatross reservoir 176
aldehydes 228
Alfa Group 82
algae 234–5
Algerian gas exports 40, 46
alkanes 227, 229, 230, 237
alkenes 230, 227
Altai pipeline 25
Alta oilfield 176
AMIGE (Arctic Marine
    Engineering–Geology Expedition) 125
AMNGR (Arktikmorneftegazrazvedka)
    56, 125
Andree Dickson aulacogen 136
animals see Arctic fauna
Arctic areas: defined 205; ecosystems in 19;
    see also Arctic region

Arctic Basin 161, 162, 165
Arctic Contaminants Action Program
    (ACAP) 64
Arctic Council 13, 47–8, 68, 99, 234;
    working groups of 64
Arctic Council Task Force 240
Arctic Deal 57
Arctic fauna; Barents Sea as habitat for 15;
    marine organisms 8, 231–2; seal hunting
    208; sea mammal distribution 232;
    zooplankton 234–5; see also fisheries; fish
    stocks
Arctic hurricanes see polar low pressures
Arctic Monitoring and Assessment
    Programme (AMAP) 48, 64, 205, 233–5,
    238
Arctic oil and gas reserves see oil and gas
    (O & G) deposits
Arctic operational environment: design for
    198–9, 201; effect on humans 186–7,
    190–1, 194–5, 241; effect on materials
    193; effect on operations 193–8; effects
    caused by remote location 195–8;
    evacuation and rescue 4, 182, 200, 219,
    220; icing 169–70, 184, 190–2, 200,
    207, 210; offshore activities 182, 198;
    petroleum production facilities 14–15,
    184–5; production and maintenance
    aspects 190–1, 201; temperature 190–1,
    236–7, 241–3; see also maintenance; oil
    and gas (O & G) production; petroleum
    production facilities; snow drifts; subsea
    production systems (SPS); weather; wind
Arctic petroleum production see petroleum
    production facilities
Arctic region: politics of 47–50; status of
    the environment 235–6; study of 8; see
    also Arctic areas; environmental issues
Arctic Response Technology Oil Spill
    Preparedness 239

For Product Safety Concerns and Information please contact our
EU representative GPSR@taylorandfrancis.com Taylor & Francis
Verlag GmbH, Kaufingerstraße 24, 80331 München, Germany